DEVON AND CORNWALL RECORD SOCIETY

New Series, Volume 56

Issued to the members for the year 2011

DEVON AND CORNWALL RECORD SOCIETY

EXETER CITY COUNCIL

New Series, Volume 56

ELIZABETHAN INVENTORIES AND WILLS OF THE EXETER ORPHANS' COURT

Part 1

Edited by Jannine Crocker

Exeter
2016

ISBN 978 0 901853 56 1

Typeset by Kestrel Data, Exeter

Printed and bound in Great Britain by
Short Run Press, Exeter

To Richard Woodgate
in memoriam
1974–2010

CONTENTS

ACKNOWLEDGEMENTS

This volume arose in the 1980s from a wide-ranging vision of the late Christopher G. Henderson, then Director of Exeter City Council's Archaeological Field Unit, in which the study of Exeter's past would be approached in a holistic way, integrating the study of documentary sources and standing historic buildings with the evidence about the city emerging from archaeological excavations. Most of the work entailed in preparing the text, from initial transcription to final production, was funded by Exeter City Council; I wish to thank Tony Ives for his fine work on graphics, Gary Young for his excellent photographs, and John Allan, who supervised the latter stages of the project, and my many former colleagues who discussed specific questions. I would especially like to thank Margery Rowe, both for generously contributing a Preface and for help and guidance, and Professor Maryanne Kowaleski, the late Chris Henderson and John Allan for assistance, direction and advice on numerous occasions. Tim Wormleighton and the staff of the Devon Heritage Centre, Exeter, were unfailingly helpful, and gave me permission to reproduce the transcripts. The RAM Museum, Exeter, and MLA Renaissance South West provided substantial financial support which allowed the transcription of the inventories to be brought to completion; Kate Osborne was especially helpful in arranging this work. Finally, I owe a great debt to Dr Todd Gray MBE, who not only wrote the Introduction but undertook much patient work to bring the volume to publication.

PREFACE

I came to Exeter as an archivist in the City Record Office in August 1956. My long stay of 40 years in the building in Castle Street was due in part to my interest in the exceptional documents I had in my care. The Exeter City Archives were described by Professor W. G. Hoskins as the finest collection of borough records outside London and after being acquainted with the documents for 58 years this week I am of the same opinion. Few collections of such archives match their medieval collection, their continuity and sheer number of documents which throw light on so many aspects of the City's history.

During the second half of the twentieth century the Devon & Cornwall Record Society undertook the publication of no fewer than five volumes based on these records: tax assessments, receivers' accounts, local custom accounts and a list of freemen covering 1266 to 1793 which was compiled from various sources in the collection. It was some years ago that a proposal to publish a transcription of the Orphans' Court inventories in the City Archives was received by the Society's Council. This was welcomed as being a popular volume but unfortunately had to be postponed at that time because of its size and expense. The Council was very much aware of the fact that so many Devon inventories had perished in the Exeter Blitz and had sought to fill the gap hitherto by publishing a volume edited by Margaret Cash in 1966 on stray 16th- and 17th-century inventories surviving in the Devon County Record Office and another in 1997 on the Uffculme wills and inventories edited by Peter Wyatt. It is most satisfactory that it is now possible to go ahead with the publication in two volumes devoted to wills and inventories of the Exeter Orphans' Court in the Elizabethan period. This is made possible by the provision of some extra financial assistance from Exeter City Council and by the co-operation of Exeter Archaeology with the Record Society.

The Introduction has been written using the skills and knowledge of both historians and archaeologists, which has produced much fuller descriptions of the items described in the inventories than would have been possible under the first proposal. The two volumes represent a most valuable addition to the collections of records in the Exeter City Archives now in print and will be well used by historians and genealogists who will no longer have to struggle with the difficult transcription.

Margery Rowe
Exeter
August, 2014

INTRODUCTION

By Todd Gray with John Allan and Jannine Crocker

In 1560 Exeter was a compact city with some 10,000 residents, many of whom were dependent upon the woollen cloth trade. It was the largest urban place west of Bristol and the capital of Devon in terms of commerce, religion and law. Exeter was growing not only in prosperity but in confidence: it had successfully supported the Crown in the Prayer Book Rebellion of 1549 and thereby proved its Protestant credentials as well as its allegiance to King Edward VI. While this may not have stood the city in good stead during the short Marian return to Catholicism, it would have endeared her to the new queen, Elizabeth I, who followed in 1558.

Two years later Exeter obtained a royal charter for the establishment of an Orphans' Court to administer the estates of all 'orphans' within the city[1] and three years later the charter was confirmed by Parliament. Even prior to this Exeter had claimed 'the charge and government of every freeman's child (after his father's death) being within the age of one and twenty years'. A substantial number of boroughs were empowered by charter to have orphans' courts: London, Bristol and Worcester before that at Exeter, and Chester, Hull, Northampton, Berwick, Coventry, Reading and Southampton afterwards.[2]

The court was a great financial help to the city because it allowed the council to use the estates of wealthy freemen. Orphans were defined as the children of freemen who were under the age of twenty-one at the time of their father's death, regardless of whether the mother was still alive. In Elizabethan Exeter retailing and the use of associated occupations were still in theory restricted to freemen, although in practice retailers who were not free could operate by paying a variety of fines for shopkeeping. However, freemen enjoyed a monopoly of trade

Fig. 1.   John Hooker, chamberlain of the city.
(*photo: G. Young, courtesy of Exeter Guildhall*).

in some articles, and of retail trade in others, and represented the wealthier citizens of Exeter during the Elizabethan period.

The administration of the deceased freemen's estates was one of the principal duties of the city's Chamberlain, and it may have been partly for this purpose that the office of Chamberlain was created in 1555. John Hooker, best remembered as Devon's first known historian and archivist, was responsible for Exeter obtaining rights for the Orphans' Court and was the first occupant of the post of Chamberlain. He held the position until his death in 1600. Among his duties was one to 'take the speciall Chardge and care of the orphanes'.[3] He is mentioned by name in the inventories.[4]

The stated aim of the court was to protect the interests of the minors: one historian has seen its primary role as a social one in trying to help 'broken families' and believed that the city had the court only because of Hooker's energy and ambition.[5] Both Hooker's father and grandfather had served as mayors in Exeter and he had intimate knowledge of how the city worked. However, the Orphans' Court was also a lucrative operation for Exeter's local government because the funds were used at its discretion and the profits retained for the city's use.[6] One corporate use of the funds was towards the establishment of the canal. Nearly £7,000 was spent by the city on the canal and of this £450 was borrowed from the Orphans' Court. The city's public financing was tight in the late sixteenth century but revenues increased and were in surplus in the 1600s. This decreased the financial need for the Orphans' Court. Perhaps this was one reason why procedures became slack and the court operated less efficiently after Hooker's death in 1601.[7]

The Orphans' Court in Exeter was governed along similar lines to those of the court which had been established in London. Hooker set down the rules and regulations for its administration.[8] The appointed executor, more often than not the widow of the deceased, was summoned by the common crier within one month after the testator's death to appear before the mayor and aldermen of the city at the next meeting of the Guildhall court, where he or she was bound over to present the will of the deceased and a true inventory of all his goods and chattels on a day appointed by the mayor. If the executor failed to appear in court, the mayor could order that he or she be committed to prison. Furthermore, if the executor was the deceased's widow and she remarried before the inventory was exhibited, she then forfeited eight shillings of every pound due to her for the use of the orphans. The inventory was to be compiled by sworn appraisers living in the ward in which the testator had died, for which service they were usually paid a small sum.

Recognised costs were paid. These could include the 'tabling', or feeding, of the children[9] or medical bills, such as those paid in 1590 for Hugh Bidwell's children. 'Mother Berry', also listed as 'Widow Berry', was given money for nursing one of Bidwell's sons, as was Peter Buckingham.[10] Occasionally items were recorded as having been pawned to cover such costs; for example, a sword and some platters, pans and saucers were pawned in 1590.[11]

According to the custom of Exeter, the goods were divided into three equal parts. The first went to the widow and the second to the children, while the third remained 'for the performaunce of the will of the testatur'.[12] If any of the heirs died before reaching the age of twenty-one, their portions were divided between the remaining heirs. The funds of the estates were then deposited with the court, which could use them to its best advantage. The common practice was for the money to be loaned out at interest to private individuals, who entered into bonds or recognisances for the repayment of the sum upon the heirs reaching their majority (or upon marriage in the case of female heirs who married before the age of twenty-one). When such a bond was entered into, the recognitors paid the fees of the officers of the Orphans' Court, such as the common crier, common sergeant and the town clerk. In 1564 the chamberlain was also granted a quarter of the fees of the other officers of the court as a reward for his service to the orphans. The recognitors were to appear in court once a year on the Monday after mid-lent Sunday, 'and yf they do make Defaulte they forfeite to the Chamber 2*d* of everye pounde of asmuche as the[y] stande bounde for'.[13] At this point 'it must be inquired whether every Orphane be lyvinge brought up guyded & instructed as he or she ought to be'.[14] If any of the recognitors died before the orphans reached the age of twenty-one (or married), the remaining recognitors were to present another man in his place within one month after any such death, who was to be bound in the same sum of money and under the same conditions as the deceased. The recognitors often included the widow of the deceased.

During the time of their minority, the orphans were in the care and guidance of the recognitors, who were to provide them not only with material necessities such as food, drink and clothing at their own cost, but also with moral education and a decent upbringing. They were paid a small allowance, the amount of which was governed by rates dependent upon the amount of money loaned out to the recognitors. The recognitors were not allowed to bind the orphans in any apprenticeship, and the orphans were not permitted to marry without the consent and approval of the court. Any female heir marrying without the consent of the mayor and aldermen forfeited 12*d* of every pound due to her to the use of the Chamber if she married a freeman, and if she married a 'foreigner' (i.e. a man not admitted to the freedom of Exeter) she forfeited 3*s* of every pound, 1*s* to the use of the Chamber, and the remaining 2*s* to the use of the other orphans, or to the use of her kin if there were no other orphans. In January 1571 it was alleged that Elizabeth Reynold, a daughter and orphan of Arnold Reynold, had married without consent, in which case the Chamber decreed that 'if it be trewe they to default so mich of her parte as by order & custome of this citie is apoynted'.[15]

Upon reaching the age of twenty-one (or upon marriage in the case of female heirs), the orphans were required to bring in witnesses to the Orphans' Court to testify on oath as to their age. Ursula Lante, for example, proved her age by the testimony of her godmother, Ursula Roberts. Once their age was established, the orphans acknowledged receipt of the portion due to them for their orphanage and the recognisance was cancelled. At the discharge of the recognisance the orphans were required to pay the fees of the officers of the court.

The men, whose wills and inventories are presented here, had some social status in the city given their status as freemen,

and some can clearly be seen to have been individuals of great standing. One such man was Henry James, a notary public, who was entrusted to keep in his house 'the crooks to hang the Mayor's Swords and Maces on'.[16]

THE DOCUMENTS

The documents are stored at the Devon Heritage Centre in Exeter. They consist of flat inventories and rolls, often with various accompanying papers. The flat inventories are made of paper, whereas the rolls (with a few exceptions) are of parchment. Several copies were made of each inventory; Elizabeth Lymett, widow of Edward Lymett, records a payment for ingrossing his inventory '3 tymes in parchmente'.[17] The appraisers toured the deceased's home room by room, making a note of all his possessions and their estimated value. As well as goods and chattels, the appraisers also listed any leases he might hold and all his debts, both those owed to him and those due from him to his creditors. Occasionally a copy of the deceased's will is present among the additional papers that accompany the inventory, as with William Lante's inventory,[18] but this is not generally the case. Many of the inventories do, however, have surviving additional papers giving details about the division of the estate and recording such payments as legacies and funeral charges, although these are not extant for all inventories. As a result it is in some instances possible to reconstruct a complete picture of the deceased's estate and its administration, while in other cases there exists only a short inventory containing little detail – for instance that of Arnold Reynold.[19] William Lante's inventory is exceptional in that it also contains a bill of sale, listing the possessions sold and the price received for them.[20] In comparing this with the estimated value in the inventory it becomes apparent that the sale price usually matched the appraisers' estimate fairly closely. Some wills have unusual details. For instance, William Lante made provision in his will for four of what he called his 'gossips'. These four, most likely men, were either fellow godparents or intimate friends.

Altogether some 216 complete inventories survive in the main series of the Orphans' Court, with partial copies of some others in the associated records. These begin on 7 April 1560 with the inventory of Thomas Grygge and the last one, for Elizabeth Cudmore, is dated 7 October 1721. The court closed in that year. Other documents relating to the Orphans' Court include the Proceedings Books, also stored at the Devon Heritage Centre. These books detail the recognisances entered into when the court loaned out portions of a freeman's estate to private individuals at interest. They also contain entries noting when the orphans returned to the court to claim their portions and prove their ages, and they often contain information about female heirs who married and subsequently returned to the court with their husbands to receive their orphanage.

The Elizabethan documents edited in this collection concern 106 individuals of whom 53 have wills and 88 have inventories. Thirty-seven men have both wills and inventories. Some of the wills were proved in the Prerogative Court of Canterbury and these are housed at The National Archives. The remainder in this collection are wills from the records of Exeter's Orphans' Court. These include the will of Joan Tuckfield which was copied into the Court records and appears here as an appendix. She was cited by Hooker in his Chronology for 1557. He noted that year 'an order was taken that the widow of every one of the 24 [councillors] should yearly at Easter and Christmastide have the half of such common bread as their husbands were want to have. The cause and occasion hereof was to encourage them by the example of Mrs Joan Tuckfield to bestow their goods to such good uses as she did'. She died in 1573 and her death is the only event that Hooker noted taking place that year. He highlighted the generous charitable aspects of Tuckfield's will.[21]

The significance of the inventories
The Orphans' Court inventories reproduced here form the most informative series of documents relating to the houses, material culture and social history of people living in Exeter during the latter half of the sixteenth century. They record in remarkable detail such matters as the names and number of the rooms in their homes, their furniture, clothing, jewellery, kitchen equipment and the pattern of their debts. These have a particular significance because almost all the other Exeter inventories of the sixteenth and seventeenth centuries were burnt, along with most of those for other parts of Devon, in the Exeter Blitz of 4 May 1942 when the Registry Office in Bedford Circus was hit by German bombs. One of the few Devon collections with which they can be compared is that of the rural East Devon parish of Uffculme, which was a Peculiar Parish in the jurisdiction of the Diocese of Salisbury;[22] these inventories thus escaped the bombing of Exeter because they were housed in Salisbury. The 33 Uffculme inventories of the late sixteenth century are nearly all of farmers and reflect their agricultural lives. By contrast, the Exeter inventories reflect the more prosperous lives of its urban freemen and thus have an added interest to historians because of the prospering nature of the city. Unlike the other Devon inventories and wills, they were moved out of Exeter, probably to Bicton, during the Second World War because of concerns about bombing.

The inventories have had little use by historians, the notable exceptions being Professor Wallace T. MacCaffrey, who was assisted by Professor W. G. Hoskins, in his study of Exeter which was published more than fifty years ago,[23] by Professor Joyce Youings in her work on Tuckers Hall,[24] and in an article and book written by Charles Carlton more than thirty years ago.[25] Carlton has described the court in terms of safeguarding the interests of those men who were running the court: 'in doing orphans good, those who ran the court were also doing well by themselves. They acted in a spirit of enlightened self-interest, fully cognisant that any day might be their last, and that on the morrow their estates would pass into the court's hands'.[26]

THE PEOPLE

Since the inventories record only the property of deceased freemen, they are not representative of all the inhabitants of Elizabethan Exeter. It has been estimated that perhaps 10%

of Exeter's adult male population were freemen in the mid-sixteenth century.[27] Nevertheless, some of the documents record the possessions of humble people. For example, the estate of Richard Hedgeland, valued at less than £4,[28] would fall into the category defined by MacCaffrey as poor. This would be equivalent at the establishment of the court to nearly £700 today.[29] John Reve, brewer, whose estate was valued at £17[30] would have been a man of modest affluence; there are many inventories of estates valued between £20 and £50 (worth between £3,500 and £8,500 today). At the other extreme, the estates of some of Exeter's most affluent citizens are represented, such as that of William Chappell, alderman, worth over £2,300 (nearly £400,000 today).[31] The inventories exhibit a variety of individuals from the wealthy merchants to the more humble artisans. The most commonly noted recorded occupation was that of merchant. Nineteen men were listed in this general category but one man was also noted as a merchant and vinter while another was recorded as a butcher and a victualler. The second highest occupation was that of baker: eight men were recorded as such. The clothing industry is represented more commonly such as the haberdasher, hatter and skinner but there was also a dyer, two weavers, two fullers and one individual was recorded as a fuller and elsewhere as a tucker. One individual was listed as a draper, another as a tailor and as a draper, and there were also three tailors. There were four men recorded as cordwainers, another as a shoemaker and a sixth man was listed as a shoemaker and cordwainer. There was also a notary public, saddler, stationer, glasier, joiner, vintner, an innkeeper, two innholders, two barbers and two brewers.

The goods listed illustrate the extensive trade which Exeter was then engaged in, but there are other indications of the city's mercantile activities. One merchant, Henry Maunder, owned a sixteenth share in the *Dragon* of Topsham,[32] while another owned half of the *George*.[33] William Chappell, another merchant, had listed his 'adventures abroad' which included an investment of £34 in the 'Isles', probably the Canaries or Madeira, and another of £321 in Spain.[34]

Many freemen had large families. Henry Maunder, an Exeter merchant who died in the 1560s, left nine children of whom at least three were under the age of twenty-one at the time of his death. William Lante, an Exeter tailor who also died in the 1560s, left ten children. The wealthier citizens seem to have had more surviving children, possibly reflecting their better diet and a healthier upbringing.

THE HOUSES

The locations of properties

Throughout the inventories there appear the names of many streets and areas which are familiar today, such as High Street, Paris Street, Longbrook Street, Goldsmith Street, Preston Street, Fore Street, Broadgate, East Gate, Friernhay and Southernhay. Some are described in unfamiliar ways such as the Island (Exe Island), Stripcoat Hill (Stepcote Hill), North Gate Street and South Gate Street (North and South Street) and Rockes or St Rocks Lane (Coombe Street). They also mention Cowkrow–Cook Row (formerly the north-eastern side of South Street), St Mary Arches Lane (Mary Arches Street), St Martin's Lane (Martin's Lane), St Paul's Lane (Paul Street), Castle Lane (Castle Street), St Pancras Lane (Pancras Street), Racke Lane (Rack Street) and Northernhay Stile. Some of the original spellings are phonetic, such as Daulyshe (Dawlish), Kirton (Crediton) and Apsam (Topsham).

The principal rooms and their functions

Many of the rooms are described in standardized terms, such as hall or parlour, but some of the inventories add additional details about their locations. For instance, one room in 1588 was listed as 'the little chamber at stair-head' and another as 'a little room at stair-head'.[35] In another items are listed under 'in the tweane doores'.[36]

The shop

The shop was usually situated at the front of the house on the ground floor. It often had a stall or 'bulk' before it to display the goods for sale; the one in Henry Maunder's shop was

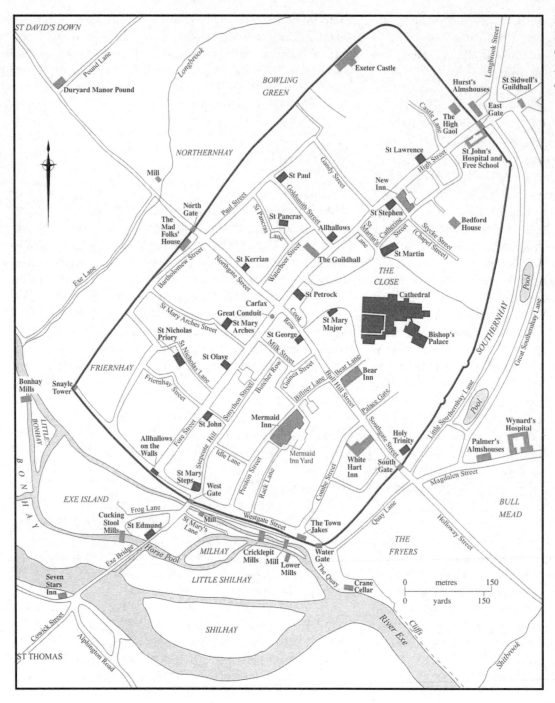

Fig. 2.   Places in Exeter in the
late 16th and early 17th centuries
(*adapted from Stoyle 2003,
Map 4; courtesy of M. Stoyle
and A. Bereznay*).

furnished with shelves.[37] In addition to being the place where goods were sold, the shop was often the workshop in which they were made. Several shops contained the tools of the trade, for example those of the saddler Edmond Berdsley[38] and of the cordwainer Richard Taylor.[39] William Lante's inventory[40] lists a higher and a lower shop. The higher one was presumably on the first floor and perhaps functioned both as a workshop and as a storeroom. Edward Lymet also had two shops, one great and the other little.[41] These contained almost identical items, although one was probably the retail shop while the other served for storage. Apart from the goods themselves and the tools of the trade, shops generally contained a board or counter, some shelves, and perhaps a pair of scales with weights. John Dynham distinguished between his shops by referring to one as the 'out shop'.[42] Thomas Byrde had three: a wool-shop, working-shop and cloth-shop.[43]

Naturally, the shop goods commonly reflected the named occupation of their owner; for example, a notary public kept a roll of parchment and 12 reams of paper in his shop, while an apothecary had an extensive list of medicines.[44] Sometimes they indicate the occupation of the owner when this is not actually stated. Richard Hedgeland was evidently a carpenter; he owned planes, saws, chisels, hammers and 'carving tools' in his (work)shop and Richard Stansby's occupation was probably a smith or cutler, judging from his shop goods of rapiers, swords, knives and daggers.[45]

Not surprisingly, cloth features fairly frequently as shop goods: William Lante, a tailor, kept more than 50 yards of kersey in his 'lower shop' as well as 22 pounds of wool in what was described as his 'higher shop'.[46] Henry Maunder's shop included nearly 150 yards of canvas,[47] John Follett had more than 500 yards of a variety of cloth[48] while John Bodleighe had more than 1,000 yards of cloth in his shop.[49] Another merchant, John Spurway, kept even more cloth[50] while in the shop of Thomas Martyn, a fuller, there was more than 2,000 yards of cloth of all kinds and yet more cloth in his warehouse.[51] The haberdasher Thomas Greenwood kept 556 hats as well as 139 caps in his shop, and nearly another 300 in his middle fore-chamber.[52]

The shop stock listed in several inventories provides striking illustrations of the significance of the leather trades. In 1568 Nicholas Marret, a cordwainer, had 67 pairs of shoes recorded in his shop[53] while Richard Taylor, another cordwainer, had 71 pairs of children's shoes, 100 pairs of women's shoes and 116 of men's shoes.[54] Hugh Bidwell, noted as a shoemaker, had nearly 500 pairs of shoes in his shop.[55] Widow Harrison had not only 67 pairs of shoes but pairs of Spanish pumps, cork shoes, boots and leather boskins (half-boots) in her husband's shop. Some of the leather for his shoes, made of lamb, goat, calf and sheepskins, came from Spain and Flanders.[56]

The hall

In late sixteenth-century Exeter the hall remained the most important room in the house. It was commonly the first to be listed, no doubt because it was usually situated on the ground floor behind the shop.[57] Many of the inventories record halls decorated with wall hangings, including stained cloths,[58] with cushions on the benches and carpets, and often a cupboard, perhaps for displaying the family's plate. In most houses the hall was the room in which the household ate their meals, and therefore it usually contained a table, at least one bench, and sometimes a chair or two. Other items commonly found there include a basin and ewer for washing hands before or after courses.

Most of the inventories suggest that by the late sixteenth century the hall served as the living room and was no longer being used for cooking; the cooking equipment was usually listed in a separate kitchen. In a number of the poorer households, such as that of the baker James Taylor,[59] however, the cooking equipment and fireside implements were kept in the hall, and no kitchen is mentioned elsewhere in the inventory.

Some of the larger dwellings had two halls, the second being known as the 'forehall', or 'higher forehall', as listed in the inventory of Thomas Greenwood.[60] This was evidently on the first floor and can be presumed to have occupied the front of the building overlooking the street.

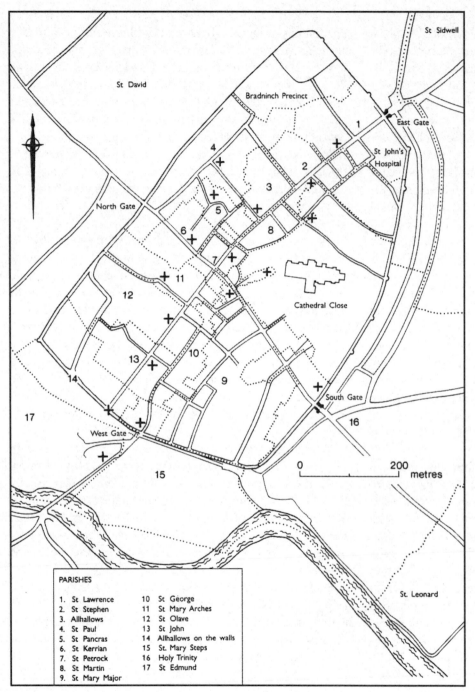

Fig. 3. The parishes of early modern Exeter (*graphic: Exeter Archaeology*).

PARISHES

1. St Lawrence	10 St George
2. St Stephen	11 St Mary Arches
3. Allhallows	12 St Olave
4. St Paul	13 St John
5. St Pancras	14 Allhallows on the walls
6. St Kerrian	15 St. Mary Steps
7. St Petrock	16 Holy Trinity
8. St Martin	17 St Edmund
9. St Mary Major	

The parlour

The parlour was second in importance to the hall, being found more frequently in the houses of wealthier citizens. It was used as a withdrawing room, although sometimes the family might dine there. A secondary function of the room was as additional sleeping accommodation, and it frequently contained a bed.[61] Nicholas Marret's parlour contained numerous beds as well as his clothes, plate and ready money.[62] It appears that the parlour was most commonly situated on the ground floor behind the hall; it was usually listed in the inventories directly after the hall, suggesting that the appraisers walked from one room straight into the other. However, it was sometimes found on the first floor. Occasionally a household would have parlours on both ground and first floors, although possession of two parlours was less common than that of two halls.

The kitchen

The kitchen was almost always found on the ground floor; architectural evidence shows that in larger dwellings it would often be a separate building lying behind a courtyard.[63] Although the kitchen was used primarily for cooking, it often fulfilled the secondary function of a brewhouse. The wide range of cooking utensils and the great quantities of metal vessels in Exeter households are well illustrated by the inventories.

The spence, buttery and larder

In one sense these three terms were interchangeable in the sixteenth century, although the term spence seems to have been supplanted subsequently by that of buttery. A spence has been defined as a room or separate place in which to keep victuals and liquor but a second definition is that it was an inner apartment.[64] Whereas a buttery could be used only for storing liquor, it could also serve for the storage of general provisions. In contrast, a larder was a room or closet which served as a storehouse for meat and other provisions.[65] Some understanding of what was meant by a spence is provided in the inventory of Henry James in 1578. In his 'utter [outer]

office' there was 'one other frame of seeling [panelling] like to a spence, with a bench and shelves round about the same'.[66]

These rooms were often contrived simply by partitioning off one end of a room, usually the hall or kitchen. For instance, Thomas Byrde's spence was within the hall in 1577, as was Thomas Jewell's eleven years later. They could often open off one of these rooms. In 1590 John Brooke had a little spence in which he kept cauldrons, crockery, pans, pewter and shelves.[67] Likewise, Nicholas Marret's spence in 1568 had crocks, a posnet, pans, skillets, buckets and tubs.[68] A spence could also be a piece of furniture.[69] In the seventeenth century the buttery was often situated next to the parlour. It was essentially a cool storage space, although both rooms provided storage space for cooking utensils and foodstuffs. In general, households had either a buttery or a spence.[70] Several men had both while Thomas Prestwood and Richard Sweete not only had a spence and buttery but also a larder.[71]

Fig. 4.   An early attempt to reconstruct an Elizabethan Exeter interior: the Nelson Atkins Museum's reconstruction of c. 1950 showing a first-floor room from 229 High Street, Exeter, built around the architectural elements of the room, transported to the USA following the demolition of the house in 1930 (*courtesy of the Nelson Atkins Museum, Kansas City, USA*).

The pastry house

The wealthy merchant Thomas Chappell had a 'pasterhouse' otherwise referred to as a 'paysteri' or a 'pastery'. In this were a cupboard, a 'pastinge board' (a board on which the pastry would have been rolled out), two other boards with three shelves, five voiders (large dishes) for paste (pastry), two pills (probably peels, the wooden shovels used to load and unload an oven), two shredding knives (rectangular knives used in making mince) and a sieve, tubs, bowls, platters, a grater, pans and pots. This room was on the ground floor and was listed separately from the kitchen.[72] In it pies and flans would have been produced; the peels suggest that it had an oven.[73]

The gallery

Many of the inventories mention a gallery or 'allyar', a covered space partly open along one side. They are most often found in larger houses, although the cook Allen Markes, whose home had only seven rooms, is recorded as possessing one. The gallery was a characteristic feature of a distinctive south-west English urban house type – the so-called 'gallery-and-back block' house, in which the main rooms on the street frontage were separated by a courtyard from a kitchen to the rear.[74] It extended along one side of the courtyard, providing access between the two blocks of the building, sometimes on two or more levels. Henry Maunder's house had two galleries, the second presumably joining the two parts of the building on the second floor.[75] The inventories show that they were generally enclosed to form a comfortable room in their own right, where furniture could be placed. On occasion the gallery could fulfil a secondary function as sleeping accommodation, indicated by the presence of beds. Galleries could even contain a secondary room, as the inventory for John Follett shows in 1589. His had 'a chamber within the gallery called a back chamber' which could have indicated that the chamber was behind the gallery.[76]

The chamber

The word 'chamber' was a general term similar in use to the word 'room' today. First-floor chambers for sleeping became common in the later sixteenth century, and the word was often

Fig. 5.   A few courtyards survive at the rear of houses in High Street, similar to this demolished example from 38 North Street, with its back block (left) joined to the main part of the house (right) by a gallery. Various houses, such as those of Thomas Byrde, Henry James and Nicholas Glanfield (OC 28, 29, 33) evidently had this feature; in Thomas Prestwood's grand house there was a great court, little court, gallery and court by the stables (OC 24).

used to denote a bedchamber. They could also be used for purposes other than sleeping, such as storage.

The principal bedchamber where the master and mistress of the house slept was usually on the first floor at the front of the house, and was called the forechamber. It would contain the best bed and bedding, far exceeding the value of that in other chambers.[77] Further bedchambers were found on the upper floors, often simply called the 'chamber over the parlour' or the 'chamber over the hall'. The servants' quarters, termed the 'maids' chamber' or the 'men's chamber', were usually to be found at the top of the house. Thomas Chappell had a 'Brushing Chamber'.[78]

The loft

The upper chamber under the eaves of the roof, sometimes known as a loft but also as a cockloft, has been defined as 'a small upper loft, a small apartment under the very ridge of the roof to which the access is usually by a ladder'.[79] In one man's cocklofts there were 'old bedsteads and other trash'. A haberdasher used his higher cockloft to hold his cloth, while in the lower cock loft was a bed, and a cordwainer stored hay in his.[80]

The warehouse and the cellar

The warehouse was used solely for storing goods, and was often found behind or above the shop. The cellar, defined in one sense as a storehouse or storeroom for provisions, was more usually found in larger dwellings, particularly those belonging to merchants. Architectural evidence shows that it was commonly below ground level at the front of the building, with direct access to the street above,[81] although it could also be found on the ground floor. It was used as a storage place, often for wine and beer, although other commodities are recorded there, including lime, pitch and timber. John Anthony, for example, kept 'wood and other trash' there in 1598.[82]

Yards and outhouses; linhays and wells

There is one reference to a linhay, an open-sided form of shed with a lean-to roof, in North Street in 1570.[83] Private wells are occasionally indicated by the listing of well-buckets, winches, ropes and chains.

Room fittings; glazing, panelling and wall hangings

Windows

The regular listing of window glass shows that it was movable, and it was a valuable feature in Elizabethan houses. It was most commonly found in the hall and parlour; the wealth of richer households is reflected in glass windows in other rooms. For example, in his Exeter house William Chappell had glass in the hall, forehall, forechamber, and several other chambers, including the maid's.[84] Similarly, William Trivett had glass in the hall, both parlours, his new chamber, and even in the kitchen.[85]

Sometimes the amount of glass is also recorded. For example, William Seldon's hall had '16 panes of glasse in the windowe by estimacion 64 foote at 6d the foote'.[86] In addition to the glass, the window casements are also frequently appraised.

Panelling and benches

Panelling, most commonly described as sealing or wainscoting, is a common feature of the more important rooms, especially halls and parlours, and sometimes with benches, which were evidently an integral feature at the foot of the panelling. The fact that panelling was regularly mentioned shows that it was regarded as movable – a point also apparent in the evidence for the resetting and adaptation of panelling visible in surviving panelling.

Wall hangings and pictures

The inventories record a variety of furnishings. Wall hangings, serving the dual function of decoration and insulation, were a common feature. They were most often found in halls and parlours, although they were occasionally also present in bedchambers. These cloths were generally dyed (stained) or painted, and were often of canvas. Bold colours were used; red and green appears to have been a popular combination, although other colours are mentioned, for example in the inventory of Henry Maunder, where yellow and blue wall cloths are listed in the chamber over his forehall.[87] Some hangings had depicted biblical or mythological scenes.

There are several references to items with 'stories' (depictions of historical scenes). In 1579 William Chappell, an alderman, kept in his hall 'two tables with painted stories' while Henry James, notary public, had in his hall 'hangings with three stories' in the same year.[88] These were probably of stained cloth. In 1564 Henry Maunder had '2 pictures of Flanders work' in his fore hall[89] and in 1591 Thomas Greenwood kept four 'Flanders pictures' in the hall.[90] Another man owned six 'painted histories' in 1591; these too were probably wall-hangings of stained cloth, and another that same year had 'one picture' which was valued as being worth 12d. In 1602 William Martin owned five pictures but altogether these were recorded as only being worth 15d.

Fig. 6. The combination of panelling, plasterwork and carved wooden overmantels in two rich late Elizabethan Exeter interiors: (a) No. 229 High Street, dating to the 1580s; (b) Bampfylde House, dating to *c.* 1600. Both houses are now lost, although the overmantel and panelling from 229 High Street are now in the RAM Museum. (*Crocker 1886, pls L, LII*).

Fig. 7. Photographs of 170–1 Fore Street, taken shortly before its demolition in the 1930s, showing its richly carved fireplace surround and superb panelling (*photos: RAM Museum, Exeter*).

Curtains

Curtains used for windows are listed in several inventories. One refers to a 'wyndowe Clothe of grene Clothe', which was presumably a curtain[91] and others are more explicit. Joan Redwood had 'the olde curtings for the window' in 1587;[92] three years later Thomas Chappell had '4 courtinges of the windowes'[93] and in 1591 Thomas Greenwood had five old window curtains in his middle fore-chamber and a window curtain in the lower hall. In some instances the curtains are listed with their rods; sometimes these are noted as being made of iron.[94]

HOUSE CONTENTS

The inventories' chief interest is in their detailed lists of possessions. Most items were valued individually but miscellaneous goods of small value were commonly listed together, referred to collectively as 'old' 'other old', 'odd', 'other trumpery',[95] 'certain trash' or 'old trash forgotten'.[96]

Furniture

The main items of furniture found in the inventories are beds, tables, stools, benches, chairs, presses, coffers, chests and cupboards.[97] Although it was no longer as rare as it had been in earlier times, furniture was still mostly of a basic and utilitarian form. At this time almost all furniture was sturdy and heavy, being usually constructed of oak, but by the 1560s most inventories record joined furniture. Rooms were often numerous but tended to be small, so that few large pieces of furniture were generally located in any one room. Occasionally timber is noted; the interesting entry of a large amount of Brazil wood, valued at £5 in 1589, suggests the arrival of wood from South America.[98]

Bedsteads

The bed of the master and mistress of the household was probably the most prized piece of furniture in many of these households. The inventories of the more affluent citizens mention beds with a tester and curtains to keep the occupants warm and protected from draughts.[99] A wide range of bedsteads can be found, from very expensive types to those

Fig. 8.   A group of finds, discarded *c.* 1600, excavated in a cesspit at the rear of a tenement in Goldsmith Street, Exeter. Although the glass, porcelain and stonewares might receive specific mention, the plainer and cheaper earthenwares seem usually to have escaped individual description, and were perhaps among the 'old trash' of some inventories. (*RAM Museum, Exeter;* © *Exeter City Council*).

more suited to the means of the humbler tradesmen. The merchant Edward Lymett possessed a bedstead with curtains and bedding worth as much as £9.[100] In a few instances beds were distinguished in the inventories by being noted as being carved.[101] However, many bedsteads were valued at much lower prices. John Denys had two bedsteads, one with a truckle bed under it, and a tester valued at only 4s.[102]

The inventories include standing beds – higher beds in comparison to the truckle or trundle bedsteads.[103] These were low beds on castors which could be kept underneath the main bedstead, and brought out for use as need required.[104] This would obviously save room, an important consideration in houses with many small and cramped rooms. Truckle beds were used by the children of the family, and perhaps by the servants. Others were described as low or side beds.

There were flock beds (stuffed with flocken fragments of wool or cloth), dust beds (filled with chaff) or feather beds. Other beds were described as being joined (made by joiners rather than everyday carpenters, and perhaps meaning they were carved) or performed (fully set-up). Other beds had become transformed in their usage: there were several referred to as death beds.

Tables & carpets

Two types of table are commonly described in the inventories: trestle and joined, the latter with the top fixed to the frame. The trestle type is usually referred to as a 'table borde', with no mention of the trestle frame. Sometimes trestles are mentioned separately, for instance in Thomas Grygge's house where they are located in two of the chambers.[105] Occasionally the type of wood is specified: one table board was made of walnut.[106] Tables came in a variety of shapes, the most common being rectangular. Nicholas Marret, however, had a 'rounde Tabell' in his hall,[107] while Roland Fabyan owned a 'Square table' in the chamber over his shop. Other tables are described as framed, joined, side, long and folding.

Many of these tables would be covered with carpets[108] – items which were too valuable to be placed on the floor, and performing an ornamental rather than a utilitarian function.

Many were coloured green but others were described variously as having been made in 'Darnax' (Dornick in Belgium), of Arras, as a 'London carpet', as a carpet of the Levant (the Middle East) and from (or in the style of) Turkey. Others are noted as being of tapestry, of 'green broadcloth' and of kersey. The most detailed description is 'a gray Kersey Carpett with a Border of needleworke edged with silke ffrenge'.[109]

Stools, benches and chairs

Stools and benches (or forms) appear more frequently than chairs, which were evidently not numerous in Elizabethan Exeter. Chairs were often still reserved for the head of the household and for important guests, while other members of the family would sit on stools, benches or even chests, often made more comfortable by cushions and covers.

The joined stool was common and was found in numerous rooms. In his hall Warnard Harrison had two small stools described as having three legs, perhaps suggesting that this was an unusual feature.[110] The inventories also record stools described as little or close. There were footstools and even 'women's stools'.

Forms are often associated with tables in these inventories. Like benches, they occur frequently but are not described in any detail. They would have been long, low seats without backs.[111] The seat in which to sit by the fire found in James Taylor's hall was probably a type of settle with a high back.[112] A settle is mentioned in Warnard Harrison's hall where it was similarly placed 'by the chymneye'.[113] Benches, however, are usually mentioned in connection with wainscot. The wooden panelling would form the back of the bench. The bench and the wainscot would be joined together and placed against the wall. These benches were probably more comfortable than forms and would afford the user some protection from draughts. Both forms and benches occur frequently but are not described in any detail.

Although not as common, chairs are described in more detail. Both turned and joined chairs are listed. In his hall William Lante had a joined chair with a leather back worth 3s;[114] in his bill of sale it is described simply as a 'lether Chere'.

Chairs made of wicker were not common but they were listed: in 1590 Thomas Chappell kept a wicker chair in his fore-chamber, in 1593 Thomas Greenwood had one in the back chamber and another in his lower fore-chamber, and in 1596 Thomas Baskerville kept a wicker chair in the chamber over the parlour and another in a different room.[115] Other chairs were listed as drilled, close, round, old, great, little or small, and others as covered with a variety of fabric. One chair of pear tree is listed.[116]

Coffers, chests and presses

Coffers and chests are common items in these inventories. They were used primarily for storage, but chests could sometimes function as additional seating. In general, coffers differed from chests in that they had a domed lid while chests were flat-lidded. These items of furniture would generally be found in the sleeping chambers and other principal rooms in the house where they would contain linen or perhaps valuables such as jewellery.

Several types of chests and coffers are recorded. The standard, such as that found in Henry Maunder's buttery, was a large chest that could be used for transporting as well as storing goods.[117] The 'fosselett' or forcer was another type of chest. It was usually small and sometimes strengthened with iron bands, often being used to store valuables such as documents or jewellery. These inventories also include instances of merchants' chests and ships' chests or coffers.

Chests and coffers were often described according to their place of origin or the material from which they were made. A 'danske chest' was probably a chest from Northern Europe imported via Danzig. 'Spruse' chests are found on several occasions; these were made from pine, which also (probably) originated from Northern Europe.[118] A 'sypres' chest is found in Warnard Harrison's shop[119] and another 'sipres chest' in Thomas Chappell's.[120] These were named after the cypress wood from which they were made.

The press was usually a tall cupboard in which clothes and household linen could be stored.[121] Fewer presses are mentioned in these inventories than chests or coffers.

Cupboards

At this date cupboards were usually simple tiered stands on which pewter or silver plate was displayed, rather than enclosed pieces of furniture. A cloth would be placed on the shelves beneath the silver or pewter. This type of cupboard would stand in the hall or the parlour so that visitors could be impressed by the householder's wealth. Robert Mathew's inventory gives a list of the items placed upon the cupboard in his hall.[122] Their value amounted to 21s and they were clearly of pewter rather than silver. The cupboard itself, along with the cloth upon it, was estimated to be worth 10s. James Taylor had a cupboard in his parlour on which he displayed three basins and three pots of latten.[123] Warnard Harrison displayed three platters upon his cupboard in his parlour.[124]

Cupboards were sometimes combined with other items of furniture. Items such as a 'Cubborde with a presse in hit', a 'cobord with a pres under' and a 'Table Borde with a Cubborde in the same' are recorded.[125]

Textiles

Bed curtains feature commonly throughout these inventories, sometimes in the popular colour combination of red and green. In addition to the bed curtains, other bed furnishings are listed including mattresses, pillows and bolsters, sheets, blankets, quilts and coverlets. Little need be said about the first three items; as noted earlier, they were often stuffed, either with feathers or flocks, depending upon the wealth of the householder. Dust mattresses were probably used only by the servants of the house. Some inventories list these items by weight, for example that of Henry James, which records 10 beds of varying weight and quality.[126]

Blankets, quilts and coverlets are also frequently mentioned. Coverlets were more numerous than blankets or quilts. Various colours are recorded, for instance white, yellow and red. Tapestry coverlets are listed and these could be quite valuable. Coverlets described as 'Thromyd' or 'thrumbe' were probably fringed or tufted. The 'Scriden' and 'screede' coverlets are harder to identify. Two examples of 'Flaunders' coverlets are found in Nicholas Marret's parlour.[127]

Other furnishings consisted mainly of carpets and cushions. As has already been noted, carpets were used to cover cupboards and tables. They were made of various materials including 'darnax' or 'dornexe' and tapestry. Red and green again appear to have been popular colours.

Cushions were common furnishings. They were made of a variety of materials including tapestry, velvet and leather. Cushions with roses, presumably embroidered on them, appear in William Lante's inventory, while 'carpet Qwishens' are found in Edward Lymett's.[128] Cushion covers are also mentioned in Hugh Pope's inventory, where two cushion 'clothes' were valued at 3s 4d.[129]

Household linen is frequently listed in a section of its own under the heading of napery and contained such items as towels, pillowcases, napkins, aprons, linen, sheets and towels. These linen storehouses were occasionally listed separately such as in 1563 for Henry Maunder and also for his wife: there was 'his napery' and 'her napery'.[130] In William Flay's napery the linen was listed separately from his woollen apparel.[131] It would most probably have been stored in a chest, coffer or press. The most common items include sheets and pillowcases, napkins, tablecloths and towels. Sheets and pillowcases were made of a variety of materials; canvas was common, as was dowlas. Sheets made of Holland cloth and cloth from Morlaix are also recorded. Napkins came in a variety of fabrics, such as canvas, diaper and Morlaix cloth (?linen). They could sometimes be decorated, an example being the two dozen 'wroght wyth blacke Sylke' found in Henry Maunder's inventory.[132] Perhaps these were embroidered with his initials. Tablecloths were made of similar materials. Diaper, Morlaix cloth, Holland cloth and canvas tablecloths are all recorded in these inventories. Towels were also fairly common. Hand towels are specified in some inventories. Where material is specified, diaper is most common, although canvas towels are also mentioned. Most towels were probably plain, but Henry Maunder had six towels 'wrowght with blacke Sylke' worth 30s, besides two hand towels 'wyth blacke lace'.[133]

Clothing

Clothing is often listed in a separate section under the heading of apparel, and is sometimes described in detail. The inventories include records of clothing adorned with fur (both rabbit's fur and fox fur are mentioned) or lambskin, or made of a wide range of fabrics including velvet, damask, lace, satin and taffeta. For those lower down the social scale, garments of kersey, worsted or wool are more common. Colours are not often mentioned, but when they are they are generally subdued. Garments coloured black, tawny, russet and 'rattes color' are mentioned. Crimson gowns are mentioned on several occasions; these were probably robes of office.

The inventory of Henry Maunder, dated 1564, provides a good example of the apparel of a wealthy merchant and his wife at the start of Elizabeth's reign. He owned four 'brown blue' gowns, ornamented with either black lace, taffeta, rabbit or 'budge' (lambskin). His other clothes included a taffeta cassock, two wool doublets, a sleeveless woollen coat, a woollen jacket, a brown blue cloak, a 'cloth' coat and a pair of hose. His clothing was worth just over £8, while his wife's was worth more than ten. She owned a cassock with 'a ffrenge of sylke', another with lace, three round woollen kirtles, a scarlet petticoat, and five gowns edged with velvet as well as one without.[134] Richard Taylor's inventory lists 'Weomens apparell' including garments made of mockado, damask, calico, chamlet, canvas and fustian.[135] A violet gown, a scarlet petticoat, a pair of red satin bodices and a red petticoat are some of the more colourful items of female attire found in the inventories.

Cloth

The shop inventory of John Follett, merchant, illustrates the range of cloth which was sold in Exeter at the end of the sixteenth century. He owned a considerable amount of canvas which was imported especially from Brittany and Normandy. This was described as being fine canvas, Normandy canvas, Vitre canvas (from the town of that name in Brittany) and Treguier canvas (from the Breton port of that name). He also sold dowlas (a coarse type of linen), calico (the cotton cloth which came from the East), Hamborowe cloth (German cloth from Hamburg), fustian (a coarse cloth made of cotton and flax), geanes, Holland (cloth from the Netherlands), durance (a stout durable cloth possibly made of wool), quilts (traditionally a thick bed covering) and 'satacocks' which have not been identified. Richard Maudytt's shop listed canvas from Normandy and Brittany but he also owned 'Kunter cloth', Scottish cloth and 'enderlyns'. Cloth was measured in the inventories by the yard, ell, piece, ballot and fardel.

Exeter's cloth industry was its main source of wealth; it would continue to prosper and grow through to the mid-eighteenth century. In the late sixteenth century the city's cloth was shifting from kersies to a more durable type of woollen cloth known as serge or perpetuanos. The city relied upon a large hinterland for production and sold to markets in northern France, the Low Counties and London. Although only a small proportion of the cloth remained in Exeter, the inventories show that some individuals owned considerable lengths, known as 'pieces'; these were kersies and not the perpetuanos which later dominated Exeter production.[136]

Lace & East Devon

The inventories help to open up the murky early history of Devon's lace-making. It has been established that there were lace-makers in East Devon by 1617.[137] The inventories not only provide valuable evidence about the types of lace in use a generation before that date but indicate that lace was made in Elizabethan Exeter. In the past the origins of the later lace-making industry have been attributed to Flemish or other European refugees, and the emergence of lacemaking has been seen as a development limited to the parishes east of the River Exe. There seems no reason to accept either view. It was only in the nineteenth century that writers began to attribute lace making with these imagined continental migrants.[138] No such individuals have been identified as being in East Devon at this time. It should also be noted that bone lace was being made not just in Devon but also to the east in Somerset: there was a bone lace teacher at 'Montague', possibly Montacute or Shepton Montague, by 1620 and at Chard by 1635.[139]

Devon lace was made from linen thread and has been described as a 'free lace', that is a lace produced by the use of bobbins made of bone. It was that type of lace which was listed in the shop contents of John Follett, who sold cloth, in 1589. He owned nine yards of bone lace as well as a quantity of 'frame lace' which, like bone lace, was made from linen thread. Not long afterwards Thomas Martyn, a fuller, owned a box of bone lace, and two other merchants also had bone lace in their inventories. Two specific entries appear to indicate lace production. As early as 1563 'a fframe for laysynge' was listed in one household.[140] Most intriguing of all is the inventory of William Seldon which includes '6 bobbings to wind silk upon'.[141] This appears to indicate that lace was being produced in Exeter a generation before it was recorded in East Devon. It is however unlikely that it had yet become significant enough to be termed an industry given that John Hooker, who oversaw the Orphans' Court, omitted any mention of it in his detailed description of Devon which he wrote in the late 1500s.[142]

Lace was used to ornament clothing and that listed in the inventories decorated gowns, jackets, hose, breeches and jerkins. There are many dozens of references to lace. Some of it is described in terms of its colour, such as gold or silver or black, while others refer to the type of material it was made from including thread and silk. Local lace, possibly from East Devon but just as likely from other parts of the county, is indicated with the aforementioned references to bobbin, bone, and possibly 'billament' lace.

Among the types of lace which are mentioned are twist lace, statute lace, parchment lace (the core of which consists of thin strips of parchment), Galloon lace (a narrow, close-woven ribbon or braid, of gold or silver used for trimming articles of apparel), purled lace (a series of small loops or twists worked in lace), biliment lace (highly ornamental lace used for trimming), crown lace (the pattern worked as a succession of crowns),[143] and cheyn lace which had been given to Queen Elizabeth as a New Year's gift in 1589.[144]

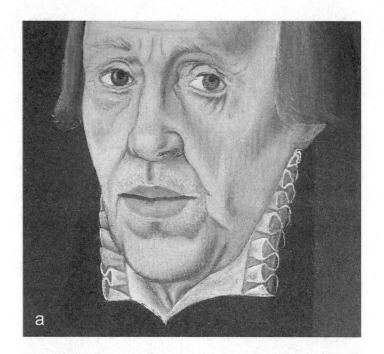

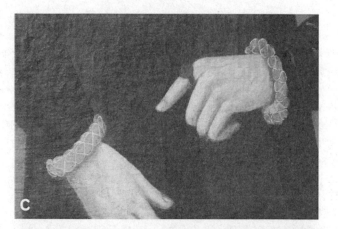

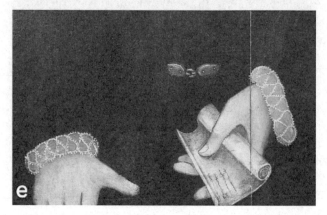

Fig. 9.   The substantial amounts of lace in some inventories, such as that of John Anthonye with its different types of lace (OC 72), or that of John Follett with its evidence for the manufacture of lace in Exeter (OC 40), are mirrored in paintings and monuments of Exeter citizens. (*photos: G. Young, courtesy of Exeter Guildhall*).

Eating & drinking

Kitchen equipment

The kitchen and spence or buttery usually housed an array of cooking utensils. Among them were cauldrons, skillets, grease pans, 'posnets', frying pans, gridirons, spits, chopping boards, tongs, toasting forks, chopping knives, and ladles. Pots and pans would often be made of tin, brass or iron. Firedogs or andirons would frequently be found in front of the open fire, which could support spits for roasting meat. Pothooks and flesh-hooks for hanging meat were other common features. Chafing dishes were used to keep food warm or to cook it. A pestle and mortar to pound herbs and spices, along with their boxes, might also be found. Bellows to fan the fire are recorded in some inventories. It is instructive to see the large numbers of cheap wooden plates, trenchers and bowls in these inventories. Trenchers were the most numerous, often numbering two, three or four dozen, with as many as ten dozen in the household of Thomas Chappell.[145]

Glass and porcelain

A number of inventories list drinking glasses: these include two drinking glasses in 1572, 'ten glasses for drink' in about 1576, water glasses also listed as '3 little glasses to keep water' in 1577, 4 little glasses, 7 drinking glasses, a 'great glass', 4 little glasses and 8 drinking glasses in 1578, 3 drinking glasses in 1583 and another drinking glass the same year.[146] Richard Maddocke owned Venice dishes valued at only 6d in 1591.[147] Another man was listed as owning a 'framed cupboard with Venice glasses and water glasses' in 1598.[148] Glass (and leather) bottles are listed throughout the inventories.

One man, Walter Horsey, a merchant, owned two 'Chyna' dishes which were valued at 3s, a considerable sum, in 1597.[149] This is an especially early record of the use of Chinese porcelain in an English merchant household.[150]

Valuables

A variety of valuables may be found in these inventories. The most common treasures were the householder's silver plate, his gold and his jewellery. Glass was another valued possession, and was often recorded by the appraisers. Books were still quite rare at this date and could consequently also be quite valuable.

Plate

The most common items of plate found in the Exeter inventories of the late sixteenth century are silver spoons, stoneware cups garnished with silver, goblets, bowls, tankards, basins and ewers, and salts.[151] Goblets and ale cups were popular pieces of plate. Almost all the inventories record at least a few pieces of silver plate. A householder's plate, along with his money and jewellery, often accounted for a large percentage of the total value of his estate.

Gilding of plate was common. Most items were only partly gilt, although one completely gilt cup appears in Richard Taylor's inventory.[152] Cups and salts would frequently have gilt covers, with perhaps gilt feet and edging as well. The price of the silver is often recorded in conjunction with the weight, giving a clear indication of both the size and quality of the piece. The high price that individual items could command is illustrated by the gilt salt belonging to the haberdasher Thomas Greenwood,[153] which weighed 21½ ozs and was appraised at £6 9s, and William Doddridge's gilt goblet worth £7.[154]

Spoons, mostly of silver but occasionally of tin, are also common items in the inventories. Many were plain, but others had decorated knops which were often gilt. One such type was the apostle spoon. These spoons were often given as christening presents. They were in sets of either twelve or thirteen, the thirteenth having a knop representing the figure of Christ. Complete sets are rarely recorded. Spoons with knops representing eagles' heads and maidenhead spoons also occur. The maidenhead knop is thought to have represented the Virgin Mary.[155] Amongst the plate recorded for one merchant in 1571 were thirteen spoons with apostle heads, six spoons with eagle heads, another six spoons with 'wreyed' knops and yet six more with maidenheads.[156] A dozen silver spoons among Warnard Harrison's plate were engraved 'wth hys leter of hys name' and were appraised at over £3.[157]

Mention of monogrammed spoons in these inventories is rare. Other oddities are six square-headed spoons, six slip spoons and others 'for cockes'.[158]

Jewellery

This is most frequently listed with the householder's plate. Gold and silver rings, including signet rings, occur on numerous occasions and appear in the Guildhall portraits. Other items include hooks and pins of silver and gilt, (waist) girdles decorated with silver and/or precious stones, and brooches. In the will of Edward Lymett he reminded his wife Elizabeth that his mother had only loaned her girdle to Elizabeth and had specified that it was to be given to their daughter Grace on Elizabeth's death.

Coinage, leases and debt

The bulk of a householder's wealth is usually found in these three items and in his silver plate. Leases were often worth a considerable sum, particularly if they still had many years to run after the death of the lessee. For example, Roland Fabyan's lease was worth £19 – almost half the total value of his estate.[159] Those householders who held several leases might have considerable amounts of money invested in them. Thomas Prestwood held leases in Exe Island and the parish of St Mary Steps, as well as a lease of thirty-two acres of land, all of which were worth around £215, almost a quarter of his total estate.[160]

Few of the inventories record large sums of ready money, although Thomas Grygge, who kept the sum of £311 15s 4d in his house at the time of his death, is an exception.[161] This sum accounted for three-fifths of the value of his estate. Henry Maunder possessed almost £40 in cash at the time of his death, which included £26 13s in Spanish currency, suggesting overseas trade.[162] Some inventories do not record any cash at all.

A great range of coins are listed. Those described in Henry Maunder's inventory may reflect his overseas interests; they included Spanish money and dollars alongside English groats and half-groats, crowns and crowns of the rose. A wide range

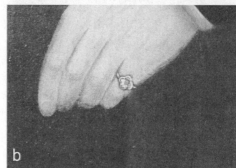

Fig. 10. Gold rings shown on the fingers of people depicted in the Guildhall portraits: (a) Joan Tuckfield, 1573; (b) Thomas White, 1566; (c) Laurene Atwill, 1588. Such rings are regularly recorded in the Orphans Court inventories. Typically, the cheaper ones cost 5–8s; towards the top end of the market, Arnold Reynolde's '2 golde Rynges one withe a blue stone and an other withe a littell stone' cost £3 8s 4d, and the three gold rings of alderman William Tryvet, 'being a turkes, a synet and a Jemye' were valued at £5 (OC 16, 28). (*Photo: G. Young, courtesy of Exeter Guildhall*).

of coins was also present in a Devon household of high status at this time: that of Henry, Earl of Bath, at Tawstock, North Devon.[163]

Debts are more likely to represent a large percentage of the householder's wealth than cash, particularly in the case of merchants. Debts are often itemised, with details of the debtors and what the debt was due for. An example of this is the account of Henry Maunder's debts which covers several pages. It shows a surprisingly wide geographical range in the places his contacts lived: they included Heavitree, Topsham, Exminster, Woodbury, Doddiscombsleigh, Honiton, Gittisham, Ottery St Mary, Chudleigh, Totnes, Brixham, Newton St Cyres, Crediton, Cheriton Fitzpaine, Bickleigh, Tiverton, Halberton and Dorchester.[164] Debts were often divided into two types; desperate debts, which were unlikely to be recovered and often had to be written off, and 'sperate' debts – those with hope of recovery, which may have been legally enforceable.[165] The two types of debt are sometimes recorded together and are therefore indistinguishable one from the other.

Debts owed by the householder are also recorded – often for items obtained on credit, or for servants' wages. In many instances the debts owed by the deceased accounted for a substantial proportion of the value of his estate, with the result that the orphans' portions would be much reduced. The cordwainer Nicholas Marret, for example, had an estate worth just over £41, but his debts and funeral costs accounted for more than £10, and so the amount payable to the four orphans was reduced accordingly.[166] The orphans of Anthony Robyns of the parish of St John's Bow fared even worse; their father's estate amounted to over £92, but over £47 of this was accounted for by his debts and other charges.[167]

Miscellaneous

Books and maps

Books were still quite rare at this time although many families did own a bible, and there are several instances of communion books, testaments, bibles (including bibles in English) and books of common prayer. Thomas Prestwood's inventory lists a Geneva bible.[168]

Other books were less common. Thomas Prestwood had several books in his counting house including William Turner's *Herbal* and 'Halls Cronycells with divers other bookes of Latten frenche and englishe'. The latter was Edward Halls' *The Union of the Two Noble and Illustrate Famelies of Lancastre and Yorke* which was commonly known as *Hall's Chronicle*. That book was already a generation old and the better-known Elizabethan work, Raphael Holinshed's *Chronicles,* appeared a year after Prestwood's death. Interestingly, John Hooker, the city's Chamberlain who oversaw the Orphans' Court, later re-edited the book after Holinshed's death in what became a more popular edition.[169] A more impressive collection of books is found in Henry James' house: he owned nearly two hundred volumes. James, a notary public, was obviously a learned and well-read man, and as one would expect he owned a fair number of law books and statute books. Besides these and his religious works he also had numerous chronicles, a copy of Erasmus' *Paraphrases* and one of Aesop's *Fables*, as well as many books in Latin and several dictionaries including a Greek dictionary. James also owned a chronicle written by Richard Grafton.[170] Prestwood and James both owned a copy of John Lydgate's early fifteenth-century poem *The Fall of Princes*, a retelling of the tragedies of nearly five hundred famous men and women. Another chronicle, unfortunately not described, was owned by Thomas Chappell, a merchant, in 1590. He also owned a bible, three service books and 'one booke of sickman Saule'.[171] Often the books, particularly the bibles, were kept in the hall but sometimes, as in the case of Richard Maudytt in 1594, they were kept in the parlour.[172]

In 1578 Henry James also had a map which was valued at 2*s* 6*d*. This was kept in the inner hall and was presumably printed. In his inner office he had 'a map of the whole world' which had a value given as 6*s* 6*d*. Interestingly, he also owned 'a card of Constantinople'. Thomas Baskerville, the apothecary, owned a map: in 1596 he was listed as having '3 tablets and a small map' worth 5*s* in his low parlour. Richard Sweete, a merchant, also owned a 'chart of the world' in 1591.[173]

Weapons and armour

During the latter half of the sixteenth century the majority of freemen would have belonged to the city's trained bands or militia and many of the inventories include items of weaponry and armour. The most common items include bills, bows and arrows, pikes, shearhooks, swords (including two-handed swords), daggers (including the 'poynado'), pole-axes, halberds, crossbows, javelins and jacks (sleeveless, leather-quilted jackets, often plated with iron). Guns are recorded on several occasions; they include arquebuses, dogs, muskets, demi-culverins and calivers (the latter both being types of small cannon). Along with these guns, flasks and touch-boxes are often recorded.

The most common form of armour found in these inventories is the type called 'almain' rivets. This was a type of light armour first used in Germany and made of small metal plates stitched to clothing. The corselet, a piece of body armour, appears in several inventories, as do sets of harness (defensive armour).

Headwear was usually either a skull (a tight-fitting helmet), sallet (a light helmet) or morion (a type of helmet without a visor). Bucklers (small, round hand-shields) also occur.

Musical instruments
Although music was popular in the Elizabethan period, musical instruments are seldom recorded in the inventories. The exceptions are a pair of virginals listed in 1576, a 'little pair' of virginals and a trumpet in 1593, and a lute in about 1576.[174] Another freeman owned a pair of virginals together with a frame (stand?) for them.[175]

Other items
Among the many commonplace items were mirrors, referred to as looking glasses, and chamber pots (those listed being most commonly of tin), which appear throughout the inventories and were located with other metal goods in such rooms as the kitchen, court and spence but most commonly in the buttery.[176] Ten dozen urinals (probably the glass vessels used in diagnosing illness), were owned by Thomas Baskerville, the apothecary, in 1596.[177] Warming pans appear less frequently.[178] Among the miscellaneous items recorded once or only occasionally are an otter net,[179] an apple roaster,[180] a cobweb brush,[181] a dog chain,[182] a mousetrap,[183] rats' bane[184] and leek seed.[185]

Food and livestock

Livestock
Livestock are recorded in a large proportion of the inventories. Cows, pigs, sheep and horses (nags, mares, geldings, colts) are most common but some inventories list poultry as well.

Foodstuffs
A variety of foodstuffs is found in these inventories, mainly dried food such as cereals and spices. Naturally, fresh food appears less frequently because it decayed quickly (unless, in the case of meat, it was preserved in salt). It would therefore be eaten as quickly as possible, and would probably be purchased on a daily basis. In one instance grain was listed in the garnard, which would more commonly be called a granary today.[186]

Meat, fish and dairy produce
Beef, bacon and mutton are occasionally mentioned in the inventories. Fish, and the chests for it, is listed including that from Newfoundland (Newland) as well as dry fish, millwell, and ling.[187] Dairy produce is mentioned a little more frequently, although it is far from common. However, there are several references to cheese and butter.

Other foods
Cereals are quite frequently mentioned. Bran, wheat, corn, beans, peas, barley and rye all occur in several inventories. The appraisers also listed unharvested crops, for example William Trivett's crops at Duryard, being 3½ acres of 'Barley Otes and beanes nowe in the grownde', which they estimated to be worth 53s 4d.[188] Bread occurs infrequently, although flour, 'meale', 'Beane flower', 'beane meale' and 'wheate meale' all appear.

There are also many instances of luxury goods. One inventory listed 2lb of sugar candy[189] while Thomas Baskerville's inventory listed not only white and red candy, but comfits, marmalade, dry conserves and brown powdered sugar. The shop of a fuller also had 235*lb* of loaf sugar as well as ginger, 46*lb* of white candy, 45*lb* of liquorice and ginger powder, 21*lb* of marmalade and 'suck', and 12*lb* of spice powder.[190] Throughout the inventories there are instances of salt and pepper, honey, saffron, mustard seed, aniseed, vinegar, treacle, raisins, figs, hops, malt and numerous other foodstuffs.

Wines, beers and cider

Instances of wines include references to malmsey, muscadine, 'eager' (sour) sack, 'Hollock' (a type of Spanish wine with a fine red colour) and 'taint' (a Spanish wine of low alcoholic content), as well as wine from Gascony. Small (weak) beer and 'Coyte', a type of thin beer, are also encountered. Cider is listed, sometimes by the hogshead.

The funeral

More detail can be found in these inventories for Elizabethan funeral practice than in any other documentary source in Devon. The funeral of Edward Lymett included costs for his shroud, making his grave, bearing his body to the church, paying the bellman and four poor people to walk with his corpse into the church, and for his coffin. His children were also given new caps and shoes to wear at the funeral and his widow had a new mourning gown. The bell ringers were also paid and there were costs in providing food and drink afterwards. Thomas Prestwood had an expensive gravestone engraved and a mason was paid for his additional work on the ledgerstone. The expenses listed for the funeral of John Dynham included paying the preacher for a sermon, providing four dozen loaves of bread for the poor and paying for the funeral dinner.

ELIZABETHAN INVENTORIES AND WILLS OF EXETER

1A. WILL OF THOMAS LAMBERT, 3 MARCH 1556

ECA, Orphans' Court Will 1

Note: Recognisances were entered into on 21 March 1564 regarding Lambert's children Joyce, Anne and Alice, William, Miles, Richard, Mary, Ezechial, Johan and Ciprian (ECA, Book 141, folio 6).

In the name of god Amen In the yere of the lord a thousand 500 hundred 55th the 3th day of Marche I Thomas Lambert of the Cittie & countie of Exon being thancks be to god of a good & perfecte remembraunce do this ordeyne & make my last will & testament. First I geve & commend my sole to our lord Jesus Christ my salvioure & redeemer & to the meryts of his dethe & passyon. And my bodye I geve to be buryed in the holy sepulture. Also I geve & bequethe to every of my daughters Anne thelder Margarett Geys Anne the yonger and Alys £5 in money to be delyvered immedyatelye after [theyre – crossed out] my dethe to the masters which every of theyme shall serve orells otherwise to be employed to theyre behoff & use as shalbe thought best by the overseers of this my will. And farther my mynd & will is that if any of thyme happens to dye before they come to lawffull age or be maryed that thence the parts & portions of theyme or any of theyme so decessynge do remayne to the overlevers equallye to be devyded emonge theyme, And if it happens theyme all to dye before they come to lawffull age or be married that then theyre parts & portyons do remayne to the rest of [my] children Myles Ezechiell Mary Rychard & the childe wherewith my wife now goeth equally to be devided emonge theyme. Also I do geve & bequethe to every of my children

Myles Ezechiell, Mary, Richard & the childe wherwith my wyfe now goethe the full some of five pownds to be employed to thyre behoff & proffytt as my wyfe theyre mother & my overseers shall thincke best. And if it happens any of thime before they come to lawffull age or happen to be married to dye that then the portion or porcons of theyme or of any of theyme so decessing do remayne to the overlevers equally to be devided emongest theyme. And if it fortune theyme all to dye before the tymes tofore expressed that then I will all theyre parts & porcons do Remayne to Christian my wyfe. Also my will mynde & entente is that after my dethe Christian my wyfe have my garden which liethe in the parishe of St Mary the More within the Cittie of Exon for the terme & during her naturall lyfe & after her deth the sayde garden to remayne to Myles my soune and to the heyres of his bodye lawfully begotten, And if it happen him to dye withoute any suche Issue that then the same to remayne to Ezechiell my soune & to the heyres of his body lawfully begotten. And for defaulte of suche Issue to remayne to Rychard my soune & to the heyres of his bodye lawfully comynge. And for defaulte of suche Issue to remayne to the childe wherwith my wyfe now goeth if it to be a manne childe & to the heyres of his body lawfully comynge, And for defaulte of suche Issue to remayne to Mary my daughter & to the heyres of her bodye lawfully borne. And lykwise for default of suche Issue of her the same to remayne to the childe wherwith my wiffe now goeth if it [be] a woman childe & to the heyres of her bodye lawfully borne, And if it happens theyme all to dye withoute suche Issue that then I will that the same garden with theappertances do remayne to the heyres generall of Christian my wyfe for ever. Farther I geve & bequeth to Mr Ambrose the physition my gowne of browne blew facid with blacke budge. Also I geve to Rychard Lymbery my soune in lawe 40s in mony to be alowed out of suche somes of mony as he oweth me under such condycon as he do trewly faythfully & quyetly pay & contente to my wyfe all suche somes of mony as he shall owe to me at the houre of my deth. Also I geve & bequethe to every of my apprentyses, John Heyle & Roger Bolte 40s under condycon as they & every of thyme do contynew faythefull & trusty in the service of my wyf

Christian during the yeres of theyre apprentheshode if my wyf do so longe lyve or contynewe the [excers - crossed out] excecysing of the Apothechary crafte. All the Resydew of my gooddis not bequethed over & above my debytts legacys & funeralls paied I geve & bequethe to Christian my wyfe whome I do ordeyne my sole & full executryx of this my present last will & testament & she to despose the same as to her dyscretion shalbe thought best & meetest. And for the Ayding & helping her herein I do ordeyne and appoynt my faythfull frends John Vowells alias Hoker & Rychard Prouse to be the overseers of this my present last will & testament desyrenge & most ernestly requesting theyme to see the performance hereof. And for theyre paynes herin I geve to every of theyme 5s. In wytnes of the premysses I have subscribed my presente testament the day & yeare above wryten in the presence of theyme whose names are subscribed. [Signed] Thomas Lamball

1B. WILL OF THOMAS LAMBERT, 19 APRIL 1560

ECA, Orphans' Court Will 5

In the name of god amen In the yer off the lord 1560 the 19 day of Aprell I Thomas Lambartt off the settye & countie of Exon being thancks be to god off a good & a perfecte Remembraunce do this ordeyne & make my last well & testament. First I gewe & commende my sole to our lord Jhesus Christ my sawyore & Redemer & to the meryts off his deth & passyon and my bodye I gewe to be buryed in the holye sepulture. Also I gewe & bequeth to ewerye off my daughters that I had by An Pryce that ys Geys Anne & Alis to ewer off them £6 13s 4d in monye to be delyvered emmedyatlye after my deth to the masters which ewre off them shall serve or else other wysse to be employed to there be houffe & use as shallbe thought best by the owarsyars of thes my will & Farther my mynde & well is that iff anye of them happed to dye beffor they come to lawfull age or be maryed that then the parts & porsyans off them or anye off

them so decesseng do Remayne to the owerlyvars equally to be dewyded emonge them & if it happen them all to dye beffour thaye come to lawffull age or be maryed that then ther partts & porcions [off them or anye off them so decesseng do Remayne to the owerlyvers equallye to be devyded – crossed out] do Remayn to the Use off my cheldren that I hawe by this [w]oman that ys Myles Ezechell Marye Wellyam Jone & Crestyan. Also I do gewe & bequeth to ewre off my cheldren Myles Ezechell Marye Wellyam Jone & Crestyan to ewre off them the Full some off £6 13s 4d to be employed to ther behoffe & proffett also my wyfe ther mother & my owarseers shall thinke best & yff it happen anye off them beffor thay come to lawffull age or happen to be maryed to dye that then the porcon or porcons off them or off anye off them so decessing do Remayn to the owerlewers equally to be devyded emongest them and yff it Fortune theyme all to dye beffour the tyme beffor expressed that then I well all the partes & porsions do Remayn to Christian my wyffe. Also my mind & well and entente is that after my deth Chrystian my wyff have my garden which lyeth in the parish off St Marye the Mor within the cyttie off Exon For the tarme & during off her naturall lyffe & after her deth the sayed garden to Remayn to Myles my soune & to the heyres off his bodye lawfullye begotten & yff it happen hem to dye withowte any suche Issue that then the same to Remayne to Ezechyell my soune & to the heyres off hes bodye lawfullie begotten & For deffautt off suche Issue to Remayne to Wellyam my soune and to the heyres off hes bodye lawfullye begotten & For defaut off such Issue to Remayn to Marye my doughter & to the ayres off her bodye lawfullye [begotten – crossed out] borne & For default off suche essue to Remayn to Jone my doughter & For defaut off such Issue to remayn to Crestyan my doughter & yff it happen them all to dye withowt Issue that then I well that the same garden with the apportinance do Remayn to the ayres generall of Crestyan my wyff For

ewer. Also I do gewe & bequeth unto Roger Bolte my prentes 40s under condycion as he do trewlye & Faythffullye serwe owt hes apprentice with Chrestyn my wyff. Yff my wyffe do so long lywe or continue the excisyseng off the appotycar crafte all the Resedew off my goods nott bequethed ower & abowe my detts legacies & funerallis payed I gewe & bequeth to Chrestyan my wyffe whome I do ordeyne my sole & Full executrix off this my present & last well & testament & she to disspoce the same as to her discressyon shallbe thaught best & metest & For helpen her here In I do ordayne & apoynt my Faythffull Frends John Blackhallar att the condett & Wellyam Trevett to be the owarsears off this my present last well & testament desyreng & moste ernestlye Requering them to se the perfformans here off & For ther paynes here In I gewe to ewre off them 10s. In wettnis off the premisses I have wretten this well with my one hand & hawe subcribed my name to thes testament the day & yer abowe wretten In presens off them whos names ar under wretten.

2A. WILL OF THOMAS GRYGGE, BAKER OF ST KERRIAN'S PARISH, 29 MARCH 1558

ECA, Orphans' Court Will 2 (and National Archives, PROB 11/44/162)
Note: the will was proved via Canterbury on 3 May 1561. The register for the parish of St Kerrian recorded 'Thomas Grege the Baker' was buried on 2 May 1558. Recognisances were entered into on 19 April 1564 regarding Thomas, Margaret, William, Michael and Johan, the children of Thomas Grygge (ECA, Book 141, folio 8).

[1] **In the name of god Amen**. The 29th day of Marche, in the yere of our lorde god a thousand five hundreth fifftye and eight. **I Thomas Grege** of the p[ari]sshe of Saynt Keriane in the cittie & countie Exetter, baker, beyng in my perfecte Remembraunce thanks be to god but sicke yn bodye do make my last wyll & testament yn man[ner] & forme folowinge **ffirst** I geve & bequeth my Soule to Almightie god my Savior and Redemer And my bodye to the holye yearthe to be buryed in the chauncell of the churche of saint Sidwells without the Estgate of the saide cittie of Exetor **to the whiche** churche of Saint Sidwells I geve to the reperacon theroof 20

sh And to the curatte of the same churche to praye for me I geve ten shillings. **Item** I geve & bequethe unto Thomas Grege my eldest sone in lawfull mony of England fiftie pounds and all my fee simple lands that lyeth in the parish of Ilsington named Colsswaye with a salte of silver wayenge 12 unces and a goblet of silver wayeng 10 unces & halfe with six silver spones having maydyns hedds with a rose **Item** I geve & bequethe to my eldest daughter Margarett Grege in lawfull money of England fortie ponds & a demye that was her grandmothers & a goblet of silve wayenge 12 unces and six spones of silver **Item** I geve and bequethe unto my

3

son William Grege in lawfull money fourscore pounds **Item** I geve & bequethe unto John Grege my Soune in lawfull money a £80 **Item I** geve **&** bequethe unto Michaell Grege my youngest Sone in lawfulll money a £80 **Item** I geve & bequethe unto every householder in the p[ari]sshe of Saint Sidwells 2*d* and to every householder withyn the parisshe of Kerans 4*d* And after my buryall to be distributed at the churche to pore people ten dosons of brede & 2 barells of ale **Item** I geve and bequethe to Elizabeth Mugge in lawfull money 53 shillings 4*d* **Item** I geve & bequethe to John Freer 20 shillings to be paide 3 shillings & 4*d* every quarter until the hole some of 20 shilings be fullie paid. **And** I geve unto the saide John Freer my works dayes gowne **Item** I geve & bequethe unto evey one of my brother William Grygges childer 20 shillings apece **And** I geve unto the same William Gregge my brother my fox furred gowne & a gowne clothe that I nowe dress **Item** I geve & bequethe unto my brother Lawe Harry Mawnder my gowne facid with Spaynyshe taffatoo & a nother gowne facid with Budge **Item** I geve & bequethe unto y Sone Wylliam Grege my house with theappurtences that I nowe dwell yn And my house with the appurtenances nexte there unto Adyoinenge whereyn nowe dwelleth the widow Stonynge to have & to holde the saide two houses with there Appurtenances to the saide Wylliam his heires and Assignes yn fee Symple for ever **Item** I geve & bequethe unto my Sone John Gryge my two houses with theyr appurtenances that stand in the Bocher Rowe with yn the saide cittie of Exeter whereyn dwelleth now eyn one of them Elys Backeley and in the other house dwelleth Widdow woman of late being John Coles wyffe to have & to *[2]* holde to the saide John his heires & assignes yn fee symple for ever **Item** I geve unto my sone Michael Grege my house with thappurtenances that standes in the Southgate Strete of the foresaide Cittie wherein nowe dwelleth John Lone peteror and my house with the appurtenances that standes uppon Stripcott Hill wherein nowe dwelleth Thomas [space] Barall bearer **To** have and to hold to the saide Michael Grege his heires and assignes yn fee Symple for ever **Item** I geve & bequeth to my yongest daughter Jone Grege all my lease &

['tithes' crossed through] termes of yeres of all my stables that I bought of William Tucker with stables I holde of the Citie of Exeter lyenge and Junynge agaynst Rocke Lane in the one Side and parte of them Standyng in the Fore Strete **To Have and to hold** to the saide Jone & to her assignes duringe all the terme thereof **Also** I geve & bequethe unto the saide Jone Grege my yongest daughter the twentie poundes that I londe to the Quenes majestie when so ever hit be reserved **And** the Rest of all my goodes (after my dettes legacies and funeralles paid) I geve & bequethe to the saide Jone Grege my youngest daughter Whom I make my hole executrix of this my Testament & last Wyll. **And Farder** my Wyll is that whereas I have geven unto my eldest Sone Thomas Grege certayne money landes and plate as before is specified and lykewise certain money & landes unto my other 3 sounes that is to say William Grege John Grege & Michaell Grege that none of them fewer shall have those bequestes untyll they shalbe & come to the full age of 24 yeres olde other than the profytt of those landes for the good bryngyng upp of them. **And lykewysse** for suche money as I have geven & bequethed unto my twoo daughters that is to saye Margarett Grege and Jone Grege as is above written **My Will is also** that they shall have none of their said legacies untyll they shalbe & come to full age of 19 yeres old **And yf it fortune** that any one or more of all my foresaide childer happen to dye before the foresaide money and legacies be dewe to be paide and delyvered unto them as aforesaid **Then my Will is** that the deddes partes shalbe delyvered emongest the rest of my childer then lyving equallie to be devided betwixt them when the rest of theire legacies shalbe dewe unto them as aforesaide or otherwise by the advice & dyscretyon of my bothe overseers or their assignes **And I make the overseers** of this my Testament and last Wyll my brother in lawe Harrie Maunder & my Brother William Grege to se this My testament & last Wyll faythfullye to be fulfilled **And** also I geve & bequethe unto Marie Grege my Brother John Grege's daughter for a Remembraunce a Golde Ringe of the valew of 20*s* or 20*s* in lawfull money **And** my Wyll is that if all my Childer fortune to dye withoute issue that then all my landes to Remayne to my Brother William Grege to his heires for ever **Item** more I geve & bequethe unto Katheryn Mander my lytle mayde fortie Shillinges yn money or money worthe **And** my Wyll is that my overseers shall se me buried according to an honest order at their discretion. **Thes** beynge wittnes Harrie Mawnder and William Grege.

Matthew by divine permission Archbishop of Canterbury, Primate of all England and Metropolitan to our beloved in Christ Henry Mawnder and William Grege, overseers named in the will and last wish of Thomas Grege, late of the City and our diocese of Exeter and Province of Canterbury deceased, greeting. Whereas Thomas Grege promised to the deceased Henry while he lived and at the time of his death goods, rights and debts in his house in this diocese and jurisdiction specified in his will, in which Joan Grege his daughter, a minor, was constituted his executrix, which as because she is still a minor cannot be committed to her as of right, therefore we are effecting that the goods, rights and debts owed to the deceased interim shall be faithfully administered and that the cost of the implementation of the administration of these goods etc by the present executors of the said deceased shall be undertaken by the present executors of the said deceased to well and truly dispose of them. And the debts of the said deceased shall be collected and levied owing when he lived and at the time of his death of Henry's legacies specified in the contents of his will as far as the goods, rights and debts of the said Henry are concerned are to be paid at the proportionate rate. We faithfully trust you to adminster the same and to compile and to exhibit an inventory of all and singular Henry's goods and debts owing to him in our Perogative Court of Canterbury on the second day after the feast of St Fides the Virgin [6 October] next coming. And to return a proven account of this to the person of Master Robert Chaffe, Notary Public, in this behalf constituted administrator of the debts, rights etc, and we ordain that the admininstrator shall hold the goods, rights and debts during the minority estate of the beforesaid executrix. Sealed under our seal and given at London the third day of May in the year one thousand five hundred and sixty one and in the second year of our Consecration.
[Signed] Thomas Argall

2B. INVENTORY OF THOMAS GRYGGE, BAKER OF ST KERRIAN'S PARISH, 7 APRIL 1560

ECA, Orphans' Court Inventory 1

[m. 1] 1560
The Inventarye & all the goods chattalls and debts of Thomas Grygge of the parishe of Saynt Kyrans of and yn the cittie & countie of Exeter baker late deceased made & praysyd the 7th daye of Aprill yn the yere of our lorde god a thowsend five hundredth and threscoer by us John Parramore & Robert Harward *alias* Colemen and Robert Chaffe

In the Hall
Firstly A Table borde with a Carpitt of olde darnax & a nother strakid carpit 10s;

Item a Tabell borde uppon a frame 2 juned formes 1 junyd Stole two chayres 2 litle Stoells & 2 fore Stoells 5s;
Item 17 quysshyns 6s 8d;
Item a Cobbord & a Cobbord Clothe 13s 4d;
Item 2 basons & 2 evers 6s 8d;
Item 4 pottell wyne potts 6 quarts 3 pynts with a lytle pott of Tyn 6s 8d;
Item the Selings of the Hall & before the Chymley with ye hangyng & one tablement 53s 4d;
Item 29 platters 23 podingers 26 saucers half a dosen podiche disshes of Tyn & 5 olde basens 40s;
£7 20d.

In the parler

Item a Carvyd Bedstede with a tester of Rede & grene saie & Courtens to the same 3 ffetherbedds a fflockebed 2 bolsters & a pilloe of fethers with 2 coverletts £4;

Item an old Cobbord with a Cobbord Clothe a Counter borde a Carpet of darnax 4 juned formes one old Coffer with an old Rounde Chair 13s 4d;

Item a Grete pere of Aundyrons & a lytle pare of Andyrons 10s;

Item 4 end of torches 12d;

Item the Selinge & the hangyngs of the parler with the binche 13s 4d;

£5 17s 8d.

In the fore Chamber

Item a juned bedstede with the Tester & Curtens of darnax 10s;

Item 4 pilloes & a lytle pilloe of fethers with a blanket 5s 4d;

Item one olde Counter bourde 3 Coffers & a lytle broken Coffer 6s 8d;

Item a presse and olde Cobbord & a forme 10s;

Item a sworde a wodknyff & 2 olde skeynes 3s 4d;

Item one dosen of kerseye 18s;

Item a kassack of Taffata garded with velvet with out sleves 20s;

Item a Gowne of newe Coller faced with Budge & a gowne of browne blewe faced with Taffata 46s 8d;

Item a Gowne of Kentis blewe faced with fox & a single gowne unmade 40s;

Item an olde gowne facid with Catts Skynns 6s 8d;

Item a Ridyng Cote of Clothe with an olde jacket of Clothe 5s;

Item a jacket of black Chamlet & a doblet with Satten sleves and one olde doblet with damask sleves 13s 4d;

Item one Blanket 2s 6d;

Item the hangynge of olde paynted Clothres 5s;

Item certayn Raynes [?] by extimacyon 8 yerds 4s;

Item 4 lytle belts 12d;

£9 17s 6d.

The Napperye

Item 14 payre of Shets 35s;

Item 5 borde Clothes whereof one is diaper 10s;

[m. 1v.] Item 5 Towells with a Berynge Shette 5s;

Item one dosen of Borde napkyns & 4 pilloeties 5s;

Item a white Tester with Courtens of Dowlas 4s;

Item a Graper for a well of Iron 6d;

59s 6d.

In the litle Chamber towards the streate

Item 2 olde bedsteds 2 fetherbedds 3 bolsters one olde pilloe of fethers with a stayned Clothe 2 olde Coverletts & 3 olde Blanketts 23s 4d;

Item 2 paire of rustie allmen rivetts without splynt 3 salletts 4 Bylls with one olde rustie two hand sword 13s 4d;

36s 8d.

In the Chamber over the entrey

Item 3 olde Beames with a Certen of olde Iron 10s;

Item a pippe of ledd with a lytle broken ledd 10s;

Item a Saddle 2 paire of styrupes a trestell an olde stayned Clothe with other trasshe 3s 4d;

23s 4d.

In the backe Chamber

Item 2 olde Bedsteds 2 olde fflockebedds & 2 trestells with an old forme 3s 4d;

Item a lytle belt with the hangyng of the same 12d;

4s 4d.

In the shoppe

Item one Tubbe one olde Rounde Chaier with a broken borde 12d;

Item a lytle Rounde Borde a Chayer a Coffer and a stayned Cloth 2s 8d;

Item a beme of Tymber a busshell a peck 2 tubbs with an olde chest yn the entrye 3s 4d;

7s.

In the brande loffte
Item a certen of branne 3s 4d;
Item 8 Busshells of Beane flower 9s 4d;
Item 7 longe bords & a pannell [?] posse 3s 4d;
Item 6 hundreth of lathes 2s;
Item by extymacyon a Busshell of Salte 12d;
Item 2 old Coffers 4 tubbs 2 Rangers 2 oven stappers with
other trashe 5s;
Item 22 pecs of Tymber in Fryrengehaye £4 8s;
£5 12s.

In the kechen
Item 2 broches 20d;
Item an olde Cobbord a Chaire & bokett a payle a forme with
other trashe 20d;
Item 12 pannes & 2 Caudrens of Brasse 53s 4d;
Item 9 Croks a possenet & a water Chaffer of brasse with
a pestell & a morter of Iron & 3 Chaffynge dysshes & a
Skyllet 55s;
Item 10 latten Bassons & 5 olde lavars 6s 8d;
Item a pair Candelstycks of latyn & one Candlestick of Tyn
5s;
Item an olde grede 2 hoks 2 hangyngs fete for broches a
brandis a flesshe hoke a paire of Tonges a fier pyke 2 gose
pannes & 2 berers 2s 6d;
£6 5s 10d.

[m. 2] In the bake house
Item by extimacon 26 Busshells of Whete onely 40s;
Item 11 olde Sacks 7s 4d;
Item 2 Buntyng hutches 2 troes with Covers 2 tubs one Cowle
a payle & 4 piells 8s;
Item 5 fre Stones for the flore of an oven 5s;
Item an olde pan of brasse with one ballens 6s 8d;
£3 7s.

In the Stable & Wodehouse
Item a pipe of lyme 3s;
Item a hutche to put Whete yn 6s;

Item Certayn olde tymber 6s 8d;
Item a pipe 2 hoggsheds 2 olde Barells & a Certayn of brome
facketts 5s;
Item a Certayn of Wallinge Stones 10s;
Item in the boucheres [?] certen Sylyngs & Staynyd Clothes
two Cobbords a Cownter borde a bedstede a paynetyd
Tester a presse a planke wyth olde Sylyngs upon the planke
42s 6d;
£3 12s 2d.

The plate
Item two Salts with one cover gilte wayenge 48 uncs at 5s 8d
the unce £13 12s;
Item two square Salts with a cover gilte wayenge 21 uncs and
halff at 5s 8d the unce £6 22d;
Item two Gobletts gilte wayenge 32 uncs at 6s the unce £9
12s;
Item one Stondyng Cuppe with a Cover gilte wayeng 24 uncs
at 5s 4d the unce £6 8s;
Item two Gobletts parcell Gilte with one cover wayng 38
unces and halff at 4s 8d the unce £8 19s 8d;
Item two Gobletts more parcell Gilte wayenge 23 uncs at 4s
4d the unce £4 19s 8d;
Item one Stondyng Cuppe parcell gilte wayenge 14 uncs at 4s
8d the unce £3 5s 4d;
Item one Salte parcell Gylte with a cover waynge 11 uncs and
halffe at 4s 4d the unce 49s 10d;
Item one ale Cuppe parcell Gylte waynge fyve uncs & halffe
at 4s 4d the unce 23s 10d;
Item two dosens & halffe of Spones with mayden hedds
parcell Gilte wayenge 31 uncs & halffe at 4s 8d the unce £7
7s;
Item a flatte pece of playne white sylver wayeng 12 uncs &
halffe at 4s the unce 50s;
Item 6 silver Spones of playne white wayenge 4 uncs & halffe
at 4s the unce 18s;
Item 6 sylver Spones more of playne white wayng 6 uncs
quarter at 4s the unce 25s;
Item two masards Bownden with sylver and gilte and one

Crewse with a cover of sylver & gylte valewed at 43*s* 4*d*;

Item 3 golde Ryngs waynge halffe an unce & halffe quarter after the value of 53*s* 4*d* the unce 23*s* 4*d*;

[m. 2v.] Item 24 Silver Stones two Sylver Ryngs and two pecs of Currell [?] waynge all to gether 2 uncs at 3*s* 8*d* the unce 7*s* 4*d*;

Item fyve payer of howks & 3 pynnes of Sylver & gilte wayenge 4 uncs & halff at 5*s* the unce one with a nother 22*s* 6*d*;

Item a Gerdell with 13 barres and a demye gilte with a Red Stone wayng 15 uncs webbe & all to gether at 5*s* the unce £3 15*s*;

Item a Gerdell of blacke velfett with barres of white sylver with mordell & buckell wayng all to gether 12 uncs at 3*s* the unce 36*s*;

Item a Gerdell of webbe with a demye of Sylver parcell gylte 13*s* 4*d*;

Item a 129 white sylver Stones & 30 stones of sylver and gylte wayeng 11 uncs and halffe at 4*s* 4*d* the unce one with a nother 47*s* 8*d*;

£82 10*s* 8*d*.

Item in lawfull monye of Englonde £311 15*s* 4*d*;

Item in debbts Sperats & deffalts £56.

Sum total of the said inventory £498 10*s* 8*d*.

Compared with the other part of the inventory which was exhibited in the Perogative Court of Canterbury witnessed by Robert Chaffe notary public

3. WILL OF HENRY HARRIS, 19 AUGUST 1559

ECA, Orphans' Court Will 3 (Also National Archives, PROB 11/43/19)
Note: this was proven via Canterbury on 16 December 1559.

In the name of god Amen the 19th daye of August In the yere of our Lorde god A thowsand five hundereth 59. And the first yere of the Raigne of our Soveraigne ladye Elizabethe by the grace of god of England France & Ireland quene defender of the faithe &c **I Henry Harrrys** of Exetter by godds permission beynge then In a perfytt Remembreance willinge to declare my will & Testament at that present tyme have desyred my frynd John Peryam to put in Remembreauns by writtinge that I wilde to be done as folowethe *Firstly* I comitt my soule unto the tuycion of Almyghtie god unto everlasting lyffe by the meritts of the death & passion of Jesus Christ Amen Settlyinge all other vayne Superstitions & Serimonies aparte. **Seconderlye**, my erthlye body unto the earthe as hit came from and to be laide in suche place as hit shalbe thought good to my wyfffe in suche sorte & order as other christians are Interyed & buried. **Thirdly, I** geve & bequethe unto the poor of the Inhabitones of this cittie of Exetter 40*s* which

fourtie shillings to be distributed by the Receyver of the cittie & one other Stuearde desiring them to take so myche paynes therein at my poor requeste. *Fourthlye* my will is that all my lands leasses & bargins & other yerelye proffyts shalbe durynge the lyffes of my wyffe & my sonne Thomas equally be devyded unto them durynge their bothe lyves always & after the decesse of my wyffe the saide lands, leasses, bargens & other yerelye profytts shall whollye remayne unto my sonne & heire Thomas Harris. **Provided** always that all my writings concerninge my lands leasses bargens & other shalbe within 15 dayes after my decesse Saffelye delyererd unto the custodye of the chamber of Exetter *Fyfelye* my will is if my wyffe Margerie overleve my childe Thomas Then I wille that all my lands leasses & bargens shall remayne whollye unto my saide wife Margerie durynge her lyffe *Sixtly* my will is after the decesse of my wyf & Thomas my sonne for asmuche as Thomas my sonne decesse with oute heires then I will that my house which Henrye Tone holdes of me by lease with the purtenanses of the same shalbe geven to the poor. I say the rent of the same for ever for a perpetuall memorie to the 12 poor men namyd Mr Thomas Androwes power men to be dystributyd to them foure tymes by the yere. I saye 4 tymes by the yere by Mr Recever & one of the stuerds of the same cities & to have for their paynes yerelye out of the same lands 2s. I say 2s for their paynes. *Seventhlye* my will is that after the decesse of my wyf & Thomas my heire dye withoute yssue The Resydue of all my lands leasses Rents & proffytts of the same & except bfore Exceptyd, shall whollye Remayne to one John Harrys Sonne & Heire to John Harrys my brother of Brystoll. **Item** ferder I will that my plate shalbe equally devyded per moyte to my wyf Margerie & Thomas my sonne. I say that Margerye my wyf shall have thone half of all my plate & Thomas my sonne thother halfe. **Item** that my will is that half of my plate the which is accordyinge geven to them by my will shalbe delivered within eight dayes after my decese unto the chamber of Exetter for the safffe kepinge of my sonne Thomas and yf my sonne Thomas dye then the saide plate to be unto my brothers sonne John Harrys of Brestolle. Reserved thershall remaine to the behofe of the cittie a flatte pece of 20 unces or nige thereunto. **Item** that

all the rest of my goods not bequethed I geve unto Margerie my wyf & do make her hole Executrix to see my detts & legacies paide without fraude & delaye. **Item** to see unto thes my hole mynde & entent furnished & to be ayde unto my sonne Thomas & to my wyf I will hartelye desire Mr John Parker of Northmolton Richard Prestewoode & John Peryam of Exetter. *In Wittness* this for my last will to be done of a perfyt remebrannce I the said Henrye Harrys have putte this my Seyne & Seale by me Henrie Harrs by me Thomas Harris **Item** after all this my will I will that the kepynge of my childe Thomas with heis Revenewes shalbe unto Mr John Parkers custodye to kepe him to his lernynge untill the age of 21 yeres & then to Render hym accompte Justlye how his Revenewes is spent in his exekussion for his well brynginge uppe in lernynge & Mr John Parker is to delyver hem his lyvynge whollye unto his hends at the age of 21 yeres havynge for his paynes 10s yerelye to se the well orderynge of the said Thomas my sonne. And yf hit be thought good by Mr Parker to putt aprents with some merchantman for certen yeres. *By me Henry Herris by me Thomas Herris* **Yf** that my wyf Margerie put in Sureties to the masters of the cittye of the plate geven to my sonne by my bequethes I will that she shall have the custodye therof untill my childe be of a full age of 21 yeres.

4. WILL OF JOHN PARRETT, OF LYME REGIS, DORSET, 20 OCTOBER 1559

ECA, Orphans' Court Will 4 (also National Archives, PROB 11/44/133)
Note: the will was proved via Canterbury on 4 April 1561.

In the name of God Amen, In the yere of our Lorde 1559 the 20th daie of October I John Parrret of Lyme Regis in the Countie of Dorsett being of whoale mynde & perfecte remembrance the Lord be thanked do make & ordeyne my Last will & testament in manner & forme folowenge. Ffirst I geve & bequethe my sole in to the hands of all mightie god & my bodye to be buried within the parish churche of Lyme Regis. Item I geve and bequethe to the same parish churche with my buriall 13s 4d.

Item I geve to everie ['person' crossed through] poore person be it man woman or childe which shalbe at my buriall 1d. Item I geve to the maior & his brethren of the foresaide towne of Lyme to be bestowed in making of a key at the end of the cawsey upon the Cobbe of Lyme for bots to Land £6 13s 4d. Item I geve to tenne of the poorest men dwelling within the towne of Lyme aforesaide to everie of them a ffryese coate & sherte. Item I geve to 10 of the poorest women of the saide towne to everie of them a peticot & a smocke which I will to be done by the descracon of the overseers & executors of this my present last will & testament. Item my will mynd & intente is that the maior & his brethren & there successors of the towne of Lyme aforesaide shall have to them in ffee & perpetuitie for ever all that my tenement with a backsyde & medow therto adioning within the towne of Lyme which I late purchased of one Edwarde Redman & being now in the tenure of Robert Coller for term of certeynge lyffs at the yerely rent of 26s 8d which rent & revenewe as also that which may be more increased thereof after the terme of Robert Coller expired my will & mynd is that in consyderacon convencon & satisfaction of the yerely revenew of 20s issuing out of certeyn my Lands in the towne of Wellington in the countie of Somerset to the use of the poore by the gyft of my late father decessed shalbe yerely employed & bestowed by the said maior his brethren & there sucessors by the advise of the oversoers & executors of this my Last will during there life to the behoffe of the poore & nedie of the saide towne of Lyme. Item I geve & bequethe to be bestowed from tyme to tyme as need shall require in paving of the Cawsey before one Legers dore at the ende of the towne of Lyme aforesaide & from thense to the crosse called the three legged Crosse the some of 40s. Item I geve & bequethe to Thomas Samfford my servant after the decesse of Thomas Trevill of the towne of Lyme all that my lease & terme which I have of and in the tenement of the saide Thomas Trevill now dwellethe in. Item I geve to the saide Thomas my servant 20s in mony. Item my will & mynd is that Thomasyn Samfford my servant shall shall have all my state & interest of & in one pece of grownde conteininge ffyftie foote in bredth & ffyfftie foote in lengthe which do lye at the end of the house off [blank] Harte of Lyme. Item I geve to her also 40s in money. Item I geve to Elysabeth Storye, John Welche and Johan Lamerton to everie of them 20s. Item I geve to everie man servant which is now in my howse dwelling 10s. Item I geve to Nycholas Chaplyn my brotherlawe & to his wyffe £5 in money. Item I geve to my brotherlaw John Blackhall my grey gelding. Item I geve to William Chapel my brotherlaw my coalte. Item I geve to Robert Perett £6 13s 4d. Item I geve unto John Follett my

godson 20s. Item I geve to be distributed to the poore people of the parish of Uplyme 10s. Item I geve to be distrubted emonge the poor people of the parishe of Wotoon 10s. Item where as John Garland is in my debt & oweth unto me certeyn somes of monye I do geve & forgeve it unto him. Also whereas ['John Garland of John Garlande' crossed through] Geffrey Carsewell oweth unto me upon his byll the some of £20 my will & mynde is that if he the saide Geffrey do quietly without reparacon or troble pay & content unto the oversoers & executors of this my Last will & testament the full some of £4 that he to be clerly dyschardged of the resydew being £16. Item my will & mynd is that John Sampford have & shall have 2 of the best oks he can chuse in Coxwell woods. Item I geve to eveie of the children of the saide John Samford 4s 4d. Item I do geve & bequeathe to Johan Perett my daughter the full some of 200s marks of lawffull mony of England to be paide unto her by the hands off the oversees & executors of this my last will & testament at the tyme or day of her mariage or ['when she shalbe of the age of' crossed through] otherwise at the descrecon of my executors & overseers. Item my will & mynd is that the said Johan my daughter shall have for & during her lyffe the house or tenement where Richard Buckford now dwelleth in yelding yerelye to John my sone & to the herres of [his] body lawfullie coming for ever [2] to the overseers & executors of this my last will during the minoritie of ['John my son' crossed through] to the behoff of the said John the some of 20s. ['And further I will that if the' crossed through] after the decesse of the saide Johan my daughter the foresaide tenement with all theappurtenances do whoalie remayne unto the said John my son & to the heres of his body lawfully cominge and for defaulte of suche issue my will mynd & intent is that all the said house or tenement with the appertenances do wholly remayne to the Residew of all my children then lyvinge & to ther heires for evermore' [crossed through] Also I geve & bequeath to Alys Perett my daughter the some of 200 marks to be paide at the dore of her mariage or ['when she be of' crossed through] otherwise at the descrecon of my overseers & executors. Item I geve to Thomasyn Perett my daughter 200 marks to be paid at the daye of her mariage or ['when she shalbe of' crossed through] otherwise at the descrecon of my executors & overseers. Item I geve to Anne Parett my daughter 200 marks ['athe' crossed through] at the day of her mariage ['to be paid or when she shalbe' crossed through] or otherwise at the descrecon of my executors & overseers. Item my will mynde & intent ['that' crossed through] is that the childe wherewith Anstys my wyffe now Goethe withall if it be a man child ['that' crossed through] and lyve untyll he be of the age of 20 yeres that then he to have & enioy to him for terme and during his naturall lyffe, the yerelye rent fee or annuitie of tenne pownds goeng & issuenge one of all my lands rents farmes & leases what so ever within the realme of England whereof I will my son John which so ver he shalbe of lawfull age do make to hym a perfect good & sufficient estate in lawe. Ittem I geve to the said my child if it be a sonne or manchild the some of £200 of lawfull monye to be paide when he shalbe of lawffull age or according to the dyscresion of the overseers & executors of this my last will & testament. Item my will & minde is that if the saide childe my wyffe now gooeth with be a mayden then she to have the some of 200 marks to be paide at the daie of her mariage or otherwise at the dyscrecon of my overseers & executors. Item ['if' crossed through] my will & mynde is that if ['the' crossed through] any of the foresaide my children Johan, Alys, Thomasyn, Anne or the children wherwith my wife now gooethe do dye before the daie of mariage of tyme & yeres of discrecon or otherwise as is before rehersed that then my will is the part or porcon of him or her so first decessing do whoalie remayne to the overseers & executors ['& executors' crossed through] of this my last will to the behoffe & use of the said John my sonne. And if it happen any more then one of them to dye then my mynde is the part in manner as before said then my mynde is the parte & porcon of everie of them so decessing do whoalie remayne to the ['children wherewith my wife now goethe if it be a man childe' crossed through] residew of all my children then surviving or the heres of them. But ['if it be a woman childe that then the parts or porcons of everie of them so decessing do remayne whoalie to John my sone & to the heires of him

lawfully comminge or if the do so dye [illegible] age. And for defaulte of suche issue John the sonne to be destrybuted emonge the Rest & resydew of my children then lyving & to the heres of my everie of them' crossed through] And for defaulte of suche Issue my will is that the one halfe or moitie thereof do whoalie remayne to Anstyse ['wif' crossed through] my wyffe if she be then a lyff & if she be dedd to the next heires of her blodde. And thother moitie to the next of my blodde. Item I geve & bequethe to Anstyse my wife the full some of fyve hundred marks of Lawffull mony of Englande to be paid to her or her assignes by the executors & overseers of this my will within one halffe yere after my decesse. Item my will mynde & intent is that the saide Anstyse my wyfe shall have the yerelye rent annuytie & some of £20 Issuenge out of all my lands & tenements Rents Revercons ffermes & Leassse whatsoever I have within this Realme of England for terme & during her naturall lyffe. And the Resydew of all my Lands tenements Rents with other the premysses I will do remayn in the hands of the overseers and executors of this my Last will during the minoritie or noneage of John Perett my son to the behoffe & use of the said John my sone. And when the saide John my son shall come to the age of 21 yeres and do then make a sufficient & good estate in law of the yerely rent annuitie & some off £20 by the yere to be paied to the foresaide Anstyse my wife, his mother, during her lyffe, also make another sufficient & good estate in law of the yerelye Rent & Revenewes of £10 by the yere to the behoffe & use of the childe my wife now goethe with if it be a manchilde during his lyffe that then my will mynd & intent is the saide Resydew of my lands Rents & other the premysses do then whoaly remayn to the saide John my son & to the heires of his body Lawffullie cominge. And after the decesse of the said Anstyse my wyffe & ['the' crossed through] of the manchilde before whersed I will the whoale lands de remayn full & whoale without all manner of ffees or annuities as is aforesaide to be paied out thereof to the forsaide John my sone & to the heires of his body lawfully And all the resydew of my Lands rents ffermes Leases or annuities over & above the forsaide 2 severall anuyties of £20 to my wyffe & £10 to her child she goethe with if it be a son I will it do remayn in the Custodie & goverment of my overseers & executors to the behoffe & use of John my sone during the tyme of his minoritie. And when he shall come to the full age of 21 yeres I will the some do whoalye remayne to him & to the heires of his bodye lawfully cominge. And after the decease of the said Anstyse my wyffe & the childe she now Goethe withall if it be a manchilde I will that all my whoale lands rents formes leases & anneties do fullie & wholly remayne to the saide John my son & to the heires of his bodye lawffullie cominge for evermore. And for dedawlte of suche Issue or if the saide John my son when he shall come to the age of 21 yeres shall refuse to make a sufficient estate of & in an yerely annuities of £20 by the yere to Anastyse my wiffe his mother as also any other sufficient esetate of a yerly fee or annuitie of £10 by the yere to be paied to the childe my wiffe now goethe withall if it be a man childe during his lyffe according to the trew purporte effect & intente of this my present Last will & testament that then I will the saide Lands tenements rents fermes & leases with other the premysses do whoalie remayn to the foresaide posthumus or childe my wyfe now goeth with And if it be amanne childe & to the heries of his bodie Lawffullie cominge. And if the saide mannchild do dye without heyres of his bodie Lawffulie coming, or if he refuse when he shall ['refuse to make a g' crossed through] come to thage of 21 yeeres to make a good & sufficient estate in the lawe of the foresaide annytie or yerly rent of £20 to be paied to Anastyse my wyffe his mother than then my will & mynde is the forsaide Lands rents fermes & Leases with other the premysses do whoalie remayn to the resydew of my children & to there heires for evermore under the lyke condicons as is before expressed saving & reserving to Johan my daughter & to the heres if she do overleve Anstyse my wyffe my too sones and the heires of ther bodyes as is before specified my terme & lease of all suche yeres then to come of the house I dwell in and if all my children do dy without heires so begotten then I will the said moitie of all my premises remayne to heires off me for ever & the moitie to the heires of Anstyse my wiffe for ever. All the Residew of my goodds

moveable & immoveable my Legacies & funerals paied my will & whoale mynde ys that thedo whoalie remayn in the government custodie & rule of my deere & welbeloved & trustye John Blackall & William Chapell of the Citie of Excester merchants & William Skryven & Henry Snowe of Lyme merchants wherin I do ordayen not onelye the overseers but the Executors of trust of this present Last will & testament to the only behoffe & use of John my sone most heartelie [?] proveing them according to the confidence & trust I have reposed in them that the will see the same to be observed in everie article & intente according to the trew meaning thereof And they not onelie do observe or kepe the partes & porcons of everie of the legacies before to my children geven [illegible crossed through] to there use but but do resyve & to reteyne to them selfes all also the whoale resydew of my gooddes my detts & legacies paied be savely kept to the behoffe of John my sone until he shalbe of lawfull yeres of age And further also have the government & educacon of everie of my foresaid chidren whom I chardge in godly behalf to obey & be ruled by the said my executors in all godlile & reasonable orders. And if any of them contrarie to the good will & consent of them or there mother my wyff foolishly do bestowe themselfs in mariage or otherwise or wilfully do refuse to be governed & ruled by them or do seeke the breach of any branche article or intent of this my last will & testament that then I will the parts or porcons of everie such stubborn frowered or disordered chile to be abated & to be employed to the resydew of my children survivinge or otherwise to the descrecon of the saide my executors ['& overseers exladinge the' crossed through] And futher I will & do request the said my executors & overssers that immediatly after my deth there be prepared a coffer with 4 keys & loks & the same to be kept in the common concell chamber of the towne of Lyme whereof one key to be allwaies remaining in he custodie of the maior or Lyme for the time beinge & theother to be in the custodie of my executors & overseers & in this coffer I wilbe kept all suche wrytinges scripts evydens leases ['& other' crossed through] as are pertaining to my Lands & livings as also all suche obligacions or writings as my executors &

overseers shall take for any parte porcon or money pertening to any my children. And for the more trust & faithfull paines of the maior for the tyme being I will be geven yerly to him 12*d* & to as all of his brethren as shall then present with him when any suche paynes shalbe taken 8*d*. And further my consyderacon of the paynes and travels of the overseers & executors of this last will I geve to everie of them 40*s* in mony.

And further my will is that if the said John my soone do dye without Issue & not married or before he be of 21 yeres of age

that then I will all suche parts or porcons of mony & goods & other things as shold have ben resyved to his use shall be resved by my said overseers to the behoff & use of the saide mannechilde until he shalbe of lawfull yeres, & if he do likewise so decess that then all the premises to be reserved as before to the resydew of my children. And if they all do dye all the said goods so remaining to be reserved the one moieties to Anstys my wyff & the other to my next heires.

5. WILL OF STEPHEN VILVAYNE, BAKER, 21 NOVEMBER 1561

ECA, Orphans' Court Will 7

Note: The Allhallows Goldsmith Street parish register was burnt during the Second World War but an earlier transcript of it recorded 'Steaphen Vilvayne' was buried on 30 November 1561. Recognisances were entered into for Agnes, the daughter of Vilvayne, on 22 May 1570 (ECA, Book 141, folio 29).

In the name of god Amen the 21 daye of Novembre in the yere of our lord god a Thowsand five hundred threscore & one [1561] And the fourth yere of the Raigne of our Sovaigne ladye Elizabeth by the grace of god Quene of Englonde Fraunce & Irelonde defendor of the feith &c. I Stephyn Vilvayne Citizen & baker of Excestre yn the Countie & Citie of Excestre beynge of whoale mynde & yn good & perfitt remembraunce lawde & prayse be to god do make & ordeyne this my present Testament Contenynge thereyn my last wyll yn maner & forme folowyng, that is to wete, ffirst & pryncipallye I commend my saule to almyghtie god my maker & redemer & my body to be buried wtyn the Churchyard of Seynt Peter yn Excestre **Item** I wyll that all suche dettes & duties as I awe of right or Consciens to any person or persons shalbe well & truly paid wtout delaye or Contradiccion And after the same is performed I geve unto Nicholas my soune thirtie poundes yn monye whereof ys payd eight poundes. Also I geve unto the said Nicholas one salt of Silver parcell gilt **Item** I geve to John my sone thirtye poundes yn monye and also a cupp of Silver or a salt of Silver **Item** I geve to

David my soune thirtye poundes yn money & one Cuppe of Silver or a salt of Silver All which legacies I wyll shalbe payd wtyn one quarter of a yere after my death at the discrecion of my overseers And if any of my said sounes dye wtyn the age of twenty & one yeres then I wyll that the porcion of hym dyenge shalbe devided emong[est – crossed out] the residue of my Children lyvynge **Item** I geve & bequeyth to Agnes my dawghter thirtie poundes yn money And also one Cuppe of Silver or salt of Silver To be delivered unto her as she shall Come to or accomplishe her full age or ells be maried And if the said Agnes happen to dye before she Come to her full age or be maried then I wyll that the porcion to her geven by this my Testament shalbe equally devyded to & emong all the residue of my Children & to the survic' [?] & survivyngs [?] of every of them **Item** I wyll & ordeyne that Richawrde my wyffe shall have holde use & occupye durynge her lyffe only [?] to her only use & behouff all my dwellynge house yn the parishe of All Seyntes yn Gouldsmythstrete yn the said Countie & Citie of Excestre whereyn I my self do dwell And also all the selyngs [?] & Coffers the presses beddynge performed & all other furnyture of houshold wtyn the same house durynge her lyffe The said house wt the bakehouse & apptennces to the same bakehouse belongynge And also the selyng of the same house yn the hall wt the best Cubbord & tableborde yn the hall after the decesse of Richawrde my wyffe I leve bequeyth & geve to Peter my soune To have & to hold all the saide house wt all & Singler the apptennces after the death of my wyffe to the saide Peter & to his heires & assignes for evermore **Item** I geve & bequeyth to the said Peter ten poundes yn money And also one salt of silver parcell gilt which salt I had of the gift & graunt of John Vilvayne my father **Item** I geve unto Julyan Robynson my dawghter one litle house yn Excestre aforesaid wtyn the saide parysshe of All Seyntes yn Gouldsmythstreate lyenge nye to the said Churche of All Seyntes whereyn Wylliam Sto[...] nowe dwellyth To have & to hold to the saide Julyan for terme of her naturall lyfe for the yerely rent of four pens to be payde to the heires & assignes of me the said Stephyn Vilvayne And the said Julyan shall repayre all the same house at her proper Costes & Charges durynge the saide terme Item I geve unto the said Julyan Robynson my dawghter fyve markes in mony & six silver spones **Item** I geve & bequeyth to Stephyn John Wylliam & Charitie Southmeade & to every of them the sounes & daughter of Edmond Southmede & Julyan his wyffe daughter of me the said Stephyn Vilvayne twentye shillynges a pece the Some of four poundes to be paide at there full age And if any any [sic] of the said Children happen to dye before the[y] Come to full age then I wyll that the parte & porcion of hym or them dyeng shalbe devyded to & among the residue of them which shalbe lyvyng **Item** I geve & bequeyth to my said dawgter [sic] Julyan Southmeade one other litle house yn Excestre aforesaid wtyn the said parysshe of All Seyntes yn Gouldsmythstreat whereyn Water [sic] Harrys nowe dwellyth To have & to hold to the same Julyan for terme of her naturall lyffe for the yerely rent of four pens to be payd to the heires & assignes of me the said Stephyn Vilvayne And the said Julyan Southmede shall repayre all the same house at her proper Costes & Charges durynge the said terme **Item** I geve & bequeyth to Thomas Vilvayne myne eldest soune & heire

all the residue of my landes Tenementes & hereditamentes rentes reversions & services wt thapptennces wtyn the Cite of Excestre & yn the paryshe of Seynt Sydwylles yn the Countye & Citie of Excester not before legatyd nor bequethyd And all other my landes Elswhere yn the Countye of Devon To have & to hold to the said Thomas & to his heires & assignes for evermore upon Condicion that the same Thomas do observe & performe my wyll & mynde hereafter mencyoned Item I give unto the said Thomas myne eldest soune sixe poundes thirtyne shillynges & foure pens yn money And also my best goblet of Silver and sixe spones of silver of the best sort And for asmytche as the house in Excestre whereyn I dwell is Inteeyled & that my gift thereof made to Peter my soune maye be doubtfull I wyll therefore & mynde that Thomas myne Eldest Sone shall knowledge a fyne & make other Convayaunce of the same house wt thapptennces to his brother Peter & his heires for evermore for his farder & better strenght & assuraunce of & yn the same house wyth thapptennces And if the said Thomas do refuse so to do then I wyll & mynde & also do geve & graunt to the said Peter & to his heires for evermore all the foresaid londes Tenementes & hereditamentes wt thapptennces which are [?] before geven grauntyd & assigned by this Testament to the said Thomas Vilvayne And my legacy of the saide landes to the said Thomas made to be utterly voyed & of none Effect **Item** I geve to Wylliam Cop [?] a Coate & a doblet & to Wylliam Richard my s[erva]unt & apprentyce I geve fortye shillynges to be payd to hym when he hath performyd his Covenant wt an honest Rewarde to be geven hym over & besides the saide 40*s* **Item** I wyll that Margarett Parker my tenaunt shall have holde & enioye my Tenement in Gouldsmythstreate [verso] whereyn she nowe dwellyth for terme of her lyfe for the yerely rent of thirtyne shillynges & four pens which she [superscript: nowe] alwayes hath borne and payed **Item** I geve to every of my godchyldren twelve pens a pece **Item** I wyll & geve to & emong the pore people yn almonshouses & elswhere yn Excestre & the suburbes of the same where bedrede [?] people & most necessitie is ffortie shillynges yn money to be distributyd by the dyscretion of my Executrix &

overseers namyd hereafter yn this my wyll The Residue of all my goodes & debtes after my dettes payd & my funerall Expences performyd & this my legacies Conteined yn this my present Testament fulfilled I whaly [sic] leave geve & bequeythe to the saide Richawrde my wyfe to her awne proper use the which Richawrde my wyffe of this my present Testament & last wyll I make & ordeyn my sole Executrix And I do Constitute & appoynt Mr Robert Midwynter Alderman of Excestre & John Anthony to be my supervisors of this my last wyll & Testament And for ther paynes yn

that behalfe to be taken I geve to every of them twenty sixe shillynges & eight pens sterlynge the Some of four markes **In wytnes whereof** to this my present Testament & last wyll I have putt my hande and Seale To this wytnesseth Richard Smart Harry Gyll & others **Yeven** the daye & yere above writen

Probate 15 December [?] 1561 [?] by Robert Fyssher, official of George Carew, archdeacon of Exeter.

6. WILL OF NICHOLAS REVE, BREWER OF ST GEORGE'S PARISH, 23 MARCH 1562

ECA, Orphans' Court Will 6
Note: there are two versions of this will. The first has a preamble and additional final few lines as below. Recognisances were entered into on 21 March 1564 regarding Reve's three children Joan, Katherine, and Elizabeth (ECA, Book 141, folio 5).

In the name of god Amen The 23th daye of Marche In the yere of our lord god 1561 and the fowerth yere of the Raigne of our Soveraigne ladie Elizabethe by the grace of god of England Frannce and Ireland quene defender of the faithe &c I Nycholas Ryve of the parishe of Sainte Georgis within the Cittie and countie of Exetter brewer, beynge in my perfit remembraunce (**thanks** be to god) **make my testament & laste will in manner and forme followinge ffirst I bequethe my sole to allmightie god** and my bodye to Christian burial Item I geve and bequethe all my fee simple lands and my tenement lands … I make my full and whole Executrix she to bestowe the same as she shall thinke hit best. Thes beinge willed. Mr Thomas Richargs clerk person of Saint Georgys aforesaid Richarde Gervis Thomas Perkyn John Lanne & Wiliam Wagland with others.

The effects of Nich. Reve
The effects of the Wyll of Nicholes Reve of Exeter brewer decessed by hym made the 23th daye of Marche 1561, toochynge his legacyes by the seid Wyll & testement

Firstly I geve & bequethe all my fee Symple lands & my tene lands unto Johan Reve my daughter to Kathryn Reve my daughter And to the childe my wiffe nowe goethe withall equally to be devyded betwyxte them. And to the heyrs of ther bodies lawfully begotten Excepte the childe my wyffe goeth with all be a man childe but and he be a man [sic] childe then I geve to the same childe my wyffe goeth withall, all my term lands wholy to hym selfe And the chylde parte of my fe symple landes And provydng to the custome of the Citie, And if any of them dye without issue of ther bodyes lawfully begotten then the seeme to remeyn to the Rest then lyvynge, And yf they dye all three without issue then my wyll ys that Kathryn Stephyns & Johan Stephens my Wyffe towe daughters should have & Injoye All my said fee symple & term lands duryng there lyves equally betwyxt them And to the longist lyver of them And after the decesse of the seid Kathryn Stephens & Johan Stephens, I geve & bequeth all my said fee symple & tene lands to my Sister Johan Cylley Margery Elknes Philpit Hethfilde & Elizebeth Mills. And to the heyrs of ther bodyes lawfully begotten for every but my wyll is that Johan Reve my wyffe shoudd have the kepynge

of all my fee symple lands and term lands to her awne use & behouff & untyll my said childryne come to the full age of Eightyne yeres. And with the same lands to brynge up my said childryne at her costes & charges And as they come to ther Ages so to enter unto there parts and porcons. ['And also I geve & bequethe to e' crossed through]
And also I geve & bequeth to the said Johan Reve my daughter Kathryn Reve my daughter And to the childe my wyffe goethe withall a nest of Gylte Gobletts there is to every of them a goblet a pease. And Johan Reve my daughter to have also the cover of the seme nest of Gobletts. And I geve to the said Johan Reve my daughter Kathryn Reve my daughter & to the childe my Wyffe goeth withall to every of them £6 13s 4d a pece lawfull money of Englonde And if any of them dye before the age of 18 yeres, that then ther parts & porcons to Remayne unto the rest lyvynge Item I geve & bequeth to ['the heyres Atkens my Sister 40s Item I geve to Johan Cylley Philpet Hethfilde & Elizebeth Mills my sister 10s to the pece of them' crossed through] John Reve clerke a standynge Cupp gilted with a cover & a hert upon & also four pounds

lawfull money of England. Item I geve to Margery Elkens my Sister 40s Item I geve to Johan Sylley & Philpet Hethfilde & Elizebeth Mills my Sister 10s to a pece of them Item I geve to Johan Chandeler wydowe 10s Item I geve & bequethe to Johan Hethfild my servant £3 6s 8d lawfull money of Englonde Item I geve to the reparaicon of Seynt Georges Church in Exeter 10s And to the parson of Seynt George for the tythes forgotten 3s 4d Item I geve & bequeth unto Nicholas Evans my sister Margerys sonne a blacke gowne fased with blacke conney
And I make my fryndes Robert Chaff Thomas Stephens the overseers of this my Testament & laste wyll wyll [sic] and they to have for ther peynes 10s a pece.
The Rest of all my goods my detts & legeacyes paide I geve & bequethe to Johan Reve my wyff whom I make my full & whole Executrix &c.

Memorandum … the court is appoynted on Thursday in the Ester wyk in the next …
promise thr recognisnances.

7. WILL OF JOHN THOMAS, 1 JUNE 1562

ECA, Orphans' Court Will 8 (also National Archives, PROB 11/45/295)
Note: the top right-hand and bottom right-hand corners of the will have been cut with a resulting loss of words. These have been supplied in brackets by the copy proved via Canterbury on 13 November 1562.

1562
In the name of God Amen The fyrst day of June in the 4th y[ere of the Raigne of our] sovereigne Lady Elisabeth by the grace of God Quene of E[ngland Frannce and Ireland deffendor of the faith &c 1562] I John Thomas thelder of the Citie of Exon beinge yn good & [parfect remembrance doe] make & ordeyne my last will & testament yn manner & f[orme following ffirst I] geve & bequethe my synfull sole to allmightie God & in the [meritts of the death of Christ my] onely redemer & savyr and my bodye beinge of earth I comende [to the yerth to be buried] yn to the seemely

sepulcure there to remayn untyll it shall please the [the Lorde by] the trumpe of the angells to rayse the sonne & to unyte bothe bodye & sole to apeare before him at the day of judgment to receve everlastinge joye & lyffe. Also I geve to the poore menns releffe 5s Also I geve to every of my children John Julian Elisabeth Joan & William the full some of £6 13s 4d which parts & porcions of £6 13s 4d so severally bequethed unto them my will & mynde is that Mary my wyff shall kepe reteyn & have yn her custodie untyll every of them shall come to lawfull yeres of age or to the tyme of mariage condycionally that she by thadvise of the overseers of this my

last will & testament do put in good and sufficient assurance by suretyes to answere the saide severall somes of £6 13s 4d to every of my children at the tymes of ther lawffull yeres or tymes of mariage and [doe also] educat & bring up the said my children during untyll & before the saide t[ymes whiche] condicons if she refuse to do them my will & mynde is that immediatly after my [death] the saide severall somes of every of my childrens legacie shalbe by my exec[utrix paide] to the overseers of this my will with severall somes to be either delyvered to th[e masters of] every of the saide my children with such assurance as by my overseers shalbe [devised or else] the same to be employed to the best beheff & use of the saide my children [with suche assurance] as the saide my overseers shall devyse & thincke good. And further my will [and mynde is] that if any of the saide my children do dye either before the tyme of mariage or y[eres of] discrecon I will the partes & porcons of everye of them so decessinge to rem[aine] to the overlivers to be equally devyded emonge them & to be employed as is before saide. And if they all dye before suche lawffull age or tymes of mariage then I will the some there porcons do wholy remayne to the executrix of this my last will & testament. The resydew of my goodds not bequethed my debts & funeralls paied I geve & bequethe to Mary my wyffe whom I do ordayn & make my sole & full exeuctrix of this my last will & testament. And for performance thereof I do pray & besche my well loved Edward Brydeeman John Hoker & John Kestle & Hew Sowithley To be the overseers of this my last will & testament and to every of them for there travells herein I geve 6s 8d. Witnesseth to the premsyss Geffrey Thomas Nichus Benson & others
By me John Thomas John Vowell *alias* Hoker Edward Brydeman Geffrey Thomas Hugh Southley

8. WILL OF ELLERY WESTCOTT, 30 OCTOBER 1563

ECA, Orphans' Court Will 9

In the name of God Amen the 30 daye of October in the yere of our lorde god 1563 I Ellerye Westcott in whole & perfett memorye do make thys my last wyll & testament. Fyrste I geve & bequeth my sowle to almyghtye god to hys mother Marye & to the hollye Companye of Heaven & my bodye to be buryed in hollye earsse. Item I geve to be buryed in the Chauncell 6s 8d. Item I geve to the mayntenance of the churche of Dunsforde my beste wether. Item I geve & bequeth to Robart Ward one brasyn Crocke namyd the molson mowithed crocke And a heyffer Byrlyzige [?]. Item I geve to Opephine [?] Hore a panne & 5 shepe. Item I geve to Marye Durynge a brasynge panne. Item I geve to John Bearne a heyffer yearelynge. Item I geve to John Gefford Wyllyam Gefford & Illarye Gefford eche a yeo shepe. Item I geve to Elizabeth Bearne a lambe. Item I geve to everye godchyld 4d. Item Rose Stephyn shall have one brasyn panne namyd the pyttyd panne valer of 3 pottells. Item I geve Agnes Gyfforde a brasyn panne & a bed of duste a peare of blancketts a Coverlett a bolster & my Tabell borde with a forme. Item I geve to James Gefford a Cowe. Item I geve to eche of Parterydge's children a shepe. Item to James Gorvyn a heyffer. Item I geve Hewgh Deart a shepe. Item I geve Agnes Gefford a Coffer. Item Tristram Tooker shall have a Cubbord & the shelves with the syde borde. The Resydewe of my goods not bequeth I geve & bequeth to Thomas Hoore Gent[leman] I make my Executor to Dyspose my goods for the welth of my sowle. Wytnes hereof Rychard Egbeare vycar of Dunsford Robart Sparke & Wyllyam Towning & Fraunces Gorvyn Thye to have 6s 8d. Item I make my over seer Roberte Sparke he to have 5s.

This has been compared with the original will remaining in the Archdeaconry of Exeter witnessed by M. Browne
Sum total £34 20d.

9. INVENTORY OF HARRY MAUNDER, MERCHANT, 24 FEBRUARY 1564

ECA, Orphans' Court Inventory 2A

Note: The register for the parish of St Mary Arches recorded 'Henry Maunder' was buried on 24 February 1564. Recognisances were entered into on 19 and 22 April and 7 July 1564 regarding Thomas, Silvester, John and Henry Maunder, sons of Henry Maunder, and for his daughters Margery, Rose and Dorothy (ECA, Book 141, folios 7, 10, 11). A dispute over the goods was taken to London (see National Archives, C3/14/37).

Thys ys the Inventorye of all & singular the goods chattalls & detts plate & redye money wyche late apptayned unto Harrye Maunder of the cyttye of Exeter merchant late decessyd made & taken the 24th daye of Februarye in the yere of our lord god a Thowsand fyve hundred Three skore & Three & praisid by George Peryman Edmond Whetcombe Andrewe Gyve marchants George Hunte Wyllyam Phyllypps & John Haydon ['praised' crossed through] appoynted accordyng to the order of Orphans withyn the Ceattie of Exeter by John Mydwynter one of the alderman of the said Cete as ffolyoth.

[1] In the Hall
Firstly a foldinge tablebord Joynyd 20*s*;
Item A wyndowe Clothe of grene Clothe 2*s*;
Item A Cubbord Joynyd 20*s*;
Item a basyn & a yewer of tynne 5*s*;
Item A Cubbord Clothe 2*s*;
Item 3 formes 3*s* 4*d*;
Item 2 Chayers Joynyd 4*s*;
Item 4 foote stooles 16*d*;
Item the hangyngs of Red & grene Saye 4*s*;
Item 6 old quisshyngs of grene 12*d*;
Item A backe of yron 6*s* 8*d*;
Item A barre in the Chimlye 18*d*;
Item A peare of doggs 16*d*;
Item An Andyron 8*d*;
Item A peare of Pottehangyngs 6*d*;
Item A hearon brusshe 4*d*;
Item the Sealyngs in the hall 30*s*;
Item A standyshe with weyghts 6*d*;

Item A nother bord with A carpett 8*s*;
Sum £5 12*s* 2*d*.

In the Allyar
Item a Coverlett of Tapstre worke 6*s* 8*d*;
Item A old Cheste 6*d*;
Item A fyne Coverlett of tapstre worke 26*s* 8*d*;
[2] Item 6 greate & 3 lyttell quisshyngs of lether old 3*s*;
Sum 36*s* 10*d*.

In the Chamber within the Allyer
Item A bedstede Joynyd 6*s* 8*d*;
Item A Tester of whyte lynnen cloth 3*s* 4*d*;
Item A fether bed 25*s*;
Item A flocke bed 5*s*;
Item A blankett 16*d*;
Item A pyllowe of downe 3*s*;
Item 2 lyttell Coffers 16*d*;
Item a countynge bord 2*s*;
Item A mattres 2*s*;
Item A greate Joyned cheste 8*s*;
Item A nother cheste 5*s*;
Item the staynyd clothes 8*s* 4*d*;
Sum £3 11*s*.

In the Chamber over the Parlor
Item A standinge bedstede 4*s*;
Item A Tester of buckeron 2*s*;
Item A flocke bed 3*s* 4*d*;
Item 2 fether pyllowes 2*s*;
Item the hangyngs of stayned cloth 6*s*;

Item A old shyppe Coffer 2s 6d;
Item 2 old coffers & 2 lyttell ffosseletts 6d;
Item 5 peare of harnys savinge a backe [?] 32s 4d;
Item A Cubbord Joynyd 5s;
Sum 58s 8d.

In the ffore Hall
Item A foldinge tableborde 26s 8d;
Item A London Carpett 5s;
Item A Joynyd Cubbord 26s 8d;
Item A Cheste 8s;
Item A benche 20d;
Item A quisshynge of tawnye & grene velvett 16d;
[3] Item A Joynyd Chayer 2s;
Item A backe of yron in the Chymlye praisyd 8s;
Item the hangyngs of Red & grene Saye 10s;
Item 2 formes 2s;
Item 2 pyctures of flaunders worke 5s;
Sum £4 16s 4d.

In the Butterye
Item 4 shelfes & 4 bordes of payntyd Canvas 3s 4d;
Item 2 sheffes of arrowes 3s 8d;
Item A standerd 8d;
Item 2 presses for Kerchers 2s;
Item A yearthen potte 6d;
Item A powitherynge tubbe with A Cover 12d;
Item A boxe & a payle 1d;
Sum 11s 3d.

Hys Apparrell
Item A gowne of brone blewe led with blacke lace & facyd with budge £3;
Item A other gowne of browne blewe facyd with budge 26s 8d;
Item A gowne of browne of browne [sic] blewe facyd with taffeta 20s;
Item A nother gowne of browne blewe facyd with Conye 25s;

Item A Cassacke of taffeta gardyd with velvett 15s;
Item A wostyd dublett with slyves of Satten 6s 8d;
Item A Chamblett coote with out Slyves 3s 4d;
Item A wostyd Jackett 3s 4d;
Item A Cloke of browne blewe 6s 8d;
Item A Clothe Coote 6s 8d;
[4] Item A wostyd dublett 2s 6d;
Item A peare of hawse 20d;
Sum £8 17s 6d.

Hys Wyffs Apparrell
Item A gowne of browne blewe lynyd with chambelett with A garde of blacke velvett 26s 8d;
Item A gowne in grayne gardyd with velvett 20s;
Item A gowne in vyolett in grayne with A garde of velvette 20s;
Item A gowne of browne blewe with A garde of blacke velvett 13s 4d;
Item A nother gowne of browne blewe with A gard of blacke velvett 13s 4d;
Item one other olde gowne of blacke without velvet 6s 8d;
Item one Cassacke of browne blewe with A ffrenge of sylke 26s 8d;
Item A nother Cassacke of browne blewe led with 3 laces 20s;
Item A Rownd Kyrtell of wostyd with A gard of blacke velvett 10s;
Item A nother Kyrtell of wostyd with out velvet with damaske bodyes 30s;
Item A Craynyd Kyrtell of wostyd with Chamblett bodyes 6s 8d;
Item A pettycotte of Skarlett 10s;
Sum £10 3s 4d.

Hys Naperye
Item 17 peare of shetts £5 13s 4d;
Item 2 dosyn of napkyns wroght wyth blacke Sylke 32s;
Item 18 napkyns without sylke 9s;
Item 6 fyne bordeclothes 40s;

Item 6 towells wrowght with blacke Sylke 30s;

Item 7 playne Towels *viz* towe of dyaper & 5 of other playne 20s;

Item 10 pyllowe tyes sume wrowght with blacke & sume with whyte 25s;

Item 8 handetowells and towe wyth blacke lace 3s 4d;

[5] Item A spanyshe Tester with 3 Courtyns of the same havynge ffrenge of grene & Red sylke 10s;

Item A Tester of grene & Red saye with Curtens to the same 10s;

Item 2 Cubborde Clothes the one wrowghte 2s;

Sum £14 14s 8d.

Her Naperye

Item 5 peces of hangyngs of whyte Clothe 8s;

Item 30 neckerchers £3;

Item 9 kerchers *viz* 13 of hulland & 6 peare of Callowcaue 50s;

Item 2 peare of whyte slyves the one wrowghte 2s;

Item 6 whyte Aperons 8s;

Item 2 peare of satten slyves the one Tawnye the other blacke 20d;

Item A 11 lynnen parteletts 13s 4d;

Item A lyttell spouse [? spruse] cheste 13s 4d;

Sum £7 16s 4d.

In the Hyer Chamber Allyer

Item A Cheste 8d;

Item A ladder 4d;

Item A Joynyd doore with A peare of Twystes 2s 6d;

Sum 3s 6d.

In the Chamber next to the hyer Allyar

Item A flockebed 6s 8d;

Item A bolster of fethers 2s 6d;

Item A Tester of buckeroun 2s 6d;

Item A playne bedstede 12d;

Item A lyttell table bord 12d;

Item 2 old payntyd clothes 4d;

Item 2 Coffers 16d;

Sum 15s 4d.

In the Chamber over the forehall

[6] Item A Joynyd bedstede 3s 4d;

Item A Tester of payntyd clothes 4s;

Item A fether bed 26s 8d;

Item 2 fether bolsters 5s;

Item 4 pyllowes of downe 10s;

Item A lyttell pyllowe of fethers 6d;

Item A Joynyd stoole with A draste 2s;

Item A Joynyd forme 12d;

Item A longe Joynyd cheste 6s 8d;

Item A smaller cheste 3s 4d;

Item A lyttell fframyd table with A Cover of buckerom 12d;

Item the hangyngs of yellowe & blewe buckerombe with A border of payntyd clothes 8s;

Item A whyte Thromyd coverlett 2s;

Item 3 old mantells 6s 8d;

Item 3 old blancketts 18d;

Sum £4 20d.

In the Maydens Chamber

Item A Joynyd bedstede with A Cover of Tymber 6s 8d;

Item A fether bed with a fether bolster 20s;

Item A peare of blancketts 2s 6d;

Item 2 Coverletts 3s 4d;

Item 2 formes 8d;

Item more A playne bedstede 20d;

Item A fether bolster 4s;

Item A flocke bed 4s;

Item A flocke bolster 12d;

Item A peare of blanketts 2s;

Item 2 Coveryd coverletts *viz* yellowe & Red 4s;

Item 2 whyte Coverletts 3s 4d;

Item An old Coverlett 6d;

Item A playne forme 4d;

Item A payntyd tester 3s;

Item the hangyngs of payntyd clothes 2s 6d;
Item A lyttell Table bord 6d;
Sum £3.

In the Parlor
[7] Item A hamer 2d;
Item 2 lanterns 8d;
Item A Cubbord with A Cubbord Cloth wrowght with blacke
  sylke 3s 4d;
Item A dressynge bord 12d;
Item 3 planks in the flower 10d;
Item 2 ffryinge pannes 2s;
Item A skower 2d;
Item 2 gose pannes 16d;
Item A goater 8d;
Item A backe of Iron in the chymblye 3s 4d;
Item A gryderon 8d;
Item An Iron barre 10d;
Item A brasyn ladell 6d;
Item A morter & A pestell 2s 8d;
Sum 18s 2d.

In the Kychinge
Item 12 barrells of swarrowe £3 14s 4d;
Item A Cage for pubtoye [? poultry] 5s;
Item A shelfe 6d;
Item A tubbe with towe yeres 4d;
Item A lettys 8d;
Item A dryssynge bord 2s;
Item A busshell 8d;
Sum £4 2s 6d.

In the Ware Howse
Item towe fardells of Canvas £28;
Item halfe a fardell of treagar [?] contayninge 4 peaces at £3
  13s 4d A pece Amounteth to £14 13s 4d;
Item 25 endes of Iron weinge 7 hundryd lackynge 4 pownd at
  10s the hundryd Amounteth to £3 9s 6d;
Item 36 gallons of Coyte at 3s 4d the gallon Amounteth to £6;

Item 12 Pannes of brasse weinge 45 lb at 6d the pownd
  Amounteth to 22s 6d;
[8] Item 3 Cawderons of brasse weinge 20 lb at 5d the pownd
  Amounteth [to] 8s 4d;
Item 3 skylletts weinge three pownds at 6d the Pownd 18d;
Item 10 latten basens weinge 42 lb at 7d the pownd 24s 6d;
Item 13 Crockes of brasse weinge A 100 & 3 quarters & 6 lb
  at 5d the pownd £4 4s 2d;
Item 4 Chaffers of brasse weinge 34 lb at 5d the Pownd
  Amounteth to 14s 2d;
Item 4 posnetts weinge 27 Pownds at three pence the pownd
  6s 9d;
Item 7 flower potts of tynne 3s 6d;
Item 4 flower potts of latten 2s;
Item 3 Chaffyndysshes of brasse 18d;
Item 2 quarte potts of tynne 2s;
Item 2 pottell potts of tynne 3s 4d;
Item 2 howpyd potts of tynne 18d;
Item 2 pynt potts of tynne 12d;
Item A flaunder beame & skales 3s 4d;
Item 2 Chamber potts of tynne 16d;
Item 4 halfe hundred weyghts of ledde & 3 qar [quarter]
  weyghts and 23 Pownd of ledden weyghts 24s 6d;
Item 4 lb of braysen weyghts 16d;
Item A barrell of okercombe weinge A quarter of A hundred
  4s 6d;
Item A hogshed of Tallowe weinge towe hundryd & A halfe &
  14 lb at 20s the hundryd Amounteth to 52s 6d;
Item A whyte maunde with brusell weinge A hundryd 13s
  4d;
Item 5 emptye hogsheds 5s;
Item A sugar cheste 8d;
Item A hogshed of lyme 2s;
Item 5 broches 5s;
Item A pecke 2d;
Item A pece of Pyche weinge 17 lb – 2s;
Item A shulle 4d;
[9] Sum £36 15s 7d.

In the Chamber over the Kychynge
Item 38 latten Candylstycks weinge 44 lb Prysyd at 26*s* 8*d*;
Item A brasyn Chalderon 12*d*;
Item 3 garnyshe of Pewter vessell £4;
Item 6 porydge dyshes with boode baynnes [?] 4*s*;
Item 12 Pewter dysshes with yeares 4*s*;
Item 2 tynnen basens 16*d*;
Item A bole of Tynne 8*d*;
Item A Chardger of Tynne 16*d*;
Item tynnen Plates fower & towe Sawcers 3*s* 4*d*;
Item halfe a dosyn of plates of tynne 4*s*;
Item 3 standynge booles of Tynne 2*s*;
Item A lyttell flatte peace of tynne 2*d*;
Item A quele turne 4*d*;
Item A byll 10*d*;
Item A Playne borde with 2 trestells 8*d*;
Item 2 Raynes for brydells 2*d*;
Item A Cappe case 1*d*;
Item A longe old Coffer 6*d*;
Item A Cappe 2*d*;
Sum £6 9*s* 11*d*.

In the Chamber next the steyer
Item A hackenye saddell 6*d*;
Item A peare of bootes 8*d*;
Item 2 sydes of A bedstede 8*d*;
Item A fframe for laysynge 12*d*;
Item A sugar cheste with shewes 3*s*;
Item A greate flanders Cuppe with A Cover 2*s*;
Item A 11 yearthen potts 2*d*;
Item A bagge of Sackeclothe 6*d*;
Item A emptye hogshed 12*d*;
Item A lyttell powderynge tubbe with A treen Platter 4*d*;
Item A docke for A hackenye Saddell with hangyngs 2*d*;
Item A boxe for spyces 1*d*;
[10] Item A peare of styrooppes 4*d*;
Sum 10*s* 5*d*.

In the Tweane doores

Item A butte of mamseye £7 6*s* 8*d*;
Item halfe A butte of Eagar Seacke halfe full 13*s* 4*d*;
Sum £8.

In the Shoppe
Item A pece of vyttrye Canvas Contayninge 71 yards at 8*d* the yard 48*s* 4*d*;
Item 6 yards of vytterye canvas at 8[*d*] the yard 4*s*;
Item one other peace of vytterye Canvas contayninge 24 yards & A halfe at 8*d* the yarde 16*s* 4*d*;
Item more 33 yards of canvas at 8*d* the yard 22*s*;
Item A peace of normandye Canvas contayninge 9 yards & A halfe at 13*d* the yard 10*s* 3½*d*;
Item 4 dosyn & 2 horse shewes 4*s*;
Item A whole peace of dowlyshe of the longe pleytte £5 13*s* 4*d*;
Item A whole peace of dowlyshe of the Shorte playte £5;
Item halfe A peace of dowlysshe of the shorte playte 50*s*;
Item halfe A peace of tregar beinge of the shorte playte Presyd at 38*s*;
Item A nother peace of tregar 36*s* 8*d*;
Item A pece of Callowe cowe cloth 12*s*;
Item A nother peace of tregar contayninge 17 yards at 8*d* the yard 11*s* 4*d*;
[11] Item 10 yards of dowlyshe at 10*d* the yarde 8*s* 4*d*;
Item 7 yards & A halfe of Callowe Cowe Clothe at 12*d* the yard 7*s* 6*d*;
Item 7 yards of Callowe Cowe Cloth at 9*d* the yard 5*s* 3*d*;
Item halfe A peace of brytten Clothe & a yard at 7*d* the yard 35*s*;
Item A peace of treagar of 6 yards 3 quarters at 8*d* the yard 4*s* 6*d*;
Item 17 Reames of browne paper praisyd at 18*d* the Realme 25*s* 6*d*;
Item 33 nestes of style at 16*d* the neste 44*s*;
Item 17 lb of Castell soope at 7*d* the Pownd 9*s* 11*d*;
Item 2 lyttell kyches of waxe weinge 4 lb at 8*d* the Pownd 2*s* 8*d*;
Item A dosyn of Playnge cards 16*d*;

Item 3 dosyn of weake yarne 6s;

Item blacke sylke 3s;

Item 2 pownd & A halfe of Redde mayle at 9d the pownd 22d;

Item A ounce of safferon 20d;

Item halfe A hundred of nayles 4d;

Item 4 pownd of blacke mayle at 8d the Pownd 2s 8d;

Item ffor Ratts bane 4d;

Item 14 yards of yryshe ffryte at 10d the yard 11s 8d;

Item 2 grosse of buttons 20d;

Item A grosse of hearyn buttons 8d;

Item A dosyn of parchement 18d;

Item 2 pownd & a halfe of Peaseminge threede 5s;

Item 2 pownd & halfe of browne threde praisyd at 20d;

Item a quarter & a halfe of Kype [?] threde 6d;

[12] Item 7 Pownd & A halfe of Rawe threde at 8d the pownd Amounteth [to] 5s;

Item halfe A pownd of Crewell 8d;

Item in gyrse webbe 14d;

Item A old face of budge 2s;

Item A pownd of blacke threde 2s 6d;

Item halfe A pownd of browne threde 12d;

Item A sume of lath nayles 14s;

Item 6 maylynge Cords 2s;

Item 2 pownd of sugar candye 2s;

Item 42 pownds of Reasons of Coryn at 4d the pownd 14s;

Item A 11 lb of the best sorte of graynes at 18d the pownd 16s 6d;

Item 9 shurts & 3 smocks at 20d A pece one with an other 20s;

Item 2 pownd of Coleryd threde at 14d the pownd 2s 4d;

Item A pownd of Agnes seede 8d;

Item 18 pownd of led 20d;

Item A grosse & 5 dosyn of whyte poynts 12d;

Item 31 barrells of triackell 5s 2d;

Item A peacke of mustard seede 15d;

Item 8 lb of weake yarne 16d;

Item A busshell of mustard seede 5s;

Item 22 Comes 6d;

Item Ratts bane 4d;

Item 3 qar [quarters] & a halfe a pownd of Peper 2s 11d;

Item 15 ffosseletts 2s 6d;

Item 4 Rounynge [?] boxes 6s 8d;

Item 5 hatts 16d;

Item A greate cheste 26s 8d;

Item A greate peare of ballance 6s 8d;

Item A nother peare lesser 4s;

Item A nother peare lesser 2s;

Item A nother peare lesser 12d;

Item A nother lyttell peare 2d;

[13] Item 2 shelfes Bownd Abowte the Shoppe with the borddes 10s;

Item 6 Surplusses 6s 8d;

Item 2 shelfes to stand uppon the bulke 4d;

Item 2 peare of Cardes 8d;

Item 7 Kyrsyes praisyd at 16s a Kersye £5 12d;

Item 3 other Kyrsyes at 20s the peace £3;

Item 2 other Kyrsyes at 25s ye peace 50s;

Item 10 other Kersyes fyne praisyd at 32s the pece £16;

Item 2 Rawe Kyrsyes 36s;

Sum £69 6s 10½d.

In the Sealler

Item 10 hogsheds of yolledge wyne A Emptye Tearse and A Emptye hogshed 53s 4d;

Item A hogshed of Lyme 20d;

Item A pottell A quarte & A pynte of Tynne 2s;

Item 4 plancks 10d;

Item An Ale Coste of 12 gallons 8d;

Item A doore 4d;

Item A shelfe bord with Ropes 6d;

Item A old Coffer 6d;

Item wood 2s 6d;

Sum £3 2s 4d.

In the Howse in Saynt Marye Arches Lane

Item A old Panne of brasse and A Ladell of yron 2s;

Item A Reke for Candells 2d;

Item A old turne 4*d*;
Item A old sugar cheste 2*d*;
Item An old Chayer 7*d*;
Item 23 Caskes leare & sume with vynegar £3 16*s* 8*d*;
[14] Item Trestells 16*d*;
Item 2 good studds 4*d*;
Item A Case to put torches in 2*d*;
Item 5 lb of waxe & 7 lb of torche waxe 4*s* 2*d*;
Item A candell mowlde 2*s*;
Item A peace of Sealinge 12*d*;
Item A hundryd of Caldellvoods [?] 1*d*;
Sum £4 9*s*.

In Shyppynge
Item halfe A quarter of A barke callyd the dragon of Tapsam
   £8;
Sum £8.

In Plate
Item A pounce [?] goblett weinge 6 ouncs at 4*s* 8*d* le ounce
   Amounteth to 28*s*;
Item 2 saltes of sylver parcell gylte with Covers weinge 23
   ouncs at 5*s* le ounce £5 15*s*;
Item A nother goblett broken weinge 12 ouncs & A halfe at 4*s*
   8*d* lee ounce 58*s* 4*d*;
Item 3 flatte peaces of sylver weinge 16 ouncs at 3*s* 8*d* le
   ounce Amounteth [to] £3 14*s* 8*d*;
Item 3 stoninge Ale Cuppes with Covers & footes of sylver
   weinge 10 ouncs at 4*s* 8*d* the ounce 46*s* 8*d*;
Item one Ale Cuppe of sylver parcell gylte with A Cover
   weinge 6 ouncs & A halfe at 4*s* 8*d* the ounce 30*s* 4*d*;
[15] Item A berell Cuppe with A foote & Cover of sylver 5*s*;
Item 2 dosyn & one spone of sylver weinge 25 ouncs at 4*s* 8*d*
   the ounce £5 16*s* 8*d*;
Item A gyrdell of sylke with A dymye of sylver 7*s*;
Item 3 peare of beades with certyn sylver stones 3 peare of
   sylver hookes gylte, the one with perells the other Ameld
   & gylte A pynne with perells & one other pynne all gyltyd

weinge 10 ouncs at 5*s* 4*d* the ounce 53*s* 4*d*;
Item A whyte stone Cuppe with A Cover of sylver gylte
   which lyeth to gage as yt ys thowght 13*s* 4*d*;
Item 6 sylver spones 26*s* 8*d*;
Item A peare of hookes gylte and 2 pynnes gylte 13*s* 4*d*;
Sum £29 8*s* 4*d*.

In Monye
Item in spanyshe monye £26 13*s*;
Item 9 yeoffendallers 39*s*;
Item 20 halfe sufferons with other Crownes £14 12*s*;
Item 19 old Crownes of the Rose £5 14*s*;
Item in Comon monye £16 14*s* 8*d*;
Item in base monye at 4½*d* A pece 54*s*;

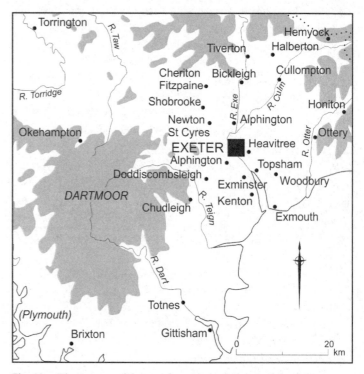

Fig. 11.   The pattern of the merchant Henry Maunder's business,
reflected in the places where people owed him money, as recorded in
his shop book (OC 2; *graphic: T. Ives, Exeter Archaeology*).

Item in halfe face grotes 10s;

Item in goune [?] holle grotes 5s;

Item in doggs 2s 3d;

Item 6 bulfords 3s;

Item in Slyppes 2s 5d;

Sum £39 8s 10d.

Detts dewe unto the sayd Harrye Maunder As Appereth by hys Shoppe booke

[16] Item Philippe Yard murse [?] beinge A weaver without Estgate oweth uppon the shoppe booke 2s 4½d;

Item Wyllyam Austyn oweth 10s;

Item mother Alse in Saynt Rockes Lane 17d;

Item Alreades wyffe oweth 6s 1d;

Item Androwe Clarke of Dodscombeleygh oweth 15s;

Item John Boyer 30s;

Item Christopher Smyth oweth 8s 6d;

Item Pettybrydge oweth 22s 3d;

Item Benett Smythes wyffe with out Estegate oweth 18d;

Item Borowe the Carryers wyffe with out Estegate oweth 26s 9d;

Item Christopher the smyth of Chudleygh 14s 5d;

Item Burte the smyth with out Estegate oweth for yron 6s 11d;

Item Rychard Brussheford of Tyverton oweth for towe shyrts 4s 6d;

Item Androwe Burnard of Cheriton Fythpayne oweth for Iron 19s 1½d;

Item John Bowcher in monye lent hym the wyche one Rychard Collyar ys sewrtye for hym 13s;

Item John Barstaple oweth upon the boke for canvas & callowecowe 18s;

Item mother Crabbe oweth for certyn wares 4s;

Item Phillippe Cane oweth for A quarter of fyggs 5s 8d;

Item mystrys Conwaye oweth for A mustard myll 3s 4d;

Item Robart Cosyns Smyth oweth for A quarter of Coles 8s;

Item Robart Cookes wyffe oweth as appereth uppon the booke 3s;

Item hys Cosyn Thomas Walrond oweth for mony lent hym 6s 8d;

[17] Item Hearcules Clement of Hevytrye oweth for monye lente hym 4s;

Item Edmond Coyles wyffe oweth for wares 4s 11¾d;

Item Thomas Canne of Woodbery oweth for Lynne Clothe 7s 2d;

Item John Crofton the shryffes baylye oweth for lynne clothe 15d;

Item Lawrence Chollys of Exmister oweth for the Rest of the Canvas 1d;

Item John Collyngwood oweth for the Rest of A peace of tynne which the pewtener ys sewrtye for 11d;

Item Sir Peter Carewe oweth for hoppes 56s 3d;

Item Edmond Coyle oweth As Appereth uppon the booke 38s 11d;

Item Wyllyam Carye with out Exe Brydge oweth 6s 8d;

Item Rychard Clyffe for the Rest of A barrell of vynegar 13d;

Item Chycks wyffe uppon Stryppecott Hyll oweth for Lynnen Clothe 12d;

Item John Cruse of Halberton oweth for Yron 20s;

Item Colwylls wyffe of Saynt Ceres Newton oweth 22d;

Item Walter Clarke of Exmister oweth for Reasons 23s for the wyche the Roper of Alfyngton ys Sewertye 23s;

Item Hubart Colwyll oweth for monye Lente hym as Appereth uppon the booke 42s;

Item Robart Cotten oweth for yolledge wyne 24s 4d;

Item Rychard Collyns the Cutteller oweth for A gryndynge stone 6s 8d;

[18] Item John Coyell of Topsam oweth for hoppes 27s 8d;

Item John Dyer Mr Custemers man oweth for wares as Appereth by the booke 3s 9d;

Item Ducke the smyth with out Sowithgate oweth 24s 6d;

Item Thomas Dyer of Shogbroke oweth for lynnen clothe 7s 6d;

Item Robart Davye the smyth with out Sowith Gate oweth for A hundryd of yron at 12s the hundryd for the wych Rowe of Hevytre ys Sewertye 12s;

Item Ducks wyffe the smyth with out Sowith Gate oweth 18d;

Item Androwe Earle of Dodscombeleygh oweth uppon the booke 8s;

Item Harrye Ellys oweth for monye lente hym £4;

Item Thomas Fursdon oweth uppon the booke 11*d*;

Item Rychard Fleacher of Honyton oweth for wares 4*s* 8*d*;

Item Hewgh Fursse of Okyngton oweth as Appereth uppon the booke 10*s* 1*d*;

Item Gaynge of Dorchester pewtener oweth for the Rest of certyn tynne as Appereth in the booke 3*s* 6*d*;

Item Gylbart the smyth with in Westegate oweth for yron 42*s* 11*d*;

Item Wyllyam Garrett of Alfyngton oweth for Canvas 3*s* 4*d*;

[19] Item Gearmyns wyffe the bowcher oweth for dowlyshe 4*s*;

Item Androwe Gyre oweth for wares as Appereth by the boke £7 2*s* 7*d*;

Item Thomas Gregorye of Honyton oweth 50*s* 9*d*;

Item Wyllyam Gregorye oweth as Appereth upon ye boke 17*s* 11*d*;

Item Walter Hanckocke smyth oweth me for one hundryd of yron at a 11*s* 6*d* the hundred 11*s* 6*d*;

Item Rychard Bragell oweth for the Reste of A pece of Reasons as Appeareth by the booke 5*s*;

Item Thomas Hockett of Exmowith oweth for 8 hogshed of yolledge wyne at 7*s* 6*d* the hogshed Sewertye Mr Drake £3;

Item Mr Hearnyman oweth for certyn lynnen clothe as Appereth by the boke 10*s* 7*d*;

Item Lawrence Hellyar oweth for certyn yron as Appereth by the booke 12*s* 9*d*;

Item Wyllyam Hoole of Heale oweth for the Reste of an old Reckenynge for seacks £4 17*s* 6*d*;

Item Hylls wyffe of Woodbery oweth for wares 12*s*;

Item Thomas Irelond oweth uppon an old Reckenynge 2*s* 2*d*;

Item John Kellye of Cheryton Smyth oweth for yron & style 16*s* 7*d*;

Item Gregorye Laye oweth for A pece of fyggs as Appereth by the booke 5*s* 8*d*;

Item Peter Lake oweth for mony lent hym as appereth by ye booke £5;

[20] Item Mr Lyle of Honyton oweth for certyn Seackes &

other wares £9 2*s* 8*d* for the which Rychard Strowberydge ye sewertye £9 2*s* 8*d*;

Item James Lake of Pynne oweth for certyn wares as Appeareth by hys booke 8*s* 4*d*;

Item John Mouncke of Awtrye oweth the 10th day of December 1563 [?] for halfe A pece of tregar 38*s* 4*d*;

Item Martyn Phyllipps smyth oweth uppon an old Reckenynge as Appereth by hys booke 28*s*;

Item John Myller of Bryxston oweth as Appereth by the booke 20*s*;

Item John Maynerd of Exeter oweth as Appereth by the boke £10 9*s* 3*d*;

Item Rychard Mortymer of Totnes oweth for safferon 3*s* 4*d*;

Item Elizabeth Moryshe yt ys marryed to A weaver oweth as Appereth by ye booke 6*s* 8*d*;

Item Pryddys of Torryton oweth uppon an old Reckenynge as Appereth uppon the booke 18*d*;

Item Wyllyam Phillipps oweth for hoppes & Reasons 25*s* 6*d*;

Item Alyce Parymore oweth for Playinge cardes 18*d*;

Item Wyllyam Parrymore oweth for wares as Appereth uppon the shoppe booke £5 16*s* 8*d*;

Item Anthonye Pynson oweth for Lynnen Clothe as Appereth by the booke 2*s*;

Item Alexander Prynge of ye paryshe of Gyttsham oweth 26*s* 1*d*;

Item Peter the smythes man oweth for the Rest of one end of yron uppon an Accompte 14*d*;

[21] Item John Parre oweth for wares & monye lent hym 13*s* 5*d*;

Item Potter of [blank] oweth for A peare of wollen cards 18*d*;

Item Edward Redman oweth As Appereth uppon the booke for yron & other wares and monye lente hym £11 10*s* 9*d*;

Item Androwe Rychards oweth for Reasons & other wares as Appeareth uppon ye booke 13*s* 4*d*;

Item Wyllyam Rychards of Byckelygh oweth uppon an old Reckeninge 18*d*;

Item Thomas Rychardson oweth as Appeareth uppon the booke £18 9*s* 8*d*;

Item Margerye Rolston oweth for monye lente her 16*s*;

Item Rudge the dyer oweth as Appereth for certyn wares 22*s* 9*d*;

Item Rowe of Alfyngton for monye lent hym oweth 2*s*;

Item Roper the smyth with out Westgate oweth for yron & Cooles the wyche Harrye Rooper ys sewrtye for to paye 4*s* quarterly the sume of 32*s* 9*d*;

Item John Shyrwell of Newton Busshell oweth for lynnen cloth £12 10*s*;

Item John Smyth of Lyngston oweth for yron £3 2*s* 10*d*;

Item John Smythes dowghter oweth for A pece of Reasons as Appereth uppon the booke 8*s*;

Item Harrye Stodden of Dodscombeleygh oweth for certyn wares as Appereth by the booke 13*s* 4*d*;

[22] Item Harrye Seaward of Woodbery oweth for certyn wares 3*s* 5*d*;

Item Mystrys Shylston of Kyrton oweth uppon the boke uppon A Reckenynge the sume of £12 10*s*;

Item Gylbart Saywell oweth uppon the booke for seake wyche Rychard Sterowberydge ys sewertye for the sume of £6 13*s* 4*d*;

Item Peter the smythe with in Westgate oweth uppon the booke 2*s* 8*d*;

Item Robert Smyth with out Sowithgate oweth for bylbowe yron the sume 11*s*;

Item Trowberfyld of Honyton oweth for Allombe £3 8*d*;

Item Agnes Treman oweth for wares as Appereth uppon the boke 4*s* 3*d*;

Item Wychalse of Kenton oweth for the Rest of A polledavye 3*s* 4*d*;

Item Nycholas Taplye oweth for yron the sume of 25*s* 5*d*;

Item Wyllyam Wyndeatt of Hemyocke oweth for certyn yron the which Robart Estchurche ys sewertye for 13*s* 4*d*;

Item Mystrys Waggott oweth for Certyn wares as Appereth uppon the booke 26*s*;

Item John Ware of Halberton oweth for yron as Appereth uppon ye booke 18*s* 4*d*;

Item Phillippe Yard of Exeter oweth for Seaks as Appereth by the shoppe booke £9 6*s* 8*d*;

Item Wyslakes wyffe of Tapsam oweth for wares the sume 3*s* 7*d*;

[23] Item Wyslakes wyffe at Ware oweth as Appeareth uppon the boke 2*s* 2*d*;

Sum £145 9*s* 11*d*.

Detts dewe unto the sayd Harrye Maunder by specialltyes as ffolloweth

Item Robart Bennett of Exeter oweth uppon A byll obligatorye 6*s* 8*d*;

Item Rychard Trosse of Woodbery oweth uppon A byll obligatorye £4;

Item Edmond Sture of Visborowgh [?] oweth uppon an obligacion £6 13*s* 4*d*;

Item Thomas Edgebastian of Collu[m]pton oweth uppon an obligacyon £4;

Item Harrye Foxe of Tapsam oweth as Appereth by A byll obligatory 7*s* 6*d*;

Item the Remaynyd in the hands of the Above namyd Harrye Maunder decessyd towe severall bylls obligatory of one George Hunt of the Cyttye of Exeter draper by the wyche bylls hyt doth Appere the sayd George Hunt to be Indettyd unto the sayd Harry Maunder in the sume of £12 10*s*.

[24] Stuffe Remayninge in the howse that John Cotten dyd late dwell in

Item the Seylynge in the hall 40*s*;

Item A bord with A fframe and A Joynyd fforme 10*s*;

Item the staynyd clothes & A old bedsteed 3*s* 4*d*;

Sum 53*s* 4*d*.

Sum of the Goods housholo fours [?] sap' [?] wars & merchandise £253 3*s* 6½*d*;

The lease for terme of yers of his mothers house nothing;

Reddy mony £69 8*s* 10*d*;

Plate £30 17*s* 4*d*;

Detts by his Bucke in the Shopp £185 9*s* 11*d*;

Detts by specialties £127 17*s* 6*d*;

[£213 7s 5d];
[Sum total] £155 17s 1½d.

ende

In desperat detts sperat [?] detts And detts by specialties £213
    7s 5d;
Clere above the detts £342 9s 8½d.

ECA, Orphans' Court Inventory 2: Item 2

Suche mony as William Paramore is bound to paye to
    Maunders children
To John Mawnder £40;
To Henry Mawnder £40;
To Rose Mawnder £40;
To Dorothee Mawnder £40;
Also paid to Elysabeth Paramore £20;
Also to her the 8 of February as appereth by obligacon £20.
Monye to be dysbursed by the Citie
To Thomas Maunder [to] Alexander Mayne £20;
To Sylvester Maunder to Jo Barsabb £40;
To Mrs Ameredeth for Margery Maunder £40.

Also remaining yn the custodye of the Citie for Thomas
    Mawnder who is with Alexander Mayne £20;
Also for William Maunders porcion £40;
Also for William Paramors wiff £20;
Which £20 stondeth to the order of the house whither the
    saide William or the children shall have.

Sum total £360

ECA, Orphans' Court Inventory 2: Item 3

[1] In 23 sovereings with crownes & pysteletts £14 12s;
In 19 old crownes £5 14s;
In royalls of plat £26 12s 6d;
In [illegible] dawlers [?] 9 – 39s 2d;

In surrd [?] mony £16 [11s 4d – crossed through] 14s 8d;
In base mony 140 [illegible] 54s;
In monye receved for stuffe solde £45 [9s 6d – crossed
    through] 13s;
In half furrd Grots [?] 5s;
In gowne [?] hole Grots [?] 5s;
In doggs 2s 3d;
In bullford 3s;
In slypps 2s 5d;
Sum £[illegible]15 23d.

Memorandum that the 22th of Aprill 1564 there was of the
    foresayd £45 13s taken out £8 which was paid to John
    Trew;
Also taken out of the same some the 24th daye £5;
Also taken out of the bagg wherein the sovereings were 23
    soverengs & 2 crownes which is £12;
Which foresaide £25 was paid to Mr Trew by thassignment of
    the masters.

Delyvered the 5 of May 1564 to John Barstabls wyff by
    Henry Ellys her servant £20;
Delyvered the 6 of May 1564 to Alexander Mayne of the bagg
    yn corrant monye £16 & of the bagg of £45 14s – £4 which
    amount to £20;
Also paid to Stephen Hodge for 13 Alphingtons for mendinge
    there hedgs 13s;
Also to Laurens Smyth for mendinge the dytches at A[d]
    lebury 20d;
Also to Mr Hert for money lent to Thomas Cruett [?] £4;
Also the 23 of May to John Bastables wiffe £20;
Sum £89 14s 8d;
Resteth £25 12s 2d.

[marginal note] 119 6s 10d
115 15 10d
70 16 4

[1v.] Also paid to Mr Holland the 4 of June £5 Also to him the 6 of June £6 – £11;

Also for makyng the hedgs at Mr Tothills marsh 20d;

Sum paid out £[illegible] 16s 4d.

So restethe £14 5s 6d.

Memorandum that Harry Mawnders goodds over & above desperat detts amount to £360;

Which some beinge equallye devyded emonge his 9 children amount to every childis porchon £40;

Wherof the 6 daie of Julye 1564 there was allowed to William Paramore upon his recognysance the some of £180;

That is to saye for John Mawnder £40;

For Rose Mawnder £40;

For Elysabeth Paramore £20;

For Henrye Mawnder £40;

For Dorothy Mawnder £40.

And thother £180 is remayninge yn the cities custodie for their childrens porcons whose names folowe

For Sylvester Mawnder which is paid to John Barstable £40;

For Thomas Mawnder which is paid to Alexander Mayne £20;

For Margery Mawnder which is paid to Mrs Ameredeth £40;

For which foresaid somes of £100 recognysancs ar taken.

For Elysabeth Paramore which remaineth yn the councell chamber £20;

For Thomas Maunder which remaineth yn the councell chamber £20;

For William Maunder which remaineth yn the councell chamber £40;

Sum £180.

Of which £180 there is £100 paid which the children as apperethe before and of the rest which is £80 there is laied out by the Citie as foloweth

Fyrst to John Trew £25;

To Thomas Cruett [?] £4;

£40 16s 8d;

To Mr Holland £11;

For certeyn chardgs in hedgeing 16s 8d;

Also resteth yn this accomptants hand for the first recept £14 5s 2d;

Also Mr Paramor ought to paie for parcell of the £180 not yet received wherof [illegible] £18 18s 2d – £24 18s 2d;

£80.

[2] In royalle plat £21 12s 6d – 7s 2d [?];

200 crowns £6;

17 [?] goune holls 5s 3d;

23 halfe faced grots 10s;

6 board 4s;

15 doggs 2s 10d;

Slypps 2s 6d;

140 percalls [?] 52[s] 6d.

In mony £7 7s 3d;

In gold 52s;

In grots 10s;

In roghm daw [?] 39s;

Bownd £13 6s 8d.

ECA, Orphans' Court Inventory 2: Item 4

The Accompte of the monye of the late Henrye Maunder received yn to the counsell Chaumber & paied by order & comaundement geven as folowethe

Fyrst received yn 23 soverines with crownes & pyseletts £14 12s;

Also received yn 19 olde crownes of the rose £5 14s;

Also yn Royalls of plat £26 12s 6d;

Also yn 9 yonghm dawlers [?] 39s;

Also yn curraunt moneye £16 14s 8d;

Also yn base monye 58s;

Also yn curraunt monye received for stuffe solde £45 13s;

Also yn halfe faced grotes 10s;

Also yn gooune [?] hole grotes 5s;
Also yn doggs 2s 3d;
Also yn bollford 3s;
Also yn slyppes 2s 5d;
Sum £115 22d.

Whereof paid the 22 of Aprill 1564 by the assignment of the
    masters to Mr Trew yn curraunt monye £13 & yn soverengs
    £12 – £25;
Also the 5 of May to John Bastables wiffe £20;
Also the 6 of May to Alexander Mayne £20;
Also to the men of Alphington for mendynge thrie hedgs &
    bancks 13s;
Also the 21 of May to Mr Hert for money lent to Thomas
    Civett [?] £4;

Also to Laurens Smyth for mendinge of the hedgs by
    Adlebury Wood 20d;
Also the 23 of May to John Bastables wyffe £20;
Also the 6 of June to Mr Holland £11;
Also for amendinge of the hedgs at Mr Tothills ground 20d.

Memorandum that the 6 of Julye 1564 William Paramore
ought to paie to this house £64 18s 2d yn full payment of £180
for the porcons of Maunders children viz
For Thomas Maunder to Alexander Mayne £20 – £40;
For Silvester to Bastable £40 – £40;
For Margery Maunder to Mrs Ameredeth £40 – £40;
For Elysabeth Paramore £20;
For William Mawnder £40.

10A. WILL OF ROBERT MATHEW, OF HOLY TRINITY PARISH, 28 MARCH 1564

ECA, Orphans' Court Will No. 10
Note: Recognisances were entered into on 2 November 1564 regarding Eleanor, Joyce and William, the children of Robert Mathew
(ECA, Book 141, folio 12).

In the name of god amen In the yeare of our Lord 1564 &
in the 28th daye of March I Robarte Mathewe perfecte of
memory of the parishe of Trinity within the cittye of Exon
do make my laste will & testament in manner & forme
followinge ffyrste I bequethe my sowle unto almightye god
& my bodye to be buryed in Christyan buryall. Item I geve &
bequethe unto my three Children £40 a peece. Item I geeve to
the mayntenaunce of the church of the Trynytie £3 4s. Item I
geeve to the poore mens boxe 12d. Item I geeve to my mayde
['servant' crossed through'] Servante ['John Coles' crossed
through] James Ebworthye £10. Item I geve to my man
servant John Colls one olde gowne of Cotton clothe & one
fryse jerkyn. Item I do assigne unto my wyffe all my leases &
tenements & she to use them acordynge to her dyscretyon all
my other ['resid' crossed through'] other goods not bequethed

I do geve unto my wyffe whom I make my hole & sole
Exequytrix. Witnesses to this my laste will Stephin Dyllet,
Sylffester Weste, & Thomas Williams Clerke Overseers of
this my laste will to be performed I make & ordayne John
German & Thomas Babcombe & for ther two paynes do geve
to eche of them 12d.

The probate of the will before us Thomas Williams master
surrogate Robert Fysher official of the Lord Archdeaconry of
Exeter the 25 day of the month of May in the year 1564

Examined by us [signed] Richard Hert John Hoker

£13 9s 8d

10B. INVENTORY OF ROBERT MATHEW, OF HOLY TRINITY PARISH, 30 AUGUST 1564

ECA, Orphans' Court Inventory 3

The Invitatorye of all & singular the goods & cattells & deptes of that latlye pertained unto one Robarte Mathewe late of the parishe of the Trinytye in the Cittye of Exeter deceased made praysed the 30th daye of Auguste 1564 by John German Sylfester Weste Thomas Babcombe & Henrye Wallter in manner & forme as followethe

In the Halle
Firstly A table borde a Carpet a framed forme & a benche 10*s*;
Item upon the Cobbarde one chardge 5 platters a basen 4 pedengers 5 sawcers 7 podenedyshes one tynen quarte a salte 2 erbe pottes 21*s*;
Item a Cobbarde with a cobbarde clothe 10*s*;
Item 4 candelstyckes a morter & a pestle & a broken chafyngdyshe 6*s* 8*d*;
Item a shyppe cheste 4*s*;
Item a peare of harnys & 2 bylls 8*s*;
Item 2 quyshens & the stayned clothes 5*s*;
Item 2 brushes & a Rubber 6*d*;
Item a ywen bowe with 18 shotyinge arrowes 6*s*;
Item an olde Chayre 4*d*;
Sum £3 11s 6d.

Item a Taffyta doblete & a canvas doblete 5*s*;
Item one cote of clothe & 2 Jacketts of clothe 16*s*;
Item one cloke 6*s*;
Item 2 gownes 27*s*;
Item 2 peare of hosen 4*s* 8*d*;
Item a cappe & a hatte 2*s*;
Sum £3 8d.

Lynnen
Item 4 bordclothes 8*s*;
Item 4 towels 4*s*;

Item 14 napkyns 5*s*;
Item 7 peare of Shetes & one odde shete 26*s* 8*d*;
Item 4 pyllowes tyes 5*s*;
Item an olde cobarde clothe 4*d*;
Item 5 shyrtes 13*s*;
Sum £3 2*s*.

Yn his chamber
Item 3 fether beddes 3 bolstrers & 3 pyllowes 53*s* 4*d*;
Item 3 coverletts one of taptyer [? taffeta] & 2 playne 16*s* 4*d*;
Item a ioyned bedstede & a tester 5*s*;
Item 2 blankets 2*s* 6*d*;
Item the paynted clothes 3*s* 4*d*;
[Item an olde flocke bedde 2*s* – crossed through];
Item 20 pownde of woole 16*s*;
Item 2 rosers & a borde 2*s*;
[2] Item a remlet of Cersye contayninge 2 yards & halffe 5*s*;
Sum £5 5*s* 6*d*.

Plate
Item one dosen of Sylver spones £3;
Item a stondinge cuppe with a cover parciall gylte £3;
Item a stond cuppe with a cover gylte 26*s* 8*d*;
Sum £7 6*s* 8*d*.

In the kychen
Item 3 brasse potts & a posnet 13*s* 4*d*;
Item 2 panes a scelle panne & 2 lytell cawdrons 13*s* 4*d*;
Item a frying panne & 2 gose pannes 20*d*;
Item 4 olde candelstyckes 16*d*;
Item 5 platters 3 Sawsers 3 podengers & a tynen quarte potte 9*s*;
Item a broche & 2 pothanginges 16*d*;
Item 2 dogges a fyer peke a fyer panne an arondyron 2*s*;
Item a table & 2 formes 2*s*;

Item a cobbarde 12*d*;
Item a borde clothe 8*d*;
Item 4 stoninge cuppes 8*d*;
Item a botell 2*d*;
Item 3 dosen of trenchures 3*d*;
Item an olde peare of bots & spores 2*s*;
Item a syltinge tubbe 6*d*;
Item in woode 6*s*;
Item a cowpe kayg & a tubbe 12*d*;
Item a mouldynge trawe & a boshell 18*d*;
Sum 57s 9d.

In the bakhouse
Item 7 sackes 6*s*;
Item a sacke of whete 20*s*;
Item in other stuffe remayninge in the bake house to the
     value of 13*s* 4*d*;
Sum 39s 4d.

In the shoppe
Item an old fetherbedde & a bolster a peare of shetes & a
     tester 8*s*;
Item an olde mantell 6*d*;
Item 2 spininge tornes 20*d*;
Item a peare of Cardes 8*d*;
Item an olde bedstede & a coffer 12*d*;
Item a horse & a saddell 26*s* 8*d*;
Sum 38s 6d.

Sum total £29 23d.
In Redy mony 12*s*;
In desperat detts 20*s*;
[Illegible] for the leases for terme of yers £6 13*s* 4*d*.

[verso] [Illegible] he allyd to Roger Mathew for a Gildyng 26*s*
     8*d*.

11A. WILL OF EDWARD LYMETT, MERCHANT, 7 JULY 1564

National Archives, PROB 11/53/284

Note: the will was proved on 25 May 1571. Recognisances were entered into on 27 August 1571 regarding his children Peter, Johan, Roger and Agnes, William, Grace and Lettis (ECA, Book 141, folios 31 dorse, 32).

[1] **In the name of god amen the 7th daye of** Julie *in the year* 1564 I Edward Lymett of the Cyttie and countie of Excetor merchante being in perfecte memorie and of good remembrance thanks be geven unto allmightie god doe make and ordeine this my testament & last will in maner & forme followinge Revokinge all other testaments and wills by me made before this present daye. First I give and bequethe my soule unto allmightie god my maker and savioure hoping by his precious deathe to be saved, and by him to enioye the kingdome of heaven, and my bodie to be buried if that I dye in Exetor in the same grave where that my father & mother were buried in the chancell of Saint Martins within the cyttie of Excetor if not, then where it shall please allmightie god to

visite me, and if I be buried in the chancell aforesaid *[2]* Then I doe geve and bequeath to the mayntenaunce of the same churche 13*s* 4*d* and to the parson of the same churche for that tyme being 3*s* 4*d* and at the same daye of my buriall I will that there be distributyd unto the prysoners of the Jayles in Excetor with the kings Jayle and unto the poore folkes of the same cytie the some of 30*s*. Also my mynde and wyll is that my children maye have and enioye all suche goods and Plate as my mother Grace Lymet deceassed have given & bequethed unto them upon her testament & last will the which is as followeth. Item unto John Lymet Robert Lymet Willyam Lymet, and Grace Lymet my children £20 in money to be equallie devyded betwene them. Item more unto John Lymet one ale cuppe of silver parcell gilte with a cover adioyninge unto him weyinge 13 ounces 3 quarters. Item unto Robert Lymet one ale Cuppe of sylver parcell gilte with a cover adioyninge unto him weyinge 11 ounces 3 quarters. Item unto Willyam Lymet one standinge cuppe without a cover of sylver, and doble gilte and is of the fashion of a bell, weyinge 15 ounces quarter. Item unto Grace Lymet one flatte bolle with a cover of sylver parcell gilte, weyinge 22 ounces. Item more unto the same Grace 1 lyttle pardon wrotte [?] with a cover and bordryd with sylver & gilte. All this forsayed money and plate is to be delivered unto them and every of them at their full age of 21 yeres or at the daye of their mariage. And if anye of them do happen to die before that he and they come unto mariage or 21 yeres, that then his or their parts so deceassed to be equallie devyded emonge the other then livinge. And if it happen that all fouer children do dye before that they receyve this money and plate aforesaied, That then it be geven and equallie to be devyded betwene suche children as I shall have then lyvinge had and begotten betwene me & Elizabeth my wyffe nowe living at the makinge of this present, And if that I have none then living, then to be devided in thre partes, The first parte unto the poore people, the seconde Parte unto the next of my kynne, and the third parte unto the discrecon of the 24 of the cittie of Excetour. And all other things that my mother Grace Lymet hath given upon her last will and testament that be not paied and delyveryd at the tyme of my deathe, That then I doe Chardge my wyffe Elizabeth whome I doe ordeine to be my sole executrix to se it paied, that she dothe knowe to paye, and with evident proffe by specyaltie. Also I doe give and bequeth unto John Lymet in money or money worthe the somes of £31 11s 3d to make up the miste some of fortie Pounds with the money and plate that was given him by my mother aforsaied. Item more I doe geve and bequeathe unto Robert Lymet £32 1s 3d to make up the mist some of tenne poundes with the money and Plate that was given him by my mother aforesayed. Item I doe geve and bequeathe unto Willyam Lymett £31 3s 9d to make up the full some of £40 with the money and plate that my mother aforesaied hath geven him. Item more I doe geve and bequeath

unto Grace Lymet my eldyst daughter in money £29 10s to make up the full some of £40 with the money and Plate that my mother aforesaied hath given her and beside one girdle conteyninge 8 barres of sylver and gilte and a demye unto the same girdell off sylver and gilte and one paier of beades of 5 setts of sylver and the pater nosters gilte The which girdle and bedes my mother aforesayed gave and delyvered unto Elizabeth my wyffe on the condicon that my wyffe shall leve them unto Grace Lymet our daughter after hir decease and do remayne in the custodie and kepinge of Elizabeth my wyffe and have done sythence that my mother did delyver them unto hir. Also I doe geve & bequeth unto Lettyce Lymet my second daughter in money or money worthe the some of fortie pounds for that she had no gyfte of my mother abovesayed. Also I doe give and bequeathe unto Peter Lymet in money fortie Pounds. More I do geve and bequeth unto Jone Lymet in money fortie Pounds and unto the childe that my wyffe dothe nowe goe with all in money £20. All theis my gyfts abovesayed to be delyvered and paied unto suche childe and children as ys abovesayed when they or either of them shall come unto the full age of 21 yeres or at the daye of their mariage, And if yt happen anye of them to dye before they come unto the age of 21 yeres or mariage That then his or their partes so deceased to be devided the one halfe unto the rest of my children then lyvinge and thother halfe unto Elizabeth my wife, And if she be not then livinge, then the whole Partes of them deceased to be whollie devyded betwene the survivours by equall porcons. And if it happen all the children to dye before they come unto the full age of 21 yeres or mariadge, That then to devyde their hole porcions into thre partes, the first parte unto Elizabeth my wyffe yf that she be then lyvinge yf not then unto the next of my kynne, the second Parte unto the poore, and the third parte unto the edefyenge and mayntenance of some highe wayes at the discrecon of the Mayor & the rest of his Brethren for that tyme being. Item more my will is That myne Executrix shall paye or cause to be payed unto Johan Smyth £6 13s 4d that Grace Lymet my mother did geve unto her upon hir testament and last will. Also I doe give and bequethe unto Reyne Smyth my servante in money or money worthe Six Pounds to be paied her at the daye of hir Mariadge. *[3]* Also I doe geve and bequeath unto everie one of my householde servants that shallbe dwellinge with me at the hower of my death over and above their wages in money 5*s*. Also my will is that John Lymet, Robert Lymet, Willyam Lymet, Peter Lymet, Grace Lymet, Lattyce Lymet, and Johan Lymett shall have and enioye after the decease of Elizabeth my wyffe my fee symple lands, that is to saye one meadow called Tadyford Meade and my howse that I have in Sainte Martins Lane that John Ryder nowe dwelleth in, unto them and everye of them by even porcons. Also my will is that my wyffe do put in sufficient suerties unto the Mayore and governors of the orphans goods for the Payment of all this my will and testament accordinge unto the orders that they have granted by the Quenes Maiestie, and past by acte of Parliament. The Resydue of all my goods Cattalls and Leases my debts and legacies being paied I do give and bequeth unto Elizabeth Lymet my wyffe, and her I doe make ordeine and constitute my sole executrix and do chardge hir conscyence to the performinge of this my last will and testament in maner and forme as ys above declaryd as she will answere before god at the generall daye of iudgement. Also I doe ordeine Mr Davyd Hensloe parson of Kenne and my cosen Thomas Richarson to be my overseers of this my last will and testament, And for their Paynes I do give either off them in money 20*s*, Desyringe them that suche poore legacies as I have there given them in this my last will and testament that they will take yt aworthe in recompence of theire Paynes and travell in and aboute the execucon of this my last will and testament, and in lyke maner I doe require my sayed executrix to take and followe the advyce and councell of my sayed overseers in all things as shalbe thoughte reasonable

and lawfull to this my Last will and testament bearinge date as is abovesaied. And to this my last will and testament I have sette my signe and seale, yeoven the daye and yere above written, By me Edward Lymet of Excetor merchaunte, Looke in the backsyde of this my last will and youe shall fynde my whole mynde & entent. Memorandum that I Edward Lymet the maker of this will herewithin written have on the last daye of August *in the year* 1564 perused this my last will and testament and doe understand that my adventure southewards & for Bordeauxe is of that value that this my will cannot be obsered onles yt shall please All mightie god to send this my adventure home in safetie. So far forthe as it shall please Allmightie god to send this my adventure home from besouthe from the Ilonds of the Cannaries and from Burdis, That then my will is that all things herewithin written to be observed and kept, and if not that then my will is my debts and legacies being paied that Elizabeth Lymet my wyffe shalbe my sole and whole executrix and to enioye my Fee simple Lands duringe her life, And after her life then unto the use of all my children that then shalbe lyvinge by even porcons, And the rest of all my goods moveable & umoveable with leases and otherwise to be praysed and devyded in three partes The first parte unto Elizabeth my wyffe the second parte unto all my children had by my wyfe that nowe is at the makinge of this present and the third parte unto my selfe, which thirde Parte my will is that it be equallie devided the one halfe unto my wyfe, and the other half unto my children. Provyded allwayes that the Poor people have and enioye their giftes that I have given by my will herewithin written by me Edward Lymet off Excetor Marchaunte.

11B. INVENTORY OF EDWARD LYMETT, MERCHANT, 17 JUNE 1571

ECA, Orphans' Court Inventory 15

The Inventorie of all and singuler the goods cattels and detts which latelie apperteyned unto Edward Lymet late of the cittie and countie of Exeter merchant decessed taken and praised the 17th daie of June in the yere of our Lord god a thowsand five hundred seventye and one by John Bentlo, John Alsop, Thomas Ratclief and William Nicholls

[m. 1] In the higher chamber
Firstly a plaine bedsteed & 2 fetherbeds & a bolster with the coverlet & the Tester of the same bed 40s 8d;
Item a standing bedsteed with a fetherbed & a flockbed with 2 bolsters, a coverlet, with the Tester & the courtyns £3 6s 8d;
Item the stained clothes in the chamber 16d;
Item 2 coffers and a ioyned stoole 6s 8d;
Item one small bord 8d;
Sum £5 16s.

In the backe chamber
Item a plaine bedsteed & 2 fetherbeds a flockbed with a fether bolster & the coverlet to the same bed £6;
Item 7 downe pillowes and a fether pillowe 10s;
Item 2 old presses in the same chamber 26s 8d;
Item a cubborde 5s;
Item 3 coffers in the same chamber 13s 4d;
Item the stained clothes and a tablet 18d;
Sum £8 16s 6d.

In the great Hall
Item the seelinge and the benches £3;
Item a cubbord 6s 8d;
Item a bason & ewer and the cubbord cloth 5s;
Item the table bord & forme with a carpet to the same 12s;
Item half a dosen of carpet Qwishens 12s;
Item half a dosen of lether Qwishens 2s;
Item a tablet in the same Hall 20d;
Item a ioyned stoole 12d;
Sum £5 4d.

His apparell
Item a Crymsen grained gowne furred with ficchals [?] and faced with foynes £3;
Item a gowne of browne blew furred with foxe and faced with foynes 46s 8d;

Item a blacke gowne furred with white lambe and faced with budge 30s;
Item a russet gowne faced with budge & furred with lamb 20s;
Item a gowne of rattes color furred with white lambe and faced with conye 20s;
Item the furre of an old gowne 10s;
Item a wusted cassecke garded with velvet 20s;
Item a dowche cloke 13s 4d;
Item a Jacket of brown blew garded with velvet 10s;
Item a Jacket of browne blew laid with lace 7s;
Item a Jacket of blacke cloth 5s;
Item an old cote 16d;
Item a fryse cote 2s;
Item a satten doublet 10s;
Item an old Kersey doublet 2s 6d;
Item a buffe lether Jerken 6s 8d;
Item a paire of hose laid with lace 5s;
Item a paire of colored hose 5s;
Item a paire of hose 2s 6d;
Item a velvet coif 2s 6d;
Item a silke coif 2s;
Item a cap and a hat 4s 8d;
Sum £14 6s 2d.

In the longher Chamber
Item a standing bedsteed with 3 fetherbeds & a mattrice 2 pilloes a bolster of fethers with a paire of blankets the courteynes & a coverlet £9;
Item the hanginges of sea with a tablet 10s 6d;
Item a cubbord & a clothe upon it 6s 8d;
[m. 2] Item a small bord & a carpet 3s 4d;
Item 5 spruise chestes £3;
Item 3 small flanders coffers 10s;
Item for a coffer 2s 6d;
Sum £13 13s 2d.

In the Parlor
Item the seelinge 18s;

Item a cubbord & clothe upon it 5s;
Item a table bord a carpet and a forme 13s 4d;
Item the hanginges 2s;
Item the tablets 5s;
Item half a dosen of Qwishens 12s;
Item a ioyned cheare 2s;
Item a paire of andyrons & the backe in the chimley 9s;
Sum £3 6s 4d.

In the litle Hall
Item 4 paire of almen ryvets & a Jacke with 5 billes to the
  same 40s;
Item a corslet and a pike 30s;
Item a blacke bill 6d;
Item a bowe and a sheafe of arrowes 3s 4d;
Item a callever and a demye Culverlyn 14s;
Item a table bord with a carpet & 2 formes 2s 6d;
Item 2 coffers 10s;
Item a merchants cheste 30s;
Item a chaire and a stoole 12d;
Item for half a dosen of old lether Quishens 6d;
Item the hanginges 2s;
Sum £6 13s 10d.

In the chamber within the Hall
Item a litle trockell bed with a fetherbed and 2 bolsters of
  fethers with a blanket & the tester 20s;
Item a ioyned bedsteed with a flockbed & 2 pillowes and the
  coverlet 26s 8d;
Item a benche to set before the fyer 3s 4d;
Item 2 coffers & a litle runner [?] 6s 8d;
Item the hanginges of the same chamber 12d;
Sum 57s 8d.

In the meale chamber
Firstly a plaine bedsteed with a flockbed a fether pillowe & 2
blankets 5s;
Item the hanginges 16d;
Item the bedsteed & the pillowe 12d;

Item 3 old coffers and a half bushell 2s;
Item a black byll 6d;
Item a cowle and an old tankerd 12d;
Item 9 tubbes one bucket & a bole 2s;
Sum 12s 10d.

In the Kytchen
Item the shelfes and 2 bordes 12d;
Item 7 pothanginges 3s;
Item 4 potcrookes 12d;
Item a toster and a grydiron 6d;
Item 2 andyrons & a dogge with a barre & the backe in the
  chimley 7s;
Item 2 fyer peekes 12d;
Item a paire of tonges 12d;
Item 6 broches 6s;
Sum 20s 6d.

The brason & latten vessell
Item one brasse pot 11s;
Item a brasse pot 7s;
Item a brasse pot 14s;
Item a brasse pot 8s;
Item a brasse pot 7s;
Item 2 brasse pots 7s;
Item 2 skillets & a posnet 6s 8d;
Item 3 of the best pans 22s 8d;
Item 2 pans 14s;
[m. 3] Item a kettell & a cawdren 8s;
Item old brasse 20d;
Item 3 latten ladels 12d;
Item 5 skillets 3s 4d;
Item a cole chaffer and a skillet 5s;
Item an ewer of brasse 8d;
Item 2 chaffers 2s 6d;
Item a small morter & a pessell 16d;
Item 2 driping pans 2s;
Item 2 scomers 8d;
Item 2 bell candlesticks 2s 6d;

Item 2 candlesticks 2s 6d;
Item 2 candlesticks 2s;
Item 2 paire of small candlesticks 2s 8d;
Item 2 flat candlesticks 16d;
Item 2 euer potts of brasse 12d;
Item foure latten basons 5s 4d;
Sum £7 10d.

Pewter vessell
Item the best pewter £4 2s;
Item the worst pewter 20s;
Item 6 eared dishes 20d;
Item 2 london quarters 2s 4d;
Item 2 london pyntes 20d;
Item 2 hooped tankerds 16d;
Item 2 old pots 16d;
Item 2 old pyntes & a quarte 14d;
Item 2 half pynte pots 4d;
Item 2 old quarte pots & a pynte 8d;
Item 2 old potts 4d;
Item a bason & ewer 16d;
Sum £5 14s 2d.

In the great shopp
Item the trashe in the shopp 52s 2d;
Item the bookes 5s;
Item the cheste 6s 8d;
Item a paire of ballance 3s 4d;
Item foure paire of old ballance 20d;
Item the brasen weightes 5s 9d;
Item the shelfes 8d;
Sum £3 15s 3d.

In the litle shoppe
Item the trashe in the shop 2s;
Item 3 barrels 12d;
Item 2 paire of small ballance 2s;
Item a morter and the pessell 10s;
Item 2 chestes 6s 8d;

Item a table borde 5s;
Item an old coffer 12d;
Item 2 old cubberdes 3s;
Item the beame and the scales 4s;
Item the ledden weightes 31s;
Item a tyn crooke 2d;
Sum £3 5s 10d.

In the seller
Item 5 tubbes and 3 barrels 4s 6d;
Item 3 paire of tressels 6d;
Item 8 bordes & 2 plankes 3s 4d;
Item a morter & a pessell 7s;
Item some glasses 12d;
Item the shelfes 3s;
Sum 19s 4d.

In the stable
[m. 4] Item the wood £4;
Item 16 leere casks at 20d the peece 44s 4d [sic];
Item a saddle and a brydell 6s 8d;
Item a wheele barrowe 8d;
Item a planke 6d;
Sum £6 11s 2d.

In the ware howse
Item 2 hogsides of egar wyne 26s 8d;
Item 4 old hogsides and an old pipe 12d;
Item the brymstone 6s;
Item 7 peeces of old tymber and a suger cheste 2s 4d;
Item the rasome 8d;
Sum 36s 8d.

The lynnen
Item 2 shertes 3s 4d;
Item 6 paire of sheets 20s;
Item 2 paire of canvas sheets 6s;
Item one paire of fustian blankets 3s 4d;
Item 2 diaper clothes & a towell 6s 8d;

Item 12 diaper napkens 6s;
Item a dosen & half of canvas napkens 4s;
Item 2 towels 12d;
Item one diaper towell 2s;
Item 3 bordclothes 2s;
Item 4 pilloties and 2 old pilloties 6s 8d;
Sum £3 12d.

Leases
Item the lease of the 2 howses which he dwelt in £30;
Item the lease of the stable 40s;
Item the lease of Androw Jeyres howse £10;
Sum £42.

Wynes & a geldinge
Item the wyne in the seller at Exeter £34 10s;
Item the wyne at Tapsam £15 5s;
Item a geldinge 40s;
Sum £51 15s.

The plate
Item 2 flatte peeces weyinge 42 ownces & half at 4s the
    ownce £8 17s 1d;
Item 2 goblets parcell gilte with a cover weyenge 38 ouncs at
    4s 4d the ownce £8 6s 10d;
Item 2 goblets parcell gilte with a cover weieng 48 ownces at
    4s 4d the ownce £10 8s;
Item 2 white goblets with a cover weyeng 67 ownces at 4s the
    ownce £13 8s;
Item 2 goblets double gilte with a cover weyeng 57 ownces at
    5s the ownce £14 5s;
Item 2 goblets double gilt with a cover weyeng 28 ownces & a
    half at 5s the ownce £7 2s 6d;
Item 2 standinge cuppes double gilte with a cover weyeng 49
    ouncs at 5s the ownce £12 5s;
Item 2 saltes double gilte with a cover weyeng 39 ouncs &
    half at 5s the ownce £9 18s 6d;
Item one ale cup gilt with a cover weinge 9 ownces & a
    quarter 5s the ownce 46s 3d;

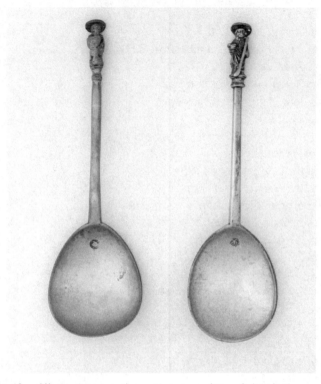

Fig. 12.   Silver spoons are the most common item of plate in these
inventories. Edward Lymet's inventory of 1571 lists 33 examples,
including Apostle, Maidenhead and wrythen-knopped spoons (OC 11B).
These silver Apostle spoons by the Exeter goldsmith John Jones date to
c. 1570 (*photo: D. Garner, © Exeter City Museums*).

Item 2 ale cuppes parcell gilte weing 25 ounces at 4s 2d the
    ownce £5 4s 2d;
Item one salte parcell gilte with a cover weyeng 13 owncs &
    half at 4s 4d the ownce 58s 6d;
Item 13 spoones with postels heds weyenge 32 ownces at 4s
    the ownce £6 8s;
Item 6 spoones with egles heds parcell gilte weing 10 ounces
    and half at 4s 4d the ownce 45s 6d;
Item 6 spoones with wreyd knoppes weyeng 8 ownces & a
    quarter at 4s 4d the ownce 35s 9d;
Item 6 spoones with mayden heds parcell gilte weyeng 12

ownces quarter at 4s 2d the ounc 51s ½d;

Item one goblet parcell gilte weyeng 11 ouncs & a quarter at 4s the ownce 45s;

Item 2 old spoones weyeng 1 ounce 3 quarter ounce 4s 7s;

[m. 5] Item a masard bended with silver 8s;

Item the garnishe of 2 stone pots weyeng 11 ounces at 4s the ownce 44s;

Item 2 goldringes 54s;

Sum £115 17s 1½d.

Dettes due unto him by booke

Item Thomas Cocke of Tawnton oweth £22;

Item Elles Rychardes of Mylverton oweth £8;

Item Constance Rewe of Tyverton £5 7s;

Item Mr Humfry Walrond esquier £3;

Item Mr Thomas Richardson for Mr Ames Pawlet £3;

Item John Barstaple of Exeter 57s;

Item Anthonie Thomas 55s;

Item Robert Daie of Charde 20s;

Sum £48 4s.

Dettes due by byll

Item Phillip Rosdon oweth £20;

Item Gregorie Lasky £10;

Item Thomas Beade [?] £4 10s;

Item Mogridge of Bramford £3;

Item Prowse of Kentsbeare £3 10s;

Item Ric Thomas 13s;

Item John Weeks of Exeter 26s 8d;

Item Greene of Eed 40s;

Item there is dewe by the cittie £50;

Item Mr Dreton scoolemaster £13 6s 8d;

Item Mr Yeard £3;

Item Agnes Coyll of Apsam £3 10s;

Item John Bastable of Exeter £6 19s;

Item John Palmer of Stocke 51s 4d;

Item Prowse of Kentsbeere £3 10s;

Sum £127 16s 8d.

Reddie monye

Item fownd in his howse at the hower of his deathe in redye monie £29 3s 6d;

Sum £29 3s 6d.

Sum total £509 4s 8d.

Off which some Elizabeth Lymett wief and executrix of the said Edward Lymet desireth to be allowed as hereafter foloweth:

For funerals *viz* his buriall and other charges:

Firstly she asketh allowance for his shroude 3s 8d;

For making his grave 20d;

For his cheste 5s;

For his bearing to church 16d;

Item to the belman 8d;

Item to 4 poore folkes to goe by him to church 16d;

[m. 6] Item for ringinge 4 knylles 2s;

Item to weomen that kept him in his sicknes & candlelight 4s 4d;

Item for 2 yerdes half & half quarter of clothe for a morning gowne for the said executrix at 18s 6d the yerd 48s 6d;

Item for fustian for the same gowne 22d;

Item for the makinge & hooks & eyes 21d;

Item for 3 cappes & newe sheos for the children at his buryall 9s 1d;

Item for meat & drinke at his buryall and 8 weeks since at 10s the weeke £4 13s 4d;

Item paid to his mayd servant for her wages due 9s;

Item for boots [?] & sheos to the children sithence the death of the said Edward 5s 4d;

Item for proving his Testament in the prerogatyve courte, the proctors fee & registring the same 23s 4d;

Item for copieng the Testament in paper, ingrossing the same in parchement, & the engrossinge of the Inventorie 3 tymes in parchemente 26s 8d;

Item to the praisers for there paines 13s 4d;

Sum £13 2s 2d.

Dettes due by the said Edward Lymet at his death

Item she asketh allowance of a dette due by him to Edward Goold of Totnes £22 15*s*;

Item to the parson of Kenne £20;

Item to Mary Petevyn £9 10*s*;

Item to John, Robert, Grace and William Lymet, to eche of them £5 geven & bequethed by Grace Lymet in her Testament £20;

Item to Thomas James 31*s*;

Item to the wido Bolte for making apparrell 20*s* 8*d*;

Item to Mr Phillip Risdon 3*s* 4*d*;

Item to Mr Harte 32*s*;

Item to Collens the hatter 2*s* 6*d*;

Item to Thomas Esworthie 14*s*;

Item to Roger Robenson 14*s* 2*d*;

Item to John Michell of Apsam 17*s* 2*d*;

Item to Wm Erell apothecarie 10*s*;

Item to Alex servant to the said Edward Lymet 48*s*;

Item to John Farrer 10*s*;

Item to the said Alex his servant for wages 40*s*;

Item to Robert Vynton for freighte 50*s*;

Item to Harry James for a dette dewe £8;

Item to the carter for a tunnes cariadge of wine 3*s* 4*d*;

Item to John Pope of Exeter by bill £13 6*s* 8*d*;

Item to Mr Chapell, & to caryers for carriadge of wood bought in his lief tyme £3 10*s*;

Item to Ric Harden 3*s* 4*d*;

Item to Mr Thomas Prestwood 6*d*;

Item to George Smythe for wares 4*s* 10*d*;

Item to John Pynson of Bovy Tracie for tynne £14 3*s*;

Sum £126 18*s* 3*d*.

Legacies bequethed by the said Edward Lymet

Item she asketh allowance for a legacie bequethed to the poore 30*s*;

Item to the churche of St Martyns 13*s* 4*d*;

Item to the person there 3*s* 4*d*;

Item to the servants dwelling with him at his deth 15*s*;

Item to his 2 overseers 40*s*;

Sum £5 20*d*.

The hole some of the allowancs cometh to £145 2*s* 1*d*;

So there remaineth in the said Elizabeth Lymets handes all thinges allowed £365 2*s* 7*d*.

12A. WILL OF EDMUND WHETCOMBE, MERCHANT, 27 JULY 1564

ECA, Orphans' Court Will 11 (and National Archives, PROB 11/47/283)

Note: the will was proved via Canterbury on 28 August 1564. Recognisances were entered into on 24 June 1565 regarding his children Margery, Alice, Joan, Elizabeth and Peter (ECA, Book 141, folios 16 & 17).

In the name of God amen The 27th day of July yn the yere of our lord god 1564 I Edmond Whetcombe of the Cytie and Countie of Exceter marchant beinge sicke of bodye but yt Lawde and prayse be unto almighty god of perfect mind and memorye do make this my will and Testamente in manor and form folowinge **Firste** I bequeth my sowle into the mercifull hands of Almightie god and my bodye to the holy yerthe. **Item** I geve and bequeathe unto the poore people of Exeter five powndes to be distributed unto them by the discretion of my Executrixe here under writen. **Item** I geve unto Mary my wife dwelling now with me Six powndes thirtene shillings and fowre pence. **Item I** Geve unto Archules Wheatcombe my servant and kinsman Ten powndes to be paid withn one whole yere at the hands of his father John Wheatcombe out of fifty powndes which he oweth me. **Item** I geve and bequeth unto Richarde Jurdon my Servant and Apprentice 40*s*. **Item**

whereas Nycolas Whetcomb my Brother doth owe me as it aperth apon my booke fortie powndes or more, of the which £40 I do allow him Twentie powndes which I must pay him apon my fathers bargain which is dew unto him after the death of my father and mother in Satisfaction of the same I frely forgeve him the rest besides the butt of hollocke **Item** I geve unto my brother John Whetcombes thre dawghters twenty shillings a pece of them and the longest liver to Inioye the same wholye. **Item** I geve unto Hary Foletts 2 dawghters Twenty shillings a pece. **Item** I geve to the poor people of Coliton ten shillings. **Item I geve** to my father and mother five powndes. **Item I geve** and bequethe the Bargayne and Bartayn that my father now holdeth set liinge and being withyn the parishe of Colitin withyn the county of Devon unto Peter Whetcombe my Sonne and to the heires of his bodye lawfully begotten fore ever withall such thinges as I have therof. **And yff** the said Peter Whetcombe my sonne die withoute Issew. Then I will that my wyffe do Inioye the same bartyn or bargain duringe hir naturall lyffe. And after hir decesse then the said bargayn or bartayne to remayne and be to my brother Archules Whetcombe and to his heires forever **And** for lacke off Issewe of the said Archules the said bartayn or bargayn to remayne and be to my brother Nycholas Whetcombe and to his heires for ever. Item I geve and bequeth unto my wyffe my howse on Northgate Striate during her life paiinge therefore yerely to Peter Whetcombe my son sixteen pence. And unto the said Peter my sone I geve & bequithe the fee Simpell of the said howse forever. **Item I** geve and bequeth unto my Cossyn John Whetcombe at Oxfforde fortie shillings **Item** I geve unto Margery my daughter Threscore powndes of lawfull monye of Inglonde to be paid hir at Eighteen yeres of hir Aige or at the day of hir mariage. **Item I geve** unto Als Jane and Elizabeth my daughters and to every of them Threscore powndes a pece to be paid them as ther sister is before that is to say at 18 yeres of Aidge or at the daye of there mariage. **Item** I geve and bequeth unto Peter Whetcombe my son Threscore sixe powndes thirtene shillinges and four pence **And** if any of these my Children ['abovewisen' crossed through] abovewriten do dy before the tyme of there mariage or before they do accomplysshe the Aidge of 18 yeres that then his or there part so doinge to be devided unto the longest lives by equall porcons. **Item** my brother of Bristow oweth me twenty two pownds Lawfull mony of Ingland of the which sum of £22 I do geve and bequeth unto him twelffe powndes and the other ten pownds to be paid to my Executrix. **The Residew** of all my goods chattalls & debts not before geven nor bequeathed my debts Legacies and funerals discharged I geve and bequeth them unto Agnes my Wyffe whom I do nominate ordayne and make my trew full & whole Executrixe And I do appynte & ordayne Mr John Peter Customer & my my [?] John Peter to be the overseers of this my Testament and last will. Desiringe them to be Ayders and helpers of my said wife and hir children Witness hereunto ar Master Simon Knight and Wm Chappell and Mr Philip Yerde & Robert Lamboll per me Simon Knight, per me William Chapel, by me Phelyp Yerd by me Robert Lambell.

12B. INVENTORY OF EDMUND WHETCOMBE, MERCHANT, 11 JUNE 1565

ECA, Orphans' Court Inventory 4

The Inventory of all the goods and Chattals of Edmond Whetcombe late of the Cytye of exeter decessyd Praysed by Androwe Geare Henry Parramore Wyllyam Parramore And George Peryman Sworne and Admytted by Mr John Periam Alderman of the southe quarter in the yere of our Lorde god A thowsand ffyve hundryd threeskore and ffyve the 11th daye of June

Fig. 13. Edmond Whetcombe's inventory of 1565 (OC 4) lists 'the sylinge (panelling) in the hall with a portall £1'. This appears to refer to an internal porch integral with the panelling, a feature known from several Devon country houses, such as this very elaborate example at Bradfield, about 25km from Exeter, but no longer represented in any city building (*engraving by Palmer, 1867, courtesy of the Westcountry Studies Library*).

[m. 1] In the shoppe
Firstly 48 yeards of treger at 7*d* the yarde Amounth to the
   sume of £1 8*s*;

Item 7 yards of blewe clothe at 2*s* the yard 14*s*;
Item 2 dossen of wykyearne at 16*d* the dossen 2*s* 8*d*;
Item 18 peces of Resons valowyd at £9;
Item 3 sorts of figgs at 15*s* the sorte £2 5*s*;
Item 2 hundryd of Newlond fyshe at 10*s* the hundryd 20*s*;
Item 1 dussen of olde breade cards valewyd at 4*s*;
Item 4 Reames of browne paper at 5*s*;
Item halfe A dussen of coveryd cuppes vallewed at 2*s*;
Item halfe a hundryd of Agnetsede vallowed at 10*s*;
Item 8 Raw Kerses £8;
Item 2 endes of yron 2*s*;
Item 2 hundryd of Allam £2 10*s*;
Item a payre of skales & 3 payre of ballons 6*s* 8*d*;
Item 1 hundryd & halfe in weights 15*s*;
Sum £27 4*s* 4*d*.

In the Hall
Firstly A tabelborde with a forme at 8*s*;
Item halfe a dussen of quysshins 6*s*;
Item A carpett 2*s*;
Item A cubborde with a cubberd clothe 14*s* 4*d*;
Item 2 candelsticks 2 basens 2 yewers 9*s* 2*d*;
Item 9 fflower potts 3*s*;
Item 1 olde cheste with 2 billes 7*s*;
Item the hangings Abowt the howse 6*s* 8*d*;
Item the sylinge in the hall with a portall £1;
Item the glasse windowes in the hall 10*s*;
Sum £4 6*s* 2*d*.

In the parler
Firstly a fether bed with a flockbed & 2 bolsters £1 13*s* 4*d*;
Item 2 coverlets with 2 payre of blancketts £1 16*s* 8*d*;
Item A bedstyde with a trockelbedstyde £1;
Item the curtings Abowt the bedd 5*s*;
Item 2 carpets 4*s*;
Item A spruse chest with 3 litle coffers £1 3*s* 4*d*;
Item A tablebord a forme with a bynche £1;
Item the hangings Abowt the howse 13*s* 4*d*;
Item halfe a dussen of gryne quysshings 2*s*;

Item 2 brusshes with a grasse 12*d*;

Item A table 2*s*;

Item A strowinge cheare 2*s*;

Item A payre of bellowes & a backe of a chimleye 3*s* 4*d*;

Item A cheare 1*s* 4*d*;

Item the glasse windowes in the parler £1;

Item A cape for A man 13*s* 4*d*;

Sum £10 1*s* 8*d*.

In the ffore chamber

Firstly A bed a bolster & 5 pyllowes £2;

Item A payre of blanckets 5*s*;

Item A coverlet & a bedstyd 8*s* 4*d*;

Item A tester of lyne clothe with the hangings 3*s* 4*d*;

Item A coffer with a Rownd table 4*s*;

Item A still with the hangings abowt ye chamber 5*s* 10*d*;

Item a payre of hulland shetts 10*s*;

Item 3 payre of morelys clothe shytts £1;

Item 2 payre of dowles shytts 10*s*;

Item 4 payre of canvasse shytts 10*s*;

Item 4 pere of pyllots tys 2 of hollond & 2 of morlys 6*s* 8*d*;

Item 2 payre of dowles pyllowtys 2*s* 6*d*;

Item 4 towels of Raprom [?] to wype hands 1*s* 8*d*;

[m. 2] Item 3 dussen of canvas napkins And 1 dussen of moreles clothe 16*s*;

Item 4 towells of fyne canvas 13*s* 4*d*;

Item 2 towells of brytten clothe 3*s* 4*d*;

Item 2 bordclothers of moreles clothe 13*s* 4*d*;

Item 2 cubbord clothers of moreles clothe 5*s*;

Sum £8 18*s*.

In the hyghe chamber

Firstly A bedstyde 5*s*;

Item A fetherbedd 10*s*;

Item A payre of blanckets with a bolster of flocks 3*s* 6*d*;

Item A coverlet & a flockbed 6*s* 4*d*;

Item A bolster with A olde coffer 2*s* 6*d*;

Item A chayer A stole with other trasshe 3*s* 4*d*;

Item 2 testers of staynyd clothers 2*s* 6*d*;

Sum £1 13*s* 2*d*.

In A nother chamber

Firstly 2 flockbeds 13*s* 4*d*;

Item a payre of blanckets with 2 corse coverlets 9*s* 4*d*;

Item A bedstyde with 2 olde coffers 4*s*;

Item A payre of almen Ryvets 10*s*;

Item halfe A sheffe of Arrowes 1*s*;

Item A pestell & a morter 6*s* 8*d*;

Item a brandyron with a Andyron 2*s*;

Item a tester of the bed & the hangings 2*s* 6*d*;

Sum £2 6*s* 8*d*.

In the spence and in the Kychinge

Firstly A garnyshe of vessell £2;

Item 2 quarte pots 2 pints & a potle pott 6*s* 8*d*;

Item one chaffinge dysshe 2*s*;

Item 3 panes 3 cowdrens & 5 potts of brasse £2 5*s*;

Item A chaffer of brasse with 2 litell skillets 4*s* 4*d*;

Item 3 broches 3*s* 4*d*;

Item 4 pothocks & 2 pothangings 2*s*;

Item 6 candelstycks of brasse 10*s*;

Item 2 watter potts of brasse 1*s* 4*d*;

Item 1 fryinge pan with 2 grydyrons 2*s*;

Item one skomer 4*d*;

Item 2 flesshe hoocks with other trayshe 4*s*;

Item a payre of Andyrons with a barr of yron 6*s* 8*d*;

Item a bord with the seylinge in the kychinge 5*s*;

Item A nagge with the saddell £1;

Sum £7 12*s* 4*d*.

detts as ys fownd by the boocke as ffolloweth

Firstly John Whetcumbe of Wonton oweth £49 17*s* 7*d*;

Item Francys Gale of Tapsome oweth £8;

Item Nicholas Whetcombe of Lyme owethe £43 9*s* 6*d*;

Item John Dyer owethe £49 16*s* 8*d*;

Item Mr Wadam of Katherstowe owethe £1 4*d*;

Item Andrewe Geyre owethe £6;

Item John Macye of Colyton owethe £1 9*s* 2*d*;

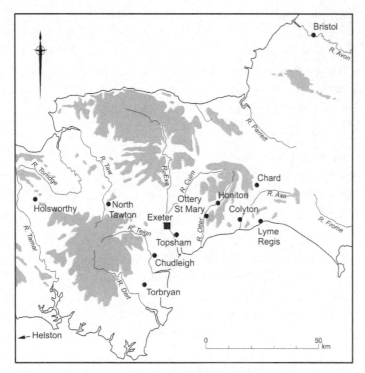

Fig. 14. Places recorded in the list of debts of Edmond Whetcombe (OC 4; *graphic: T. Ives, Exeter Archaeology*).

Item Mr Mapowder of Holsworthye oweth £5 15s 10d;
Item Mr Beade owethe £3 10s;
Item Thomas Grygge owethe £37 6d;
Item Mr Peters of Torbryant oweth £2 7s 11d;
Item Whetcombe of Brystowe oweth £22;
Sum £230 7s 6d.

desperate debts as are found by the boocke as fowllowethe
Firstly William Izacke of Tapsom oweth £4;
Item Richard Whetcumbe owethe £3 11s;
Item John Bastables brother in lawe owethe 2s 4d;
Item Jeffrye Froste of Tapsome owethe 18s;
Item Richard Delfe of Welskome owethe £1 3s 4d;
Item John Dare owethe 12s 9d;

Item Symon Whyt of Lyme owethe 5s;
Item Harrye Grene of Northtawton owethe 8s 5d;
Item Robert Grestowe owethe 5s 2d;
Item Margaret Stevens with owt Est Gate owethe 7s;
Item Richard Fyshe owethe 8s 4d;
Item Peares Martyn of Helston owethe 5s;
Item John Ransberye owethe £1;
Item William Fryer owethe 5s 5d;
[m. 3] Item John Hill Husbandman withowt Estgate £1;
Item Davye Paslowe owethe £2;
Item William Chollyshe owethe £7 10s;
Item Lawrence Raffe 11s 6d;
Item Hughe Tyder owethe £1 2s 4d;
Item Alse osteler owethe 2s;
Item Cocks of Owtrye owethe 12s;
Item Boyere of Tapson owethe 4s 4d;
Item John Whetcombe of Colyton oweth 8s;
Item John Toucker merchant owethe 18s;
Item Mr Blackaller owethe 8d;
Item John Stevens owethe 3s;
Item John Hoper [?] of Tapsom owethe 15s 6d;
Item Roberte Dorsell of Collyton owethe £1 13s 4d;
Item Chollys the boocher owethe 3s 4d;
Item Harrye Lopus [?] of Chagford owethe £1;
Item John Glasse of Bawnton [?] owethe £1 17s 7d;
Item George Palfrye owethe £4;
Item Mr Peter of Chard owethe £21 6s 11d;
Item Tryggs of Tapsom owethe 6s 8d;
Item Harrye Chugge withowt Estgate 9s;
Item Robert Cotten oweth £2 14s 4d;
Item Mr Francklyn owethe 9s 4d;
Item John Toucker owethe 11s;
Item Thomas Myller owethe £4 11s 11d;
Item Thomas Ford owethe £1;
Item Mr Wadams man owethe £2 18s 8d;
Item Mr Trobelfilde of Honyton owethe 18s;
Item Molton corne hocker [?] owethe 15s;
Item Boysell Mr Larders myller 3s 1d;

Item Bennet Graunt of Chydleghe £3 5*d*;
Item William Gregorye owethe 15*s*;
Item Edward the sawer withowt Est Gat 6*s*;
Item Thomas Coyle owethe 10*s*;
Item Christoffer the pyllet 1*s*;
Item James Sprage owethe £1 10*s*;
Item William Haimond £1;
Item William Chaffe 8*s*;
Sum £81 7*s* 8*d*.

Plat and all such wares as ar to be solde as followith
Firstly 3 goblets containing 40 ouncs & a halfe at 4*s* 4*d* the
    ounce A montethe to the sume £9 9*s*;
Item a salt gilte 13 owncs 3 quarters at 6*s* the ownce
    Amontethe to the sume £4 2*s* 6*d*;

Item 8 spones 8 owncs & halfe at 4*s* 6*d* the ownce Amontethe
    [to] £2 2*s* 9*d*;
Item fyrst in 30 peces of dowlys in the short playte vallewyd
    at £147;
Item in 16 peces & haffe of treger at the short playt vallewyd
    at £3 15*s* the pece £61 17*s* 6*d*;
Item 2 serons of sope £6;
Item 13 whytt Kerses £14 10*s*;
Item there ys dewe by yron & ode as will apere by accompt
    £72 7*s* 10*d*;
Item there ys owinge in the cytye as by accompt will appere
    the sume £100;
Sum £417 10*s* 7*d*.

Sum total £791 7*s* 1*d*.

12C. INVENTORY OF EDMUND WHETCOMBE, MERCHANT, 15 JUNE 1565

ECA, Orphans' Court Inventory 5

The Inventory of Edmond Whecombe ['1565' crossed
through] the 15th of June 1565

Goodds plat mony debts specalties & desperat and yn the
    whole £791 7*s* 1*d*;
Whereof yn debts & desperat £81 7*s* 8*d*;
So rem[ains] above the debts desperat £709 19*s* 5*d*;

Whereof
In funeralls £10;
To the poor £5;
£15 5*s* [*sic*];
So remaineth £694 19*s* 5*d*.

Which £672 [*sic*] must be devyded 3th parts & the[y] are as
    folowith:
To the wyff £231 9*s* 10*d*;
To the admynesters £231 9*s* 10*d*;

To the children £231 9*s* 10*d*.
Whereof geven yn legacyes
To Mary Whetcombe £6 13*s* 4*d*;
To Hercules Whetcombe £10;
To Rychard Jourdan [?] 40*s*;
To Nycholus Whetcombe £20;
To John Whetcombes daughters £3;
To Henry Folletts 2 daughters 40*s*;
To his father & mother £5;
To John Whetcombe at Exson 40*s*;
To Margery Alyce Jane & Elysabeth his daughters every of
    £60 – £240;
To Peter Whetcombe his sone £66 13*s* 4*d*;
To his brother of Brystowe £12;
Sum £369 6*s* 8*d*.

By which accompt he hathe geven yn legacies more then the
testators 3 part doth amount unto the some of £137 16*s* 10*d*

which some might be rebat hout of the testators 3th part after the rate of the pound & then yn every £ geven yn legacies there is lost 7s 5¾d;

Wherfor is dew to the children as foloweth:

To Peter Whetcombe £66 13s 4d – £37 11s 1½d;

The 4 daughters £240 – £150 4s 6d;

Also emonge them for the 3th – £231 9s 10d;

£419 5s 5½d.

Edmond Whetcomb is Children

One Recognysanc for Margery & Alic every of them £60 – £120;

One other Recognysance for Jane & Elyabz every of them £60 – £120;

One other Recognysance for Peter Whetecomb for £66 13s 4d;

£306 13s 4d.

ECA, Orphans' Court Inventory 6

Edmond Whetcombe, 1565

The Inventorie of the goodds & cattalls of Edmond Whetcombe of the Citie of Exon decessed praysed by Andrew Geere, George Peryman, Henry Paramore & William paramore praysors apoynted by Mr John Peryam Alderman of the south quarter & sworne to do the same, 1565

Goodds housholde stuffe wares plate & debts £791 7s 1d.

Whereof

In debts desperatt £81 7s 8d;

So remaineth clere the desperatt debts allowed £709 19s 5d.

Whereof

In funerealls £10;

Item geven to the poore £5 10s;

£15 10s;

So remaineth cleere the detts & funeralls allowed £694 9s 5d.

Which some of £694 9s 5d must be devyded yn to three equall partes & porcons as folowethe:

To the wiffe of the testator for her 3rd parte £231 9s 10d;

To her for the executryx 3rd parte £231 9s 10d;

To the fyve children for theire 3rd parte £231 9s 10d;

£694 9s 6d.

Whereof geven yn legacyes

To Mary Whetcombe £6 13s 4d;

To Hercules Whetcome £10;

To Rycherd Jourdon 40s;

To Nychus Whetcombe £20;

To John Whetcombes daughters £3;

To Henry Folletts 2 daughters 40s;

To the testators parents £5;

To John Whetcombe of Oxford 40s;

To Margery (£60) Alyce (£60) Jane (£60) & Elysabethe (£60) £240;

To Peter his soune £66 13s 4d;

To his brother of Brystow £12;

£369 6s 8d.

Of which £369 6s 8d is geven yn legacies more then the the [sic] testator coulde geve because he can dispose at his wyll onely one thirde parte the some of £137 16s 10d;

[2] Which £137 16s 10d beinge more then the testators 3rd parte must be deducted & robard out of the saide testators 3rd parte that is out of £231 9s 5d after the rate of the pounde & then there is lost yn everye pounde geven yn legacye 7s 5¾d;

By which accompt the children for their porcons & legacyes must have as folowethe:

Peter Whetcome of £66 13s 4d must have £37 11s 1½d;

The 4 daughters of £240 must have £150 4s 6d;

Also they must have emong them for one 3 parte £231 9s 10d;

Sum £419 5s 5½d.

And for asmych to the Courte helden the 22 day of June in the 7th year of Queen Elizabeth 1565 before the mayor & the more parte of the comen Councell by gad & sufficiet

Testymony that thentent & will of Edmund WheteCumbe the testator was & by hem declirid att Bristawe in his deyth bedd that he dyd by good coniecture thincke he hadd geven the 3rd part of his goodds to his sayde children & wolde the same sholde for theire full satisfaction of the 3rd part which they might lawffully clayme by the custome of the Citie which the order of which custome was to hym then unknowen, and for asmich also as it apearethe that the sayde legacys of £306 13s 4d dothe excede & is more then the 3rd parte by £75 3s 6d as appeareth by the inventorie it is therefor ordred & agreed that according to the mynde & will of the sayde Edmond & yn consyderacon of the premyss that the saide children shall stande contented with the sayde legacys & accept the same as their full & lawffull porcons.

[3] The 22 of June in the 7th year of the Lady Elisabeth 1565 Mr Levermore maior, Mr Jo Mydwynter, Mr Peter, Mr R Mydwynter, Mr Jo Blackall, Jo Ulcot, Ryc Prestwode,

Thomas Rycherdson, John Smyth, Robert Chaff, Rychard Helierd, Edward Lynett, Symon Knight, William Seldoune, William Tryvett, Tho Prestwode

Noted that on 22 June in the 7 year of Elizabeth Andrew Goode of the city of Exon merchant, George Peryman of that city merchant, Philip Yard from that city merchant, and Richard Swete from that city merchant, came into the presence of the Mayor and 24 of the council and recognised themselves to be bound to John Hoker, chamberlain of the said city, in the sum of 300 marks;
The condycon is if the sayd recognyters do pay or couse to be payed to thuse of Margery & Alyce the some of £120;
The condicon is that if the saide Recognistors do pay or cause to be payed to thuse of Jane & Elysabeth the some of £120;
The condycon is that if the sayde recognyters do pay 100 marks to the use of Peter Whetcombe [tails off].

13A. WILL OF GEORGE HUNTE, DRAPER OF ST PETROCK'S PARISH, 3 MARCH 1565

National Archives, PROB 11/48/260
Note: Hunte's will was proved on 12 October 1565. Recognisances were entered into on 9 April 1565 regarding his son Hannibal otherwise known as George (ECA, Book 141, folio 14). The register for the parish of St Petrock recorded George 'Hunt' was buried on 8 March 1565. An Inquisition Post Mortem survives (National Archives C142/141/54 and see C43/6/72).

[1] **In The Name of God amen The thirde** day of Marche in the yere of oure Lorde god a thowsande fyve hundreth three skore & foure. I George Hunte of the parishe of Sainte Petrocks in the Citie of Exeter being sicke in body and yet neverthelesse god be thancked of good and perfecte remembrance doe make and ordeine this my present Laste will and testament in manner & forme Followinge. Firste I geve and bequeath my soule into the handes of Almightie god my maker and Redemer and my earthly bodie to be buried in the churche yarde of St Peters in Exeter. Item I give and bequeath unto Alice my wiffe one hundereth marckes of Lawfull money of Englande to be firste paide before any

other of my Legacies be paide. Item I give and bequeath to Elizabeth Fursdon my wiffes sister tenne pounde to be delyvered unto her within one halfe yere after my decease. Item I give and bequeath to Johne Fursdon my wifes mother six and twentie shillings eighte pence. The residue of all my goodes moveable and unmoveable I give and bequeath to Haniball Hunte otherwise called George Hunt my soune whome I make and ordeine to be my hole executor. And if it happen the saide Haniball otherwise George Hunte to decease befor he doe accomplishe the full age of one & twentie yeres then my will is that the same residewe of my goodes so before given unto him shall hollie remaine come and be to the use of

47

Alice my wiffe. Item I make and ordaine my unckell Thomas Ratcliffe and Thomas Martin to be my overseers to see this my will performed and doune in everythinge accordinge to to [sic] the trewe meaninge hereof and I give and bequeath to every of them tenne shillinges apeice for theire paines. Item I give and bequeathe to the poore prisoners in the quenes Gayle of the Castell of Exeter, tenne shillinges that is to wite, twoe [2] shillings weakly to be paide untill the saide some of tenne shillinges befulled paide. Item I give to the poore prisoners in the quenes Gaile of the Citie of Execeter, fyve shillinges, that is to wite twelve pence to be paide weakely, tyll the saide some of fyve shillinges be fully paide. Item I give to the poore of the Mawdelyn withoute the Sowithegate of the Citie of

Exeter fyve shillinges that is to wite twelve pence to be paide weakely till the saide some of fyve shillinges be fully paide. Item my will is that my wiffe Alice shall have and enioye duringe her Lyffe one howse a stable orcharde and gardyn and twoe Lyttell croftes of grounde sett lyinge and beinge in Faringdon wherein one Richarde Sladde nowe dwelleth in, the same Alice payinge to my Heires and assignes during her Lyffe the some of twentie shillinges yerely to be paide for the same. In witnes whereof to this my presente Laste will I have sett my Hande geven the daye & yere above written in the presence of Thomas Marten, Thomas Ratclife, Peter Longe, John Hole, Martyn Browne, John Fursdon withe other, by me George Hunte.

13B. INVENTORY OF GEORGE HUNTE, DRAPER OF ST PETROCK'S PARISH, NO DAY OR MONTH GIVEN, 1565

ECA, Orphans' Court Inventory 7 [Item 1]
Note: There are seven versions of this inventory but Item 1 has notes added after the inventory was made. This version has patches of discolourisation.

The Inventory and Devysion of the goods & [chattals – crossed through] of George Hunte late of the Citye of Exeter decessed Accordynge to the order of Orphanes of the Cytye of Exeter 1565

Goodes householde Stuffe Weeres detts sperate and desperate £255 14s 4d.

Whereof
In debts desperate dewe by the Shoppe boke £25 5s;
Item for the debte of Richarde Strobridge £26 6s 8d;
Item for the debte of the halffe of the ship called the George £30;
£81 11s 8d;
So there Ramayneth yn goods & debts payable £174 2s 8d.

Whereof
In Charges for the funeralls 12s 8d;
Also geven to the poore 20s;
Also for debts owed by proffs £15 9s 4d;
Item for debts owed uppon specialties £76 15s;
Also for severall Rents of his house & Ten[emen]ts 25s;
Also for probate of the Testament & ingrossynge of the Inventory 18s 8d;
£96 8d.

So there Remaineth over & above the funeralls the debts which the Testator owed and the debts whiche is owynge & not Receavyd £78 2s.

Whiche some of £78 2s must be devyded yn three Equall parts & then there Remayneth to every parte as folowethe:
To the Wyffe of the Testator for her 3rd £26 8d;

To Hanyball the Childe for his 3rd £26 8*d*;
To the same Hannyball the Admynystrator for his 3rd £26 8*d*;
£78 2*s*.

Whereof *[verso]*
Gevyn in legacy by the Testator to his Wyffe £66 13*s* 4*d*;
Also to Elizabeth Furssedon £10;
Also to Johan Furssedon 26*s* 8*d*;
Also to the overseers 20*s*;
£79.

Off whiche £79 there is geven in legacies by the Testator more then the thirde parte whiche only he myght dispose £52 19*s* 4*d*

Whiche £52 19*s* 4*d* must be rebated after the Rate of the pounde out of the foresaid £79 geven in legacies And then there is lost in every pounde 13*s* 5*d* over & above 7*d* uppon the Whole by Whiche Accompte the legatories must have of every pounde but 6*s* 7*d*.

[So then the wiff for her 3rd must have £26 8*d*
Also for the rent of her bargayne at 6*s* 7*d* the £ £21 18*s* 10½*d*
Also for the 3rd part of the debts when the be recovered £26 18*s* 2½*d*
Also for her part of her legacie when the debts are… 6*s* 3½*d* the £ £22 11*s* 8*d*
Sum £97 8*s* – crossed through].

[Later notes on the administration of the child's portion]

After our hartie Comendacions, we have herwith sent unto you the Division of the goodds of George Hunt decessed, by you to be throughly examyned and to be amended: for we do doubt myche therein what to do concerninge the wiffe to whom the testator gave yn legacye for her full porcon & payment 100 marks which in deed is now they will aryse of the gooddss onlie the debts be recovered, and therefore if we sholde the devisyon before made she sholde have a great debt more then the legacie, and the poor childe who is the executor & standeth to the bronte of all shall not have much more then his 3rd part the testators 3rd part being altogether spent yn answeringe the legacies. What your opinyon & idgement shalbe herein we pray you to be certyfied for untyll your further advertysment we mynd to stay yn proceding any further herein. And bysides the debts the testator owed beinge before recyted it is thought that there be others which upon specialties wilbe sued & demanded. This present day Thomas Holmer & Olyver have verye ernestlye requested the sight of the examynacons taken before Mr Maior agayne them & yn the behalfe of Ryc Taylor and though the same be denyed yet that is not thought reasonable to them who mynde otherwise to have the same will we or will we not. If what you shold thincke reasonable to be donee send your letter & it shalbe done it were not reasonable that suche an advantage should be given to that [obscured] Concerninge the copie the charter of St Sydwells fee you shall receave by the carier this next weke together with an answere to all your artyclrs and whereas there are too wrytes brought by [?]Salter agayne Pope & Martyn for certyn lands there shalbe nothinge done therein without your advise of the copies of the protestations & answeres shalbe sent up unto you for your advise therein before any thinge shall passse. And this endyinge we [?]pray the lyvinge [?] child to have yt yn his keeping. From Excester the 9th of April 1565
Your Lovinge ffrendes Richard Hext
John Vowell *alias* Hooker

I dyd by my letters sent by Mr Haydon's servant request you to advertise me of any questyon yn a cause of [contr – crossed through] doubt dependinge yn the court of Exiland and sythence I dyd the lyke by my letters to Mr Haydon who as I now perceve is at London. I pray you open these letters & if he be there lett him have them & lett me be advertysed of bothe your opinyons.

14. INVENTORY OF JOHN REVE, BREWER OF ST EDMUND'S PARISH, 23 SEPTEMBER 1566

ECA, Orphans' Court Inventory 8

The Inventory of all and singuler the goodes and cattalls which latlie appertayned unto John Reve brewer within the parishe of St Edmondes upon the bridge decessed made and praised by John Edames Millar and Robert John Bonyfant & Richard Fry the 23 daie of September in the yere of our lorde god 1566

Firstly for 2 cobbordes the price 26*s* 8*d*;
Item for one fether bedde withe 3 pillowes 26*s* 8*d*;
Item for one flocke bede 3*s*;
[Item for a flocke bedst – crossed through];
Item for a bedstede and the testar with the hangins to it 10*s*;
Item for 2 formes 3*s* 4*d*;
Item for a chaire 8*d*;
Item for a borde and a stowell 12*d*;
Item for a trockell bedde 16*d*;
Item for the hangins abowte the hall 5*s*;
Item for one pott of brasse the price 11*s*;
Item for a nother pott of brasse 6*s*;
Item for a nother potte of brasse 2*s*;
Item for 3 littell pottes 4*s*;
Item for 4 fryinge pannes 4*s*;
Item for a fier picke and a fier shovell 2 addises 12*s*;
Item for 3 paire of pothockes 3 paire of hangins and 3 [tails off];
Item for 2 broches 2*s*;
Item for 2 fleshehockes 4*d*;
Item a bason and ever 6*s* 8*d*;
Item for 7 platters 7 poddingers 5 saucers and a charger 20*s*;

Item for a levent [11] flower pottes 4*s*;
Item for 2 saltes of tynne 12*d*;
Item for a pottell pott and 2 quarts 5*s*;
Item for 5 candelstickes 4*s*;
Item for a panne 6*s* 8*d*;
Item for 3 caudrons a littell panne and a chafer 6*s*;
Item for 3 peaire of shetes 10*s*;
Item for 3 bordclothes 2 towills and 6 napkinges 8*s*;
Item for 3 flocke beddes 2 pillowes and a bolster 26*s* 8*d*;
Item a bedstede and a trockell bedstede with the clothers in the chamber 10*s*;
Item for 2 coffers in the said chamber 2*s* 8*d*;
Item for 2 clokes 5*s*;
Item for a carpet 2*s*;
Item for 3 coverletts 3*s*;
Item for 5 cosshinges 20*d*;
Item for his gowne 20*s*;
Item for the borde and the binche in the chamber 3*s* 4*d*;
Item for 3 blanckets 18*d*;
Item for 6 coborde clothes 5*s*;
Item for 2 daggers 20*d*;
Item for a stayll 12*d*;
Item for a borde 10*s* [?];
Item for 2 hogges 10*s*;
Item for the malte and the garner and 2 hogshedes 31*s*;
Item for the coffer and a torne and a bord 2 tressells 5*s*;
Item for a gowne that is at plagge for 30*s* and there is paide of the said goune 20*s*;
Sum £17.

15. WILL OF JOHN BEDECOME, 21 OCTOBER 1566

ECA, Orphans' Court Will 12a

Note: an accompanying copy of this will, which follows, has slight differences in wording including omitting his soul was 'foolish and sinful'. The register for the parish of St Mary Major recorded 'Johne Biddycombe' was buried on 2 November 1566. A parish copy of the register noted his surname as 'Bydecombe'. Recognisances were entered into on 10 March 1567 regarding his children John the elder, John the younger, Robert, Mary, Joyce, Thomasyne, Alice and Katherine (ECA, Book 141, folio 18 dorse).

In the name of God Amen The 21th of October 1566 I John Bedecome of the Citie of Exon do make & ordayne my last will & testament yn manner & forme as foloweth, ffyrst I geve & bequeth my foolys & synnffull sole yn to the handes of my lorde & almightie God to be partakers of the remission of sinnes through the deth & merytts of Christ Jesus my onely saviour and redemer. And my bodye beinge earth I comend to the earth shewing therein seemely to be buried my hope of the resurrection therof to lyff everlastinge. Item I geve the some of 6s 8d to be destrybuted emonge the poore prysoners, of the Quenes gaole of the Castle of Exon & the Southgate of the saide Citie as by my wyffe shalbe thought best. Item I do geve the some of 12d to be distybuted emonge the poore lazar people of the Magdalen without the Southgate of the Citie of Exon. Item I geve to Rychard Plympton & Johne his wiff my sister either of them 2s. Item I geve to every of their children 2s saving to Jane their daughter to whom I geve 6s 8d whereof I will the 3s 4d to me bequeathed by my late father Andrew Bydcom to be parcell thereof. Item I geve to Jane [?] Branscombe & Elisabeth his wiff my syster every of them 2s. The resydew of my goodds my debts & funeralls paied I geve & bequethe to Margarett my wyff & to John, the elder, John the younger, Robert, Mary, Joyce, Thomasyn, Catharane, Alys, my children equally to be devyded emonge them that is to wyte to the said my wiff there moytie & to the said my children theother moytie which my saide wiff & children I do makce & ordayne to be the full [executrix – crossed through] executors of this my last will & testament. And for the better performance thereof I do request & pray John Hoker & Mathew Drake to be the overseers of this my last will & testament and to every of them for their paynes I geve 6s 8d

In wytnes whereof I have subscrybed to these presents yn presence of them whose names do ensewe.

Orphans's Court Will 12a

John Bedecome, 21 October 1566

In the name of God Amen, The 21th of October 1566 I John Bedecome of the Citie of Exon to make and ordyne my last will & testament yn manner & forme as foloweth. Ffyrst I geve & comende my sole yn to the handes of allmightie God to be partaken of the remyssion of synnes through the dethe & merytes of Jesus Christ my onely Lorde and redemer. And my bodye yn hope of a blyssed resurrection I comende to be seemely buryed yn the comon sepulcure of St Peters churchyarde. Item my will is that the some of 6s 8d be equally destybuted emonge the poore prysoners yn the Quenes Gaole of the castle & Southgat of the Citie of Exon. Item I geve to Richarde Plympton of St Georges Clyst & Jone his wyff my syster eche of them 2s as also to everye of their children now lyvynge 2s savynge to Jane theyre daughter to whom I geve & bequethe the some of 6s 8d whereof I will that 3s 4d to me bequeathed & geven by my late father Andrew Bedcombe to be parcell of it. Also I geve to [blank] Bronscombe of Edesleighe & Elysabeth his wyff my syster every of them 2s The resydew of my goodds my debts & funeralls payed I geve & bequethe to Margarett my wyff, & to John thelder John the yonger Robert Mary Joyce Thomasyn Alys & Katharen my children equally to be devyded betwene them that is to saye there moytie to the said my wyff & thother moytie to the saide my children wyllinge & requiringe that thadmynystracon of all my goods & chatalls after my deth be taken accodrynge to this my last will & meanynge.

16. INVENTORY OF JAMES TAYLOR, BAKER, 17 DECEMBER 1566

ECA, Orphans' Court Inventory 9

Note: Recognisances were entered into on 27 November 1567 & 13 January 1570 regarding his son Simon (ECA, Book 141, Folios 19, 21).

1566 The Inventary of all the goods and Chattalls of James Teallor late of the Cyttye of Exete baker deacessed taken & praysed by [Robert [illegible] & Phillip [illegible] of Hevytre – crossed through] John Bonyscombe, William Milbury John Bettye and Henry Dabenot the 17th daye of December in the sivnthe yere of the Raigne of the Sovereigne lady Elizabeth the queens majestie that now is

In the halle
Firstly a Table bourde with a Joyned forme 13s 4d;
Item a Cubbourde 14s;
Item a lyttell Syde Cubbourd 2s;
Item a Seat to Sytt by the ffyer 5s;
Item the Sealyng in the halle 10s;
Item a hangyng Candelstycke in the halle with foure Snowfes 8d;
Item too Stayned Clothes 2s;
Item too Brasen Crocks & a possenet 11s;
Item an Iron Barr & three Andyrons 3s;
Item 8 lattyn Candelstycks 6s 8d;
Item too Broches too pothangyngs too Brandyses a ffrye pan, a fyre pyke & a peare of Belowes 4s;
Item 6 brasen pannes too Cawderyns & a Skyllet 20s;
Item too Gose pannez & a fryyng pan 8d;
Item a leasse for terme of Certayne yerez it to Come of the Ten[emen]t in Exon in ye whiche the Testator dwelld £10;
Sum £14 13s 4d.

In the parler with in the halle
Firstly a Cubbourde with three latten Basens and three latten potts 6s 8d;
Item a Iron morter with a pestell 8d;

Item 15 platters & 14 podyngers 6 Sawcers of Tyn three Tynnen potts & 2 Salts of Tyn 22s;
Item a bourde a Joyned forme & 2 Carpetts 2s 6d;
Sum 31s 10d.

In the Inner parler
Item a fflocke Bed with a Bolster of ffeathers a peare of Shets & a pere of Blancketts 10s;
Item a rounde bourde with a Carpet a Chest & a Chayre 6s 8d;
Item three Coffers 4s;
Item Certayn Stayned Clothes 2s;
Sum 22s 8d.

In the Inner Chamber
Item a Bedstede & a ffetherbed & a bolster of ffethers 20s;
Item a Chest & Cover & Cheare 4s;
Item Certayn Stayned Clothes 2s;
Item a peare of harnys 6s 8d;
Item 6 bourde Clothes 8s;
Item a dosen of bourde Napkyns 2s 6d;
Item 2 Cubbourd Clothes & too Towells 20d;
Item foure pillatyves 2s 6d;
Item six peare of Sheats 20s;
Item his apparell £3 6s 8d;
Item a Goblet of Sylver & a Salt of Sylver & a halff a dosen of Sylver spones £6;
Item a maser Tapp[ed] with Sylver and a Cup Coveryd with Sylver & 9 Sylver spones 46s 8d;
Sum £15 8d.

In the fforth Chamber
Item two ffetherbeds & a fflocke bed & too bolsters of
    ffeathers & to Coverlets 33s 4d;
Sum 33s 4d.

[verso] In the Chamber over the Shoppe
Item a ffetherbed a flockebed & a doust bed a bolster of
    ffethers & 2 bolsters of flocks 20s;
Sum 20s.

In the Chamber over the spence
Item a fflocke bed 5s;
Sum 5s.

In the Shoppe
Item three hoggyshids sixe pounde of Woulle and too Tornes
    with other Trasshe 10s;
Sum 10s.

In the Spence
Item too Standers with three lyttell Costs 4s;
Item a hutche with other Traysshe 3s 4d;
Sum 7s 4d.

In the loft over the Stable
Item foure Trusse of haye 30s;
Sum 30s.

In the Bake house
Item one brasen pan 10s;
Item more three Sacks of meale 30s;
Item more 4 Sacks & 2 peare of panyers 6s 8d;
Item 2 bourds & too hutches & too Trawes with too Tubbes
    with other Stuffe 10s;
Sum 56s 8d.
In the Curtilage
Item Certayn Woode 20d;
Item yn pottrye 2s 4d;
Item a grendyng Stone 2s;
Sum 6s.

Sum total £40 16s 10d;
Item min[us] [?] yn dyttes £3.

17. INVENTORY OF NICHOLAS MARRET, OF THE PARISH OF ST JOHN'S BOW, 24 JUNE 1568

ECA, Orphans' Court Inventory 10 [Item 1]
Note: Recognisances were entered into on 7 August 1568 regarding Margaret, John, Joan and John [?; sic], the children of Nicholas 'Marreke' (ECA, Book 141, folio 20).

The Inventory of all & singuler the goodes & Cattalls of
Niclas Marret late of the Paryshe of St Johns Bowe in the
Citty of Exceter decessed praysed the 24th day of June in the
yeare of our Lorde god 1568 by Robert Cotton, John Budlye
& John Turner and John Barstabell

In the Hall
Firstly a Tabelbord & a forme 6s;

Item 4 old Carpetts 4s;
Item a rounde Tabell & a Plancke borde a forme 4 Chairs 3
    Stowles 2s 6d;
Item a old Cubborde a Benche with seelinge 10s;
Item a mans Harneis a sallet a sherehooke and a Bill 6s 8d;
Item a Towell & a Course Cuppbord Clothe 12d;
Item a Bason a yewer 2 tynnen dishes 4 square Saucers 2
    tynnen saltes 2 flower potts of Tynne 8s;

Item a old Bason 2 quartes of Tynne 2 Pynts of Tynne 8 stone
    Cuppes & parte of them Covered 3s 4d;
Item 7 Candelsticks of Brasse 2 of old Tynn 2s;
Item a Bason 8 Platters 8 saucers and a Poddenger 15s;
Item a Barre of Iron 3 old doggs of Iron 3 Pott Croks 2
    Pothangers a fier Pike a Toster & a fiershowle 2s 6d;
Item 3 old stayned Clothes 2s 6d;
Item 15 old Tynne spones 4d;
Sum £3 3s 10d.

In the Parler
Item a Tabelbord with a old forme a Carpet & a Benche 6s 8d;
Item a Bedsteed a ffetherbed a Bolster 2 Pillowes & a
    fflaunders Coverlett with a stayned Tester 26s 8d;
Item a Trokell Bedsteede a fflockebedd a Bolster a Pillowe of
    ffethers and a scriden [?] Coverlett 6s 8d;
Item a Bedsteede with a Dustebed a paire of Blanketts a
    fflaunders Coverlett a Bolster 2 Pillowes a stened Tester
    12s;
Item a grett Cheste 2 Coffers a old Cupord & a fforme 6s 8d;
Item 4 BordClothes 2 Towells & 10 Napkins 10s;
Item 4 Pillobeares 19ene Shetes 2 hande Towells a Bone
    Tabell Clothe & 2 sherts 20s;
Item 6 Plattes 4 Poddingers & 6 saucers 10s;
Item a Cassake of wosterd a Cassak of Clothe a rounde
    Kertell of wasterd a mapron of wosterd 2 Clothe Cappes
    a old silke hatt a peire of redd satten Bodies 3 Kerchers a
    Partlett a Hedbande and a paire of old knitt Slyves 30s;
Item 2 old Mantells 9 old Quishions 5 old Blancketts 5s;
Item a Gowne facid with foxe a Jerkinge of Tawny Chamlet a
    Jerkin of blacke worsterd a nold dublet sleved with Tawny
    Taffata 2 Clokes of Clothe a Waste Dublet of Saclothe a
    nother of Canvas a payre of blacke hose a blake Capp &
    felte Hatt 46s 8d;
Item in redy money 27s;
Item a Goblet of Silver parcell gilte 53s 4d;

Item 2 stened Clothes 2s;
Sum £13 2s 8d.

In the Chamber over the spence
Item 3 Bedsteedes with 3 fflockebedes 3 Coverletts with
    Bolsters & pillowes 26s 8d;
Item in Wolle & Yearne 6s;
Item in Rye & Drie fishe 3s;
Sum 26s 8d.

In the Chamber over the Parlor
Item 4 olde Bedsteedes 2 Dustbeddes one ffloke bedd 2
Blanketts 3 old Coverletts 13s 4d;
Sum 13s 4d.

In the spence
Item 3 Brason Crokks a Posnett 13s 4d;
Item 5 brasen Pannes a litell skillet & a Skymer 20s;
Item a frying Panne 2 Broches a gridyron a Brandyse & a
    ffleshehoke 3s 4d;
Item a old Bedsteede a old fflokebed a Course Coverlet a
    bounting whiche [hutch] 6 tubbes 2 Bucketts 2 bolls 4s 6d;
Item 2 old goose pannes 6d;
Sum 41s 8d.

In the Stabell
Item in Haye 10s;
Item 3 spining Turnes & a vate 4s;
Item Racks mangers & other plancks 5s;
Sum 19s.

In the Shoppe
Item in the shopp a Dosen & ½ of shewes at 8d the peire 12s;
Item 2 Dosen & halfe of Showes at 6d the pere 15s;
Item 19 paire of small shoes at 6d the pere 8s;
Item Lethere there 16s;
Item other trashe there 3s 4d;
Sum 54s 4d.

Detts owed to the Testator upon his Booke
Firstly Richard Gifford for shewes 20s;
Item Eustas Oliver 4s 6d;

Item Mr Muncks [?] House for shewes 7s 6d;
Item Thomas Wescotts house 5s 4d;
Item Harry Sewards house 5s 10d;
Item Hew Snedalls house 5s;
Item Mr Cokeson of Barly 2s 4d;
Item Nichas Vilvayne 2s 4d;
Item Thomas Ellet for shewes 16d;
[verso] Item Bennet of Whitstone for shewes 6d;
Item Ball the Lymer 6d;
Item Mr Clement Snedall 6s;
Item James Olyver of Garnezey [? Guernsey] 8s 2d;
Sum £3 9s 3d.

Sum Total £28 7d.

Item the Lease of the House £13 6s 8d;
Sum Total £41 7s 5d.

Wherof
In ffuneralls 36s 4d;
In severall detts to severall persons which the testator ded
    awne in his lyve tyme to the power 10 [?] £7 19s;
Sum £10 5s 4d.

So Remaynyth Cler £28 13s 5d.

ECA, Orphans' Court Inventory 10 [Item 2]
Nicholas Marrett

The Inventarie & devysyon of the goods of Nicalas Marrett
decessid accordyng to the order of orphans withyn the Cetie
of Exeter

The goods plate & detts speratt (£3 9s 3d) & desperat
household stuff &c (£24 11s) amounts in the hole as apperith
by the Inventorie £28 9d;
A lease for yers £13 6s 8d;
Sum Total £41 7s 5d.

Wherof yn detts desperat 48s 8d;
So remaynyth £38 18s 9d.

Wherof
In ffuneralls 36s 4d;
In detts to severall persons which the testator ded awe £7 19s;
To the poure 10s;
£10 5s 4d.

So Remaynyth Cler £28 13s 5d.

In 2 parts
One part £14 6s 8½d for the executrix;
Of which £14 6s 8½d the legacyes must be payd.

Memorandum the other £14 6s 8½d to be devydid to 4
    Chylder in 4 parts;
Legacy To Johan his syster 26s 8d;
Memorandum legacy to be taken oute of the testators parte;
To John his Elder son A Sylver Cup weying [blank] oucz 53s
    4d & his best gowne a dyshe performyd;
To John his yonger son 28 [?] marks;
To Elizabz Davy of Kirten the best Cassack the best hatt the
    best Slevys one partlett 20s in mony;
To Margaret his wyff the lease of his house & beyng
    executrix;
Sum of the legacies [blank].

[verso] Nicholas Marret
Sum Total £28 in 2 parts devided viz
To the executrix Margaret his wyffe £14;
One other parte viz £14 to be devided amongs 4 Childerne as
    foloyth:
To the seid Margarett £3 10s;
To Johan £3 10s;
To John his Elder son £3 10s;
To John the yonger £3 10s.

18. INVENTORY OF EDMUND BERDSLEY, SADDLER, 14 AUGUST 1568

ECA, Orphans' Court Inventory 11

Note: Recognisances were entered into on 13 January 1569 regarding his sons Richard, Nicholas and Edmond (ECA, Book 141, folio 20 dorse).

The Inventory Indented of all the money Juells Plate Goodes Cattalls and debts of Edmonde Berdsley Sadler late of the Citty of Exceter decessed made the 14th day of August in the Tenth yeare of the raigne of our Soveraigne Lady Elizabeth &c praysed by Robte Edmonds John Harte Thomas Nicolls and John Haukeridge as foloweth

[1] Fyrste halfe a Dosen of Silver Spones a Salte & Cupp of Sylver weing 28 ouncs at 3s the ounce £5 12s;
Sume £5 12s.

The Halle
Firste one Beddsteed with 2 ffether Beddes £3;
Item 2 Chestes price 13s 4d;
Item one Cubbord pryce 5s;
Item one Basen & Ewer 3s 4d;
Item one pere of white Candlesticks 2s;
Item 6 fflower Potts 16d;
Item one Table borde with 2 fourmes & a Binche 10s;
Item the Stayned Clothes aboute the Hall 3s 4d;
Item a pere of Harnes with 2 Salletts and a Bill to the same 7s 2d;
Item 2 Carpetts 2s;
Item one Tynen Pottell Pott 2 quarte Potts one Pynte Pott three Tynnyn Cuppes 4s 8d;
Item 2 Quishions 8d;
Sum £5 12s 10d.

The Kytchin
Firste 14 Platter dyshes price 9s 4d;
Item 6 Porrengers 3s;
Item 8 Sawcers 2s 8d;
Item one Latten Bason with 8 Candlestiks 4s 4d;

Item 4 Brasse Potts 10s 8d;
Item 2 Pannes & 2 Cawdrons 7s 8d;
Item a litle Skillet 6d;
Item 2 Driping Pannes 18d;
Item one Andiron & 2 Doggs of Ieron 14d;
Item a Broche with three Potthangers & other old stuffe of Ire for the Kitchin 16d;
Item a pere of Bellowes 10d;
Item a Boorde a forme a bynche with other woden Dressers in the kitchin 3s 8d;
Item a Cuppord there 20d;
Item 2 Dawe Tubbes a Pecke a sarger & a Syve 22d;
Sum 9s 2d.

[2] Stable & Backehouse
Fyrst three Cheares 15d;
Item for Tymber in Plancks and woode 12s;
Item 22 Butter Barrells & leer Cases & 3 Costs 5s 6d;
Item old wast formes 4s;
Item 4 Boketts & one Boale 10d;
Item one Bushell of Rye 16d;
Item 11 Kersies £13 15s;
Sum £14 19s 11d.

Chamber
Firste 5 paire of Sheetes 16s;
Item 9 Pillowes 7s 8d;
Item a dosen of Table Napkins 7s 6d;
Item 3 borde Clothes & 3 towells 10s 8d;
Item 3 Shirts 5s;
Item a Cuppord Clothe 2s 4d;
Item a ffetherbed with his furniture & a stayned Clothe 30s;

Item a Trokelbed a fflockebed and a bad fetherbed with a pere
  of Blanketts and a Coverlett 13s 4d;
Item a standing Presse 6s 8d;
Item 3 Coffers 3s 4d;
Item a glassing bottell 8d;
Item 30ti Poundes of Wolle 20s;
Item 18 peecs of Tallo weing 6 C lying in a Pawne ffor £5;
Item one Bedsteede 10d;
Sum £11 4s.

Apparrell
Item a Gowne furred with Lambe 10s;
Item a doblet of fustian blacke 3s 4d;
Item 2 peire of Hosen 3s 8d;
Item a frise Gowne a bad wosted doblet 3s 4d;
Item a Cloke 8s;
Sum 28s 4d.

Debts owed to the testator
Firste by a Obligacon of Roberte Bagwill £30 13s 4d;
Item by a Obligacon of Dennys Pasmere £5;
Item by a Obligacon of Roberte Uffington £15;
Item Mr Farringdon 30s;
Item John Weste for seeling 35s;
Item Michael Smote 32s;
Item Nicolas Jones 47s;
Item John Trapp 13s 4d;

Item Roberte Snilliam 8s;
Item Richard Collyns Cutler 43s 4d;
Item Baker of Daulyshe 9s;
Item William Sadler of Treiro [?] 24s;
Sum £62 15s.

[2v.] The Shoppe
Firste newe Saddells reddy made £4;
Item for Spurrs Buckells Bitts stiroppes and other small ware
  redy made 46s 8d;
Item the Lether unmade 10s;
Item Sadle Tryes 16s;
Item old Sadles & implements with the Tooles 8s;
Sum £8 8d.

[Sum total] £112 11s 11d.

Wherof in debts desperate £25 11s;
Sum remeyneth £77 11d.

In funerals;
In debts to severall persons;
To the poore;
£4;
Remaynyth above the debts & funeralls £69 11d;
The devision in to 3 equall parts as Apperith by the bucke of
  Orphans.

19. INVENTORY OF WILLIAM LANTE, OF ST STEPHEN'S PARISH, 26 MAY 1569

ECA, Orphans' Court Inventory 13
Note: Recognisances were entered into on 14, 17, 21 April, 19 July and 22 December 1570 regarding his children Thomas, William, Mary, John the younger, Ursula and Grace (ECA, Book 141, Folios 24 dorse, 25, 26, 27 dorse).

[1] The Inventorye of all & singullar the goods cattalls & detts of which latelye apptayned unto Willyam Lantte late of the paryshe of St Stephens within the cyttye of Exeter made & presyd by Henery Ellycotte John Jones Goldsmythe Roger Robynson & Thomas Johnson the 26th daye of of Maye in the yere of our lord god A thowsand fyve hundryd three score & nyne

1569

The Inventorie of the Goods of William Lante deceasesed the 26th daie of Maie and praised by Henry Ellacott, John James Goldsmith, Roger Robinson and Thomas Johnson

Kearseis in the Shoppe

Firstly a yearde 3 quarters ½ of carnacon Kearsey 6*s*;

Item halfe a yearde & ½ quarter of Stamell 16*d*;

Item 6 yeards 3 quarters of englishe Stamell at 5*s* the yearde 33*s* 9*d*;

Item 12 yeards of coorse carnacion Kearsey at 18*d* the yearde 18*s*;

Item a dosen of coorse Skye colorid Kearsei 24*s*;

Item 8 yeards & a halfe of vassey color Kearsei at 2*s* 10*d* the yearde 24*s* 1*d*;

Item 2 pecis of yeolowe Kearsey 44*s*;

Item 6 yeards of Aishe color Kearsey in Groine at 4*s* the yearde 24*s*;

Item on yearde and a halfe of Blacke Kearsei 5*s*;

Item halfe a yearde of coorse Blacke Kearsey 8*d*;

Item a paire of yeolow Stookes 14*d*;

Item 7 yeards and a halfe of russett Kearsey at 2*s* 6*d* the yearde 18*s* 9*d*;

Item a yearde of Grine Baies 16*d*;

Item 2 yeards quarter of Osett Redd Kearsey 2*s* 8*d*;

Item 4 yeards of Blacke ffrisse 2*s* 8*d*;

Item 2 yeards quarter of Grine Bokeram 8*d*;

Item a Dosen of Blacke Kearsey 40*s*;

Item 3 Dosens of colorid Kearseis £4 10*s*;

Item 4 Skye colorid Kearseis £5 6*s* 8*d*;

Sum £22 4*s* 9*d*.

In the parlor

Item a Table Borde and the Seilings with Benchis and painted Clothes 26*s* 8*d*;

Item a Lookinge Glasse 15*d*;

Item a presse for Kearseis 16*d*;

Item a paire of Tappers 2*d*;

Sum 29*s* 10*d*.

In the Hall

Item the Seilings and hangins with a Butterie Seilin and a Cubborde with a presse in hit £6 13*s* 4*d*;

Item a Table Borde and a fframe with Drillid pillors 10*s*;

Item a Lesser Table Borde with a square fframe 4*s*;

Item a paire of fflaunders Andirons with a Backe of Iron 13*s* 4*d*;

Item a Bible in Inglishe 8*s*;

Item 6 Quosshins with Rooses 8*s*;

Item 6 coorse Grine Quosshins 2*s*;

Item a Carpett of Tapestrie for the longe Borde 10*s*;

Item a Carpett of Redd ffrise Adee for the Shorte Borde 3*s* 4*d*;

Item a Brasen Candellstike to hange in the hall 16*d*;

Item 3 Joynid formes 2*s* 6*d*;

Item a Joynid Cheare with a Backe of Lether 3*s*;

Sum £9 18*s* 10*d*.

[1v.] In the Chamber within the Hall

In the hangins of Redd Saie and Grine with paintid Borders 33*s* 4*d*;

Item a Joynid Bedsteade with a Tester of Gilinge 20*s* 6*s* 8*d* [*sic*];

Item a ffether Bedd a Bolster & 3 pillowes 40*s*;

Item 5 Curtaines of Redd and Grine Sarsnett 40*s*;

Item A Coverlett of Tapestrie 40*s*;

Item A Blankett 12*d*;

Item A Coffer 5*s*;

Item A Joynid portall in the same Chamber 6*s*;

Item A water potte of Brasse 6*d*;

Item 2 olde Curtaines of Grine Saie 6*d*;

Sum £9 13*s*.

In the greate Chamber within the Hall

Item a Bedsteade 6*s* 8*d*;

Item a fether Bedd 30*s*;

Item a Coverlett 8*s*;

Item a Bolster 6*s* 8*d*;

Item a Redd Coverlett 4*s*;

Item a Trokelbedsteade 3*s* 4*d*;

Item 3 Coffers 6s 8d;
Item hangins of paintid Clothes 20s;
Item a Table Borde with a Cubborde in the same 3s 4d;
Item A Grine Carpett 2s;
Item 2 pillowes 3s 4d;
Item A wollen Blankett 18d;
Sum £4 15s 6d.

In the Chamber within the great Chamber
Item A Bedsteade 5s;
Item A ffether Bedd 10s;
Item A Bolster 4s;
Item A Coorse Coverlett 16d;
Item an olde Coffer 8d;
Item A Cubborde 20d;
Item an olde Testor 2s;
Item 2 welshe hookes 16d;
Item A pyke 4d;
Item A Corslett furnished 10s;
Item an olde Coffer 12d;
Item 2 olde Curtaines of Strakid Canvas 8d;
Sum 38s.

[2] Apparrell
Item A Gowne facid with Damaske 40s;
Item A Caape Edgid with Sattaine 26s 8d;
Item A Dowblett of Kearsey 2s;
Item A waste knite peticote 16d;
Item A Russett Gowne 2s 6d;
Item an olde nighte Cape of velet 2d;
Item 2 olde Girdells 16d;
Item an olde Comunion Boke 4d;
Sum £3 13s 4d.

In the wooll Chamber
Item a Joynid Trokelbedsteade 20d;
Item A flocke Bedd with a Bolster of flocks 2s;
Item 2 white Rugges 12d;
Item an olde Lanterne 2d;

Item an olde Blewe mantill 8d;
Sum 5s 6d.

In the Butterie
Item 2 Chargers 2s 8d;
Item 18 platers 12s;
Item 12 podingers 6s;
Item 10 pottage Dishes 4s;
Item 17 Saucers 3s 4d;
Item 2 pye plats 16d;
Item A Custarde Dishe 12d;
Item A Chaffinge dishe with a foote 5s;
Item 20 fflower pottes 4s;
Item 2 pottell potts 2 quarts 2 pynts 2 Tankerds of Tynne A Cruet of Tynne for Oyle and A Salte of Tynne 6s;
Item A deape Bason of Tynne 12d;
Item A Bason and Ewre of Tynne 3s 4d;
Item A Bottell of Tynne for *Aqua Composita* 20d;
Item A piper Boxe of woode and A Doosen of fruite Trenchers in A Boxe 4d;
Sum 51s 8d.

In the Larder
Item A Coope for Pulterie A Litell Coffer 2 Shelfes 5 Litell Costes 2 Tubbes and 2 pecks and A Buntinge Tubbe 6s 8d;
Sum 6s 8d.

In the Seller
Item A Remnaunte of A Butt of Secke contayninge 50 Gallons £3;
Item A Remnaunte of A Butt of muscadill 40s;
Item A hoggeshed of small Beare 6s 8d;
Sum £5 6s 8d.

[2v.] In the Kitchine
Item 3 Brasse pannes And 3 Cawderons 14s;
Item 4 Brasse potts 15s;
Item 3 Skilletts 2s 6d;
Item 5 Candelsticks 3s 4d;

Item A Litell Brasen mortar 8*d*;

Item 3 Brochis 2*s*;

Item A Grater 4*d*;

Item 3 Litell dogges and a peace of Iron with 3 feate to torne the Broche in and a paire of Tonges withall 6*d*;

Item 2 potte hangins and 3 Cottrells 12*d*;

Item A fryinge panne 6*d*;

Item A Gridiron 8*d*;

Item a peace of Iron with 2 feate to tourne the Broche in 2*d*;

Item A Dripinge panne of Iron 6*d*;

Item A Litell Table Borde A Joynide Stoole And 3 Dressinge Bords 4*s*;

Item A mortar of woode with a pestell 2*d*;

Item an olde Chappinge knife 2*d*;

Item A Brandisse 6*d*;

Item A Litell Barre of Iron 18*d*;

Item an olde water Tankerde 6*d*;

Sum 48*s*.

In the Chamber within the Kitchine

Item an Olde Bedsteade with 4 pillers 20*d*;

Item A Bigge Cheste with A ffewe Bands of Iron an olde Cubborde A Baskett with A Cover A fyne Ranger & 2 Tearses with ffethers 4*s*;

Item A Boxe of Ledd for a plumpe 2*s*;

Item A Bruinge vate 12*d*;

Item A Spade for the Gardyn 2*d*;

Item 5 hoggesheds at 16*d* a peace 6*s* 8*d*;

Item 6 Tearsis at 6*d* a peece 3*s*;

Item A pipe 20*d*;

Item 2 Tubbes 8*d*;

Item A Bookinge Tubbe 4*d*;

Item 18 Inche Bords at 3*d* A pece 4*s* 6*d*;

Item A poderinge Tubbe 4*d*;

Item A Bilhooke 2*d*;

Item an olde paire of Belowis 2*d*;

Item an olde Ranger 2*d*;

Item 2 hampers 8*d*;

Sum 27*s* 2*d*.

In the Stabell

Item an olde Saddell a horse Combe A hedstall and Raines 2*s*;

Item A mare 43*s* 4*d*;

Item an olde hurdell to swinge woolle 4*d*;

Item 12 olde Tressells 12*d*;

Sum 46*s* 8*d*.

In the lower Shoppe

Item a Shoppe Borde 2*s*;

Sum 2*s*.

[3] In the higher Shoppe

Item 3 paire of Stoke Cards with theire Stockes 2*s*;

Item A Beame with a paire of Schalles 12*d*;

Item 2 olde Cheares 8*d*;

Item A Turne 8*d*;

Item 20 pounde of white wooll 18*s* 4*d*;

Item 2 pounde of colorid wooll 2*s* 4*d*;

Item 2 Inche Bords and an olde planke 9*d*;

Sum 25*s* 9*d*.

Plate

Item 2 Gobletts of Silver percill gilte wayinge 24 oncs at 4*s* 10*d* the once £5 16*s*;

Item A Standinge Cuppe of Silver parcill gilte 14½ oncs starse wighte at 4*s* 10*d* the once £3 10*s*;

Item A Trencherde Salte all gilte one once and a halfe Bate thereof 4*d* – 6*s* 8*d*;

Item A white Silver Salte with a Cover 9¾ oncs at 4*s* 6*d* the once 41*s*;

Item 11 Silver Spounes with gilte knappes 14 oncs 3 quarters at 4*s* 4*d* the once £3 3*s* 11*d*;

Item A Bigge Stone Cuppe with a Silver Cover one once 3 quarters at 4*s* 4*d* the once and the Cuppe 4*d* – 7*s* 11*d*;

Item A Litell Stone Cuppe with a Cover mouthe and foote of Silver 4 onces at 4*s* 4*d* the once 17*s* 4*d*;

Item A Cover mouthe and foote of Silver for A Cuppe 4 oncs at 4*s* 4*d* the once 17*s* 4*d*;

Item A Bruche of Golde halfe an once at 52*s* the ounce 26*s*;

Item A Silver Tankerd 13 ouncs and a halfe Bate 4*d* at 5*s* the ounce £3 7*s* 2*d*;
Item in monye £9;
Sum £30 13*s* 4*d*.

Naperie
Item 2 Diaper Borde Clothes 15*s*;
Item 6 plaine Borde Clothes 10*s*;
Item a Dosen diaper napkins 10*s*;
Item a Doosen of ffyne frangid napkins 6*s*;
Item 22 coorse olde napkins 3*s* 4*d*;
Item a 11 pillowties 6*s* 8*d*;
Item a 11 Sheats 10*s*;
Item 5 Towells 7*s*;
Item A Cooborde Clothe with a frange and a Border of Stoole worke 5*s*;
Item 3 Sherts 2*s*;
Sum £3 15*s*.

Leasis
Item A Lease of the howse wherein he Dwellid at his Deathe of the which there is 51 yeares to come the Rente for the yeare is 53*s*;
Item there is more to be paide oute of the same howse Duringe the liffe of an olde woman 5*s* by the yeare;
Sum £40.

[3v.] Item A Lease of the howse wherein William Parsons nowe Dwellithe of the which there was to come the 4th Daie of Aprill Laste paste 16 yeares the Rente is 40*s* by the yeare £6 13*s* 4*d*;
Item A Lease of the Corner Shoppe under parte of the howse Laste above written of the which there was to come at midsomer Laste 8 yeares the Rente 20*s* by the yeare £4;
Sum £10 13*s* 4*d*.

Sum total £154 16*s*.

Debts Sperat and Desperat
Item Mr Thomas Williams Chauncelor 5*s* 8*d*;
Item Richerde Bartlett 19*s* 9*d*;
Item Mr John Upton 38*s* 6*d*;
Item Mr John Courtnaye 20*s*;
Item Mr John Sidnam of Brempton 40*s*;
Item Mr John Copleston of Lamberds Castell 38*s*;
Item Mr Chedson 14*s* 10*d*;
Item Richerd Hexte 20*s*;
Item William Grynwoode 7*s* 2*d*;
Item Mr Waller the minister 10*s* 6*d*;
Item Mrs Trelawnye thelder wyddoe 6*s* 8*d*;
Item Mr John Prouse of Clayforde 21*s* 10*d*;
Item John Bordfilde 4*s*;
Item Mr Snedall thelder 3*s*;
Item William Pannell 22*d*;
Item Mr Acklonde servaunte to Mr Amys Pawlett 4*s* 11*d*;
Item Mr Sidnam of Dulverton 4*s* 1*d*;
Item Mr Roberte Yoe 32*s* 7*d*;
Item Alexander Torker 40*s* 9*d*;
Item Mr Hercules Ameridethe 4*s* 8*d*;
Item Mr Markes Slader £4 19*s* 8*d*;
Item my Lorde Fytzwarren upon his Bill 47*s*;
[Item more to Hym as appereth by ye Boke £3 8*s* 4*d* – crossed through];
Item to hym more as appereth by the Boke £3 8*s* 4*d*;
Item more to Mr Sidnam of Brempton as apperethe by the Boke 9*s*;
Item Sir William Courtnaye 41*s* 9*d*;
Item Richarde Berrett of Bristowe merchaunte upon his Obligacon the Bande £30 – £24;
Item William Knolles 11*s*;
Item William Earle 8*s* 3*d*;
Item John Heale 5*s* 5*d*;
Item Stephen Hatche servaunte to Mr Trelawny 38*s* 3*d*;
Oliver Hoskyns 46*s* 8*d*;
Item John Carrewe 3*s*;
Item Humfrie the Tooker 2*s* 9*d*;
Item Mr Saunders of Brigwater 6*s* 5*d*;

Item Mr Amys Pawlett 4s 5d;

Item Mr John Tremaine 2s 6d;

Item the Curate of Upton Pyne 7s;

Item Richerde Hackley 43s 7d;

Item John Ameridethe 29s 4d;

Item Churchill sometyme servante to Mr Chidley 8s;

Item Fountaine sometyme servante to Mr Ayshe 17s 7d;

Item Hughe Sowithhaye 15s 11d;

Item Mr Kelley servaunte to Mr Trelawnye 2s 4d;

Item Sir John More Knighte 7s;

Item Mr Kyllegrewe 14d;

[4] Item Mr William Gibbes £4 2s 2d;

Item John Cater servaunte to Sir Thomas Denys 16d;

Item William Prise sometyme servaunte to Sir Peter Carewe 10s;

Item Mr Yeardley servaunte to my lorde Voysey Busshope of Exeter 18s;

Item Prescott servaunte to Sir John S[aint]tleger 10s;

Item Mr Richerde Fortescue 20d;

Item Mr Roger Tremayne 10s;

Item Mr Richarde Strechley 38s 10d;

Item Mr Roger Gyfforde 10s 4d;

Item Mr Pawlett sometymes servaunte to Mr Henrie Champernowne 20s;

Item Mr John Wyvell 7s 11d;

Item Mr William Arundell £3 15s 7½d;

Item Mr Tooker 2s 6d;

Item Mr Nicolas Fortescue 10s 2d;

Item John Rowlande the Baker 6s 6d;

Item Mr Wa[l]ter Rawley 5s 9d;

Item Mr John Raynolds 5s;

Item Edwarde Foxe 11s;

Item Mr Hughe Earthe [?] 11s;

Item Harknolle servaunte to Sir John Saintleger 4s 10d;

Item Garlonde servaunte to Sir John Saintleger 7s 8d;

Item Mr Giles Grainfilde 7d;

Item Mr Hexte of Staverton 2s 6d;

Item Mr Dawbney sometymes servaunte to Sir William Courtneye 4s;

Baker sometymes servaunte to Sir Richerde Chidley 8s 4d;

Item John Ameridethe 18s 10d;

Item Mr Richerde Dillon 7s;

Item Mr Carewe Courtneye 4s 8d;

Item Nicolas Benson 5s;

Item Roberte Norcott 20s 4d;

Item Roberte Grestoke 7s 11d;

Item Mr Rowpe 12s;

Item John Veysey 4s;

Item Mrs Carewe of Bickley 8d;

Item Rugge the dier 15s 8d;

Item Geraunce Bowhaye 20s 10d;

Item Thomas Richerds Taylor 9s 2d;

Item William Adams dothe owe to William Lante as hit Apperethe by his Bill 53s 9d;

Item Mr Thomas Harvy 17s;

Sum total of the debts sperat & desperat £95 8s 11½d.

Sum total £250 4s 11½d.

[4v.] The apparell of Wm Lante gevyn by legacye

Item a gowne facyd with taffata 12s;

Item a Jackyt gardyn with velvyt 5s;

Item a black cote edgyd with sattyn 3s 4d;

Item a spanyshe lether gerkyn 20d;

Item a sattyn doblett 5s;

Item a blacke cloke 4s;

Item A Cappe 16d;

Item A taffata hatte 2s;

Item a skene [?] 2s;

Item A boke of the new testament 8d;

Item a sygnett of golde 27s 6d;

[Item a pec of harnes 3s 4d – crossed through];

Sum £3 [7s 10d – crossed through] 4s 6d.

ECA, Orphans' Court Inventory 13 [Item 2]

[2] The Sum of the goods praysed £154 16*s*;
The gayne by the sale of the same £64 12*d*;
Sum total £218 17*s*.

Abate therof for his funeralls 15*s*;
Remaynith £218 2*s*;
The thridde [third] part therof £72 14*s*;
And yf the[y] will take place then take awte of the sayd thridd
part for the legacyes £8 18*s* 4*d* & for the debts £36 or nere
therabowte;
Sum of the legacies & debts £44 18*s* 4*d*.

Then Remaynith of that thridd part £27 15*s* 8*d* then put the
same to the Chyldernes thredde part wych is £72 14*s* the hole
for theyre part by this devycon £100 9*s* 8*d* besyde £6 gevyn to
three of the doughters.

And yf the[y] will be not alowyd then take awt of the hole
Som for the debts & funeralls £36 15*s* then remaynith £182 2*s*
devyde the same into 2 parts for the wyffe & the chylderne
the halfe therof for the Chylderne by this devycon £91 12*d*;
Memorandum that suche debts as were dew to theyre father as
yt may be recovered the Chylderne shall have 2 parts therof.

The will
I will and ordene that all my goods & leases to be solde &
to be devyded into three parts according to the order of this
Cyttye;
Item I geve to my gossyppe Heryt [?] my gowne faced with
taffata;
Item I geve to my gossyppe Kechell my Jackett gardyd with
velvyt;
Item I geve to my gossyppe Grenewod a black cote edgyd
with sattyn;
Item I geve to my Webbe [*sic*] my spanyshe lether Jerkyn;
Item I geve to Robert Dew my skene [?];

Item I geve to Alexander Tocker my boke of the new
testament;
Item I geve to my brother Randell Lant 26*s* 8*d*;
Item I geve to John Hondeler my Ryding cloke;
Item I geve to my fatherynlawe my best sattyn doblett;
Item I geve to John Bartlett my best Cappe;
Item I geve to Anastarye Bartlett my taffata hatte;
Item I geve to Papall [?] Bartlett 5*s* to mak hyr a Ryng with
all;
Item I geve to my elder soune John my sygnet of golde;
Item I geve to my three doughters to eche of them 40*s* a pece;
Item I geve to the pore 20*s* to be devydyd accordyng to the
dyscressyon of myne overseers;
Item I geve to the taylers hall a per of harnes & the Rest of my
part of the goods I will to paye my debts & legacyes & the
Rest to be devydyd equally emounge my chylderne;
Item I mak myne overseers my gossyppe Heryd [?] my
fatherynlaw Ric Bartlett my gossyppe Webbe & Wm
Grenewadde;
In wytnes wherof &c.

[3] The bill of sale of the goods of Wm Lant deceasyd
Firstly 2 peces of yelowe Kersey 50*s*;
Item a pere of yelowe stocks 16*d*;
Item a lyttell trencherde salt 7*s*;
Item a bruche of golde 26*s*;
Item a byble yn Inglyshe 8*s*;
Item 2 emtye hoggsheads & one tearse 4*s*;
Item 3 lyttell olde quosts & one tubbe 3*s*;
Item 3 colored Kerseis £5 8*s*;
Item one cowarse skye coler Kersey 26*s* 8*d*;
Item for fyve candelstycks 4*s* 2*d*;
Item for a fetherbedde a bolster 3 pelowis a wollyn blanket
and the best coverlett fyve £ syxe shelings eight penc – £5
6*s* 8*d*;
Item for a fetherbedde a bolster 2 pelowis a wollyn blankett
and a Redde coverlett fyftye shelings – 50*s*;
Item the second coverlett ten shelings 10*s*;

Item a brasyn morter 10*d*;

Item 2 flower potts 6*d*;

Item 2 pye plats 20*d*;

Item a lyttell bottell for *aqua composita* 2*s*;

Item for 2 chargers ten new platters & fyve new podyngers 15*s*;

Item a bason & yewer of tynne & a depe bason of tynne 5*s*;

Item a Joyned stole 10*d*;

Item for eight olde platters & 6 newe potage dyshes 9*s* 4*d*;

Item for 2 podyngers & 4 sausers 2*s* 8*d*;

Item a sylver salt wyth a cover 41*s* 9*d*;

Item the least fetherbedd with the bolster tester & a badde coverlett 20*s*;

Item one olde podynger & 2 olde saucers 13*d*;

Item a pere of olde tappers 2*d*;

Item 4 sausers & 2 podyngers 2*s* 8*d*;

Item 4 potage dysshes & 6 olde grene quosshens 4*s* 8*d*;

Item the chest yn the fore chamber 8*s*;

Item a bygge coffer yn the great chamber 4*s* 8*d*;

Item a pycheforke 4*d*;

Item a lyttell coffer 20*d*;

Item for 2 flowerpotts & an olde brokyn pynt potte 12*d*;

Item for 6 flowerpotts 21*d*;

Item a quart potte & halfe a pynt 18*d*;

Item a lyttell tablebord & an olde coffer 3*s*;

Item a lether Chere 3*s*;

Item a brewynge vate 16*d*;

Item a candelstyck to hange in the hall 2*s*;

Item a pottell potte of pewter 2*s*;

Item a lyttell tankerd of tynne withowt cover 6*d*;

Item 12 Inche bords 4*s*;

Item an Iron broche 16*d*;

Item the mouth fote & cover of sylver for a cuppe 17*s* 11*d*;

Item a dyaper tablecloth a towell & a dosyn of napkyns 40*s*;

Item a lyttell alde beame with a pere of skales to wey wolle withall 8*d*;

Sum £30 7*s* 8*d*.

[4] Item a grene Carpyt 2*s* 8*d*;

Item 2 gobletts parcell gylt £5 18*s*;

Item 6 sylver spones with knappes 36*s* 6*d*;

Item tenne olde pelowties 7*s*;

Item an olde dyaper bordeclothe 2*s* 6*d*;

Item a lyttell crewyt for vyneger 6*d*;

Item a drypping panne of Iron 12*d*;

Item a tablecloth of canvas 2*s*;

Item a brasse potte 5*s* 4*d*;

Item a longe cottrell 8*d*;

Item a lyttell olde Cauderne & 2 pere of potte hangings 12*d*;

Item an olde tubbe 2 olde pecks & 3 lyttell doggs of Iron 18*d*;

Item a olde cubbord 12*d*;

Item an olde pere of tongs & 2 lyttell cottrells 10*d*;

Item an olde coffer an olde flockbedd a bolster 2 old whyt Ruggs & a welshe hoke 8*s* 10*d*;

Item an old grydyron 2 lyttell Irons to turne the broche yn 14*d*;

Item an old welshe hoke 6*d*;

Item a salt of tynne with a cover 9*d*;

Item a Joyned forme 16*d*;

Item a carpyt for the longe bord 15*s*;

Item 6 quosshyns with Roses 12*s*;

Item a Joyned forme 11*d*;

Item an olde Russett gowne 6*s*;

Item a coffer 18*d*;

Item a bedstedd 10*s*;

Item a turne to spynne withall 11*d*;

Item a brasse panne 8*s*;

Item 22 olde napkyns 3*s* 4*d*;

Item a chafyngdyshe with a fote & a hurdell to swyng wolle on 5*s*;

Item a lyttell panne of brasse 2*s* 4*d*;

Item a custerde dyshe 14*d*;

Item an olde bordcloth a towell & a pelowtye 4*s*;

Item a Cawderne 2*s*;

Item an olde blew mantell 16*d*;

Item a lyttell coffer 16*d*;

Item a forme 8*d*;

Item a lyttell cauderne 18*d*;
Item an olde quarte potte & a pynt 14*d*;
Item for 60 lb of fethers 25*s*;
Item for fyve lyttell sausers 15*d*;
Item a hoper [?] boxe of wall [? wool] 2*d*;
Item an olde powdryng tubbe 6*d*;
Item a troclebedstede 4*s* 6*d*;
Item an old coffer 6*d*;
Item an olde lanterne 2*d*;
Item 2 olde podyngers & 2 sausers 18*d*;
Item 6 Inchebords 2*s*;
Sum £15 6*s* 10*d*.

[5] Item an olde knytte petycote 16*d*;
Item 2 olde grene curteines 6*d*;
Item a bedstede 7*s*;
Item a dosyn frute trencherds 4*d*;
Item a lyttell olde brokyn skyllett 4*d*;
Item a Crocke 4*s*;
Item ten flower potts 2*s*;
Item 3 olde sherts 2*s*;
Item 11 olde shets 10*s*;
Item a pere of andIrons & a backe of Iron 13*s* 4*d*;
Item a cubbordcloth with a frynge of stole work 5*s*;
Item 2 old curteynes of straked caunvas [?] 8*d*;
Item an old brandIron 6*d*;
Item an old fryeng panne 6*d*;
Item a grater for the Kechyn 4*d*;
Item a lyttell byrdbroche 4*d*;
Item 8½ yards of vassye coler Kersey 24*s* 1*d*;
Item 6½ yards of Russett Kersey 18*s* 9*d*;
Item a yard [and] ½ of black Kersey 6*s*;
Item a yard of grene bayes 18*d*;
Item a lokyng glasse 2*s*;
Item a tablebord 3*s* 6*d*;
Item 3 hoggsheads 5*s*;
Item 2 old tearses 16*d*;
Item an olde hoggsheade & an olde tearse 2*s* 2*d*;
Item a pype 2*s*;

Item a dosyn of cowarse carnacon Kersey 18*s*;
Item an old water tankerd 6*d*;
Item a dosyn of black Kersey 40*s*;
Item a yard 3 quarters of carnacon Kersey 6*s*;
Item halfe a yard & halfe a quarter of stamyn [?] 16*d*;
Item 6 yards 3 quarters of Inglyshe stamyn [?] 33*s* 9*d*;
Item 6 yards of ashe coler Kersey 24*s*;
Item ½ yard of cawarse black 8*d*;
Item 2 yards quarter of osett redde 2*s* 8*d*;
Item 4 yards of olde blacke fyrse 2*s* 8*d*;
Item 2 yards quarter of olde grene bockram 8*d*;
Item 20 lb of whyt wolle 18*s* 4*d*;
Item 2 lb of colored wolle 2*s* 4*d*;
Item a pere of harnes 11*s*;
Item an olde saddell with headstall & Reynes 2*s* 6*d*;
Item a shoppe bord 3*s* 4*d*;
Item a mare 44*s* 4*d*;
Item a brasen crocke 7*s*;
Item a standyng cuppe of sylver parcell gylt £3 10*s*;
Item a lyttell stone cuppe with a mouth cover & fote of sylver
    17*s* 4*d*;
Item a sylver tankerd £3 7*s* 2*d*;
Item a Redd carpytt 3*s*;
Item 12 old t[r]essells & an old borde 18*d*;
Sum £24 11*s* 7*d*.

[6] Item an olde communion boke 4*d*;
Item an olde tubbe 4*d*;
Item an olde longe coffer 16*d*;
Item a plumpe of leade 3*s*;
Item a gawne faced with damaske £3;
Item an olde pottell potte of pewter 14*d*;
Item a crok of brasse 6*s*;
Item 2 olde cheres 8*d*;
Item a spanyshe cloke 23*s* 4*d*;
Item an olde panne of brasse & a lyttell old skelytt 5*s* 6*d*;
Item for an other Skellytt 2*s*;
Item a presse for Kerseys 2*s*;
Item an old pere of stock cardes with theyre stocks 16*d*;

Item a gowne faced with taffata 15*s*;

Item an old Kersey doblett 2*s*;

Item the hangyngs of the chamber withyn the hall of saye 33*s* 4*d*;

Item a remanant of a butte of secke contening by estemacon 50 gallons £3;

Item a remanant of a butte of muscadell 40*s*;

Item the lease of the great howse with these Implemets folowing the sylings of the hale & borders with a buttre syled & a cobbord with a presse yn yt & 2 table bords yn the same with a Joyned portall yn the chamber next withyn the halle & the hangings of the chamber over the parler of paynted clothis & the hangings of the parler of paynted clothis with the table bord with the benches & sylings there – £100;

Item for the lease of the corner howse with the 2 shoppes £14 10*s*;

Item yn Redy money £9;

Item for the bedstede in the chamber withyn the hall with fyve curtaynes of Redde and grene sarsenett 58*s*;

Item for fyve sylver spones 27*s* 7*d*;

Item for foure cowarse skye coler Kerseys £7;

Item for an old Cubbord 12*d*;

Item a trocle bedsted 18*d*;

Item 2 pere of old stocke cards with theyre stocks 16*d*;

Item 2 old table clothis 2 old cubbord clothis & 3 old towells 3*s* 4*d*;

Item a stone cuppe with a sylver cover 7*s* 6*d*;

Item 3 bords yn the Ketchyn with 2 shelfes 2*s*;

Item a lyttell broche 4*d*;

Item a cope for pultre 12*d*;

Sum £148 10*s* 11*d*.

Sum total £218 16*s*.

ECA, Orphans' Court Inventory 13 [Item 3]

The Inventorie of the goodds & cattalls of William Lante late of the citie of Exon decessed 1569

Goodds housholde stuff £51 8*s* 7*d*;

Plate £21 13*s* 4*d*;

Money £9;

Debts owed to the testator £95 8*s* 11½*d*;

Wares £22 4*s* 9*d*;

Leasses £50 13*s* 4*d*;

Apparell geven yn Legacys £3 17*s* 6*d*;

£254 2*s* 5½*d*.

Whereof

In debts sperat & debts desperat £95 4*s* 11½*d*;

Also the testator dyd owe £33 6*s* 5*d*;

£128 11*s* 4½*d*;

So remaineth £125 11*s* 1½*d*.

Geven yn legacys £12 9*s* 6*d*;

So there remaineth to be devided £113 19½*d*.

Which £113 19½*d* beinge devided yn to 3 equall parts there amount to everie part as foloweth:

To the wyff for her part £37 13*s* 10½*d*;

To the children for the 2 parts £75 7*s* 9*d*;

£113 19½*d*.

By which divisyon there cometh to everye of the children being tenne yn nomber as foloweth:

To Geffrey Lante for his porcon £7 10*s* 9¼*d*;

To George Lant for his porcon £7 10*s* 9¼*d*;

To John thelder for his porcon £7 10*s* 9¼*d*;

To him for his legacy 27*s* 6*d*;

£8 18*s* 3¼*d*;

To John the yonger £7 10*s* 9¼*d*;

To William Lant for his porcon £7 10*s* 9¼*d*;

To Thomas Lant £7 10*s* 9¼*d*;

To Ursula for her porcon £7 10*s* 9¼*d*;

To her for her legacie 40*s*;

£9 10*s* 9¼*d*;

To Mary for her porcon £7 10*s* 9¼*d*;

To her for her legacy 40*s*;

£9 10s 9¼d;
To Grace for her porcon £7 10s 9¼d;
To her for her legacy 40s;
£9 10s 9¼d;
To Jone for her porcon £7 10s 9¼d;
To her for her mothers third £37 13s 10½d;
£45 4s 7¾d.

[verso] The goodds of William Lant bysids the debts
The goodds housholde stuff leasses wars plat & money £154 16s;
Which devyded in to 3 parts every part is £37 12s 4d [?];
Whereof to the wyffe £38 5s 4d;
To the children £38 5s 4d;
To the admynestrator £38 5s 4d;
Sum £154 16s.

Of which thadmynestrators part is to be deducted for legacys

£8 11s 8d;
Also for debts by estymacon £35;
Sum [blank].

To the wiff £51 12s;
To the chyldren £51 12s;
To the admynestrators parte £51 12s;
£154 16s.

Of thadmynestrators part deduct for the legacys £8 11s 8d;
Also for debt by estymation £35;
£43 11s 8d.

So remaineth £8 4d which with the 3rd is £59 12s;
So then to the wyffs child for her mothers part £51 12s;
For her childes part of the father £5 8s 2½d.

20. INVENTORY OF HARRY WALCOTE, OF ST KERRIAN'S PARISH, 30 OCTOBER 1569

ECA, Orphans' Court Inventory 14
Note: Recognisances were entered into on 5 November 1570 regarding John, Richard, Alice, Mary and Agnes, the children of Harry 'Wolcott' (ECA, Book 141, folio 36. Also see folio 31).

Thys ys the Inventery of all the goods cattells & debts of Harry Walcote of the parishe of St Kyryions in the Citty of Exeter late Decessed made & preysed by us Robert Chaffe & John Martyn the 30th day of October In the yere of our lord god 1569 And the 11 yere of the raigne of our Sovereigne Lady Elizabeth by the grace of god of Ingland Frannce & Ireland queen & defender of the fayth &c

Firstly A Carvyd bedstede A trokellbed a fetherbed a bolster 4 pylloes of fethers a Coverlett of Tapystry a whyt lynen tester and thre Courtens of whyt lynen 40s;
Item a shorte tabell borde uppon a frame a Juned forme & a Juned stole with 2 olde carpets 13s 4d;

Item a cupborde with a Cupbord cloth 8s;
Item too chests 6s 8d;
Item 8 payer of shetes and one odd shete thre bordeclothes too Canvas towells 6 pyllotyes 6 bord napkyns & thre hand Towells with 2 olde Coverlets 33s 4d;
Item too payer of blankets 6s 8d;
Item too spruse chests 20s;
Item a gowne fased with budge 2 cassakes one of mocado & the other of cloth 3 olde Jerkyns too dubletts a cloke thre payer of hose too cappes & a hatt 26s 8d;
Item a too hand sworde & a backesworde 10s;
Item a bedstede A paynted tester an olde quylte & a olde mantell 6s 8d;

Item A Coverlet of Tapstry with thre curtens of paynted callocowe clothe 16*s*;

Item a flockebedd a bolster of fethers 2 bolsters of flocks & one flock pyllow 6*s* 8*d*;

Item A Turned chayer 4*d*;

Item A haquebutt with a box 8*s*;

Item a lytyll square borde 16*d*;

Item a shorte Tabell borde uppon a frame with a Juned forme 10*s*;

Item A nother olde flockebedd 3*s* 4*d*;

Item a basen & ever of Tynne 4*s*;

Item 6 platers 2 podyngers & 12 sawcers with 2 plates 12*s*;

Item 21 podysshe dysshes & a butter dysshe of Tynne 8*s*;

Item 2 pottell potts 2 quarte potts a pynte a halffe pynt 2 pynt Tancards a halffe pynt Tancard A wassinge bason 4 flower potts too Salts & too water potts of Tynne 6*s* 8*d*;

Item 7 candelsticks good & badd 3*s* 4*d*;

Item 5 crocks of brasse too cawdrens too lytyll pannes A posnet a broch too payer of pott hookes & crowkes a gredyron a flasshe hooke a chafing dysshe a fryeng panne a scummer a ladell & a payer of doggs 40*s*;

Item a olde coffer 12*d*;

Item a goblet of Silver parcell gilt wayeng 17 unces £4 2*s* 2*d*;

Item more 6 spones of Silver callyd Slyppes 28*s*;

Item one goblett of Silver £3 10*s*.

Sum total inventory £23 2*s* 2*d*.

21. WILL OF ELIZABETH BRICKENELL ALIAS TAYLOR, WIDOW, 30 OCTOBER 1569

Orphans Court Will 14

[1] 1569
In the name of god Amen the 30 daie of October in the Eleventh yere of the Raigne of our soveraigne ladie Elizabeth by the grace of god quene of England Fraunce & Irelond defender of the ffaith &c I Elizabeth Brickenall of the Cyttye of Exceter Widowe beying of perfytt mynde & memory thanckes be unto almyghtie god make and ordeyne this my last Wyll & Testament in maner & forme as foloweth: ffirst I Comytt my Sowle in to handes of almyghtie god my Saviour & Redemer & my Body to buried in St Thomas Churchyard Item y geve & bequeth to Symon Taillor my Sone the leasse & terme of yeres Whiche I have yet to Come of & yn the Tenement wt thapptennces wheryn y nowe dwell Item I geve & bequeth to the said Symon ffyve poundes of lawfull money of Englond Whiche remayneth yn my brother John Duckes handes Item I geve & bequeth to Margaret servaunt to John Courtes Cordewayner one Red petycot Cloth Item y geve & bequeth to Ellyn my servaunte my best Cloth kyrtell Item y geve & bequeth to my brother John Duckes Eldest daughter my best gowne Item y geve & bequeth to his daughter Thomasyn my wosted kyrtell wt damaske bodies & my best petycot wt Taffiti bodies Item I geve & bequeth to John Tremayn is wyffe my Second best petycote Item y geve & bequeth to Isebrand Grenes wyffe my third best petycot Item y geve & bequeth to Wylmot my servant [3 kerches – crossed through] three kerchers three Neckerchers & a petycott Item y geve & bequeth to John Goby *[2]* my servaunte a pere of hosen & a doblet Item y my Wyll [*sic*] is that my overseers shall bestowe towardes the poore people threscore dossen of 6*d* The residue of all my goods moveable & unmoveable not geven nor bequethed my funeralles paid I do wholy geve & bequeth to my said Sone Symon & to the Childe wherewt all y nowe goo And them y make & ordeyne to be my Executors of this my said Wyll & Testament Item y make Constitute & ordeyne my overseers my brother John Ducke & William Lange of Ken [?] & y geve & bequeth to every of them for

their paynes 2s a pece In witnes hereof John Hole John Courtes & Robert Copland.

[3]
Dettes owed unto me Elizabeth Bricknall as foloweth

Inprimis William Brickenall oweth me for a gowne whiche he bought of me in price of 36s 8d;

Item more [blank] Thatcher of Ken oweth for 10 lb & a halff of yarne at 20d the pound 17s 6d;

Item more John Ector oweth for foure dossen of whit bred 4s;

Item more he oweth for [illegible] [dossen of – crossed through] horsse bred [18d – crossed through] 14d;

Item John Saterley [?] oweth for bred 3s 4d;

Item William Milford Capper oweth for 6 dossen of horssebred 6s;

Item John Hunte Carpynter oweth for bred 2s 8d;

Item more for bred 18d;

Item Ambrosse Howell oweth for 5 dossen of [horssebred – crossed out] whit bred 5s;

Item a mason dwellyng yn John James house the Shomaker oweth me for bred 2s 8d;

Item Jesper Rede my servaunte oweth uppon a Skore betwene hym & me 38s.

M[emoran]d[um] there remayneth yn my brother John Duckes Custody a pere of Bedes of Corell Bawdred wt Sylver whiche were geven to my said Sone Symon by his ffather James Taillors wyll and one [gold – crossed out] ryng wt a Signet.

Item Richard Robyns of Alphington oweth me for a moyle [?] whiche he bought of me in price of 20s–10s.

Sum £6 8s 6d.
[4] M[emoran]d[um] that the 21th daye of November in the yere of our lord god a Thousand fyve hundred threscore & nyne and yn the 12th yere of the Raigne of our Soveraigne lady quene Elizabeth that nowe is Elizabeth Bricknall Wydowe

after the makyng of her last Wyll & Testament dyd geve & bequeth over & bysides her legasy mensioned yn her said last Wyll & Testament These parcelles of goodes hereafter ensuyng That is to Weyt I geve & bequeth to Cables wyffe a Smocke Item I geve to Saterley [?] a bearyng Blancket Item y geve one other bearyng bancket [*sic*] to Toker Item y geve to Johan Hunt my old Cassacke Item y geve to Anne my servaunte my Cloth kyrtell Item y geve unto Elizabeth Marten one Smocke & a blacke apron Item y geve unto Thomasyn Courtes my best hatt Item y geve unto my said servaunt Anne and Wylmote too peare of Sylver Hokes Item y geve to Johan Taillour my other best pyn' & a peare of Hokes Item y geve & bequeth to the said Wylmote a pere of grograyne slevys & a whit apron & a whit petycot Item y geve to Johan Chard one old red petycot Item y geve to Isebran' Grenes wyffe one Red petycote Item I geve to Jesper my servaunte a pere of hosen

Dettes owed unto me

Inprimis Style the Toker oweth me 19d;
Item Xpian [?] Hethfild 8d;
Item Richard Ambrose 9d;
Also I forgeve halff the dept of Touker whiche is 10s;
Stansby oweth me 13d;
Harry Poore 2s 4d;
John Ector 2s 3d;
Thatcher of Ken oweth for 9 lb & 3 quarters of yerne at 18d the pound 14s 3d ob[olus] & more he oweth 18d – 15s 9d ob[olus];
Sum 34s 5½d.

[1] Thomas Wyllyams, official of Robert Fisher: John Ducke and William Lange, supervisors of the last will of Elizabeth Bryckenell *alias* Taylor, lately of the parish of St [lost], Exeter, widow, are also constituted as executors of that will. They are to well and faithfully administer all and singular the goods of the deceased during the minority of Simon. They are to administer the same according to the will, and they are to

collect, levy and demand the debts due to her and to use the same to pay the debts which she owed. An inventory of her goods and chattels is to be made.

Dated 2? [part of figure obscured at edge of page] November 1569.

22. INVENTORY OF HUGH POPE, OF ST KERRIAN'S PARISH, 15 FEBRUARY 1570

ECA, Orphans' Court Inventory 12

Note: The register of St Kerrian recorded the burial of 'Mr Hughe Pope' on 10 February 1570. It also noted that the plague occurred that year. Recognisances were entered into on 17 April 1570 regarding his children Bartholomew, William, John and Thomas (ECA, Book 141, folio 28).

The Inventorie of all & **singuler** the gooddes cattalls and debtes which lately apperteyned unto Hughe Pope late of the parrishe of Sainte Kyrian within the Citie of Excester decessed Made & praysed by John Redwodd John Budley, Godfrey Harman and John Felde. The 15th daye of February in the yeare of oure Lorde god a thowsande ffyve hundred three score and and [*sic*] Nyne, and in the twelveth yeare of the reigne of oure sovereigne Ladye Queene Elizabeth &c

[m. 1] **In the Haule**
Firstly a cubborde 20*s*;
Item a tableborde 6*s* 8*d*;
Item an other litle cubborde 2*s* 4*d*;
Item a cheste 8*s*;
Item a litle coffer 12*d*;
Item the Bynches 6*s* 8*d*;
Item a forme and a chayer 12*d*;
Item a carpet and 3 cussions 2*s*;
Item the stayned clothes 2*s*;
Item in the chymney one barr of Iron 2 doggs of Iron, a ffyershovell a payer of tonges, 2 crokes of Iron 12*d*;
Item 2 basons and one ewer of pewter 3*s*;
Item 2 cubborde clothes 8*d*;
Sum 54*s* 4*d*.

Fig. 15. Hugh Pope lived in St Kerrian's, a parish composed largely of long narrow properties on Northgate (now North) Street. Edward Ashworth's painting shows Nos 18–20 North Street in 1887. *(courtesy of the Devon and Exeter Institution).*

In the parler
Item a presse 20*s*;
Item a bedstede 15*s*;
Item a cubborde 3*s* 4*d*;
Item a coffer 3*s* 4*d*;
Item 2 litle coffers 12*d*;
Item a tableborde 4*s*;
Item 2 bynches 2*s* 6*d*;
Item 2 ffetherbeddes and 2 bolsters 26*s* 8*d*;
Item 4 pyllowes 2*s*;
Item 3 curtyns of saye with 3 roddes of Iron 5*s*;
Item 2 coverletts & a payer of blancketts 3*s* 4*d*;
Item a chayer and 2 stoles 8*d*;
Item a forme 6*d*;
Item a bason and a ewer 20*d*;
Item a cubberde clothe 4*d*;
Item the stayned hangyngs 12*d*;
Item 2 coverlets & a payer of blanckets 10*s*;
Item 1 barr & 2 doggs of Iron in the chymney 8*d*;
Item 6 cusshyns 12*d*;
Sum £5 2*s*.

In the chamber over the parler
Item a presse 4*s*;
Item a bedstede and a trokelbed 5*s*;
Item 6 coffers 2*s*;
Item 2 fosletts 6*d*;
Item a rounde borde, and a carpet 10*d*;
Item 4 ffetherbeddes 26*s* 8*d*;
Item 2 bolsters & 4 pyllowes 2*s*;
Item 2 cusshyn clothes 3*s* 4*d*;
Sum 44*s* 4*d*.

In the chamber over the shopp
Item a corselet, and 2 almon ryvets and a pyke 26*s* 8*d*;
Item 2 bylls, a sherehooke 2 olde sordes and other trasshe 2*s*;
Sum 28*s* 8*d*.

In the chamber over the spynnyng howse

Item a bedstede 2 formes, & other trasshe 2*s*;
Item 3 bowes, and a sheafe of arrowes 20*d*;
Sum 3*s* 8*d*.

[m. 2] Pewter vessell
Item 2 dozen of platters 12*s*;
Item 6 pottengers 2*s* 6*d*;
Item one dozen of potage dysshes 4*s*;
Item 14 square dysshes 5*s*;
Item 2 dozen and fower sawcers 4*s*;
Item one dozen plates, and one dosen of Jelly dysshes 6*s*;
Item 6 olde pottyngers, and an olde bason 2*s*;
Item 5 pottell potts 5*s*;
Item 2 quarte potts and 2 pynte potts and an olde pott 2*s*;
Item 6 flower potts 12*d*;
Item 13 candlestickes 6*s*;
Sum 49*s* 6*d*.

In the kytchyn and in the spynning howse
Item 11 crockes 40*s*;
Item 5 cawdrons 8*s*;
Item 4 pannes a skyllet, & 2 skymmers 10*s*;
Item 5 olde basons of brasse 2 chafendysshes and a flower pott 4*s*;
Item 2 dryppyng pannes & a fryeng pan a grydiron and 2 potthookes 20*d*;
Item a brason morter 4*d*;
Item 3 spynnyng tornes 12*d*;
Item a cubborde and a coffer 12*d*;
Item 3 broches & 2 andyrons 6*s* 8*d*;
Item a crowe of Iron 12*d*;
Item olde tymber and bordes 20*s*;
Item tubbes and other trasshe 3*s* 4*d*;
Sum £4 17*s*.

In the backside and in two other howses in Northgatestreate
Item a ryke of woode, and a pyle of stones in the backside £3 6*s* 8*d*;
Item tymber and bordes, being in a lynny in the backside of

Thomas Jordyns howse in Northgatestreate £4;
Item 2 olde cubberdes, and one borde in John Jones howse in Northgatestreate 4s;
Sum £7 10s 8d.

In a **litle chamber** behinde the parler
Item a trokelbedstede with a flockbed 16d;
Item a coffer 8d;
Item a halfe hundred wayght of ledd and a quartern 4s;
Item a Sestron of ledd 18s;
Sum 24s.

In the Shopp
Item a cubborde 10s;
Item wole 8s;
Item litle tubbes and other trasshe 12d;
Sum 19s.

Apparell
Item a blacke gowne welted with velvet 26s 8d;
Item a blacke gowne furred with lame 13s;
Item a dublet of tawnye sattyn with vellet sleves 13s 4d;
Item an olde velvet dublet with bramiche [?] damaske sleves of tawnye 5s;
Item a wosted dublet 2s;
Item a chamlet Jacket garded with velvet 8s;
Item an olde wosted Jacket of wosted [sic] 2s;
Item an olde gowne faced with fox 5s;
Sum £3 15s.

[m. 3] In naperye
Item 11 payer of Sheetes 20s;
Item 2 diaper bordeclothes 8s;
Item 6 bordeclothes 12s;
Item 9 towells [blank];
Item 15 olde diaper napkyns 4s;
Item a dozen and a halfe of canvas napkyns and one dozen of morles clothe 5s;

Item 6 pylloweties 2s;
Item 3 cubberde clothes 3s;
Item a tablecloth for a rounde borde and fower handetowells 10d;
Item 2 shyrtes 3s 4d;
Sum £3 6s 2d.

Plate
Item a salte of sylver, with a cover gylte conteyning 36 ounces and a quarter at 4s 10d the ounce £8 15s 2½d;
Item a standing cupp of sylver with a cover gylte containing 29 ounces and a halfe at 4s 10d the ounce £7 2s 7d;
Item 2 covers and 2 feete of sylver & gylt to two stone cupps containing 10 ounces at 4s 10d the ounce 48s 4d;
Item 2 covers and 2 feete of sylver and gylte to 2 litle stone cupps conteyning bothe 5 ouncs at 4s 10d the ounce 24s 2d;
Item a cover of a litle whyte cuppe of stone, sylver and gylte containing one ounce 4s 10d;
Item 2 bowles of sylver parcell gylte containing 27 ounces & a quarter at 4s the ounce £5 9s;
Item 2 saltes of sylver parcell gylte containing 31 ounces at 4s the ounce £6 4s;
Item a masser the edge of sylver and gylte containing one ounce 4s;
Item 4 gobletts of sylver parcell gylte containing 50 ounces & a halfe at 4s the ounce £10 2s;
Item 2 dozen of sylver spones and one containing 28 ounces at 4s the ounce £5 12s;
Sum £47 6s 1½d.

Leases
Item the assignement of a lease of twoo tenements wherin John Filde and John Martyn taylor doeth nowe enhabit, in Northgatestreate of the which ther was to come at mychalmas laste 33 yeres the rente of bothe is £4 13s 4d – £6;
Item a lease of 2 gardens one lyinge behinde Robert Lambetts howse, in Saint Powles parrishe, and the other lyeth

behinde Mr Yeoes howse in the parishe of Saint Johns Bowe, the rente of bothe is 5*s* 4*d* of which ther is to come about the terme of 60 yeares 40*s*;

Item a lease of a seller by the Brode Gate in Excester, nowe in the teanure of John Well taylor 13*s* 4*d*;

Sum £8 13*s* 4*d*.

Sum of all gooddes and cattals £91 13*s* 9½*d*.

Sperate debtes and Desparate debtes

Firstly Robert Drewe of Exon oweth £4 10*s* behinde of an obligacion to be paied 10*s* a quarter – £4 10*s*;

Item Thomas Fitzdavye *alias* James of Exon oweth by obligacion £10;

Item John Webb, and the saide Thomas Fitzdavy owes by obligacion £20;

Item Richarde Keyser by Northgate 40*s*;

Item Richarde Mayo oweth £8 to be payed eight yeares hence £8;

Item John Pill of Exon and Richarde Whytinge owes by a bill £22;

Item [blank] Flynge of Newton Saint Seers 8*s*;

Item John Tooker merchant of the parishe of Saint Oules, by a bill obligatorie £8;

Item Mistris Staplehyll wydowe £5;

Item Richarde Wylcocks 53*s* 4*d*;

[m. 4] Item Ralfe Sandyforth £6;

Item William Scobbell 20*s*;

Item George Frenche of Kyngesbridge Anthony Thomas of Exon & William Frenche of Kingesbridge £6 13*s* 4*d*;

Item Jane Hewet wydowe £4;

Sum £100 4*s* 8*d*.

Sum totall of all gooddes cattalls and debtes amounts to £191 18*s* 5½*d*.

[Signs of] John Redwodde John Bodley

By me [signatures of] Godfre Herman John Felde

Wherof ther is to be allowed, as followeth

Firstly the saide testator owed at the tyme of his decesse to Elizabeth Helyer his sarvante £3 6*s* 8*d*;

Item to William Lange late of Exon £8;

Sum £11 6*s* 8*d*.

Funerall expences

Item paied for mornyng blackes and other charges aboute the buryall £12 9*d*;

Item to the poore 40*s*;

Item to the overseers 20*s*;

Sum £15 9*d*.

23A. WILL OF ARNOLD REYNOLD, SHOEMAKER OF ALLHALLOWS IN GOLDSMITH STREET PARISH, 8 AUGUST 1570

ECA, Orphans' Court Will 15

Note: 16 is a copy of this will. The register for the parish of Allhallows Goldsmith Street was burnt in the war but an earlier transcript published by the Devon & Cornwall Record Society in 1933 recorded 'Arnold Reynold' was buried on 17 October 1570. On 5 October 1570 recognisances were entered into for William and Richard, the sons of Arthur 'Renell' (ECA, Book 141, folio 34).

In the name of god amen the 8th day of August in the yere of our lord god a thowsand fyve hundred threescore and tenne I Arnold Reynnold of the parrish of Allhallowes in Goldsmyth Streate within the cyttie of Exeter shomaker beinge hole of mynd perfet of remembrance thanks be geven to almightie god do revoke adnychillate & make voyd all former willes

Fig. 16. Goldsmith Street, the street between St Paul's and Allhallows, where the cordwainer Arnold Reynold lived (OC 15), shown in Braun and Hogenburg's view of the city (*courtesy of Exeter City Museums*).

and legacyes by me heretofore made and doe make this my laste will and testament in manner and forme folowinge ffirst I bequeath my soule to almightie god and my bodie to holy grave Item I geve and bequeathe to the poore people of Exeter £3 6*s* 8*d* Item I geve and bequethe to my wief Julyan tenne powndes of laufull money of England and all my howshold stuffe in consideracion of all and singuler her parte porcyon of my goods that may growe unto her by reason she is my wief and no more for that she hath myche mysused me when she was dwellinge with me and spoyled me of suche goods as I had for which causes and dyvers others I have apoynted

her the legacyes above wryten and that she shall not make or medle with any part or percell of my goods otherwise then the said legacies by me before to her given. Item I geve to my man Laurence Mathew £4. The residue of all my goods, chattels & dets whatsoever my dets, legacyes & funerals discharged I doe geve and bequeathe to William Reynold, Rychard Reynold, and Elizabeth Reynold my children whome I make my executors equallie to be devyded amonge them by my overseers hereunder wryten at suche tyme and when as they and everye of them shall severallye accomplishe the age of twenty & fower yeres & not before. Item, I do no[m]i[n]ate & apoynt my fryndes Harry James and Hewghe Wylson to be the overseers of this my present Testament & laste will charginge and requyringe them in gods name to take all my said goods c[h]attels & dets into there safe custody & kepinge presently upon my Deathe and they to pay and Delyver the same as I have above apoynted to my wief and children and no[t] otherwise, & for there paynes takynge in the same I do geve unto every of my overseers 20*s*. In wytnes this to be of trewghe I have to this my will put my seale and marke being witness

[Sign of] wytnes William Hunte
[Sign of] Gustas Olyver.
Agreed with the original will and witnessed by Henry James, Notary Public, sworn by me Thomas Williams, official of the Archdeacon of Exeter.

23B. INVENTORY OF ARNOLD REYNOLDE, CORDWAINER OF ALLHALLOWS IN GOLDSMITH STREET PARISH, 30 SEPTEMBER 1570

ECA, Orphans' Court Inventory 16

This is the Invletory of all the goods and cattells of Arnolde Reynolde Dwellynge in Goldesmythe Stret made the laste daye of September in the 12 yeare of the Raigne of our soveraigne ladye Elizabethe by the grace of god quene of

England Frannce and Irelond defender of the faythe &c

Firstly a hundred pound in angelets in on bige;
Item 3 score pound ten pound and a marke of that 3 score

pound and ten pound and a marke ther ar 29 Riolds and 29 angelets of that golde William Reynoldes must have a mark and Richard Reynoldes must have a marke geven to them by a kynsman that did die in my house;

Item geven unto Besse Reynold 26s of her kynsman that did die in my house;

Item a hundred pound of whit mony in a shert slefe;

Item £1 of whyt mony in another shert slefe;

Item £13 of spanyshe monye in a littell byge.

Off all dettes

Item lond to master Robert Hunt upon a goblete duble gelt £6;

Item lond to Thomas Germon upon 2 golde Rynges one withe a blue stone and an other withe a littell stone £3 8s 4d;

Item lond to John Scinner of Tavlnebriddge upon a salt of selver 26s 8d;

Item lond to Harrye Robarts upon a selver cupe 40s;

Item lond to Harrye Tanne upon a goune 40s;

Item a byll of oblitory of Thomas Germons of £5 lacke 8d;

Item a byll of oblitary of Harrye Robarts of £3 6s;

Item a byll of oblitory of master Lennet and master Nicholas Marten of 40s.

24. INVENTORY OF RICHARD TAYLOR ALIAS FARRINGDON, CORDWAINER, 30 OCTOBER 1570

ECA, Orphans' Court Inventory 17

Note: Recognisances were entered into on 21 November 1572 regarding Esayae Taylor, the child of Richard 'Taylor *alias* Farryngdon' (ECA, Book 141, folio 35).

The Inventories of all and singular the goods Chattells And leases of Richarde Taillor otherwise Farringdon late of the countie and citie of Exeter deceassed cordewayner praised the thirtie daie of October, the yeere of our lorde god a thowsande ffyve hundreth and seventie by Richarde Moggridge, Warnarde Harrissoune, Roberte Toocker And Richarde Bowdon the daie and tyme abovesaide

[1] Stuffe in Johan Peeters shoppe

Firstly Woode in the same shoppe 3s 4d;

Item 6 hogsheads 5 withoute heads 4s;

Item 2 litle tubs and salte in them 12d;

Item a litle Standarde with a cover 12d;

Item 2 litle dawe tubs, and a litle tub of lyme 4d;

Item a trie to sette Bacon in 2s;

Item a Hamper full of Shreds and a Bridell 12d;

Item an Earthen Crocke, and tallowe in the same 4d;

Sum 13s.

Stuffe in the lower Bowure

Firstly a white strakede featherbede and a Bolster to the Same 14s;

Item another featherbed, and a Bolster to the same 15s;

Item a cubborde with a Shilf 6s;

Item a table borde and a frame 5s;

Item a fourme 12d;

Item a Carpette 6d;

Item Seallings and Binches 23s 4d;

[2] Item a Bedsteade, and a Borde by the hearth 16d;

Item a Staignede cloth about the howse 2s 6d;

Item 2 iron dogs, and a tongs 16d;

Item a cheste in the same Bowure 8s;

Sum £3 17s.

Apparell

Firstly a gowne of london Russette laced and faced 38s;

Item a gowne of Browne Blewe faced with Budge 38s;

Item a cloke of fyne Blacke, with a Standinge coller 30s;

Item a Blacke cloke with a cape 6s;
Item a cloke of a sad newe cullor 4s;
Item a dubblette with tawnie damaske Sleeves 4s;
Item a dubblette of Blacke Kersye 4s;
Item a pair of hose of Black Kersy 4s 8d;
Item a cappe 2s;
Item one olde cappe 4d;
Item a Hatte, lyned with tafferta 16d;
Sum £6 12s 4d.

Weomens apparell
Firstly a Browne Blewe gowne, a plackette and ruffs 4s;
Item a cassacke with a villette cape 18s;
Item a worsterde Kertill with a chamblette Bodies 4s;
Item a petticoate with a mocadowe Bodies 6s 8d;
Item a petticoate with a chamblette Bodies 4s;
Item a Silke ffelte hatte 12s;
Item a coverlette of arrasse 13s 4d;
Item another coverlette 5s;
Item a yarde and quarter of course cloth 4s;
Item 2 yerds and half of white cloth 3s 9d;
Item a sheete to wrappe thapparell in 6d;
[3] Item the glasse in the windowe 5s;
Item a Baskett and a Bread kniffe 6d;
Item 2 ledde wights 2d;
Item 2 white cappes 12d;
Item a pair of damaske Sleeves 16d;
Item a pair of gloves 4d;
Item another pair of gloves 1d;
Item 2 Smocks 12d;
Item a cubborde cloth 6d;
Item 3 aprons of dowlis 21d;
Item an apron of creasse 4d;
Item one Kerchiffe of callacowe 16d;
Item another of callacowe 8d;
Item a Kerrchiffe of Hollonde 16d;
Item another Kerchiffe 3d;
Item 2 neckerchiffs of Hollonde 2s;
Item a neckerchiffe of Hollonde 10d;

Item a neckerchiffe of dowlis 8d;
Item a neckerchiffe of Hollonde 6d;
Item 5 crosse clothes 2s;
Item 2 paste Kerchiffs of callacowe 12d;
Item 3 partelets 9d;
Item 2 heere clothes 3d;
Item a waste petticoate of fustian 10d;
Item 3 course table napkins and a Hande towell 8d;
Item a canvas apron 3d;
Item 2 canvas Borde clothes 2s;
Item a dowlis sharte 2s 8d;
[4] Item a coyffe for a childe 4d;
Item 6 pillatise 4s;
Item 12 table napkins 3s;
Item a Borde towell 12d;
Item a table cloth of Hollonde 18d;
Item a table cloth of diaper 12d;
Item 2 pair of canvas sheets 2s 6d;
Item 2 pair of canvas sheets more 3s 8d;
Item a sheete of dowlis 10d;
Item 2 pair of dowlis sheets 10s;
Item another pair of dowlis sheets 3s 4d;
Item a pair of sheets of Hollonde 9s;
Item another pair of course canvas sheets 12d;
Item a tester and vallaunces to the same 2s 6d;
Item an olde sharte 8d;
Item 3 coffers 4s;
Item another sheete 12d;
Sum £7 14s 7d.

Gaidgs [?]
Firstly certeine writings of Roberte Molls 8s;
Item a womans gowne Whereof thone half is his and thother
     William Shepeherds 8s;
Item a pair of damaske Sleeves 5s;
Item a womans cappe 5d;
Sum 21s 5d.

Other Stuffe of his owne
Firstly 7 Kusshings 2s 8d;
Item a dawe sheete and 3 Bags 20d;
Item a Standinge Bedsteade, and a truckle Bedstead 28s;
Item a whitell 18d;
[5] Item a pair of graie hose 12d;
Item a pair of Russette Breeches 4d;
Item a flocke bed of a canvas tie, 3 Bolsters 4s;
Item a pair of Blaunckets 4s;
Item a pair of olde blaunckets 20d;
Item 6 pilloes 2s 8d;
Item a thrumbe coverlette 4s;
Item another graie Blaunckette 16d;
Item a Carpette of an olde vestmente 2s;
Item a water cowell 12d;
Item a Stoole 4d;
Item 3 Boxes, and a pecke 6d;
Item a Rendger 2d;
Item a welshe hooke, and a Blacke Bill 8d;
Item 3 spilts 2s;
Item an olde tub 1d;
Item an almonde rivets and a scull to the same 4s;
Item 2 andirons, 2 olde gridirons, 2 pothangings 2 cottrells a
    hooke of iron, and a Brandise 2s 8d;
Item a fryinge panne 6d;
Item a pottle potte 4s;
Item a Quarte potte 12d;
Item an Ewer 12d;
Item 3 greate brasse crocks 14s;
Item another brasse crocke 3s;
Item 2 porscnets 3s;
Item 2 Skillits 6d;
Item an Earthen crocke 1d;
[6] Item two cawdrons 2s 6d;
Item a brasse panne 3s 4d;
Item 7 candellsticks 4s;
Item a scoomer 4d;
Item a chaffinge dish 6d;
Item a morter withoute a pestell 2s;

Item a grater 2d;
Item a peppercorne a dozen of trenchers and a trene dish 4d;
Item a hamper 3d;
Item 9 pieces of corke 2s 8d;
Item 2 salte Sallerds of tinne 2d;
Item one pinte pot and a salte of tinne 12d;
Item 2 coats one tawnie and another of a skie cullor 3s;
Item a cheare 4d;
Item 12 pair of boots at 3s 6d the pair 42s;
Item 48 lb of pewter dishes at 4d half farthing the pound 15s
    10d;
Item a studde 1d;
Item a brushe with a Rubber 4d;
Item a table borde and a fourme in the chamber 5s;
Item 3 curteins of Saie, greene and red 6s;
Item a Quilte 2s 8d;
Item a peair of Blaunckets 3s 4d;
Item a flocke bed 2s 6d;
Item a bedstead and a testor to the same 4s;
Item 2 screede coverletts 2s;
Item a flocke bed and a bolster 3s;
Item a trucle bedsteade 12d;
[7] Item a table Borde and 2 binches in the fore chamber 5s;
Item a hoope and a Borde 2d;
Item a cubborde 20d;
Item a lettis 12d;
Item the glasse in the windowe 2s;
Item a water Buckette 2d;
Item 2 Butter crocks 2d;
Item a duste bed and a flocke bolster in the hier chamber 2s;
Item a flocke bed and bolster 2s;
Item 3 Bedsteads 2s;
Item 5 couple of milwill and half 2s 8d;
Item 5 lengs [?] 2s 8d;
Sum £11 3s 2d.

The Shoppe
Firstly a hundred pair of weomens shoes at 7d the pair 54s
    2d;

Item a hundred 16 pair of mens shoes at 12*d* the pair £5 16*s*;

Item threscore and eleven pair of childrens shoes at 5*d* the pair 29*s* 7*d*;

Item a dozen and half of calf Skinnes 17*s*;

Item the cuttinge Borde 2*d*;

Item twentie paers of Sole leather 40*s*;

Item the Boote trees in the shoppe 12*d*;

Item 16 pair of shoes yorkke 3*s* 4*d*;

Item 9 calf Skinnes alreadie curried 9*s*;

Item certeine soles alreadie cut and other peecs 2*s*;

Item 2 Shoppe hammers 10*d*;

Item 2 Raspes 8*d*;

Item a botome of a Shoppe threede 3*d*;

[8] Item a hatchette 4*d*;

Item a hammer a dresser a stoppinge sticke and a sockette 8*d*;

Item 2 cuttinge kniffs with hafts 10*d*;

Item a litle tub and 12 lb of tallowe in the same at 2*d* the pounde 2*s*;

Item 2 shoinghornes 2*d*;

Item 6 Stoolls 10*d*;

Item the leasts and the Realls 2*s*;

Item a daggar with a dugill hafte and a villet scabarde 20*d*;

Item a drie sak in Harie Savoudgs house 4*d*;

Item Harie Savaidge muste paie for michaellmas quarter 16*s* 8*d*;

Item certeine Bords at Mr Gibs that wee sawe not 3*s*;

Item certeine housholde stuffe at Otterton 10*s*;

Item a deeker of leather, and a dozen of calf Skinnes that were set frome the curriers £3 10*s*;

Sum £19 2*s* 6*d*.

The plate

Firstly a cuppe all guilte £3 15*s* 4*d*;

Item a salte parcell guilte £3 15*s* 8*d*;

Item a dossenne of Spounes £3 8*d*;

Item a gobblette parcell guilte £3 18*s* 1½*d*;

Item broken Silver and curell 2*s* 6*d*;

Item in money £12 18*s*;

Item lente to John Commelte 40*s*;

Item receaved in money 12*s* 4*d*;

Sum £30 2*s* 7*d*.

The Leasses of his howses

Firstly the howse wherein Harie Savaidge dwelleth £15;

Item hys owne howse £13;

Item the Leasse of the gardinge which he helde of William Tooker 6*s*;

Sum £28 6*s*.

Item one white blancket a peece of tafferta and 2 peecs of blacke velvet 3*s* 4*d*.

[9] Certeine debts due unto hime as it appearith uppon his Shoppe Booke all which debts we do here prayse and nominate doubtfull and desperate: insomuche as wee do not knowe the veritie and true writinge of them:

Firstly Adams oweth for shoes and pumps 19*s* 10*d*;

Item Mr Sawnders for Shoes 2*s* 8*d*;

Item Anthonie Lowe 2*s* 6*d*;

Item Mr Seawarde for Shoes and pumps 2*s* 6*d*;

Item Mr Huckemor for shoes 19*d*;

Item Jefferie for shoes and boots 9*s* 10*d*;

Item William Beelughe for shoes 22*d*;

Item Bartrem for shoes 9*s* 4*d*;

Item Margarette Hampton 6*s* 1*d*;

Item Ellinor Upton for Shoes 10*d*;

Item Mr Hardwike for shoes and pumps 12*s* 4*d*;

Item for a Wairs [?] childe a paire of Shoes 4*d*;

Item Pese for Shoes 20*d*;

Item a pair of Shoes for his boie 12*d*;

Item Mr Gibbs for Shoes 12*d*;

Item Mr Samuell for boots 5*s*;

Item for himeSelf 4*s* 11*d*;

Item Mr Goffe for Shoes 9*s* 6*d*;

Item Mr Browne for Shoes 2*s*;

Item Mr Commelte for shoes 2*s* 6*d*;

Item John Fyshe for shoes 9*s* 5*d*.

The hole some [**besides** – crossed through] of **the** doubtfull and desperate debts expressed uppon his shoppe Booke is [scrubbed out];
Item William Wair oweth 18*s*;
Sum duly debe £6 4*s* 8*d*;
Sum total £115 7½*d*;
Whereof owing desperate £6 4*s* 8*d*.

ECA, Orphans' Court Inventory 17 [Item 2]

The Inventorie of the goodds & Chattalls of Richard Taylor *alias* Faryngton of the citie of Exon late decessed shomaker: 1570.
Goodds houshold stuff, plate leases debtts & money £115 7½*d*.

Whereof
In legacies to the poore 5*s*;
To his father £10;
To Mogredg (5*s*) Bowden (5*s*) & Woolocomb (5*s*) 15*s*;
To his too overseers 10*s*;
£11 10*s*;
Also yn debts desperat £6 4*s* 8*d*;
Also for his funeralls & chardgs of the admenestration & praysing of goodds 7*s* 5*d*;
Also yn debts which he dyd owe £6 6*d*;
Also for chardgs yn lawe yn the Guildhall £3 5*s* 1*d*;
Sum £29 17*s* 8*d*.

So there resteth to thuse of Esanas [?] thorphane & executor £85 2*s* 11½*d*.
Whereof
Layde out by thadmynestrators for fyndinge & scholynge of the said Esayns [?] from the dethe of the testator untyll the 10th of November 1571 £3 19*s* 11*d*;
Also laied out & paied by the praysers yn suets & expenses of Lawe 6*s* 4*d*;
Sum £4 6*s* 3*d*.

Sum total £34 3*s* 11*d*;
So remaineth cleere £80 16*s* 8½*d*.

Whereof delyvered & paied to William Shepherd & John Toker the admynestrators the 21th of November 1571 yn presence of Mr Bruerton maior Mr Symon Knight Nychus Martyn John Hoker Edward Hert George Dodrudg Robert Rawe Laurens Barcombe & others £42;
So remaineth yn the cities hands £38 16*s* 8½*d*.

ECA, Orphans' Court Inventory 17 [Item 3, note this is listed as Inventory 20, Item 3]

The Inventorie of Richard Taylers *alias* Faryngdons goodds 1571
Goodds plate money houshold stuffe leases debts £115 7½*d*.

Whereof
Geven yn legacies £11 10*s*;
Also yn doubtfull detts £6 4*s* 8*d*;
Also yn chardgs for his funeralls praysing of the goodds & for the admynestracon 57*s* 5*d*;
Also yn debts which he dyd owe £6 6*d*;
Also for chardgs yn the law betwene the praysors & the admynestrators £3 5*s* 1*d*;
£29 17*s* 8*d*;
So remaineth £85 2*s* 11½*d*.

[Illegible words crossed through.]

Whereof laied out by thadmynestrators for fyndinge & scholinge of Esanas [?] the chyld & orphane of the foresaide Richerd Taylor from the dethe of the testator untyll the 10 of November 1571 the some of £3 19*s* 11*d*;
Also layed out & payed by the praysors for suets & expenses yn the law 6*s* 4*d*;
Sum £4 6*s* 3*d*;
So remaineth cleere £80 16*s* 8½*d*.

Whereof delyvered 21 of November 1571 to William Shepherd & John Toker the some of £42;

So remaineth yn the Cities hands £38 16s 8½d.

25. INVENTORY OF JOHN WEST, BAKER OF HOLY TRINITY PARISH, 8 NOVEMBER 1570

ECA, Orphans' Court Inventory 17A

Note: Recognisances were entered into on 26 May 1571 regarding West's son Thomas (ECA, Book 141, folio 42).

The Inventorie of all and singuler the goods cateels and detts which latelie appertyened unto John West late of the parrishe of the Trynitie in the cittie of Exeter decessed taken and praised the 8th daie of November in the yere of our Lord god 1570 by Richard Horwell William Bricknoll John Lynne and John Fishmore hereafter folowethe

[m. 1] In the Hall
Firstly a tablebord & 2 formes 5s;
Item the bench and seelinge 10s;
Item 2 cubbordes 20s;
Item a chaire and 2 litle stooles 8d;
Item the hanginges in the hall 3s 4d;
Item 4 flowerpotts 12d;
Item 9 Qwishens 5s 8d;
Item 2 carpets 3s 4d;
Sum 49s.

In the parlor
Item the benche and the seelinge 5s;
Item a standing bedsteed 6s 8d;
Item a dowstbed 16d;
Item a coverlet a tester & the hanginges of the bed 8s;
Item the hanginges about the parlor 2s;
Item a bowe a sculle & 13 arrowes 4s 2d;
Sum 27s 2d.

In the chamber over the shoppe
Item 2 standing bedsteeds & a litle stoole 10s 6d;
Item 2 testers and the hanginges 8s;

Item a cheste & a sworde 4s 4d;
Item foure pillowes of fethers 6s;
Item a coverlet 14s 8d;
Sum 43s 6d.

Woollen Clothes
Item a furred gowne 20s;
Item 2 dublets 10s;
Item 2 cotes 5s;
Item a paire of hose 5s;
Item a hat and a cappe 3s 4d;
Sum 43s 4d.

Pewter vessell
Item the pewter vessell is valewed in 34s;
Item the crocke bras is vallewed in 20s;
Item 2 other crockes of bras geven unto 2 of John Wests children by legacies 24s 8d;
Item pan bras by weighte 13s;
Item 10 candlesticks 6s 8d;
[m. 2] Item a pottoll pot 2 quartes a pynte & a tynnen tankerd & an old ewer 4s;
Item a morter and a pessell 16d;
Item 9 stoning cuppes 18d;
Sum £5 5s 2d.

In the kichen
Item 2 broches 16d;
Item 2 dogges of yron 20d;
Item a bord & a benche 2s 2d;

Item a chaire & a stoole 8*d*;
Item 3 boles & a litle tubbe 20*d*;
Item a paile a ladel & 3 treen plates 8*d*;
Item a cage and 2 shelfes 16*d*;
Item a salte barell & a pecke of salte and 2 chopping bordes 8*d*;
Item a fire pike a fire shoole a brandys 3*s*;
Item 3 crooks of yron & 4 paire of cotrels 3*s* 6*d*;
Item 2 grydirons & a fleshhooke 12*d*;
Item 2 drypinge & a fryeng pan 3*s* 4*d*;
Item a chaffen dishe and a scoomer 10*d*;
Item 2 chamber pots 16*d*;
Sum 23*s* 2*d*.

In the Chamber over the Hall
Item a bord a benche a forme a carpet 4*s*;
Item one fetherbed 2 bolsters 2 coverlets & one bedsteede 20*s*;
Item the hanginges of the chambr and tester 3*s*;
Item a truckel bed steed 10*d*;
Item a sheave of arrowes 20*d*;
Sum 29*s* 6*d*.

In the chamber over the parlor
Item a flockbed and a dowstbed & 2 bed steeds with the coveringes 5*s*;
Item 3 blankets 2*s*;
Item 2 bagges of woolle 8*s*;
Item a forme 12*d*;
Item a tester and a stained clothe 12*d*;
Sum 17*s*.

In the chamber over the kechen
Item a fetherbed & a bedsteed bolster & coverlet and blankets 20*s*;
Item a litle fetherbed & bedsteed and a coverlet 10*s*;
Item a chaire 4*d*;
Sum 30*s* 4*d*.

In the backe chamber
Item a doustbed & bedsteed a tester *[m. 3]* & a stained cloth 3*s*;
Item 5 bordes of elme 3*s*;
Item a hackney sadell & bridell 2*s*;
Sum 8*s*.

Naperye
Item a cubbord clothe 12*d*;
Item 8 paire of sheets 22*s* 3*d*;
Item 5 pillowbeeres 3*s* 8*d*;
Item 3 bordeclothes 6*s*;
Item 5 towels 7*s*;
Item a dosen & half of napkens 6*s*;
Item 3 sherts 6*s*;
Sum 51*s* 11*d*.

Woode
Item the wood £3;
Item the haie 40*s*;
Sum £5.

In the bake howse
Item a furnace 16*s*;
Item wheate meale 20*s*;
Item bunters 14*d*;
Item half a bushell of beane meale & a sacke of stuffe 2*s* 8*d*;
Item 2 sacks 18*d*;
Sum 41*s*.

In the spence
Item a cubbord 3*s* 4*d*;
Item a grater & 2 shelfes 6*d*;
Item 2 dosen of trenchers & 7 hall dishes 3*d*;
Sum 4*s* 1*d*.

In the Shoppe
Item 2 bandes & a basket 6*d*;
Sum 6*d*.

In the alehowse
Item 6 trendles a bote vate & 6 small costes a tunner & a powdring tubbe 5s [illegible; 4d];
Item 2 clokes 5s;
Sum 10s 4d.

Certeine implements left in the howse of Mrs Mowntsteven
Item a bed steed the seeling and a tester 6s 8d;
Item a cubbord and a forme 5s;
Item 2 painted clothes 2s;
Item an old cheste 2s;
Sum 15s 8d.

In the barne at Hevitree
Item the wheate 20s;
[m. 4] Item the barly & beanes 20s;
Item 2 horses with there apparrell 46s 8d;
Sum £4 6s 8d.

The plate
Item 2 goblets & foure spoones of silver £6 10s;
Item a salte of silver with a cover parcel gilte £4;
The said salte being laid to gage for 40s;
Sum £10 10s.

Detts sperate
Item detts sperate owed to him 34s;
Sum 34s.

Desperate dets
Item in dets desperate 30s;
Sum total £46 19s 4d.

Detts owed by John West
Item to the house of the corporacion of bakers £4 10s;
Item owed for rye 20s;
Item in scores at his deathe owed 30s;
Sum £7.
Legacies geven by John West
Item geven to his too sounes £13 6s 8d;
Item geven unto them 2 brasse crocks praisd in 24s 8d;
Item geven to 3 of Roberte Mathewes children 20s;
Item due to the said 3 children by John West for there fathers legacie £15;
Item for redeming of a silver salte 40s;
Item the funeralls 13s 4d;
Item to the ordenary [?] 10s;
Sum £33 14s 4d.

Sum total of the debts and payments £40 14s 8d.

26. INVENTORY OF JOHN DENYS, OF ST MARY STEPS' PARISH, 5 MAY 1571

ECA, Orphans' Court Inventory 18

The Inventorye of the goodes and Cattells of John Denys decessed late of the paisshe of Sayne Marysteppes vewed and praised by Wyllyam Dodrydge, James Torryton, John Curtys and Androw Mory the 5th day of May *in the year* 1571 as ensueth

In the Hall
Firstly a Table borde a fforme a benche with the sealyng 16s;

Item a Coborde 10s;
Item Peuter vessell 73 lb – 24s 4d;
Item 2 Aundyrons 4s;
Item a Wyne quarte pott of pewter, 2 Salts and 3 Covered cuppes of Tynne 2s 8d;
Item 13 Candelstyckes, 2 Chafyng dysshes of latten 12s;
Item 6 fflower potts of Tynne 12d;
Item 3 lytle brasse pannes, weyng 13 lb – 6s;

Item 2 Chayers 6*d*;
Item 2 stayned Clothes over the borde 2*s* 6*d*.

In the Chamber within the Hall
Item a standyng bedstede with a ffetherbedde 2 bolsters 3
    pellowes with a Coverlett and a payre of Blanketts 30*s*;
Item a nother bedstede, with a fflockebed, a Coverlet a payre
    of Blanketts and a Tester 10*s*;
Item 4 Cofers and a Chayer 10*s*;
Item 2 Gownes, 3 Cotes, a dublet, a Jerken & a Cloke 30*s*;
Item 11 yeardes of housolde Cloth 12*s*;
Item 7 Shetes, 2 Towells, 6 dyaper Napkyns, 6 Canvas
    Napkyns, 4 pylowbers, a bordecloth, and a Cappe 26*s*;
Item 16 lb of whyte & Colored woll 16*s* 8*d*;
Item 16 lb of Russett woll & yearne 16*s* 10*d*;
Item 18 lb of yearne 19*s*;
Item a Carpett & a beryng Blanket 6*s*.

In the Kytchen
Item 38 lb of Crocke brasse 12*s*;
Item a Cawderen, a Skyllet & an Iron Crocke 2*s* 6*d*;
Item a broche a payre of Andyrens, a Gredyren;

Item 2 Crookes for the Chymny, a payre of pott hangyngs,
    and a ffryyng panne;
3*s* 4*d*;
Item a borde in the Kytchen 16*d*.

In the bakehouse
Item bruyng pan 8*s*;
Item a brondeyron 12*d*;
Item 2 Standerdes 2*s*;
Item 2 brewyng Tubbes, 3 lytle Trendell, a buntyng hutche, a
    dowe Tubbe a boll a Buckett, and a Coste 5*s*;
Item wylly, a borde and a planke 2*s*.

In the Shoppe
Item 2 payre of lowmes 36*s*;
Item 6 Slees in harnys 10*s*;
Item 2 quylyng Turnes & 2 Spynnyng Turnes 3*s*;
Item one dosen 36*s*;
Item a payre of lowmes, in the kytchen 4*s*;
Item one other dosen 26*s*;
Item for the terme of the house, that he dwelled in 40*s*;
Item for the terme of the huse, that Thurssell dwelleth in 40*s*;
Item another leace, whyche is betwyne Cove and Denys, now
    beyng in the law [blank];
Item other small Trasshe in the house 2*s* 6*d*;
Sum total £24 10*s* 2*d*.

The debts dew to the testator £5 4*s* 4*d*;
Sum £29 14*s* 6*d*.

[*verso*] Debtes sperat & desperat owyng unto hym
Firstly Robert Locke 30*s*;
Item John Thrussell 25*s*;
Item John Lynche 24*s*;
Item Robert Coryer 4*s* 4*d*;
Item John Wescote taylor 15*s*;
Item Robert Westote taler 6*s*.

Debts wych he dyd owe
Item to Wm Toker of Thorverton 46*s* 8*d*;
Item payd to sondre other persons wych my hosband dyd owe
    40*s*;
Item the funeralls 20*s*;
Item the probate of the testement 5*s*.

27. INVENTORY OF WIDOW HARRISON, 26 JUNE 1571

ECA, Orphans' Court Inventory 19

1571 An inventorye of all suche goods as we Geofferye Thomas John Watkyns John Hart and Wm Budgyll made in expectation the 26th day of June in the year 1571 to the wydo Harysson

[2] *Firstly* in the hall a table bord with 2 formes [with a benchd bedsteed – crossed through] all worthe 6s 8d;

Item a Joyned square syde bord at 2s 6d;

Item a Joyned chayre 16d;

Item a Joyned cobord with a pres under 16s – 16s;

Item a coffer worthe 2s 6d;

Item a bason and yeower of tyn and 2 flower potts 2s;

Item a spyce boxe 6d;

Item 2 tables of storyes 2s 8d;

Item a shellfe with 21 pupetts 20d;

Item a byble of the small volume 6s 8d;

Item a pycke 20d;

Item a sestorne of led to washe hands to 12d;

Item all the seelyngs and benchys in the hall 10s;

Item the glas yn the wyndowe 16d;

Item 2 lytle stoolles with 3 legs & a planke 6d;

Item in the chymneye an Iron bar 20d;

Item a browne byll 8d;

Item a benche & settle by the chymneye 3s 4d;

Item a cobord clothe with a brusshe [?] 7d;

Som of all suche thyngs in the hall £3 3s 3d.

Item in the parler a tablebord with a planke benche 18d;

Item a Joynd stoole and a Joyned chayres [*sic*] 3s;

Item a cobord with a cobord clothe 4s;

Item upon the same 3 platters 4s;

Item 2 laton candellstycks of laton [*sic*] with a laton Ryng to set a dyshe upon worthe 2s;

Item 3 tyncupes for ale & a tyn salte and 2 old dysshes or gobbets 12d;

Item a galon pot for byeare 2s;

Item a pottle a quarte & 2 pynts london present potts all worthe 3s;

Item 4 flower pots at 8d;

Item a bras morter with a pestle of bras 4s;

Item a old botell & 2 glasses 3d;

Item a lytle Joyned bord at 2s 6d;

Item a danske chest worthe 3s 4d;

Item a lytle coffer worthe 16d;

Item 6 old cusshyns with a carpet 2s;

Item all the hangyngs in the parler 2s 6d;

Item a lookynke glas 2s 6d;

Item in the chymneye an Iron bar 4d;

Item 6 tapesterye cusshyns and a carpet of dornexe all worthe 12s;

Item all the glas in 2 wyndowes 4s;

Item a bed steed with a truckle bed under 20s;

Item 2 fether beds with a floke bed 2 bolsters 2 pyllowes and a bolster of floxes £3;

Item a per blankets a per sheets 2 coverlyts 5 cortyns a quylt a sheete & a blanket 20s;

Item 8 dosen 3 spanyshe skyns at 48s the dosen amonts to £19 16d;

Item a dosen of skynes callyd flanders skyns at 40s;

[3] Item mor in the parler 3 dosen callyd spanyshe skynnes at 40s the dosen £6;

Item 16 bathames skyns colored at 2s pyce 32s;

Item 2 payr sheets at 5s a payre 15s;

Item mor 10 payre and a ode sheete and a pece of an olde sheete all worthe 33s 4d;

Item mor 8 pyllowtyes at 8s;

Item mor 7 old corse pyllowtyes at 2s 4d;

Item mor 2 bord clothers fyne canvas at 8s;

Item 6 corser bord clothers at 3s 4d;

Item 18 bord napkyns at 3s;

Item mor a dos better napkyns at 5s;

Item mor a dos napkyns 5s;

Item mor 9 old tablenapkyns 18d;

Item mor 2 bord clothers 3 towelles of dyaper corse at 12s;

Item a bord clothe and a Rolled towayll 2s 6d;

Item 5 yards calaco clothe at 12d – 5s;

Item 3 yards ¼ hornesdalle at 2s 9d;

Item 27 yards Rome clothe at 12d yard – 27s;

Item 9½ yards canvas at 6s;

Mor 2 yards canvas 14d;

Item 4 shurts at 4s 8d;

Some of all that we fynd in the parler monts [to] £44 9s 6d.

Item in the chamber over the buterye a bedsteed with a tester 2s 6d;

Item a fether bed 2 floke bolsters & a fether bolster and a pyllow 20s;

Item 2 coverlyts a blanket 8s;

Item a whyt too Ryd Kerzye 20s;

Item a Joyned chest at 6s 8d;

Item a cobord worthe 3s 4d;

Item a shype chest 12d;

Item a old forme old Iron & other trasshe 6d;

Item a gowne lynyd with saye 6s 8d;

Item a gowne facyd with foxe & lyned with lam 20s;

Item 2 old gownes and hys best gowne fured budge 25s;

Item a casake old mocado & another grograye 4s;

Item a cote & Jyrkyn of clothe 2s;

Item a spanyshe cape at 5s;

Item 2 clokes wherof one hathe slyves 16s;

Item a old frysado cape 2s;

Item 2 por bryches 2 per stokyns & 2 bad old cloks all ys 3s 4d;

Item a cape hatt a petycote wast doblets and other thyngs belongyng to hys bodye not wroten 16d;

Item a sword dager poynado 3s 4d;

Item a payntyd clothe at 2s;

Item the glas in the wyndowe 3s;

Item 75 skynes callyd flanders skyns at 8d – 50s;

Item a whyt spanyshe skyn ½ at 7s;

Item a boxe with threed and a come to come flaxe 8d;

Som of all that we fynd in this chamber monts [to] £10 [12 – crossed through] 18s 4d.

[4] Item in the chamber over the shope a bedsteede with a tester over the bed 16d;

Item a floke bed with 4 pyllowes with a bolster of floxe all worthe 10s;

Item a payntyd clothe a seeve a range a bottle a lytle forme a pyce of bacon & other trashe 3s 4d;

Som in thys chamber monts to 14s 8d.

Item in the galerye a trokle bedsteed a floke bed 2 floke bolsters a blanket a sheete a coverlet a powderyng tobbe 6s;

Item 3 quarters C tallow at 18s;

[Item a torne to spyn thred 12d – crossed through];

Item 2 butts lether 10s;

Item in whete peeson tobes and other trashe ther 5s;

Item a ½ bosshyll measure 4d;

Some in the galerye monts to 41s.

Item in another chamber 2 bedsteeds with one trokell bed under one of them and one tester stayned 4s;

Item a bad fether bed at 5s;

Item a floke bed a fether bolster a per sheetes & 1 shete 1 blanket 2 coverlyts all worthe 10s;

Item a payntyd clothe worthe 4s;

Item a turne a hamper a bord & other trashe 2s;

Item a companye of lesses 18d;

Item a sadell styropes gyrses 3s 4d;

Som in thys chamber monts to 29s 10d.

Item in the upper chamber 20 lb awker [?] 6s 8d;

Item in corke 5s;

Item an Iron pan to cast led in 12d;

Item a old bras pan a salet and brydell 10d;

Item 6 cheeses 2 toobes & butercroxe 20*d*;

Item mor in peers & skreeds & 2 old sadell tries 5*s*;

Som 20*s* 2*d*.

Item in the Kychyn 4 broches 2*s* 8*d*;

Item 2 drypyn pans of Iron 2*s*;

Item a per andyrons a fyer pan a per tongs an Iron bar 4 pot crooks 2 per pot hangyns a gredyron and a fleshe hooke all worthe & a brandys 6*s* 8*d*;

Item 2 bras crokes 13*s* 4*d*;

Item 12 studs at 18*d*;

Item a per of byllowes at 12*d*;

Item an old forme bords & other trasshe with a coope 18*d*;

Some 28*s* 8*d*.

Item in a old backe chamber a hyde at 6*s* 8*d*;

Item 28 calves skyns at 26*s* 8*d*;

Item stadgs skyns wood & other trasshe 5*s*;

Item mor in the stable in wood coles a Racke and an aunger [? manger] and other thyngs worthe 6*s*;

Item a cowle a tob a cowlestafe 2 boldysshes a forme and 4 stone cuppes 2*s* 6*d*;

Som 46*s* 10*d*.

[5] Item in the Spence 17 platters 11 podgers 26 sawsseres weyng £92 at 5*d* 1 lb – 38*s* 4*d*;

Item 5 platters pawned for 8*s*;

Item 11 podydge dysshes of tyn at 2*s*;

Item a perye basson at 8*d*;

Item in old broken peoter 18*d*;

Item 2 chamber potts of tyn 16*d*;

Item a quarte and a pynt of wyne potts 12*d*;

Item 7 payre of latton canstycks at 5*s*;

Item a lyon of bras to hold a canstycke 4*d*;

Item 2 coderons 3 lytle panes 2 skyllets and a skemer all of bras worthe 10*s*;

Item a greate croke 3 lytle croks 2 posnetts 33*s* 4*d*;

Item a fryeng pane 8*d*;

Item an old Irone beame 8*d*;

Item a powderyng tobe shellfes & other trasshe 12*d*;

Som £5 3*s* 10*d*.

Item in the seller 7 galons butter at 14*s*;

Item sartayne bords of corke 13*s* 4*d*;

Item in lyme 12*d*;

Item in tobbes pych tymber atrye and other wooden vessell befe and other thyngs 2*s* 6*d*;

Item in a baryll sertayne gre soxe 10*s*;

Item a laton chaffyndyshe 12*d*;

Item an Iron chaffyndyshe 3*d*;

Som £2 2*s* 1*d*.

Item in the shoppe 7 dos 8 payre man shewes at 11*d* the payre amonts to £4 4*s* 4*d*;

Item 52 payre women shews at 8*d* payre 34*s* 8*d*;

Item 34 payre Rase pompes of calves lether at 8*d* the payre monts to 22*s* 8*d*;

Item 2 dosen spanyshe lether pompes for women at 12*d* the payre monts to 24*s*;

Item 30 payre corke shews and pantofes at 12*d* the payre monts to 30*s*;

Item 8 payre new boots at 4*s* the pere 32*s*;

Item 2½ dosen callves lether Jyrkyns at 24*s* the dosen 30*s* [*sic*];

Item a dosen [and] ½ calves lether old buskyns skollen [?] and of small valew 5*s*;

Item 10 dosen skynes whyte at 16*d* pyce 13*s* 4*d*;

Item a payre spanyshe lether boskyns at 3*s* 4*d*;

Item 2 boffe Jyrkyns at 24*s*;

Item 10 dosen lames skynes at 2*s* dos 20*s*;

Item 16 spanyshe lether Jyrkyns and a payr of slyves spanyshe lether at 10*s* pyce £8;

Item 4 dosen lames skyns at 2*s* dosen 8*s*;

Item 10 dry lether callves skyns fo[r] Jyrkyns at 16*d* the pyce monts to 13*s* 4*d*;

Item 9 dosen shepes skyns at 5*s* dosen 45*s*;

Item 9 dosen large gote skyns at 13*s* dosen £5 17*s*;

Item 12½ dosen small gottes at 11*s* dosen £6 17*s* 6*d*;

Item 3½ dosen whyt flanders skyns at 14s dosen 49s;

Item 3 dosen 4 skyns Red muttons at 2s dosen 6s 8d;

Item 1½ dosen blake flanders skyns at 14s dosen 21s;

Item 2 dosen old layd shepes skyns at 2s dosen 4s;

[6] Item mor in the shope 4 payre of falles and preett [?] lether skyns all worthe 6s 8d;

Item 3 chestes worthe 14s;

Item a sypres chest worthe 10s;

Item a pres worthe 2s;

Item 9 cuttyn knyves at 16d;

Item 4 pere bowte tres & boskyns 4s;

Item a dosen [and] ½ chyssylles 18d;

Item 2 shop hamers 12d;

Item a led and a whetstone 2s;

Item 3 Rapes 12d;

Item 4 dosen of lesses at 5s;

Item 4 cuttyng bords at 16d;

Item 6 scoolles at 6d;

Item a payre trestles with shelfes 12d;

Item a payre vellvet pantoffes 2s;

Item 2 botton mouldes 16d;

Item a deske coveryd with glas with loke and keye 5s;

Item in the same deske 100 dosen old sylke botons 4s;

Item 30 dosen of glas botons at 2s 6d;

Item a groce [and] ½ whyt sylke botons at 3s;

Item 2 groce grene sylke botons at 2s;

Item a dosen sylke poynts at 6d;

Item 2 owncs yelow sylke 3s;

Item ownce Redsylke at 2d;

Item 3 pownes 6d;

Item a dosen [and] ½ sylverlace at 6s;

Item a groce of botons wrought with gold syllver and sylke worthe 4s;

Item all the cutt worke in the spon un wrowght with som other thyngs forgoten 6s 8d;

Item for 2 new lokes 16d;

£49

Som of that we fynd in the shop £49 [6s 7d – crossed through].

Item in plate fyrst a dosen of sylver spownes with hys leter of hys name weyng 16 owncs 3 q[uarter]s at 4s 5d the ownce monts [to] £3 13s 11d;

Item 6 sylver spownes of the postles weyng 12½ owncs of the tythe at 4s 8d ownce £2 18s 4d;

Item 4 old spownes weyng 3 owncs quarter at 4s – 13s;

Item we fynd 7 spownes of sylver wher upon she saythe she hath lont 20s;

Item 2 whyt goblets weyng 23 owncs at 4s 4d ownce £4 19s 8d;

Item a goblet parsell gylt of the tyshe weyng 13 owncs q[uarte]r at 4s 8d ownce £3 1s 10d;

Item a salte parsell gylt with hys cover weyng 11½ owncs at 4s 8d ownce £2 13s 8d;

Item a standyng cuppe with a cover gylt weyng 15 owncs at 5s 2d ownce £3 17s 6d;

Item a flat pyece weyng 7 owncs at 4s – 28s;

Item the syllver abowte 3 stone pottes by estymacyon 16 owncs at 4s ownce £3 4s;

Item in monye and gold £98 – £98;

Item a sylver Ryng with 2 lettres of hys name at 16d;

Item a gold Rynge at 5s;

Some amonts to £125 16s 3d.

[7] Item a leasse of a tenement in the which John Northe goldsmythe now dwellethe and late the tenure of Richard Faryndon allyas Tayler valluyd in £10;

Item apromys of a leasse in the howsse which Warnard Haryson late dwelt in 26s 8d;

Item a leasse of a howsse in the which one Rychard Raynoll now dwellythe in the paryshe of Saynt Stevons valewyed 40s;

Item in the same tenement the glas in a wyndowe worthe 2s 6d;

Item mor in the same tenement a planke benche a bord 2 latysyes & a spence 20d;

Some amonts to £13 10s 10d.

Item in good dettes declaryd by her with owte specyealltyes whos name she wyll not declare £28;

Item Garet Joyner awith in good det £10;

Item Wm Not of London awith by a byll of hys awne hand good det £5;

Item she hathe Rsd [received] of the detts dew upon her booke syns the deathe of her late hosband the some of £3 1s 4d;

Some amonts to £46 1s 4d.

Some totall amonts to £309 6s 7d.

Item her booke amonts to £128 12s 8d besyds the some above wryten which she accomptes to be desperate detts bot shee wyll be countable for that she maye Recover therof £128 12s 8d.

[8] Detts broght by the Sayd Warnard Harysson late dessecyd as foloythe:

Item he owght unto Wm Symes of Chard by a specyaltye £40;

Item he owght to Geordge Cornysshe £7;

Item he owght John Garet £4 13s 10d;

Some amonts to as apyrythe £51 13s 10d.

[10] Thomas Henry Walter William James Grace Willmot [? his children; tails off].

28. INVENTORY OF ROLAND FABYAN, CORDWAINER, 28 SEPTEMBER 1571

ECA, Orphans' Court Inventory 20 [Item 1]

Note: Fragments of a copy of the inventory accompany this document. The will of Rowland 'Fabiom' was proved in the Principal Registry of the Bishop of Exeter in 1571 (E. A. Fry (ed), *Calendar of Wills and Administrations relating to the Counties of Devon & Cornwall*, British Record Society, 1908, Vol. 35, xviii). Recognisances were entered into on 28 January 1573 for his daughters Elizabeth and Mary (ECA, Book 141, folio 42).

The Inventory indented of All the goods and Cattalls of Rowland Ffabyan late Citizen and Cordwayn of the Citie of Excester deceassed praysed by Wyllyam Byckenall John Lyn Edward Wylls and John Gaydon the 28th daye of September in the 13th yere of the raigne of our Sovaigne lady Elizabeth by the grace of god Quene of England Frannce and Irlond defendor of the faith

In the Hall

Firstly A framed borde with the Selyng and a forme 10s;

Item A Cubborde 5s;

Item A presse 6s 8d;

Item 2 Chaires A framed Stole and A Cofer 2s;

Item A syde borde A fote Stole 8 trene dysshes A Choppyng knyfe A ladell and A ffleshehooke 16d;

Item 2 Cauldrons A basen A skyllet and A skomer 6s 8d;

Item 7 Candelstyckes and A Chafer 5s;

Item A barre of Iron 2 Crooks 2 peire of pothooks An Andyron twoo dogges and A fyrepyke 18d;

Item 2 bords and A tubbe of Salte 12d;

Item 3 quysshyngs 18d;

Item A peire of bellowes and 20 trenchers 3d;

Item A broche A gose pan A grydiron A Choppyng knyfe A Choppyng borde a lanthorne and A peire of Sheres 2s 4d [?];

Item 2 pottells potts A quarte pott and A Cuppe 20d;

Item A brasse pott of Rychard Chapells in gaydge of 6s;

Item 2 flower potts and A Salte 16d;

Item An Almayne ryvett and A pollaxe 6s 8d;

Item the pewter vessells wayeng 13 pounde 17s 8d;

Sum £3 16s 7d.

In the Chamber over the Shoppe

Firstly a ffetherbed A flocke bolster and 2 pyllowes of ffethers 13s 4d;

Item A bedstede and the testerne 6s 4d;

Item A Square table and a borde upon hym 2s 6d;

Item A Chest 6s 8d;

Item 4 olde Coffers 4s;

Item A framed forme and an olde Chayer 16d;

Item 5 olde stayned Clothes 2s;

Item 3 bords before the fyer and a brandys 16d;

Item A ioyned forme and A benche 8d;

Item A Serche 6s;

Item An olde knyfe and A brusshe 6d;

Item A blacke furred gowne 10s;

Item An olde fyrse gowne 3s;

Item An olde Cloke 6s 8d;

Item A blacke peire of hose And A blacke dublet 8s;

Item A Jerkyn of Clothe and An other of lether and A peire olde breches 3s 4d;

Item 2 hatts 4s 8d;

Item 2 kassecks of brode Cloth 33s 4d;

Item A olde fyrse kassecke 2s;

Item 2 rownde Kertells 10s;

Item A red petycote 2s;

Item 2 peire of Stocke sleves 2s;

Item A blacke Wosterd Apren 10d;

Item A Waste gyrdell of velvet 6d;

Item A Shurte 20d;

Item A beryng Shete 6d;

Item A towell of diaper 2s 8d;

Item 5 Shetes 8s;

Item A borde Cloth And A Cubborde Cloth 16d;

Item 3 Smockes and A Wastecote 3s;

Item A pyloweby 4d;

Item 6 borde napkyns and 2 towells 16d;

Item 5 kerchyffes 2s;

Item 4 neckerchyffes 5s 4d;

Item A peire of sleves of lynnen 4d;

Item A bande of A Shurte and A peire of gloves 12d;

Item 7 partletts and 2 knytte Cappes 3s 4d;

Item A Whytte Cappe for A Woman 3s;

Item An olde brasse pott 4s 8d;

Item A Coverlett 5s;

Item 2 Carpetts 16d;

Item An ewen bowe 6d;

Item 3 blanketts and an olde Coverlett 4s 8d;

Item an olde flocke bed and the bedstede 3s 4d;

Item the Woode 6d;

Sum £8 19s 4d.

In the shoppe

Firstly 4 dozen of mennes Shoys and 5 peire 48s;

Item 18 peire of Wemens Shoys 12s;

Item 21 peire of Shoys for Chyldren & pompes 8s;

Item 2 peire of bootes 9s;

Item A dozen of Calfes Skynnes undrest 5s;

Item 2 Slytters of lether and other peces of hide lether 20s;

Item 3 Whole butts and 6 peces 18s;

Item for the leases and 2 peire of bottres 6s 8d;

Item 6 Stoles and 2 trestoles 16d;

Item 2 Cuttyng bords and 4 other bords 16d;

Item 4 Cuttyng knyves A hammer A drawer and a rape 16d;

Item 2 Whetstones A cuppe and A pan 16d;

Item all the peces of lether 2s;

Item a Coffyn a Blied [?] a rake and A mattocke 2s;

Item A Cuttyng knyfe A Wymbell with the pooles and rayles 10d;

Sum £7 3s 6d.

Plate and money

Firstly A bolle of Sylver Wayeng 8 unces at 4s 2d a unce 33s 4d;

Item a lyttell Salte of Sylver parcell gylte Wayeng 6 unces at 4s the unce 24s;

Item 2 Covers of Sylver for 2 Stone Cuppes Wayeng 3 unces at 4s a unce 12s;

Item halfe a dozen of Sylver spones Wayeng 5 unces quarter and halfe A quarter at 4s a unce 21s 6d;

Item yn money 9s 6d.

The leasse of the house
Item the lease of the house yn £19;
Sum [blank].

Debts Sperate and Desperate
Firstly Michell Mydwynter oweth for Shoys 17s;
Item George Braston master Lusens man for Shoes 3s 4d;
Sum 20s 4d.

Sum £36 1d.

ECA, Orphans' Court Inventory 20 [Item 2]

[1] Chargs payde by Wyllyam Niccolls after the death of
Roland Fabyan for nurssyng of hys doughter Elizabeth and
other expencs of thag [the age] of a yere & halft at the deth of
her father

Firstly payde for a Shrowde 3s;
Item paide to the bell man 4d;
Item paide for makyng of hys grave 4d;
Item paide for a brest of mutton 5d;
Item paide to Beatrice for her Wags 10s;
Item paide to Mr Chaunceler 4s 6d;
Item paide to the Gardyner 6d;
Item paide to mother Hatche for bred and drynke 6d;
Item paide to Mighell hys servante 3s;
Item paide for bred geven to the Gayle 6d;
Item paide for a petycote and a peire of Sleves for Elizabeth
    Fabyan 4s 6d;
Item paide for the norsyng of the saide Elizabeth for one
    moneth endyng the fyrst daye of August in the 14th year of
    Queen Elizabeth [1571] 4s;
Item paide to the norse for one moneth more endyng the 29th
    daye of August then nexte insuyng 4s;
Item paide to the norse for one moneth more endyng the 26th
    daye of September then nexte insuyng 4s;

Item paide to the norse for one moneth more endyng the 24th
    daye of October then nexte insuyng 4s;
Item paide to the norse for one moneth more endyng the 21th
    daye of November then nexte insuyng 4s;
Item paide to the norse for one moneth more endyng the 19th
    daye of December then nexte insuyng 4s;
Item for my paynes taken 3s 4d;
Item paide for a partlet 8d;
Item paide for a Crosse cloth 6d;
Item paide for a smocke 14d;
Item paide for a Corner Kercher 6d;
Item paide for 2 blawe aprens 8d;
Item paide for a neckekercher 12d;
Item paide for a peire of hosen [6d – crossed through] 4d;
Item paide for a peire of shoys 4d;
Item paide for a knytt Ball' [?] for her hed 4d;
Item paide for a hed Cloth Wrought 12d;
Item paide for 2 partletts 16d;
Item paide for a blacke Worsted apron 4d;
Sum £3 3s 1d.

[2] Item paide for a peire of hosyn on newe yers daye 4d;
Item paide for Wrytyng of thys byll 4d;
Item paide for nursyng of the saide Elizabeth for one moneth
endyng the 19th daye of January then nexte insuyng 4s;
Sum 4s 8d.

[Sum total] £3 7s 9d.

[3] Layde oute by me Nicholas Hatche for Rowland Fabyan &
for Mary his daughter of thag of [one yere – crossed through]
3 quarters at the deth of the saide Rowland

Firstly for Sope 4d;
Item for the bearynge of hym to the Churche 16d;
Item for a leg of mutton & a pece of befe 12d;
Item Johan Trott had for tendynge of them 6d;
Item for 2 Seames of woode 12d;
Item the Clarke had for the buryenge of him & his boye 6d;

Item for a pounde of Candells 3*d*;

Item layde oute for the provinge of hys wyll 2*s* 8*d*;

Item paide unto Michell hys man 16*s*;

Item paide Johan Androwe his keper 5*s*;

Item paide to the nurse the 13th of July for kepynge of the Chylde and for sope 3*s* 4*d*;

Item paide for the dressinge of hys garden 20*d*;

Item for a yarde of clothe to make the chylde a petycote 16*d*;

Item for the mockado 7*d*;

Item for the inner lynynge 2*d*;

Item for the makinge 6*d*;

Item the 17th daye of August for the nursinge of the chylde & for Sope 3*s* 4*d*;

Item for a peire of hosen 3*d*;

Item for a peire of shoys 3*d*;

Item paide the 15th daye of September for nursinge of hys chylde & for Sope 3*s* 4*d*;

Item for the makinge cleine of hys house 12*d*;

Item for a seme of woode 6*d*;

Item paide the thyrde daye of October for nursynge of hys Chylde & for Sope 3*s* 4*d*;

Item for 2 shurtes for the chylde 2*s* 10*d*;

Item the 26th of October for the nursinge of the chylde & for Sope 3*s* 4*d*;

Item for 2 Aprens 6*d*;

Item for 2 Byggyners [?] 8*d*;

Item paide to the Praysers of hys goods for theire paynes 8*s*;

Item for my paynes 3*s* 4*d*;

Item paide for the wrytinge hereof 4*d*;

[Sum £3 3*s* 9*d* – crossed through];

Item paide to the Sumner [?] 8*d*;

Item paide to Mr Bordfilde for rent 10*s*;

Sum £3 17*s* 10*d*.

[4] Item payde one the 5th daye of November for nurssyng of the chylde 3*s* 4*d*;

Item payde to Sir Thomas the pryst for michelmas quarter 13*d*;

Item payde the 21th daye of December for nurssyng of the chylde 3*s* 4*d*;

Item paide to the pryst of Saynt Stephyns for Chrystmas quarter 13*d*;

Item payde the 18th daye of January for nurssyng of the Chylde 3*s* 4*d*;

Item payde to Davy Cooks for a hyde of lether that Roland dyd owe 9*s* 6*d*;

Item for twoo partletts 8*d*;

Item for two Kerchers 12*d*;

Item for twoo aprons 6*d*;

Item for a yeard and half of cloth to make her a pettycote 2*s*;

Item payde for the makyng of the same 6*d*;

Item payd for a peyre of hossen 3*d*;

Item a peyre of shoyes 3*d*;

Item payde for one Weks nurssyng the 25th day of January 10*d*;

Sum 27*s* 8*d*;

Sum Total 105*s* 6*d*.

[5] For Rollen Faben

Item pyed tow the cheansler 7*d*;

Item pead for a smoket 14*d*;

Item for to yaerdes of fryes to make her a karset 2*s* 8*d*;

Item for haeffe a yaerd of lenkloes 6*d*;

Item for the maken of the saem 8*d*;

Item for to Kargeres 7*d*;

Item for a yaerd and haeff of kloes for make her a petekoet 2*s*;

Item for the bodes and for the linen ther of 12*d*;

Item for the maken ther of 8*d*;

Item for to partlattes 10*d*;

Item for to apperens 8*d*;

Item for a payer of shues 4*d*;

Item for a payer of hosen 4*d*;

The suem is 12*s* 10*d*.

[7] Rowland Fabyans Inventory 1571

Goodds housholde stuffe &c £37 9*s* 2*d*.

Whereof
In legacyes 29s 4d;
For chardgs £7 16s 9d;
For desperat debts 20s 8d;
For the recognysancs 9s 8d;
£10 16s 5d;
So rem[aine]th £26 12s 9d.

Whereof
To Elizabeth Fabyan £13 6s 4½d;
To Mary Fabyan £13 6s 4½d.

28 [?] January 1571 £53
Willms Nycholls, Nychus Hatche, Edwards Ward, Fyt Lendon
Recognyters for the awnswering of £26 12s 9d to the use
of Elyzabeth & Mary the children and orphans of Rowland
Fabyan cordwayner decessed.

29. INVENTORY OF ALLAN MARKES, COOK, 22 NOVEMBER 1571

ECA, Orphans' Court Inventory 21
Note: Recognisances were entered into on 24 December 1571 regarding his on John (ECA, Book 141, folio 36 dorse).

The Inventorie of all the goods and cattels of Allen Markes
of the cittie of Exeter cooke decessed taken and praised by
Thomas Odam Harry Paramore Edward Warde and Wm
Masters the 22th daie of November in the 14th yere of the
raigne of our soveraigne Ladie Elizabeth the Quenes Majesty
that now is

In the parlor
Firstly a tablebord a cubbord and a forme 7s;
Item a fetherbed performed 20s;
Item a flockbed performed 10s;
Item a Coffer 2s 6d;
Item a cubbord and a chaire 2s;
Item 2 litle andyrons 8d;
Item 2 litle coffers 12d;
Item a handgoone [?] 2s;
Item the seelinge in the parlor 4s;
Item the stained clothes 3s 4d;
Item 6 Qwishens 12d;
Item 3 bordeclothes 6 napkens 3s;
Sum 56s 6d.

In the Hall
Item a tablebord 2 formes and a carpet 8s;
Item 2 Silver goblets parcell gilte conteyning 25 owncs, 2
   stond cuppes covered with Silver containing 5 owncs, a
   dosen of silver spoones containing 13 owncs & a salte of
   glasse garnished with silver to the valewe of 2 owncs £9;
Item 2 litle side bordes with 2 litle formes to the same bordes
   2s;
Item 2 andyrons, 2 dogges, a barre of yron 4 pothanginges
   and a fyre shoole 5s;
Item 2 cubbordes & 2 cubbord clothes thereunto belonginge
   6s 8d;
Item the seelinge about the Hall 8s;
Item the stained clothes 3s 4d;
Item a towell a chaire & a glasse 2s 6d;
Item a brushe and a welshooke 8d;
Sum £10 6s 2d.

In the gallerie
Item a Cheste and 5 lb of course woolle 3s;
Item 3 old coffers 16d;
Item a beame of yron & an old buckler 8d;
Sum 5s.

In the chamber over the Enterye

Item a flockbed performed 2 Coffers and 2 old bedsteedes 10s;

Sum 10s.

In the chamber over the parlor

Item 2 old fetherbeds performed 20s;

Item an other old bed arownd tableborde & 2 formes 5s;

Item an other table borde a forme a bench and a clothe upon the same bord [blank];

Sum 29s.

[verso] In the chamber over the stable

Item an old fetherbed a litle table bord & two formes a cheste 3 fether pillowes a cubbord and an old bedsteed 10s;

Item in brasse potts crocks pannes one hundred & ten powndes weight at 3½d the pownde in the hole 32s;

Item in pewter pots 19 lb weighte at 1½d the pownde 2s 4½d;

Item in pewter dishes 91 lb weight at 4d the pownd 30s 4d;

Sum £3 14s 8½d.

In the brewhouse

Item a furnes 13s 4d;

Item in the same howse 10 Tubbes 6s 8d;

Item 3 half barrels a Tunner [?] and a litle Coste 3s 4d;

Item an yron barre a pothanginge a crooke of yron 2 broches & a goose pan 2s;

Item a musterd myll and a stone morter 4d;

Item an enterclose and a litle bord 12d;

Item a fleshooke and a seeve 3d;

Item an other Tubbe a coole 3 buckets a dungepike an old bad borde 12d;

Item all his apparrell that is to saie an old gowne 2 clokes 2 dublets a cassecke of clothe a paire of hose a sherte 20s;

Item more in certeyne mooldes & a shriding knief 12d;

Item the lease & terme of the howse for 8 yeres & half yet therein to Come 20s;

Sum £3 8s 11d.

The hole Total some is £23 3½d.

Detts which Allane Markes doth owe

Firstly to George Peryman £4 10s;

Item to John Dorre 38s;

Item to Thomas Chapell 5s;

Item to Morish Downe 20s;

Item to George Elliot 20s;

Item to Edward Warde 6s 3½d;

Item to William Shepperd 7s;

Sum £8 16s 3½d.

[enclosure] For proving the will 3s 6d;

For new & sumpners fee [?] 8d;

For An obligacon 12d;

For Writinge a copie of the will & of the Inventrie 12d;

Sum 6s 2d.

30. INVENTORY OF JOHN BODLEIGHE, OF ST PAUL'S PARISH, 16 MARCH 1573

ECA, Orphans' Court Inventory 22

Note: the register for the parish of St Petrock recorded 'John Budley' was buried on 25 January 1573. Recognisances were entered into on 15 March 1573 for Robert, Margaret and Katharine, the children of John 'Budlye' (ECA, Book 141, Folio 53).

The Inventorie of all and singuler the gooddes cattalls and debtes which lately appertained unto John Bodleighe late of the parishe of Sainte Paule within this citie of Excester decessed made and praysed by John Davye, Richard Bevis, John Chapell and John Ffelde the the Sixteenth day of Marche yeare of our Lord god, a thowsand ffye hundred threescore and twelve, And in the ffyvetenth yeare of the rayne of our sovereigne lady Elizabeth by the grace of god queene of Englande Fraunce and Irelande defender of the faieth &c which praysers were sworne before Mr John Peryam maior of the saide citie of Exon for the trewe praysinge of the saide gooddes and cattalls.

[m. 1] **In** the Haule
Firstly a cubbarde 4s;
Item a table borde and a forme 6s 8d;
Item 3 Joyned stoles 2s;
Item 2 chayres 10d;
Item the Seelinges of tymber with certen cubbordes in the same seelinges with lokes 26s 8d;
Item a dozen of cusshens and a carpet 13s 4d;
Item a backe of Iron in the chymney a [illegible] barr a paier of Andirons, a paier of dogges, a paier of tonges, a fier showell and crokes 8s;
Item the stayned clothes 3s 4d;
Item a Calever with flaskes and an olde carpet 10s;
Item the glasse in the wyndowe and an olde curtyn 10s;
Sum £4 4s 10d.

In the chamber over the haule
Item a feather bed with a tye underneath, a bolster and 2 pyllowes 20s;
Item a paier of blancketts and a coverlet [illegible]s 4d;
Item a bedstede 8s;
Item a fetherbed, a bolster, and 2 pylowties 33s 4d;
Item a coverlet 26s 8d;
Item 2 paier of Blancketts 6s 8d;
Item a bedstede, with a trockelbedd and the teaster 6s 8d;
Item a cubborde 3s 4d;
Item an olde table borde and 2 formes 20d;
Item an olde coffer and 2 litle fforsetts and other trashe 2s 6d;
Item 2 chayres 16d;
Item the stayned clothes 12d;
Item the glasse in the wyndowe and 2 dryncken glasses 6s;
Sum £6 6d.

In the backe chamber
Item a fetherbed, a bolster and 2 litle pyllowes 16s 8d;
Item a coverlet & a paier of blancketes 5s;
Item the bedstede and teaster 18d;
Item a trokelbedstede a flockbed a coverlet, and one blancket 3s 4d;
Item 2 coffers 2s 6d;
Item a Jack and a bill and the stayned hangyns 3s 4d;
Sum 32s 4d.

In the hyer Kytchyn
Item a paier of andyrons and an olde caudron and a pot croke 5s 8d;
Item 2 broches 2s;
Item an [o]lde flockebed a bedstede, coverlet, and a paier of blancketts 3s 4d;
Item 2 olde coffers a forme, and other trashe 3s 4d;
Sum 15s 4d.

In the lower kychyn
Item 4 brasen crockes and 2 skylletts 26s 8d;
Item 5 pannes of brasse 2 caudrons and a chafindishe 23s 4d;
Item 8 candelstickes of Brasse 5s 4d;
Item 2 lattyn drypen pans, a fryinge pan, a skyllet, a gredyron, 3 pot hanginges and a fleshoke 2s;
Item 4 tubbes with other trashe 3s 4d;
Item 3 stone cuppes 18d;
Sum £3 2s 2d.

[m. 2] **In** the hier Shopp
Item in vitery canvas 275 yardes ½ at 7d ½ the yarde – £8 12s 2¼d;
Item normandye canvas ell brode 51 yardes ½ at 10d the yarde – 52s 11d;
Item other canvas 33 yardes ½ at 7d the yarde – 19s 6½d;
Item broune hollande 17 yardes at 20d the yarde – 28s 8d;
Item in broune canvas 10 yardes at 12d the yarde – 10s;
Item in Gentys cloth 21 yardes at 13d the yarde –22s 9d;
Item in morles clothe 21 yardes at 14d the yarde – 24s 6d;

Item in morles cloth 52 yardes at 13*d* the yarde –56*s* 4*d*;

Item in gentis clothe yardes 5 at 12*d* – 5*s*;

Item in hollandes 16 yardes at 2*s* 6*d* – 40*s*;

Item in fyne dowlas 56 yardes at 12*d* the yarde – 56*s*;

Item in common dowlas 205 yardes ½ at 9*d* the yarde – £7 14*s* 1*d* ½;

Item in treeger 2 peces ½ longe playte at £4 the pece – £10;

Item in treeger 163 yardes at 8*d* [?] the yarde – £4 15*s* 1*d*;

Item in Bryten clothe 19 yardes at 6*d* the yarde –9*s* 6*d*;

Item in Inderlans 44 yardes at 2*d* ½ the yarde – 12*s* 10*d*;

Item in canvas 11 yardes at 5*d* the yarde – 4*s* 7*d*;

Item in sackcloth canvas 10 yardes at 6*d* the yarde – 5*s*;

Item in sylke sackcloth 3 yardes at 14*d* the yarde – 3*s* 6*d*;

Item in castell sope 26 pounds 11*s* 3*d*;

Item in twyne 21 raunes 8*s*;

Item in maylinge cordes 3 dozen 9*s*;

Item ropes 4 dozen 4*s*;

Item in small ropes 4*s*;

Item in gyrssewebb 3*s* 4*d*;

Item a ramnant of mockadowe 14*s*;

Item in weke yarne 5*s*;

Item in knyves 7*s*;

Item a Tylte [?] 2*s* 6*d*;

Item 3 remnantes of brode lyninges 20*s*;

Item 7 shertes, 5 bannes 16*s* 8*d*;

Item in Inckell poyntes and broune threade 3*s* 4*d*;

Item in trenchers a paier of wooll cardes, paper, brusshes and cuppes 8*s*;

Item 3 vyrkyns of sope 30*s*;

Item two remnantes of bunter 6*s*;

Item a morter and a pestell 6*s* 8*d*;

Item one dozen of fflannen and a remnante of sackcloth 6*s* 8*d*;

Item in gynger and pepper 3*s*;

Item in fygges, reasons and prunes 6*s*;

Item a paier of scales, 2 paier of Balans, and smale waightes and other trashe 11*s*;

Item 100 quarter ½ of great lead wayghts 12*s*;

Item 2 chestes with a plancke and one olde cheste 24*s* 2*d*;

Sum £59 14*s* 1¼*d*.

In the lower Shopp

Item 16 dozen batters treces 16*s*;

Item 5 dozen small naylinge cordes 16*s* 8*d*;

Item 6 rundes of twyne 3*s* 6*d*;

Item 2 dozen of weke yarne 3*s*;

Item a hundred of hoppes 36*s* 8*d*;

Item a hundred of bristowe sope 20*s*;

Item in lathes 20*d*;

Item 2 olde chestes, olde tubbes, a torne, and other trashe 8*s*;

Sum £5 6*d*.

In the litle howse at the gardyn without Eastgate

Item bords, tymber, and woodd 9*s*;

Item 3 lere hoggesheddes, yron wedges and other trashe 3*s*;

Item a litle reke of ffaggotts 2*s*;

Sum 14*s*.

Item in the grounde without Eastgate 2 kye[n] £3;

Sum £3.

In Pewter vessell

Item 2 basons of pewter, and an euer 4*s*;

Item 22 platters, 18 pottengers & 19 sawcers wayinge in the whole 121 pounde, at 5*d* the pounde 50*s* 5*d*;

Item 6 potage dysshes 2*s*;

Item 9 flower potts 2*s* 3*d*;

Item 2 tynnen cuppes, a salte, a quarte pot, a pynt pot and other pot of tyne 4*s*;

Sum £3 2*s* 8*d*.

[m. 3] **Naperye**

Item a paier of shetes of dowlas and one paier of hollande 30*s*;

Item 8 paier of canvas shetes 20*s*;

Item 3 courtens of dowlas 5*s* 4*d*;

Item 10 piloties 10*s* 4*d*;

Item 8 table clothes of Dowlas 20*s*;

Item 4 table clothes of canvas 6*s*;

Item 6 towells wrought with silke 15*s*;

Item 8 playne towells 5*s*;

Item 3 coberde clothes 2s 6d;
Item a dozen napkyns wrought with silke 12s;
Item 4 dozen and half of napkyns 9s;
Item 5 hand towells 8d;
Sum £6 15s 10d.

Apparell
Item a gowne of blacke faced with budge 35s;
Item a gowne faced with chamlet 10s;
Item an olde gowne faced with budge 4s;
Item a gowne faced with lame 3s 4d;
Item 3 cotes 5s;
Item 2 paier of hosen, and 2 dubletts 4s;
Item 3 cappes 4s;
Item 2 shyrtes 5s;
Sum £3 10s 4d.

Plate and readye money
Item an ale cupp of sylver gylt with a cover conteynes 14 ounces at 5s 2d – £3 12s 4d;
Item a salt with a cover gylt wayinge 11 ounces at 5s the ounce –55s;
Item a goblet of sylver parcell gylt conteynes 16 ounces and a half at 4s 10d the ounce – £3 19s 8d;
Item a goblet parcell gylt conteynes 16 ounces at 4s 4d – £3 9s 4d;
Item a dozen spones with knappes gylt conteynes 14 ounces quaarter at 4s 2d the ounce – 59s 4d;
Item a stone cupp with a cover and foote of sylver conteynes 5 ounces at 4s 6d the ounce – 22s 6d;
Item stone cup with a cover gylt 12s;
Item in ready money £20;
Sum £38 10s 2d.

Sperate debtes and desperate debtes
Item Harry Roche of Crikehorne in the countie of Somerset yoman oweth by his bill obligatorie £6;
Item Thomas Saintclere of Exon oweth by his bill obligatorie 40s;

Item William Erle of Exon apoticarie hath in his handes for an assignement of a lease by hym to be made of certen tenementes withoute Eastgate £6;
Item Mr Richarde Hert townclarke oweth of an obligacion yet to paye £3 6s 8d;
Item there was by the testator paied to one John Hayne of Exon spurrier £3 in consideracion to have 10s a yere, oute of a certen tenement in Sowithgatestreate, there is aboute 28 yeares yet to come, for the payment therof John Smyth of Exon mercer is charged therwith, and for that wee see noo good assurance, we prayse the same at 40s;
Sum £19 6s 8d.

Sum total of all gooddes cattalls and debtes amountes [to] £155 14s 5¼d.
[Signed] John Davye Rychard Bevis John Chapell John Felde

Allocations
Fyrst the Executrice asketh allowance for morninge blackes for 2 cassockes and 3 cotes £3 14s;
Item paied for rynginge of knylles 12d;
Item to the Bell man 6d;
Item to the pit maker 6d;
Item to the vicars of Saint Peters for synginge at the Buryall 6s;
Item to the parson of Saint Petrocks for buringe 6d;
Item for drawinge & engrosing the testament 15s;
Item for provinge of the saide testament 5s;
Item for an obligacion for the assurance of the legacies 12d;
Item for wex, the somners fee & the sealle 8d;
Item for makinge of the Inventories, & for writinge the same twise in paper & three tymes in parchment 26s 8d;
Item to the fower praysers 2s a pece for their paynes 8s;
Sum £6 18s 10d.

[m. 4] **Debtes** auen by the testator at the tyme of his decesse
Item the saide testator owed to Leonarde Lovys esquier £10;
[Tails off].

31A. WILL OF RICHARD MOGRIDGE, CUTLER OF ST MARY MAJOR'S PARISH, 20 DECEMBER 1575

ECA, Orphans' Court Will 18

Note: 17 is an imperfect copy. The register for the parish of St Mary Major recorded 'Richard Moggridge' was buried on 19 July 1576.

In the name of God Amen the 20th daie of December in the yere of our Lord 1575 I Richard Mogeridge of the Cittie and Countie of Exeter Cutler being of hole mynde and in good and perfet remembrance Lawde & prayse be unto Almightie God doe make & ordeyne this my presente Testermente conteynenge herein my laste wille & testament in manner & forme folowenge, that is to saye firste I comend my Soule to Almightie God my savior and only redemer and my bodie to be buried within the churche dore of St Marie the More within the Citye of Exeter wheareas the beareres doe now stand. Item, I do geve to send emong the poore aswell in the prisons as ells where, where my executors thereunder named shall thinke most needful. Item, I geve & bequeath unto Jone my wief my howse that I now dwell in during her life together with the halfendeale of my goods & ymplements being in the same howse. Item I geve and bequeth to my cosen Jane Bonamye the other halfendeale of my goods & ymplements now being in my said howse and also my howse at Westgate after my decesse & Jone my saide wief to the said Jane Bonamye for terme of her lief. Item I geve & bequeth to Edmond Bonamye my howse whereyn Christopher Scoble and Clements and Gaye now dwellyth after my decesse, & Jone my said wief to the said Edmond for & durenge the the terme of yeres then to come in the same. Item I geve & bequeathe to Edith Bonamys after the deceasse of my said wief & me my howse wherein Mother Nicholes late dwelled to the said Edeth during the terme of yeres then to come yn

the same. Item I bequethe to my brother Laurens Mogrudge my worst gowne of brode cloth & my best of broadeclothe. Item I give to my brother Laurens Mogrudge in monye 5s. Item I geve to my cosen John Wharton my second best gowne & a sworde & dagger worthe 10s or 12s. Item my will is that if Jone my wief do happen to marrye & my goods to my children by me as aforr geven & bequethed or any parcels thereof doe then at her sayde marriadge remayne in her sayde handes & undelyvered shold forthwith be delyvered to my sayde children viz Jane Bonaymye Edmond Bonamye & Edith Bonaymye. And if anye of my saide children Jane, Edmond & Edith happen to die before they have their porcions of the said goods to them geven by me as aforesaide cleere to there hands & possession, then his and there parte so decessed to remayne & be to & emonge the survivors of them. The residewe of all my goodds cattells & dets after my debts paid my funeral expenses performed & theyse my legacyes conteyned in this my present Testament fullfylled, I holie geve & bequethe to Jone my sayd wief & Jane Bonamy my cossen whome I make my whole executaries. And of the execution of the same I make and ordeyne John Shorte John Lynne & Thomas Clarke overseers and for theire labor on that behalf I geve to everie of them 5s. And I utterlye revoke & annul all & everie former testament wills legacies bequestes executors & overseers by me in any wise before this tyme made named, willed & bequethed witnesses Thomas Clarke the writer.

31B. INVENTORY OF RICHARD MOGRIDGE, CUTLER OF ST MARY MAJOR'S PARISH, 20 DECEMBER 1575

ECA, Orphans' Court Inventory 26

An Inventorye of the goods & cattels of Richard Mogridge of the citie of Exeter Cutler decessed taken & praysed by Fyte Lenden, Richard Stanesbye Richard Bowdon and Richard Collyns the 17th Daye of August 1576

[1] The Hawll
Firstly a foldinge Bourd with a frame 12s;
Item an olde Carpett of Turkey worke 6s 8d;
Item 6 Cusshings of tapstrie worke stuft with ffloxe 5s;
Item the Bentches about the Table 10s;
Item 2 Cobbards with a pece of seling 8d;
Item one ioynd Chaier 12d;
Item one ioynid fforme 16d;
Item foure Pyctures 8s;
Item 10 golden leaves of leather to make Cusshings 6s 8d;
Item the hangings about the hall beinge Stayned Clothes 2s;
Item fyve Targetts 12s 6d;
Item foure eard disshes of tyn 20d;
Item one london Pottell pott, one london quart pott, & one Ewar of Tyn 5s;
Item 3 olde tyn bell Cansticks 16d;
Item 85 lb ½ of Pewter at 5d – 33s 4d;
Item fyve bell cansticks of brasse 5s one preckett cansticke of brasse 3s 4d & fyve other brasse cansticks 16d – 9s 8d;
Item two Chafingdisshes 2s;
Item one Brush 8d;
Item the grate, Shelves & dore of the Buttrye & shelve Clothes 2s 6d;
Item the glasse in the wyndoe with the casements 20s;
Item 20 Cheses 13s 4d;
Item one dossen Round Trenchers & one little tablement of a face and a litle stoole 4d;
Item vyell glasses 4d;
Item the ende of an Olefants tothe 16d;

Sum £8 12s 4d [entry crossed through];
Sum £9 3s 4d.

The Chamber within the Hall
Item one standinge bedstede with a tester of waynscote, one feather bed one flock bedde, 3 bolsters of feathers, one pilloe of feathers & a Keverlett 40s;
Item one other standing bedstede with a tester of Cloth, 2 feather beds, 2 feather bolsters, one feather Pilloe, one blanket, one red Keverlet, one mantyll and a litle rug mantyll 60s;
Item a close Presse 6s;
Item a round Table 2s;
Item 2 close stoles & a chaier 8d;
Item a close chaier 12d;
Item fyve chests greate & smale 4s;
Item the hangings being paynted clothes 4s;
Item the glasse in the wyndoe with a casement 5s;
Item 2 Capcases 6d;
Item certaine Bookes 6d;
Item a pole Axe 2s 6d;
Sum £5 6s 2d.

[2] The backe Chamber
Item a bedstede with a Tester of Saye, a flockebed, a feather bolster with a mantyll & a keverlett 6s 8d;
Item a forme & a Presse 6d;
Item a Turne & Chawke 8d;
Sum 7s 10d.

The fore Chamber
Item a bedstede, a Cowpe 2 Boles, 2 tubs & other traysh 20d;
Item a vyce 2s;
Item a Styll 18d;

Item a quylted Jacke 20*d*;
Sum 6*s* 10*d*.

The Kytchinge
Item a table Bourd, a bentche & a forme with the seelinge 5*s*;
Item a foldinge Bourd & a forme 20*d*;
Item 2 Cobbards 10*s*;
Item 2 paier of goldsmyths Belloes 2*s*;
Item 2 Powdringe Tubs, 1 waishing Tubbe 2 Chayers, dishes
    trenchers and other traysh 2*s*;
Item paynted Clothes about the wals 3*s* 4*d*;
Item 14 flower pots good & bad 16*d*;
Item 3 broches, 1 paier of tongs, 1 fier shovell, 2 pott hangers,
    2 Andyrons, 1 frying pan, one drypinge pan, 1 gredeyron,
    2 paier of pott hokes, one flesh hoke, 1 latten ladell, one
    belloes, 1 dog of yron & 1 paier of Snoffers 7*s*;
Item 2 blacke Jacks, one Cupp, one baskett & a Bottell 6*d*;
Item a Chaffer of brasse & one yron glewe Pott 2*s*;
Item 5 pannes greate & smale, 2 Cawdyrons, 3 Crocks & one
    leasse flower Pott 26*s* 8*d*;
Item a bible & other Bokes 5*s*;
Item 3 olde Cusshings & a Carpet 12*d*;
Item the glasse in the wyndoes 3*s* 4*d*;
Sum £3 15*s* 10*d*.

The lofte over the Shoppe
Item 60 bunches of skales and other traish 10*s*;
Sum 10*s*.

The Shoppe
Item 2 quarters and ½ of coles 12*s*;
Item 4 paier of Almon Ryvets and 3 skuls 13*s* 4*d*;
Item 3 moryans 6*s*;
Item 2 Kalyvers 8*s*;
Item one Buckler 20*d*;
Item one dagge, with a flaske & Case 3*s* 4*d*;
Item 10 Sword greate and smalle readye trymmed 20*s*;
[3] Item six swords blades 12*s*;
Item 10 dagger Blades 5*s*;

Item 17 daggers ready trymd 20*s*;
Item olde skynes & blades 6*s* 8*d*;
Item ffyles & hammers 4*s*;
Item 1 dossen of hilts & pomels 14*s*;
Item 3 Sawes, 1 paier of plate Shears & 1 burnysher 12*d*;
Item 3 vices & a Byckhorne 12*s*;
Item a fote glasier 8*d*;
Item 2 Coffers, 1 Beame & the Shelves 5*s*;
Item 3 dossen of handells & wyer 4*s*;
Item Glewe & other traish 2*s*;
Item 1 Cowle, 1 Javelinge staf & 10 knyves 8*d*;
Sum £7 10*s* 4*d*.

The Forge
Item a paier of Belloes the Racke staf and the Turon 8*s*;
Item an Anvill & a Bickhorne 13*s* 4*d*;
Item [5 hammers – crossed through] 2 Sledges & 3 hamers, 2
    payer of tongs, 1 fier sklyce, and 1 Clift 5*s*;
Item 1 hatchett & a Coletroe 6*d*;
Item 1 Anvill stocke, & a bickhorne stocke 6*d*;
Item a gryndinge stone with a spill 8*d*;
Item a holloe whele, with a spyll & the glasiers that belongeth
    thereto 4*s*;
Item 1 gryndinge stone with 2 turners and a Spill 5*s*;
Sum 37*s*.

His leasses
Item the terme of his leasse to come of his house in Preston
    Streate wherein Thomas Gyll nowe dwelleth £8;
Item the terme of his leasse to come of his houses in Preston
    Streate aforesaide which he had by the graunt of Thomas
    Ratclief £10;
Item 10 white Kersies £16 2*s*;
Sum £34 2*s*.

His apparell
Item a townes gowne with a welt of velvett 30*s*;
Item a gowne with a standing coller furd thorough out with
    white lame 16*s*;

Item an olde gowne 4s;
Item a slyveles Jackett 5s;
Item a blacke Cloke 12s;
Item a Canvas doblet & a leather gerkinge 2s 6d;
Item a doblet with damas slyves 20d;
Item 2 velvet night Caps and a cloth Cappe 4s;
Item 2 sherts & an olde doblet 2s;
Sum £3 17s 2d.

[4] Naperye
Item 4 longe table Towels 3 bourd clothes, 1 dossen of bourde
    napkyns, and 2 paier of Sheets 20s;
Sum 20s.

Plate
Item a stone Cupp covered with silver & gilt and a fote to the
    same by estymacon 26s 8d;
Item a litle stone Cuppe covered with silver, & a fote to the
    same by estymacon 13s 4d;
Item half a dossen silver spones 20s;
Sum £3.
Sum total £70 16s 6d.

Debts which he oweth
Item to Mr Trevet & Mr Hoker £19 11s 4d;
Item to Willm James 31s 4d;
Item to Barthelmewe Filde of London £3 13s 11d;
Item to Richard Cover 34s 8d;
Item to a Hallmishere man 16s;
Item to Jerome Wilcoks 22s;
Item to Anthonye Pyers of Tyverton £15;
Sum £43 9s 3d.

ECA, Orphans' Court Inventory 26 [Item 2]

Debts which Were owing by Richard Mogridge when he died
Firstly to Mr Trivet and Mr Hooker [rest lost];
Item to Willm James the [illegible; rest lost];
Item to Barthilmew Filde of London £4 [rest lost];

Item to Richard Cover 34s 8d;
Item to a Hallomshire man 16s;
Item to Jerome Wilcoks 22s;
Item for the legacies of John Weyes children £15;
Item to Wodham of Yde 17s;
Item Mr Radford demaundeth £4 but there is but 10s due to
    him – £4;
Item to Mr Buckeford £6 13s 4d;
Item to John Mogridge 26s 8d;
£57 10s 4d.

The legacie of Richard Mogrige geven unto Jane Bonamye
Firstly a fether bedd a bolster and 2 pillowes and a standinge
    bedsteed 40s;
Item a Croke a pann & a spitt 9s;
Item two bell Candlesticks and a laten chafendishe 5s;
Item 3 platters 3 powngers 3 saucers 2 spice platters 3
    porredge disshes of tynne a salte seller & a wyne quart pott
    16s;
Item the Cubourd in the Kytchin 20s;
Item a basen and yeuer & 3 flower potts 6s;
Sum £4 16s.

ECA, Orphans' Court Inventory 26 [Item 3]

[1] Memorandum that Richard Mogredge of the Citie of
Excester Cutler who dyed the 19th of Julye 1576 dyd by his
last wyll and testament geve and bequethe to Edethe Bonamy
the daughter of Nychus Banamye of the same Citie cutler the
lease & termes of yeres which he had then to come of & yn
one tenement yn Prestone Streete yn the Citie of Excester
which sometyme Thomas Nycholls dyd inhabyt and is holden
of Mr Forteskew of Fylleygh [?] by the yerelye rent of 10s 8d
To have & to holden to the sayde Edethe & to her assignes
immedyatly upon the dethe or mariege of Jone Mogryg the
then wyff of the sayde Rycherd Mogrydge;
Lykewyse under the same order manner & condicion he gave
& bequethed to Edmond Bonamy the sonn of the foresayde
Nychus Bonamye that lease & termes of yeres which he had

then to come of & yn one tenement yn the sayde streete of Prestonestreet which is holden of Thomas Ratclyff lat of the Citie of Excester decessed & now of Hannyball Ratclyff his sonne for the yerely rent of 20s.

It happened that the same Jone Mogrydg wydow dyd after the dethe of her husbonde namely yn 28th of September 1577 marie with Richard Gifferd of the saide Citie and by that meanes bothe the foresayd Leasses sholde have come to the foresayd Edethe & Edmond but the effect of the will & testament of the foresaid [2] last will & testament of Richard Mogrydg being not then knowen to the Chamberlayn & other the officers for orphanes of the Citie the sayde Richard Gifford received the rents of bothe the sayde too tenements dew at michaellmas next foloweng after their mariege: but from thenseforthe the tenements were forbydd by the chaumberlayn of the Citie to pay any more rent unto the saide Richard Gifford or to his wyff but onely unto the sayde Chamberlayn to the use of the sayde children untyll that the sayde Richard dyd put yn sufficient suerties for awnswering of the same Rents to the use of the sayde chyldren according to the chartor of the orphanes & orders of the And [land] by which meanes the foresayde Chamberlayn from the sayde feast of St Michaell dyd receve the sayde rents and chardgethe hym selffe as folowethe

[3] 1578
The Tenement yn Prestonstreet geven to Edethe Bonamy & holden of Mr Forteskewe
Received of John Salter for one yeres rent for the moytie of the sayde tenement ended at Michaelmas 1578 & for one quarters rent dew before which was not payed unto Richard Gifford 33s 4d;
Received also of [blank] Clapp for one yeres rent ended at Michaelmas 1578 for the other moytie of the sayde tenement 26s 8d;
Sum of this yeres rent £3.

Whereof payed to Mr Forteskewe for one yeres rent ended at our lady daye 1578 10s 8d;
Also allowed to the foresayde Clapp for sundry reparacons by hym doune as appeareth by hys byll [blank].

1579 Receved of John Salter for one quarters rent dewe at christmas 1578 when he departed out of the tenement & left the same wholy to Clapp 6s 8d;
Received of Clappe for one whole yere for the one moitie and 3 quarters for the other moitie 46s 8d.

[4] Firstly paid to Mr Forteskew by his servant Thorne the 28 of Marche for one yeres rent ended at the feast of our ladye last past 1579 10s 8d;
Item the 9 of Marche 1579 [1580] for one yeres rent dew at our lady last commyng paid to Mr Forteskew 10s 8d;
Item the 9th of Marche 1580 paid for one yeres rent dew at our ladie daye next cominge and which monie I received then of John Clapp 10s 8d.
[6] 1578 The Tenement yn Prestonestreet geven to Edmonde Bonamy
John Clement holdethe the moitie of that part of the tenement which is next adioyning to the howse which Frauncys Geffrey holdethe and paiethe by the yere 15s;
John Doble holdethe the other moitie of the same tenement & payeth by the yere 15s;
Mychaell Wolston holdethe the next tenemente being the mydle tenemente & paiethe by the yere 26s 8d;
Garrett Collyns holdethe the higher pare of the lowest tenemente & paiethe by the yere 8s;
Wydowe Langefford holdethe the lower parte of the said 3rd tenemente & paiethe yerly 8s;
Sum £3 12s 8d.

Whereof paid for one whole yeres rent dew at Michaelmas to Hannyball Ratclyff 20s.

Item for mending & repayring of the howse to John Serell helier for 12 dayes at 12d – 12s;

Item to John Bagwell for 6 daies 5s;
Item to John Smote for 12 daies at 8d – 8s;
25s.

Item for lyme 6s 8d;
Item for pynnes 6d;
Item for crestes 9d;
Item for Rafters 8d;
Item for 200 of laths 12d;
Item for 800 of lathe nayles 16d;
Item for 1000 of stones 5s;
Item for sande 12d;
Item for hache nayles 3d;
17s 2d;
[7] Item for 4 bordes to mak new wyndowes at 8d the pece –
    2s 8d;
Item for hatche nayles 8d;
Item to Symon Blackmore for 2 daies 2s;
5s 4d;
Sum [paid out] £3 7s 6d.

Also there remaineth yn the handes of Garret Collyns &
    wydowe Langfford for one yeres rent & yet unpayed 16s.

Sum of the reparacons & arrerages for this yere £4 3s 6d;
And so this account is yn surplusag for this yere 10s 10d.

John Clement & Nycholas Bonamye for one yere at
    Michaelmas 1579 15s;
John Dobell for one yere ended at Mychaelmas 1579 15s;
Mychaell Wolston for one yere at 17 November 1579 26s 8d;
Garret Collyns for one yere 8s;
Wydow Langefford for one yere 8s.

Item paid to Hannyball Ratclyff for chrystmas quarters rent
    1578 5s;
Item to him the 13 of May 1579 by his wyff for our lady
    quarter 5s;
Item to hym by his wyff the 21 of August 1579 5s;
Item the 14 of October 1579 to Hannyball Ratclyff for
    Michaelmas quarter 5s;
[8] Item paied to Hannyball Ratclyff the 28 of January 1579
    [1580] for Christmas quarter 5s;
Item paid to Hannyball Ratclyff the 20th of Aprill 1580 for
    our lady quarter 5s;
Item paid to Hannyball Ratclyff 13 July 1580 for mydsomer
    quarter 5s.

32. INVENTORY OF WILLIAM SELDON, MERCHANT OF ST PETROCK'S PARISH, 16 MARCH 1576

ECA, Orphans' Court Inventory 23
Note: The register for the parish of St Petrock recorded 'Wm Seldon' was buried on 1 February 1576.

[m. 1] **The Inventorye** of all & singuler the goods & cattells
which latlie appertened to one William Seldon late of the
parrishe of St Petrox within the cittie of Exeter decessed made
& praised the 16th daie of March in the year 1575 by John
Watkins & Christopher Weste as foloweth

In the [Hall – crossed through] Shope
Firstly a course coverlett 3s 4d;
Item 6 thrumed Cusshens unstoffed 6s 8d;

Item 2 carpetts of Listeinge 5s;
Item 4 dossen of wimble Irons 12d;
Item a dosen & ½ of fariners [?] & gowges 2s;
Item 2 dosen of golde ffyles 16d;
Item one neste of boxes 20d;
Item in one boxe [illegible] 400 of white garnished nailes 6d;
Item one sute of buckells 6d;
Item a 100 of muster Heads 12d;
Item 3 showemakers Knyves 6d;

Item one pesse & 2 bounches of surge[n]ts Instruments 2*s*;

Item 5 pare of small tressell garnishe 10*d*;

Item 6 paier of Inside butts 4*d*;

Item 6 fyer Irons 3*d*;

Item 6 mowlds for callivers 18*d*;

Item 10 stele plane Irons 2*s*;

Item 10 pare of small campasses 12*d*;

Item 3 brassen cocks 9*d*;

Item 6 Rustie penknyves 4*d*;

Item 6 dagger Handells 6*d*;

Item half a grosse of threde buttons 2*d*;

Item 24 dossen of crane chappes 8*s*;

Item one dossen ½ of sadlers buckells 6*d*;

Item a dosen ½ of chaier nailes 6*d*;

Item 3 dosen of shanks 3*d*;

Item in one boxe one dosen of ffyles & 6 Rapes 2*s* 4*d*;

Item 2 dosen of bowe strings 10*d*;

Item 4 peare of taylers sheers & 2 choppinge knives 3*s*;

Item 6 lb of blacke Leade 12*d*;

Item 6 lb of Reddinge stone 12*d*;

Item 5 lb quarter of yealowe waxe 3*s* 6*d*;

Item 6 bobbings to winde silke upon 3*d*;

Item in 2 barrells ½ *C* of yealowe Auker 2*s* 6*d*;

Item 2 Lookeinge glasses 4*d*;

Item 4 lb of Crosbowe Twyne 2*s*;

[m. 2] Item 2 lb of Kyppe threed 2*s* 6*d*;

Item 6 lb of Leyll for courtin Rings 3*d*;

Item 6 salte sellers of Tynne 3*s*;

Item a standinge 4*d*;

Item 3 boxes with an owence ballance 6*d*;

Item 14 paier playinge cards 2*s* 4*d*;

Item 6 mane Combes 6*d*;

Item 2 roles of gerse webbe 2*s*;

Item 2 Rolles of gerse webbe [entry crossed through];

Item 6 rounde litle lookenge glasses 3*d*;

Item ½ a pounde of red waxe 8*d*;

Item 3 dosen of buttons for hunteinge hornes 6*s*;

Item A greate grose of Amilde buttons 10*s*;

Item 6 dossen of blacke glassebuttons 3*d*;

Item a 100 of blacke bullings 3*d*;

Item 4 sewtes of buckells 2*s*;

Item 2 dossen of buckells for bouts 12*d*;

Item a 1000 of rose nayles 12*d*;

Item a 1000 of harnis nailes 2*s*;

Item a greater Leike a peare of billowes 3*d*;

Item 4 litle graters 4*d*;

Item 4 gold smyth brawches of Heare 6*d*;

Item 2 lb quarter of crewell motheaten 3*s* 6*d*;

Item 2 ownces ½ of silke frendge 2*s* 6*d*;

Item 10 ownces of blacke bottom threde 10*d*;

Item a grosse of crewell parchment lace 2*s*;

Item a dosen & ½ of statute pomett 8*d*;

Item 4 dosen of parchemente gerdlenge 16*d*;

Item 2 yerds of bobbinge Lace 4*d*;

Item 3 dosen of Armore poynts 6*d*;

Item a dosen of threede gerdelinge 6*d*;

Item 2 yerds of white Thride ffrenge 6*d*;

Item 4 pound ½ of peceminge threede 10*s*;

Item 3 mocado nighte cappes mothe eaten 6*d*;

Item a dosen & ½ of leather lace 3*d*;

Item 3 yerds & half of carrell 3*s* 6*d*;

Item a painted border & another for a bed 2*s*;

Item a dosen of leather gloves 12*d*;

Item a dosen of rings for halters 3*d*;

Item 3 dosen of harnis buckells 12*d*;

Item a dosen & ½ of Serills at 4*s* 6*d*;

Item 3 combe brusshes 3*d*;

Item 7 pare of barbers sisters 2*s* 4*d*;

[m. 3] Item a pare of gylte sycers 6*d*;

Item a dosen of Koper flewes 12*d*;

Item in cop[per?] spones for cockes 4*d*;

Item 6 dogge coples 6*d*;

Item a dosen of buckells for girdells 6*d*;

Item 2 pare of course spectakell cases 4*d*;

Item a gate loke 4*d*;

Item 4 white candell plates 4*d*;

Item a boxe with 6 pare of ballance 12*d*;

Item 3 cappe whocks [?] 6*d*;

Item 6 lb of spanyshe browne 12*d*;

Item 4 wembells 12*d*;

Item 5 grehounde collers 6*d*;

Item 2 breade graters 8*d*;

Item 6 lb of matches 18*d*;

Item 10 dogge crooks 10*d*;

Item a goose pan of white plate 6*d*;

Item 7 hand sawes & graffinge sawes 2*s* 4*d*;

Item more 2 Iron Ladells 4*d*;

Item 6 brassen showinge hornes 16*d*;

Item in a follett 2 grosse of buckells 9*s*;

Item a pare of Tinkers sheares 20*d*;

Item 4 duche lockes 2*s* 4*d*;

Item a neste of boxes contenynge 21 – 2*s*;

Item an other neste of boxes containing 32 – 3*s* 6*d*;

Item an other neste of boxes containing 12 – 12*d*;

Item a quarte tyninge bottell 16*d*;

Item 2 glassen bottells 12*d*;

Item 3 portall gymmoyes 9*d*;

Item one dosen of Tyninge spones 6*d*;

Item 12 lb of glewe 2*s* 6*d*;

Item a vice of Iron 3*s*;

Item a becke horne 12*d*;

Item 2 blacke plats 6*d*;

Item 3 pare of sworde hangings 21*d*;

Item 10 longe blacke wastes 20*d*;

Item 5 samgnyne [?] waste 8*d*;

Item 3 anviles 21*d*;

Item 2 anvyles for poynters 8*d*;

Item a barrell of Turpentyne 15*s*;

Item 6 Inke hornes 12*d*;

Item 3 robbars 6*d*;

Item a greate grosse of [illegible] combes 12*s*;

Item a pare of pointers pynsers 3*d*;

Item 2 fyshe skimes 12*d*;

[m. 4] Item 6 chaines for Kyes 12*d*;

Item a money backe 4*d*;

Item a reame of writinge paper 4*s*;

Item 6 lb of fraunkeine sence 2*s*;

Item 8 dosen of ringe thimbells 2*s*;

Item 9 dosen of Tappe thimbells 3*s*;

Item a pounde of Angletts 10*d*;

Item a dosen of arrowe heades 3*d*;

Item 2 dosen of harpers for Jives [? Jews] 2*s*;

Item a boxe of trenchers 6*d*;

Item 2 hacke lockes 6*d*;

Item a horse combe 4*d*;

Item 2 chestes & a litle olde borde 6*s* 8*d*;

Item ½ *C* of ottrome 2*s* 6*d*;

Item a 100 gloviers neildes 6*s*;

Item 4 dosen of cammells [?] 8*d*;

Item one dosen of bobbinge lace 12*d*;

Item 6 hooks & eyes for clokes 3*d*;

Item a dosen yerds of moth eaten bouler [?] 10*d*;

Item 600 of comunion breade 2*s*;

Item a pounde & ½ of campeheire 15*s*;

Item a 1000 of fyshe hooks 8*d*;

Item a 100 of chawlke 12*d*;

Item ½ a grosse of carnyshe poynts 10*d*;

Item 2 dosen of silke poynts 4*d*;

Item 5 papers of whissells & pynes 10*d*;

Item 13 lb of brasse waights 8*s*;

Item a beame with skales 2*s*;

Item a 100 & 19 lb of Leade waights 10*s*;

Item all the shelves & shelvebords 5*s*;

Item 3 pare of ballans 4*s*;

Item 2 other pare of ballans 8*d*;

Item 2 pounde of wiat & 1 lb of knittinge nelds 18*d*;

Item 3 goldesmyth hammers 6*d*;

Item 2 square packe [?] neilds 3*d*;

Item a hangenge candellsticke 10*d*;

Item 2 dosen of leane boxes 6*d*;

Item ½ a some [?] of Laste nayles 5*s*;

Item 12 lb of Reddinge 12*d*;

Item 2 handhatchetts 12*d*;

Item 3 spoke shaves 6*d*;

Item 3 Iron Raches to make showebokells 12*d*;

Item 3 hammers 3 pare of plyars 12*d*;

Item a pare of Iron Tongs 6*d*;
Item 5 rottinge Irons & a borrier 12*d*;
Item a burnyshinge Iron 2 planes & other olde Ire 12*d*;
[m. 5] Item 12 olde barrells 12*d*;
Item an olde hamper 4*d*;
Item in agricke for potticaries 2*s*;
Item in dragons blude 6*d*;
Sum £15 13*s* 8*d*.

In the noyar howse behinde the shoppe
Item a plancke with certen olde timber and bords 3*s* 4*d*;
Item a fframe 12*d*;
Sum 4*s* 4*d*.

In the Hall
Item a presse with 2 cubbords 33*s* 4*d*;
Item a gowne faced with damaske 30*s*;
Item an other gowne faced with budge 30*s*;
Item an other olde gowne faced with budge 10*s*;
Item a cloake with brodcloth 6*s* 8*d*;
Item a cassocke of silke chamlett 15*s*;
Item a damaske Jackett 6*s* 8*d*;
Item a clothen cassocke garded with velvet 5*s*;
Item a wosterd cassocke 5*s*;
Item 3 dobletts slived with silke 13*s* 4*d*;
Item 3 pare of hosen 13*s* 4*d*;
Item 3 pare of showes & a pare of slippers 3*s*;
Item 6 shurts 30*s*;
Item 2 wollinge capes & 2 velvett nighte capes 10*s*;
Item a greate Joyned cheste 6*s* 8*d*;
Item all the seelinge benches 10*s*;
Item a longe Table borde & a forme 12*s*;
Item a litle side table bord 3*s* 4*d*;
Item 3 litle Joyned stooles 18*d*;
Item 2 grene carpetts 13*s* 4*d*;
Item A dosen of greene quysshens 4*s*;
Item a bason & yeower of Tyn 5*s*;
Item a hanginge yeower of tynne 2*s*;
Item a coffer 2*s* 6*d*;

Item a latten candleplate 20*d*;
Item the bordes over the seelinge & a peice of hangeinge 5*s*;
Item 14 flower potts 2*s* 4*d*;
Item a longe bowe & two sheife of arrowes 5*s*;
Item 3 beere glasses 6*d*;
Item a backe of Ire 5*s*;
Item 2 litle Andirons 2*s*;
Item an Iron barre in the chimney 16*d*;
[m. 6] Item 2 pare of Almont Rivetts 13*s* 4*d*;
Item 2 browne bills 2*s*;
Item a corselett with a peicke 25*s*;
Item a calliver 10*s*;
Item 16 panes of glasse in the windowe by estimacion 64 foote at 6*d* the foote 32*s*;
Sum £18 17*s*.

In the Parlor within the hall
Item a Joyned bedsteed with a tester of seelinge & a truckelbed underneth worth 26*s* 8*d*;
Item 2 fether beds 43*s* 4*d*;
Item a coverlett of ares 33*s* 4*d*;
Item a coverlett of Tapistrie 6*s* 8*d*;
Item 2 bolsters of feathers 6*s* 8*d*;
Item 2 pillowes of fethers 4*s*;
Item a pare of blanketts 2*s* 6*d*;
Item a quelte 2*s* 6*d*;
Item a litle cubbord 5*s*;
Item the seelinge 10*s*;
Item an olde chaire 8*d*;
Item a rounde Table borde 2*s*;
Item a bible 6*s* 8*d*;
Item a comunyon booke 2*s* 6*d*;
Item a booke of John Dewgs [?] 5*s*;
Item 2 Iron doggs in the chimney 2*s*;
Item an Iron backe in the chimney 3*s* 4*d*;
Item a fier showell with a pare of tongs 2*s*;
Item a pare of bellowes 6*d*;
Sum £8 5*s* 8*d*.

In the greate chamber over the hall
Item a bedsted with a truckell bed & Tester of sellenge 20*s*;
Item a fether bed with a bolster & 2 pillowes 23*s* 4*d*;
Item an olde coverlett 3*s* 4*d*;
Item a pare of blanketts 2*s*;
Item a litle foldinge table borde 2*s* 6*d*;
Item a pare of virginalls 15*s*;
Item a close stoole 4*s*;
Item an olde coffer 12*d*;
Item an olde hamper 4*d*;
Item a presse with a closett of seelinge 20*s*;
Item 10 thrumed quyshens 16*s* 4*d*;
Item a presse for capps 2*s*;
[m. 7] Item 4 lardge downe pillowes 20*s*;
Item an olde carpett of darnixe 12*d*;
Item all the seelinge there 10*s*;
Item the glasse in the windowe 10*s*;
Sum £7 10*s* 10*d*.

In the Litle chamber at stare hedd
Firstly one truckell bed steede 5*s*;
Item a fether bed a bolster a pillowe of fethers & a quylte 20*s*;
Item a pare of blanketts 20*d*;
Sum 26*s* 8*d*.

In the Litle chamber within that
Item a bedsteed with a flocke bed & a bolster & a pillowe of flockes 10*s*;
Item a pare of blanketts & a quylte 5*s*;
Sum 15*s*.

In plate
Item a silver salte parcell gylte wayinge 13 owences at 4*s* 6*d* the owence – 58*s*;
Item a goblett parcell gylte wayinge 11 awncs 50*s*;
Item a salte doble gylte with a cover weinge 22 owncs 3 quarters at 7*s* the ownce £7 18*s* 9*d*;
Item a standenge cupp doble gilte weinge 15 owncs at 7*s* an ownce £5 5*s*;

Item a litle Ale cupp with a cover parcell gilte wayinge 10 owncs at 4*s* 8*d* ye [?] ounce 46*s* 8*d*;
Item a dosen of spones with gilte knappes weinge 14 ouncs at 4*s* 8*d* the ownce £3 4*s* 8*d*;
Item a goblett parcell gilte wayinge 15 owencs 3 quarters at 4*s* 8*d* ye ownce £3 3*s* 6*d*;
Item the foote cover & mouth of a stone cup gilte estemed 6 ounces at 5*s* the owence 30*s*;
Item the foote cover & mouth of a stone cupp grarnyshed [*sic*] with silver beinge 5 owncs at 4*s* 8*d* the ownce 23*s* 4*d*;
Sum £30.
The Pewter vessell & candelstickes
Item 4 Lattin candelstickes 8*s*;
Item 5 pewter candelstickes 5*s*;
Item 20 platters 20*s*;
Item 13 podgers 8*s* 8*d*;
Item 19 sawsers 6*s* 4*d*;
Item 12 porridge dishes 6*s*;
Item 2 olde platters of Tyn 12*d*;
[m. 8] Item 2 olde basons of Tin 2*s*;
Item a chamber pott 12*d*;
Item 10 fruyte sawsers 3*s* 4*d*;
Sum £3 1*s* 4*d*.

The naperie
Item 9 pare of sheets 45*s*;
Item 6 borde clothers 24*s*;
Item 6 pilloties 6*s*;
Item 21 table napkens 10*s* 6*d*;
Item 5 cubbord clothes 5*s*;
Item a dowlasse towell 18*d*;
Sum £4 12*s*.

In the kytchen
Item 2 pans of brasse 10*s*;
Item 3 cawdrons of brasse 10*s*;
Item a brasse buckett 3*s* 4*d*;
Item a cop[per] kettell 6*s* 8*d*;
Item a skillet 8*d*;

Item a fryinge pan 12*d*;
Item 2 andirons 5*s*;
Item 2 broches 2*s*;
Item a grediron 8*d*;
Item 2 pare of pothooks 2*s*;
Item 2 dripinge pans of plate 12*d*;
Item 4 pott crowks 4*s*;
Item 3 brasse crockes 30*s*;
Item 3 tubbes 12*d*;
Item a borde & a cubbord 2*s* 6*d*;
Item a chaffinge dishe of lattin 20*d*;
Item a pare of bellowes 12*d*;
Item a powdringe tubbe 12*d*;
Item a pare of Tongs 8*d*;
Item a brandise 10*d*;
Item an Ire to lie before the dripinge panns 10*d*;
Item a chaffer of brasse to heate water in 3*s* 4*d*;
Item a brewinge Tubbe 3 coasts & other wooden vessell 4*s*;
Sum £4 11*s* 10*d*.

Item the lease of the howse for 30 yeres yet to come of the same lease worth £10;
Item in money & golde 20*s*;
Item in wood 6*s* 8*d*;
Item a greate cupp of stone with a cover of tynne 6*d*;
[m. 9] Item an other greate stonenge pott 4*d*;
Item 2 quarte potts of Tynne 2*s*;
Item 2 pynte potts of Tynne 12*d*;
Item a latten braunce worthe 2*s* 4*d*;
Item 2 olde coffers at 3*s*;
Sum £11 16*s* 10*d*.

Sum total £106 15*s* 2*d*.

It agrees with the original inventory of the goods of the aforesaid William Seldon deceased remaining with the registry of the archdeaconry of Exeter.

Witnessed by me Jaspar Bridgeman, Notary Public and Registrar.

33A. WILL OF HARRY JAMES, NOTARY PUBLIC, 11 OCTOBER 1576

National Archives, PROB 11/60/457
Note: The will was proved via Canterbury on 24 September 1578. Recognisances were first entered into on 20 November & 1 December, 1578, and 24 January 1579 for Agnes, Judith, Robert and Mary the children of Henry James (ECA, Book 141, folios 63 dorse to 67) but there is extensive subsequent administration.

[1] ***In the name of God Amen*** The 11th daye of October in the yeare of our Lorde god <u>1576</u> I Harry James of the citye of Exeter notary publique being whole of minde and perfect of memorye thancks be given to Almightye god doe revoke adnichilate and make voyde all foremer wills testaments Legaceis and executors by me heretofore made and doe make this my Last will and testament in manner and forme as followeth. First I bequeathe my sowle to Almightye god and my bodye to Christian buryall. Item I give to the poore people of Exeter 40*s*. Item to the poore sick people of the Mawdlen in Exeter 6*s* 8*d*. Item to the poore prisoners of the kings gaile in Exeter 6*s* 8*d*. Item to the poore prisoners in the cityes gaile 6*s* 8*d*. Item I give to the poore people of Blandford Forum in Dorsytshyre 20*s*. Item to the poore people of Cheriton Bisshopp 6*s* 8*d*. Item I give to every of my children Agnes Judeth Robert and Marye a hundred pounds of Lawfull money of England to a peece of them, And if any of my saide children happen to dye before he or she doe accomplishe the age of 21 yeares or be marryed, Then I will that his or her parte so dying to remaine to them then Lyving

by equall porcons. Item I will that my Father Nicholas James shall have the use and occupacon of the rent of my howse or howses in Sowithgate Streete wherein William Trosse nowe dwelleth in and a tenement apperteyning to the same wherein one Abraham a shoemaker dothe nowe dwell in during his naturall Lyffe, my saide Father to paye to the chuche of St Marye Michells in Exeter the Rent of the same being 41*s* and to do suche things as I *[2]* am bounde to doe by my Lease and after his decease I give the same Lease to Judeth James my daughter. Item I give to my saide Father Nicholas James £6 13*s* 4*d* of Lawfull money of England to comforte him withall in his olde age. Item I give to Agnes my daughter my Lease for terme of yeares whiche I have of the tythe sheafe and tithe haye of St Sidwells St David Dirwood Sowithenhaie and Ruxon. Item I give to Robert my soune my Lease and termes of yeares of a peece of grounde whiche I boughte of Elizabeth Parramore the executrix of the testament of William Parramore deceased Lying withowte Sowithegate by the Mawdlen. Item I give more to my saide soune Robert the Lease of my chamber in the churche yarde whiche I doe nowe kepe my office in. Item I give to Marye my daughter the Lease of a peece of grounde Lying in the parrishe of St Thomas nere Exeter whiche my Late M[aste]r Mr Michaell Browne gave me by his saide testament and Last will. Item I give and bequeathe to every of my sisters Agnes Anne and Margeret yf they be lyving at my deathe £13 6*s* 8*d* of lawfull money of England to a peece of them to helpe and comforte them and theire children. Item I give and bequeathe to my brother William James £5 of Lawfull money of England. Item I give to Joane Jeames my brother John Jeames daughter my servaunt £10 of Lawfull money of England over and above £6 I doe owe her. Item I doe give to the goodwyffe Knolls an olde angell. Item I doe give to Thomas Trosse my

man 40*s*. Item I give to William Grenewoode 40*s*. Item I give to Richard Fletcher 40*s*. Item I give to my olde frende Mr Thomas Williams an olde ryall in golde. Item I give to Elizabeth Haselwoode my Late wyves Daughter over and above her Fathers Legaceis £10 of Lawfull money of England. Item I give and bequeathe to James Bydelcobbe 10*s*. Item I give and bequeathe to Christopher Tiffen 10*s*. Item I give to my brother Bowden and to his wyffe an olde angell to a peece of them. Item I give to every godchilde that I have 12*d* to a peece of them. Item I give to every servant that I have at the time of my decease 6*s* 8*d* a peece of them. Item I give to the reparacon of St Stevens churche 10*s*. Item I give all the residue of my goods chattells Leases and Debts whatsoever they be (my debts and Legacies paide and perfourmed £10 of Lawfull money of England excepted and reserved to my executor underwritten) to my foure children above named equally to be devyded amongest them and every of them by my executor hereunderwritten at suche time and when as they shall accomplishe theire severall ages of 21 yeares or be marryed. Item I do nominate, constitute and make my very trusty frend Ewstice Oliver of the citye of Exeter merchant my whole and sole executor to whome I doe give the £10 above excepted Requesting him to see this my will and testament to be accomplished in every thinge and he to paye my debts and Legacies owte of all my goodes and chattells as also Requesting him to see the placing and vertuous bringing upp of my saide foure children whiche I hope he will doe for that he hathe faithfully promised me so to doe. In wittnes this to be of truthe I have wrote this my Last will and testament with my owne hande and putt thereunto my seale and subscribed my name yeoven the daye and yeare above written. *By me Henry James Notary Public.* John Watkens *witness* Thomas Trosse William Cove *by Me John* Trosse.

33B. INVENTORY OF HENRY JAMES, NOTARY PUBLIC, OCTOBER 1578

ECA Orphans' Court Inventory 29 [Item 1]

The Inventory of all the goods & chattalls of Mr Henry James late of the cittie & countie of Exeter decessed praised the [blank] daie of October 1578 by Mr Phillippe Yearde Thomas Chapell John Sampforde and Thomas Turbervile

[1] In the Hall
Firstly one tabell borde with twoo leaves 40*s*;
Item all the seelings 15*s*;
Item one Cubborde 26*s* 8*d*;
Item twoo other tabell bordes 8*s*;
Item 3 fformes 2*s* 6*d*;
Item the hanginges with 3 stories [?] 17*s* 4*d*;
Item a mappe 2*s* 6*d*;
Item a greate glasse 3*s*;
Item 6 Quishings of the Kings armes 10*s*;
Item a backe of Iron 4*s*;
Item a paire of Andirons 6*s*;
Item a barr of Iron 2*s*;
Item a skryme to sett before the ffyer 8*d*;
Item the Crowkes to hange the maiers swordes and maces on 6*d*;
Item a Targett 2*s* 8*d*;
Item 9 olde Quishins 6*s* 8*d*;
Item 3 Cheares, one portugall & one ioyned with one ioyned Chear 6*s* 8*d*;
Item twoo litell ioyned stooles 2*s*;
Item a Coffer deske 12*d*;
Item one olde paire of Tabells 4*d*;
Item 3 old Carpetts & a Courtinge one of the Carpetts of Sattyn of bregs 4*s*;
Item a Basson and Ewer 3*s* 4*d*;
Item 4 litell glasses 12*d*;
Item 2 litell tynninge bottells 8*d*;
Item one Carpitt of Grene 3*s* 4*d*;
Item 8 yeardes of black Kearsey 48*s*;

Item 5 yeardes of northerne broade 16*s* 8*d*;
Item 19 kearsies at £31 3*s* 4*d*;
Item one Kersey recovered from Myller 33*s* 4*d*;
Sum £44 11*s* 2*d*.

In the Parlor
Item a ioyned tabell borde of nutte with 2 leaves 23*s* 4*d*;
Item a Cubborde 16*s*;
Item a ffourme 18*d*;
[1v.] Item a litell borde hanginge to the Seelinge with Iron barres 20*d*;
Item a dubbell fforme to putt potts on 2*s* 6*d*;
Item a paire of Andirons 5*s*;
Item a paire of doggs a Barr of Iron and a backe of Iron 3*s*;
Item a Corten and a rodde of Iron 6*d*;
Item the sellinges with a litell hanginge borde to the same £4;
Item a Carpett 6*s* 8*d*;
Item 6 Grene Quishens 8*s*;
Item a ioyned Cheare 5*s*;
Item a womans stole and foote stole 6*d*;
Item a Bason and Ewer 5*s*;
Item 6 drinckinge glasses 12*d*;
Sum £7 19*s* 8*d*.

In the Buttrey within the Parlor
Item a longe Cubborde 12*s*;
Item 2 litell tabell bordes 6*s* 8*d*;
Item a Cheare 16*d*;
Item a fforme 8*d*;
Item the shelves and borders 2*s* 6*d*;
Item one fflaskett 4*d*;
Item twoo ioyned stooles 2*s*;
Item one litell Cheare 2*d*;
Item 2 stoned Jugges and a stonnyng cuppe Covered with tyne 18*d*;

Item a bottell 2*d*;

Item 5 penttyd dishes 12*d*;

Item 2 drinckinge glasses 2*d*;

Item 45 platters 131 lb – 54*s*;

Item 27 podingers, 2 basons 2 broade plates 70 sawsers, spise plattes squar saucers, & litell sausers, one litell bolle 11 pottaige dishes, 112 lb at 5*d* per pounde 46*s* 8*d*;

Item 2 pottelles, 4 pyntes, 2 quartes, 1 Cuppe 3 saltes 1 bottell, 1 olde ewer, 3 Chamber potts 11*s*;

Sum £7 2*d*.

In the kytchen

Item the dressinge bordes and shelves and Rackes to hange the Spittes 10*s*;

Item a rounde tabell borde 3*s* 4*d*;

Item the Benche before the ffyer with the borde therunto 6*s* 8*d*;

[2] Item a paire of Racks of Iron 16*s* 8*d*;

Item a barr of Iron in the Chymney 5*s*;

Item a Candelstick of Iron 4*d*;

Item 11 Spittes 86 lb – 13*s* 4*d*;

Item 6 gredirons, a ffyer showell a ffyer pick, 2 tosters, 3 fleshe howkes, 7 pott hangings, 8 pott Crowkes a ladell 83 lb – 12*s*;

Item a paire of Andirons, a pair of doggs a paire of Racks, 2 Brandises, twoo Irons to sett before the drepinge pans containing 72 lb at 6*s* 8*d*;

Item 7 drepinge pannes, 3 frienge pannes containing 54 lb at 9*s*;

Item 2 brockinge gratters & one litell whole one 6*d*;

Item one Iron Crowk 6*d*;

Item a kittell of Iron 2*s* 6*d*;

Item 2 fformes 20*d*;

Item 9 olde pannes containing 72 lb at 4½*d* – 27*s*;

Item 5 good pannes containing 140 lb at 8*d* the pounde £4 13*s* 4*d*;

Item 6 Cawdrens of Brasse with rings of Iron containing 40 lb at 13*s* 4*d*;

Item 5 Chaffyn dishes, 2 morters a leave & a litell pestell

containing 20 lb at 13*s* 4*d*;

Item 6 good Crocks of brasse Containing 141 lb – 58*s*;

Item 3 olde Crocks and a possenett containing 56 lb – 13*s* 3*d*;

Item a Chaffer & a skillett of Brasse 6*s* 8*d*;

Item 2 Copper kittells, one with a ringe of Iron containing 30 lb – 16*s* 8*d*;

Item 9 paire of Candellstickes containing 39 lb at 15*s*;

Item 4 skilletts a ladell & skower of brasse 3*s*;

Item a Chaffyndishe of Iron 12*d*;

Item a ffane and a pestell of tymber 2*d*;

Item 2 ffishescomers 6*d*;

Sum £17 9*s* 6*d*.

In the Larder nexte to the Court

Item a Chese wrynge 16*d*;

Item the bordes and shelves 3*s* 4*d*;

Item 4 Bottells 16*d*;

Item a dawe sheite 18*d*;

Item certen sacks, weyninge sheits seaves with other Trashe 3*s*;

Sum 10*s* 6*d*.

[2v.] In the Boutinge howse

Item 6 sacks 3*s*;

Item a bountinge huche 12*d*;

Item 5 tubbes, 3 barrells 2 Bangers and 2 bounters 3*s* 4*d*;

Sum 7*s* 4*d*.

In the ffoare Buttrey

Item 11 Costes and barrells 11*s*;

Item the shelves and borders the barers and racks, 2 tressells with a longe borde 4*s*;

Sum 15*s*.

In the Seller under the Buttry

Item 7 Caskes with salt 3*s* 6*d*;

Item 5 of them full with salte containing 17tene boushells at 21*s*;

Sum 24*s* 6*d*.

In the Larder under the Backe Chamber
Item 7 gallondes of Butter 15*s*;
Item 3 standerds emptie 3*s*;
Item a verkyn with Hollock 6*d*;
Item 6 halfe barrells 6*s*;
Item 3 other olde vessells 3*s*;
Item certen shelves barers and bords to make partysions 5*s*;
Item a trendell a greate one 5*s*;
Item a brack 6*d*;
Item a paire of Canhowkes 2*d*;
Sum 38*s* 2*d*.

In the greate Courte
Item 12 toubbes, 15 barrells, 5 hogsheds good and badd 15*s*;
Item 2 Cowles, with 2 pailes 12*d*;
Item a greate block 8*d*;
Item 3 hogeheds to Mr Oliver 4*s*;
Item a litell badd tabell borde 4*d*;
Item a dubbell Coupe for pultrey 4*s*;
Item lyme and stones of buck with the cask 2*s*;
[3] Item a mattock 2 hachetts a axe a thorowe sawe, 2 wymmells [?] 2 pranges for pickes, a borryer 3 howkes, thone a reape hooke, 10 Iron wedges, with other trashe in the Courte as olde Coffers, tymber Tressells with a badd fforme 9*s* 8*d*;
Sum 36*s* 8*d*.

In the Brewehowse
Item a ffornace to Brewe in 30*s*;
Item a still of ledd 5*s*;
Item a sesterne of ledd and plompe of ledd to the same £4 6*s* 8*d*;
Item 7 tubbes and keves 2 caskes 2 barrells with other brewing Trashe 10*s*;
Sum £6 11*s* 8*d*.

In the Back Courte and Stabell
Item a Saddell, and 2 badde briddells 3*s* 6*d*;
Item a Cole racke 2*d*;

Item twoo showles and a donge pik 8*d*;
Item a whilebarrow 16*d*;
Item 3 pigges trawes 8*d*;
Item a rick of woode with other woode by the same 53*s* 4*d*;
Item a horse come 4*d*;
Item 148 ynche bordes £2 10*s*;
Item certen howpes 6*d*;
Item certen seame stones with other stones theirby 6*s* 8*d*;
Item 8 planckes 6*s*;
Item 3 paire of woode Crowkes 2*s*;
Item 40 posses with 14 other cutt in thende 13*s* 4*d*;
Item 4 [illegible] ffor a Crubbe 5*s*;
Item other Trashe 12*d*;
Item a backe Stabell with woode 30*s*;
Item in the same a olde dor 8*d*;
Sum £8 15*s* 2*d*.

In the Garden
Item a wodderick £2;
Item 2 vates 20*d*;
Item a sowe and a hogge 24*s*;
Item a gryndinge stone with one seame stone [?] 3*s* 4*d*;
[3v.] The posses standinge uppe in the Garden 3*s* 4*d*;
Item a longe poole at the dor 3*d*;
Sum £3 12*s* 7*d*.

In the Barne
Item a ricke of Rye 35*s*;
Item a ricke of Beanes 33*s* 4*d*;
Item a blocke within the gate 2*s*;
Sum £3 10*s* 4*d*.

In the Chamber over the Larder
Item 3 paire of olde Almont Rivetts 10*s*;
Item 2 paire of Briggendens olde 3*s* 4*d*;
Item a Jacke 6*s* 8*d*;
Item 2 racks for Cheses 2*s*;
Item 12 seelinge bordes 4*s*;
Item 2 Joyned Stooles 2*s*;

Item a Candell Coffer and 2 fishe chests 2s 6d;
Item 6 bedd staves 2d;
Item 3 olde Tubbes with ffeathers 12d;
Item 40 millwills and linge 20s;
Item his ridinge saddell ffurnished with the Briddell 13s 4d;
Item a fframe for Armor 12d;
Item a paire of Bootes 2s;
Sum £3 8s.

In the Lower Chamber over the office
Item a stille of ledd 3s 4d;
Item a olde tabell borde with a leave 3s 4d;
Item the one half of prese 5s;
Item 5 ffree stones 16d;
Item a thowsande of lastes 2s;
Item a dossen of Crestes 16d;
Item 2 olde hampers 6d;
Item one Cheste without Lock 16d;
Sum 18s 2d.

In the higher Chamber over the office
Item Barley malte and boushells 20s;
Item 5 peckes of Rye 2s;
Item in otten malte 14 boushells 17s;
[4] Item a litell barrell of beanes with the Barrell 12d;
Item a whitt vate with 2 heades 6d;
Sum £2 6d.

In the Shoppe
Item a greate Cheste with 2 locks 13s 4d;
Item one other Cheste with 2 locks 4s;
Item one Corsselett performed with his pike 19s;
Item a hedd pece 2s 6d;
Item a hande bawe and a sheafe of arrowes 3s 4d;
Item a role of parchement containing 20 lb skynnes 5s;
Item 12 reames of wrettinge paper great and smale 20s;
Item a weight of Basse [sic] containing 8 lb – 5s 4d;
Item of ledd weights 28 lb 14 lb and 4 lb at 4s;
Item 6 shelves with borders & hangings 6s 8d;

Item 2 paire of ounce Ballance 6d;
Sum £4 3s 8d.

In the utter office
Item a newe square fframe of seeling with shelves, a seelinge
    benche with one borde 23s 4d;
Item one other fframe of seelinge lik to a spence, with a
    benche and shelves rounde aboute the same 5s;
Item a litell borde 2s 6d;
Item a ioyned Cheare 2s 6d;
Item a fframed stolle & a litell desk 12d;
Item a Carde of Constanttinoble 2s 6d;
Sum 36s 10d.

In the Inner office
Item a tabell borde of wallenutt tree 16s;
Item the seelinge and benches in the same, with the whole
    frame of shelves aboute the same 15s;
Item a mappe of the whole wourlde 6s 8d;
Sum 37s 8d.

[4v.] I[n] the ffoare Chamber
Item a Bed steede with a Truckell bedd with the Courten
    roddes of Iron 26s 8d;
Item a presse 26s 8d;
Item a tabell borde 26s 8d;
Item a greate Cheste 20s;
Item a Ilande Cheste 5s;
Item [illegible] chestes 6s 8d;
Item 2 picters in tables 2s 8d;
Item the merchaunts adventurers armes 16d;
Item the hangings of staiened clothes 5s;
Item the storrie of Samaria [?] 20d;
Item the Courtens of redd & Grene sea of the windowes olde
    53s;
Item 4 olde Courtens to the bedd 6s 8d;
Item a Course Coverlett 3s 4d;
Item a womans Chear 8d;
Item a whitt rugge 6s 8d;

Item 2 paire of blancketts 7s 6d;
Item one other Coverlett 3s 4d;
Item a backe for a Chymney 3s 4d;
Item a litell paire of dogges 12d;
Item a paire of olde tungs 8d;
Item a paire of Billowes 2d;
Item a plancke before the hea[r]th 2d;
Item a olde Carpett 12d;
Sum £8 10d.

In the litell Chamber by the foare Chamber
Item 2 lawe beddsteedes 3s 4d;
Item 2 olde Coverletts 3s 4d;
Item a olde fflockebedd & 2 bolsters 10s;
Item the hangings & stayned clothes 6s 8d;
Item a olde paire of dogges 16d;
Item a Clost stoole with a pane in hyme 12d;
Item a olde badd ffetherbedd 10s;
Item a hanger with a vellett girdell 6s 8d;
Sum 42s 4d.

In the Countinge howse in the ffoare Chamber
Item one olde Courtinge borde 5s;
Item one olde Cheste 16d;
Item a silke pouch 3s 4d;
Item 2 spanishe lether pouches 2s 8d;
Item a hearen brish 8d;
Item the hangings and shelves 10d;
Item one other pouch 12d;
Item the portall 2s 6d;
Sum 17s 4d.

[5] In the higher Chamber over the ffoare Chamber
Item a Bed steede with Iron roddes £2;
Item a Coverlett of Tapestrie 13s 4d;
Item a olde Coverlett of Imegerie 5s;
Item a paire of Blancketts 4s 4d;
Item 4 Courtens of red and yeollowe sea 3s 4d;
Item a litell ffolden borde 2s 6d;

Item a olde Cheare 6d;
Item the portall to the Chamber 3s 4d;
Item the hangings to the Chamber 5s;
Item a paire of Iron doggs and one ffyer panne 12d;
Item in the Studie within the Chamber a litell tabell borde,
    with a benche and shelves 16d;
Sum £3 19s 8d.

In the mens Chamber
Item 2 olde bedstedes with a Couche bye [?] 2s 6d;
Item a olde Coffer and a Cubborde 12d;
Item one olde Close Cheare 6d;
Item 3 olde fflock beddes with bolsters 13s 4d;
Item 2 olde Coverletts 5s;
Item a thrummynge rugge & a olde whitt rugge 3s 4d;
Item one olde blewe Quilte 8d;
Item 2 paire of blancketts 2s 6d;
Item the hangings in the Chamber 20d;
Item 2 testers of 2 beddes 20d;
Item courtyns for the wyndowe 4d;
Item a walkinge staff with a blade in the same 3s 4d;
Sum 35s 10d.

In thother highe Chamber
Item one olde bedd steede with 3 roddes of Iron to the same
    13s 4d;
Item a olde Cheare & 2 olde fformes 8d;
Item a litell olde borde 2d;
Item the hangings of the same Chamber 6s 8d;
Sum 20s 10d.

In the Brushinge Chamber
Item a olde borde, a paire of hampers one olde Troncke, a olde
    broken presse & the hangings aboute the Chamber 3s;
Item a Capprast for a woman 12d;
Sum 4s.

[5v.] In the plompe Chamber
Item one Bedsteede with the roddes of iron 26s 8d;

Item a fflockebedd 5*s*;
Item 2 Courtens to the bedd 20*d*;
Item one wollinge Quilte 5*s*;
Item one Coverlett 3*s* 4*d*;
Item one blanckett 2*s* 6*d*;
Item one litell Joyned Chest 4*s*;
Item a litell olde Cupporde 2*s*;
Item a olde Chear 12*d*;
Item a olde Quishion 12*d*;
Item 2 Courtens for the wyndowes 2*d*;
Item the hangings of Sea aboute the Chamber 3*s* 4*d*;
Sum 55*s* 8*d*.

In the Gallarye
Item 2 Joyned stooles 2*s*;
Item one greate Chest 6*s* 8*d*;
Item a longe Chest 12*d*;
Item one other greate longe Chest 6*s*;
Item one other lesser Chest 3*s* 4*d*;
Item a olde fflaunders Chest bounde with Iron 3*s* 4*d*;
Item the hangings of stayned clothes 16*d*;
Item a welshe Hook 12*d*;
Item a Jallinge 6*d*;
Item a polle axe 20*d*;
Item 3 black billes 2*s*;
[Item a Clock 13*s* 4*d* – crossed through];
Item a Tiller Bawe 6*s* 8*d*;
Item a Gly 2*s*;
Sum [£2 10*s* 10*d* – crossed through] 37*s* 6*d*.

In the broade Chamber
Item a standinge bedsteed with 3 Iron rodds and a Truckell bedstede £3;
Item a greate presse 20*s*;
Item a ffoldinge tabell borde 20*s*;
Item a Cheste banded with Iron 10*s*;
Item one other ioyned Chest 5*s*;
Item one Chest of Iron £2;
Item a side tabell 12*d*;

Item 4 shorte fformes 5*s*;
Item a paire of Andirons 3*s* 4*d*;
Item a Chear 12*d*;
Item all the seelinge with the borders over the same £2 5*s*;
Item a Close Cheare 2*s*;
Item 6 Quishions of nylde work 12*s*;
Item a longe Quishion of lether quilt 2*s* 6*d*;
[6] Item a newe yeollowe Quilt 4*s*;
Item a Coverlett of yeollow and blewe 4*s*;
Item one olde Coverlett 18*d*;
Item one olde Carpett 2*s* 6*d*;
Item one olde longe Carpett 15*s*;
Item one olde Coverlett lyned 6*s* 8*d*;
Item a olde paire of blancketts 7*s*;
Item 2 paire of newe blancketts 10*s*;
Item a olde paire of blancketts 2*s*;
Item 5 Courtyns of mockade ffranged 30*s* 4*d*;
Item 3 bad Courtens of saye 6*s* 8*d*;
Item 3 olde windowe Courtens 18*d*;
Item a lyninge clothes about the courtens 3*d*;
Item one other Coverlett 4*s*;
Item a great Coverlett 26*s* 8*d*;
Item a pir [?] of bedtys 16*d*;
Item a olde Carpett 2*s* 6*d*;
Item a litell olde Chest 8*d*;
Sum £17 13*s* 5*d*.

The Beddinge
Item a bed with a bad tick no 1 waienge 50 lb at 4*d* per lb – 16*s* 8*d*;
Item a bedd with a olde tick no 2 waieng 50 lb at 4*d* per pounde 17*s*;
Item one other bedd no 3 with his bolster a ffyne Tick wayenge 89 lb at 6*d* per lb – 44*s* 6*d*;
Item one other bedd with his bolster a good tick no 4 Containing 119 lb at 5*d* per lb – £2 9*s* 7*d*;
Item one other bedd with his bolster indifferent good no 5 waienge 100 lb at 5*d* per lb – 41*s* 8*d*;

Item one other bedd with his bolster a good tick no 6 waienge 129 lb at 5*d* per lb – 53*s* 9*d*;

Item one other bedd with his bolster a good tick no 7 waienge 98 lb at 5*d* per lb – £2 10*d*;

Item one olde bedd with his bolster no 8 cont 83 lb at 4*d* per lb – 27*s* 8*d*;

Item one olde bedd with a olde bolster no 9 waienge 84 lb at 4*d* per lb – 28*s*;

Item 6 bolsters and a pillowe wherof 3 of Canvas ticks waienge 70 lb at 4*d* per lb – 23*s* 4*d*;

Item 6 pillowes wherof 3 of ffustyne waienge 42 lb per lb [*sic*] – 14*s*;

Item 5 pillowes of downe wherof one of ffustian waienge 22 lb at 8*d* per lb – 14*s* 8*d*;

[Sum 14*s* 8*d* – crossed through];

[6v.] Sum £18 11*s* 8*d*.

The apparrell

[Item a preste Clok 10*s* – crossed through];

Item 4 Jerkings of Spanishe lether 20*s*;

Item a dublett of silk mocade 3*s* 4*d*;

Item a satten dublett 20*s*;

Item one other Satten dublett 6*s* 8*d*;

Item a Kearsey delivered his ffather [blank];

Item a taffita dublett 6*s* 8*d*;

Item a Jerkyn of taffita 10*s*;

Item a Cassock of damask garded with vellett 13*s* 4*d*;

Item a Jerkinge of damask 15*s*;

Item a Jack of grawgren 5*s*;

Item a paire of Breches of mockade 4*s*;

Item a paire of Kearsey Bree[c]hes with a billiment lace [?] upon them 20*s*;

Item a gowne of mocado faced with Cony with a lace 26*s* 8*d*;

Item a olde mocado gowne 8*s*;

Item a olde russett gowne 10*s*;

Item a olde black gowne 15*s*;

[Item a olde gowne bought of Duckenfeilden appoincted for the olde ffather James – crossed through];

Item a blacke gowne faced with boudge and lyned with blacke lamine [?] with a welte of vellett £3;

Item one other gowne faced with ffoynes and lyned with whitt lame with a welte of vellett £3 13*s* 4*d*;

Item 3 paire of olde stockings 3*s*;

Item 3 olde Cappes 4*s*;

Item a silk hatt 5*s*;

[Item a vellett nightcappe delivered the olde James – crossed through];

Item a black Clok delivered to John Grubham vallewed at 30*s*;

Sum £17 19*s*.

The Lynninge

Item 9 sherts £3;

Item 7 paire of litell Course shetts 12*s*;

Item 3 paire of dowlis sheits 18*s*;

Item 2 other paire of dowlis sheets 10*s*;

Item a paire of morleis cloth sheits 6*s* 8*d*;

Item a paire of hullande sheits 12*s*;

Item a paire of morleis cloth sheits 5*s*;

Item a olde ffyne longe sheit of hullande 2*s* 6*d*;

[7] Item 3 paire of Canvas sheits 20*s*;

Item 3 paire of Canvas sheits 12*s*;

Item 3 canvas sheites 8*s*;

Item 3 Canvas sheits 6*s*;

Item a paire of Course Canvas sheits 4*s*;

Item 5 paire of olde sheits woringe 13*s* 4*d*;

Item 2 olde borde clothes 16*d*;

Item a olde borde clothe 12*d*;

Item one other Bordecloth 20*d*;

Item 2 other Bordeclothes 3*s* 4*d*;

Item one other Bordecloth 2*s* [6*d* – crossed through];

Item one other bordeclothes [*sic*] 2*s* 6*d*;

Item one other bordecloth of morles cloth 2*s* 8*d*;

Item a Canvas Bordecloth 2*s* 4*d*;

Item a bordecloth at 4*s*;

Item one other Bordeclothe 2*s* 4*d*;

Item one other bordecloth 3*s* 4*d*;

Item one other broade bordeclothe 8*s*;

Item a longe bordecloth of morles cloth 10*s*;

Item a olde diaper Bordecloth 12*d*;
Item one other diaper Bordecloth 5*s*;
Item one other diaper Bordecloth 4*s*;
Item a litell olde diaper bordecloth 12*d*;
Item a longe Towell 2*s*;
Item one other Towell of dowlys 20*d*;
Item 2 Towells wraghte with black 4*s*;
Item one other Towell 20*d*;
Item a shorte Towell of dowlis 12*d*;
Item one other Towell 18*d*;
Item a longe Towell of diaper 20*d*;
Item 6 shorte Towells 4*s*;
Item 7 handetowells 16*d*;
Item 5 hullande pillowties 13*s* 4*d*;
Item 3 hulland pillowties 5*s*;
Item 2 morlys pillowties 4*s*;
Item 3 hollande pillowties 4*s* 6*d*;
Item 4 Canvas pilloweties 3*s* 4*d*;
Item 4 olde pillowties 16*d*;
Item 4 shelf Clothes 8*d*;
Item 9 franged [Bordeclothes – crossed through] borders for
    Cubbords 2*s*;
Item one Cubborde cloth 3*s* 4*d*;
Item a old Cubborde cloth 8*d*;
Item 6 other Cubborde clothes 4*s*;
Item a paire of lynnen hossen 4*d*;
Item half a dossen of borde napkings of Brittaine Clothe 3*s*;
Item 6 napkings of whitt work of Brittaine Clothe 5*s*;
Item 6 napkings of black work 4*s*;
Item 12 napkings of Canvas ffranged 5*s*;
Item a dossen of weavinge napkings 3*s*;
[7v.] Item 9 plaine napkings 2*s* 6*d*;
Item 10 olde napkings 16*d*;
Item 11 course tabell napkings 4*s*;
Item 6 olde diaper napkins 12*d*;
Item 9 borde napkings 2*s* 6*d*;
Item 9 other borde napkings 12*d*;
Sum £16 18*s* 8*d*.

In the Gutrey [*sic*]
Item 2 lanterns 8*d*;
Item one Ewer of ledd 12*d*;
Item 2 Corne pikes 16*d*;
Item a huntinge staff 6*d*;
Item a morles longe awne 3*d*;
Sum 3*s* 9*d*.

The guildinges and Mares
Item one baye Colte £6 10*s*;
Item one Baye guildinge £6 13*s* 4*d*;
Item a graye Colt £3 10*s*;
Item a black mar 26*s* 8*d*;
Item a bright baye mar £2;
Sum £20.

The plate
Item one Tanckerde dubble guilt waienge 17 ouncs at 6*s* 8*d*
    per ounce £5 13*s* 4*d*;
Item one Salte dubble guilte with a Cover containing 9 uncs 3
    quarters at 6*s* 4*d* per unce £3 21*d*;
Item a Cuppe with a Cover duble guilt 13 uncs and half a
    quarter at 5*s* 4*d* the unce £3 12*s* 8*d*;
Item one Goblett duble guilt containing 11 uncs at 5*s* per unce
    55*s*;
Item one salte dubble guilt with a Cover containing 3 uncs
    and half a quarter at 5*s* 8*d* per unce 17*s* 8*d*;
Item one salte dubble guilt with a Cover containing 11 uncs
    one quarter at 5*s* per unce 56*s* 3*d*;
Item 3 gobletts parcell guilt containing 56 uncs at 5*s* 6*d* per
    unce £15 8*s*;
Item 2 gobletts parcell guilt containing 20 uncs and half at 4*s*
    6*d* per unce £4 12*s* 3*d*;
Item one Beer cuppe parcell guilt containing 12 uncs half
    quarter at 5*s* per unce £3 7*d*;
[8] Item one standinge whitt Cuppe containing 17 uncs at 4*s*
    8*d* per unce £3 19*s* 4*d*;
Item a garnishe of a stonyng cuppe guilte containing 4 uncs
    and halfe a quarter at 4*s* 10*d* per unce 20*s*;

Item 6 spones with squar heddes containing 7 uncs & a
  quarter at 5*s* the unce 36*s* 10*d*;
Item 8 spones of thappostells containing 12½ uncs at 4*s* 6*d*
  per unce 56*s* 3*d*;
Item 7 olde spones containing 7½ uncs at 4*s* 2*d* per unce 31*s*
  3*d*;
Item 3 Cuppes garnished, wherof one guilte quart 12 uncs at
  4*s* 2*d* per unce £2 10*s*;
Item 5 olde spones takinge out of a Chest 4 uncs 3 quarters at
  4*s* 2*d* per unce 19*s* 9*d*;
Item one signett containing one unce and a ffarthinge weight
  of golde 56*s*;
Item one silver ringe 3*d*;
Item a paire of Brasseletts of golde £6;
Sum £65 7*s* 3*d*.

In redy money
Item received of Mr Marston Chauncellor £20;
Item receaved of Thomas Baskervile £10;
Item Mrs James hath in paune [?] £2;
Item ffound in one boxe in whit money £25 10*d*;
Item in a nother bagge £2;
Item in one other bagge £3 13*s* 10*d*;
Item in one other bagge in groats which was delivered Mr
  James £7;
Item in twoo baggs delivered Mr James £8 14*s* 11*d*;
Item Mrs James had in money £6 6*s* 5*d*;
Item Mrs James receaved for the rent of a howse 10*s*;
More she receaved for shillingestones 6*s* 8*d*;
Item 3 thowsande of shillingstones solde at 12*s*;
Sum £96 5*s* 8*d*.

[Mor for shillingestones 53*s* – crossed through].

In the Chamber which he had at Mr Williams
Item certen olde Iron stuff 2*s* 6*d*;
Item one olde tourne 6*d*;
Item 2 Cheares solde to the meaden 10*d*;
Item one litell bed steed 3*s*;

Item one whitt vate with other Trashe and bordes 3*s* 4*d*;
[8v.] Item in thother Chamber ther one olde caige 6*d*;
Item 9 *C* of Brick 15*s*;
Item certen Charcoll 2*s*;
Item of Black and whitt woll 56 lb at 9*d* per lb – 42*s*;
Item in the Stabell 6 Trosse of heye £4;
Sum £7 9*s* 8*d*.

The Bookes
Item Grastons Cronckell 9*s*;
Item his smale Cronackell 8*d*;
Item one Englishe Bibell 7*s*;
Item Elletts dixionary 2*s* 6*d*;
Item Howletts dixionary 1*s* 6*d*;
Item golden epistells 1*s*;
Item 2 books of the poor mens liberarie 6*s*;
Item Cramer and Wynchester 2*s*;
Item the paraphras of Erasmus [?] 2*s*;
Item Isoppes ffables 2*d*;
Item Concedence of scriptur 3*d*;
Item a newe Testament in Englishe 20*d*;
Item the Image of governaunce 4*d*;
Item a Testament in lattaine 6*d*;
Item a prevese prevaltie in lattaine 6*d*;
Item the some of devinitie 2*d*;
Item Nowells Cathachisemaye 4*d*;
Item 2 of ffreithe Bookes 4*d*;
Item Cramer upon the Sacrament 2*d*;
Item a merror for maiestrase 8*d*;
Item Elletts governor 4*d*;
Item the Comunyon book in lattaine 8*d*;
Item Langwitts Crownickell 8*d*;
Item Cornewe Copia 18*d*;
Item the ffall of princs bog 20*d*;
Item a bibell in lattaine 20*d*;
Item a newe Testament in Englishe 6*d*;
Item a bibell in lattaine 5*s*;
Item the Rule of reason 2*d*;
Item Peter Lambert at Corenthami [?] 12*d*;

Item Tullies retrik with a Coment 6*d*;
Item Marshall with a Coment 6*d*;
Item Terrances with a Coment 6*d*;
Item Arast [?] with a Coment 12*d*;
[9] Item Tulles office with a Coment 12*d*;
Item Tullies Epistells with a coment 6*d*;
Item Virgell with a Coment 6*d*;
Item the declaracon of Hoppers Tenne comaundements 6*d*;
Item a grick dixionary 2*s*;
Item Laurence Vallewes cometorie 4*d*;
Item Laurence Vallewes *delingua' lattinu'* 6*d*;
Item Lucyon with a Coment 12*d*;
Item Stytons with a Coment 12*d*;
Item Volantarnos works 12*d*;
Virgell with a Coment 6*d*;
Item Textes Epitions 6*d*;
Item *allos gellos* 4*d*;
Item Daunysens workes 4*d*;
Item a Bridgement of Statuts 3*s* 4*d*;
Item 2 of Henry the VIIIth statuts 6*s* 8*d*;
Item the Statuts frome Henry the thirde to Henry the VIIIth 2*s* 6*d*;
Item 7 remenetts of Statuts 1*s* 6*d*;
Item 14 Kathachisemes 7*d*;
Item a book for Justices of peace 2*d*;
Item 4 Singinge books 2*s* 6*d*;
Item 2 smale Bookes 3*d*;
Item 65 olde lawe Books bounde with bordes 20*s*;
Item 12 olde books bounde with parchement 6*d*;
Item 19 boks for scollers 8*s*;
Item one Book of Mohamitts Lawe with 3 other Statuts of Quene Marie 2*s* 6*d*;
Sum £5 10*s* 11*d*.

In the Counter by the Hall
Item a greate Lock for a Counter dor 4*s* 6*d*;
Item a dubble lock to hange upon a dor 2*s*;
Item a Candelstick of Tymber 2*d*;
Item a Kallender with a fframe 2*d*;

Item a yenck horne 3*d*;
Item the hedd of a seale a dust boxe, and a boxe for the poor 3*d*;
Item one other Candelstick of tymber 2*d*;
Item 6 boxes to putt wrettinges in 6*d*;
Item a presse to putt letters in 2*d*;
Item a nett and a prechell 4*d*;
Item a paire of Jemyes with other Trashe in a purse 8*d*;
[9v.] Item a Certen pece of lether 6*d*;
Item a tymber desk 2*d*;
Item 6 boxes in one, and 3 in one and 3 rounde boxes 12*d*;
Item a fflask with a tuch boxe of horne 2*d*;
Item a nother desk with a box 6*d*;
Item a litell pile of weights 3*d*;
Item the borde in the Counter 3*s* 4*d*;
Item the seelinge, benchinge and shelves 16*s* 8*d*;
Sum 31*s* 7*d*;
Sum total of the goodes £410 12*s* 10*d*.

In detts good and badde as ffolloweth
Item Anthony Halstaff by a obligacon £23 9*s*;
Item Robert Smithes bill for £38;
Item Valentyne Tuckers bill for £42 7*s* 10*d*;
Item John Levermoores bill for £37 15*s*;
Item William Martyns Bill for £41 2*s*;
Item Michaell Harts bill for £18 6*s* 5*d*;
Item Eustas Oliver ffor £38 19*s* 8*d*;
Thomas Johnson doth rest to paie of a bill 16*s*;
Item Froste of Creley aweth by book 20*s*;
Item John Kaychell per book £2 15*s* 4*d*;
Roberte Prediaux by book 13*s* 4*d*;
Item John Grey per Bill £2;
Item Symon Wrinche per Book 15*s*;
Richard Braye per bill £2;
John Dyer per book and bill £18 17*s* 2*d*;
Item Clement Scutt rest per bill 10*s*;
Androwe Skutt per Bill 20*s*;
John Oliver reste per bill 20*s*;
Thomas Raymont per Book 26*s* 8*d*;
Sum £272 13*s* 5*d*.

George Southecott per book £3;

Richard Duck per Book 13s 4d;

[John – crossed through] Peter Cortyn per book £6;

John Mylhewes per Book £2;

Item Mr Williams per Bill £55;

[More he aweth by book £10 19s 8d – crossed through];

Thomas Baskervile by obligacon £10;

Item Mr Dotton by his letter £10;

More he aweth per Book £13 12s 1d;

John Weston per bill £5;

Henry Roberts rest per bill £2 2s;

[10] Item Parson [?] Ellis per bill reste 2s 6d;

Item Robert Sabeth per bill 2s;

Edward Marshe per bill 6s 8d;

Richard Gibbons by bill 5s;

Item Mr Penwarringe per book 20s;

Item [blank] Sware per book 46s 8d;

Item John Crosse per bill 10s;

Item Richerd Bartletts bill £2;

William James per book £2 4s 4d;

Item Ellett per Bill 13s 4d;

Item William Bande per bill 9s;

Item Mr Rawe per book £3;

Roger Triche per bill £10;

John Batt aweth per book 10s;

Item Cornell Bradye per bill £3;

Howssen aweth per bill and book £3 10s;

Item Hall aweth per bill £3 6s 8d;

John Tooker reste per bill 8s;

Item Wilcocks reste per bill 20s;

Item John Harvie per book 46s 8d;

Item Pherant Reste per bill 13s 4d;

Item Elizabeth Parramoor per book 45s;

Hughe Trowe and John Stronge per 2 billes 22s 8d;

Item Mr Marsson per Book 54s 9d;

Nicholas Marsson per Book 10s;

Vyncent Marsson per Booke 10s;

Item John Sandye Rest per bill £5 3s;

Walter Jones per bill 9s;

Edmonde Fowler with John Fowler reste per bill £2;

John Gribbell per book and bill £3 6s 8d;

Sir Richard Egbear per Book 30s;

John Chambers per bill 13s 4d;

Sir Borell per book and bill per accompte £20;

Item Kayever per bill 20s;

Henry Tyffen per bill £3;

John Herdwick per bill 3s 4d;

Roberte Fulforde per Book 10s;

William Edmonds per Book 5s 8d;

Roberte Easterbrook per book 16s;

Hughe Trowe per book 25s;

Richard Bowdon per book £5;

More in a nother place per book £5;

[More he aweth per bill £4 8s – crossed through];

Richard Carter per Book £3 13s 8d;

Sum £199 3s.

[10v.] Item John Semell per book 21s;

Edmonde Smithe per Book 8s;

William Spanyer per book 20s;

Wilmont Drak per Booke 9s;

William Kenswell per book 3s 6d;

Peter Esswarie per booke [illegible];

Margarett Wolcott per book 7s;

Henry Pafforde 2 boushells of Rye 3s 4d;

John Pafforde ½ a boushell of Rie 10d;

John Blackedone a boushell of Rie 20d;

Sir John Fulford for malt 21s;

John Marker per bill and book 10s 8d;

John Heale uppon his letter 20s;

Mr Clevelande aweth for a panne [?] 53s 4d;

Humfrey Bassell per book and bill 25s;

William Martyn merchaunt and Martyn Rawe per book £16 5s;

[Thomas Halse – crossed through];

Richard Hobbes per bill 10s;

Mr Langdon upon a bill condicionall of assumpcon £6 13s 4d;

Langdons obligacon for the office £100;

Item paid unto Laurence Bonifeild by Mr James, which was for Mr Langdons Bill 5s;

Item one other obligacon beinge Mr William Grenewoods hands £2 10s;

[John Tothill per book and bill – crossed through];

Richard Strowde per book 6s 8d;

Thomas Stawkes aweth per book £24;

Mr Bodley of Whittstone per 2 billes 44s;

John Watkings reste per book £4 18d;

More he aweth per bill £10;

Huberte Collwill per book and bill £2 10s;

Thomasyne Welshe per bill rest 10s;

Marker of Cheriton per bill 9s;

Henry Parramoor per bill £2;

Richard Edgescombe per book 47s 10d;

John Fuller per bill £2;

Parker aweth per book 10s;

Anthony Parker per book 19s 6d;

John Thatcher per Book 20s;

Item Mr Harvye per book 53s 4d;

Nicholas Oliver per bill £2;

Frauncis Geffrey per bill 20s;

Item Richard Hobbes per bill 26s 8d;

[11] Item John Bralards obligacon for 25s;

Roberte Eslys [?] per bill 3s 4d;

Sir William Swynson per book 18s;

Meryck upon a salt 47s;

William Ryve per book 10s;

Mr Kealt per 2 Bills £10;

Sum [£211 5s 6d – crossed through] £209 5d.

Item William Grenewood aweth upon accompt per book or bill £6 2s 4d;

Mr Symon Knight per 2 billes £300;

John Prynce per bill 20s;

Sampson Leigh by bill 15s;

More upon ring [?] 10s;

Mr Hughe Wiott aweth per book £4 4d;

Mr Staplyn rest per bill 4s 4d;

Richard Flatcher per book 6s 8d;

John Kaeth per bill 4s;

Agnes Jones per bill £20;

John Shapley per bill 20s;

Item Mr Cheame of Blandeford doth awe for fishe £6 13s 4d;

Item Mr Fisher for a hoxehed of wyne £4;

Item Thomas Trosse upon his last accompt £7;

Sum £334 2s 8d.

The leasses

Item the lease Mr James his dwelling howse £66 13s 4d;

Item the lease of St Sidwills £80;

Item the leasse of Winckeley £80;

Item the lease of a Close at Maudelyn £22;

Item the lease of a Close in St Thomas parishe £6 13s 4d;

Item 2 Closes at Cherington 20s;

Item one other medowe at Cherington 13s 4d;

Item the lease of the Chamber in the Churche yeard of St Peters £16;

Item Essworthies lease of certen grounde at Poslowe £12;

Item the leasse of a howse at St James Corner beinge in lawe £6;

Item the lease of a Courte and stabell for 10 yeares £5 16s;

Item a lease of a close without Southgat 5s;

Sum £285.

[11v.] Item the Glasse in the holle howse worthe £3 6s 8d;

Sum £294 8s 2d.

In thother howse wher Henry James dwelled before

In the Kitchen

Item the shelves, Caige, a badd fforme and a badd borde 4s;

Item a borde Portingall making 2s 6d;

Sum [blank].

In the Buttrie by the Kitchen

Item one longe Cupporde and one shorte Cupporde with a
   borde 8*s*;

Sum [blank].

Item the Seller 2 shelves & a Trye 6*d*;

Sum [blank].

In the parler

Item a borde with a fforme 10*s*;

Item a Bed steede with 2 roddes of Iron 20*s*;

Item the stayned clothes with a pece of seelinge wherin ther
   are certen Cubbords with benches £2;

Item one planck befor the Chymney 8*d*;

Sum [blank].

In the Hall

Item one borde 12*s*;

Item one littell Cupporde solde to the maide of the howse 6*s* 8*d*;

The hangings aboute the same 13*s* 4*d*;

Item one Iron Crowk of a bassen 2*d*;

Item a planck befor the ffyer 8*d*;

Item in the Buttrey by the Hall 9 shelves 18*d*;

Sum [blank].

[12] In the ffoare Chamber

Item one Bedsteede with a truckellbedd 26*s* 8*d*;

Item one Presse 33*s* 4*d*;

Item a borde 5*s*;

Item the Counter with the shelves and a litell borde 10*s*;

Item a Cheste 6*s* 8*d*;

Sum [blank].

Item in the maidens Chamber a Couches with certen bords 2*s*
   6*d*;

Sum [blank]

Item in the Backe Chamber 2 slender bedsteddes with one
   Truckell bedde 8*s*;

Item a litell borde with the hangings and 4or Chests 10*s*;

Sum [blank].

Item in a litle howse by the Chamber certen shelves 16*d*;

Sum £11 3*s* 6*d*;

Sum total £1,755 14*s*.

Whereof the Testatorr oweth £116 2*s* 7*d*;

Also for his funeralls £39 11*s* 2*d*;

Also for chardges of the howse £9 13*s* 11*d*;

Also for extraordinary chardgs £3 15*s* 6*d*;

Also yn desperat debts £217 9*d*;

Sum £385 15*s* 1*d*.

So remaineth £1,369 18*s* 11*d*.

Wherof

To the wyff £456 12*s* 11¼*d*;

To the orphans £456 12*s* 11¼*d*;

To the testator £456 12*s* 11¼*d*;

£1,368 5*s* 6*d*.

Out of the testators 3rd the legacys ar to be payd

To his Kyns folke & frendes £99 18*s* 4*d*;

To his childern £423 13[*s*] [rest illegible].

ECA, Orphans' Court Inventory 29 [Item 2]

The Inventory of Henry James

The goodds comprysed yn the Inventary £1,764 15*s*;

Also left out of the Inventery & receved of Sir B[illegible]
   25*s* for hoggshedds 3*s* for haye £4 of Mr Waldron for
   procuracion 10*s* 10*d* of Mr Bodley 16*s* 6*d* – £7 6*d*;

Also of Stoks mony not mencioned £6;

of Richerd 35*s* of Lane of Kyrton 30*s*;

of Mr James man 40*s*;

£11 5*s*;

Sum £1,783 6*d*.

for funeralls £63 11s;

for debts & the wydowes money £534 15s 11d;

for legacys £622 13s 2d;

for desperat debts £291 14s 7d;

[for Expenses yn law – crossed through];

[for debtes of – crossed through] expenses yn lawe £62 3s 7d;

for allowauncs £128 7s 10d;

Also of £15 dew by Jo: Watkyns he was thereof dyschardgd upon his oth £12 18s [rest lost];

of Richerd Bowdon for the debt of £10 he oweth £3 17s [rest lost];

Also of £24 chardged upon Stokes he hath payd but £21 the rest he denyeth £3;

Also Mr Hew Wyet is chardged upon the Inventory & hath not payed it £4 4d;

Also for an annuytie of 3 yeres 3 quarter yeres payed to Joan Awtrey at 26s 8d per annum £5;

Also paid to Stoks for caryag of tymber by order of Mr mayer 6s 8d;

[£157 11s 5d];

Sum £1,732 9s 8d.

So remaineth £50 11s 11d.

Whereof there is demaunded to be allowed for monye dew & paied to Cove of Hevytree as appereth by his byll & not allowed nor befor paied £4 7s 4d;

Also for a nother byll paied to William Greenewod £4 8s 7d;

Sum £8 15s 11d.

So remaineth £41 16s.

[verso] The abbreviat of Mrs Olyvers accompt

ffirst she oweth for the whole good comprysed yn the Inventory £1,764 15s;

Also she hath receved for goodds not mencionid yn the Inventory £7 6d;

Sum £1,771 15s 6d.

Whereof paid for funeralls £64 11s;

dew to certeyn credytors [?] & paied £534 15s 11d;

dew for legacys £622 13s 2d;

desperat debts £291 14s 7d;

Expenses yn lawe £62 3s 7d;

Certyn allowancs £133 7s 10d;

Sum £1,708 6s 1d.

So she oweth £63 9s 5d;

Also she oweth for mony received of Stokes which is not yn the Inventory £6;

Also of Richerd May 35s;

Also of Lane of Kyrton 30s;

Also of Mr James man 40s;

Sum £11 5s;

So she oweth £74 14s 5d.

Whereof she is to be allowed of somich of £15 as whereof John Watkyns, upon his oth was released £12 18s 8d;

Also of the debt of Richerd Bowdon charded at £10 & he released of £5 17s 11d;

Also of debts released of Tho: Stoks [blank].

ECA Book 141 [130v.] (126v.)

Inventory of Henry James

To Judythe James for her Orphanage £100;

To her for her Legacye £57 15s 2½d;

To her for the profittes of her Lease of two tenements £19 13s 6½d;

To her for her thirde parte of Robert James his porcon £59 13s 1½d;

Sum £237 22½d.

Wherof you are to abate for Charges in Lawe sithens the generall Accompte of Mrs Olyver £9 22d;

Also for marrienge the Orphan withoute Consent after 12*d* the Pounde only where there is 3*s* dewe for every pound and so £22 16*s* geven – £11 8*s*;

Sum £20 9*s* 10*d*.

And so restethe £216 12*s*;

which is to be receaved as followeth *viz.*

Of Mr John Peryam £34 1½*d*;

Of Mrs Olyver £79 17*s* 3½*d*;

Of Valentyne Tooker £14 2*s* 7½*d*;

Of Mr Maior £88 12*s*;

Sum £216 12*s*.

Wherof you are to leave in the posite for A Clayme made by Jasper Bridgman unto A fowerth parte beinge Symon James his porcon £26 13*s* 4*d*;

So you are to receave of Mrs Olyver £53 3*s* 11½*d*.

[131] (127) To Mary James for her Orphanage £100;

To her for her Legacye £57 15*s* 2½*d*;

The profits of her Lease £10 12*d*;

The 3 parte of Roberts porcon £59 13*s*;

Sum £227 9*s* 2½*d*.

Wherof in Mr Prouze his hands £100;

In Mr Peryams hands £40 15*s* 11½*d*;

In Valentyne Tokers hands £14 2*s* 6½*d*;

In Mrs Olivers handes £63 9*s*;

Also for the 3 parte of Charges £9;

Also to allowe for marrige withoute leave after the rate of 12*d* of every pounde £11 7*s*.

To Agnes James for her Orphanage £100;

For her Legacye £23 16*s* 10½*d*;

The third parte of Roberts porcon £59 13*s* 1½*d*;

Sum £183 10*s*.

Wherof payd in money £100;

Also of Mrs Oliver £24 5*s* 9¼*d*;

Also to allow for the thirde parte of Charges £9 22½*d*;

So restethe £51 2*s* 6½*d*.

Wherof in Mr Peryams hands £5 3*s* 11½*d*;

In Valentyne Tokers hands £14 2*s* 7½*d*;

In Mrs Olivers hands £30 15*s* 11½*d*;

Sum £50 [*sic*] 2*s* 6½*d*.

34A. WILL OF THOMAS PRESTWOOD, 13 DECEMBER 1576

ECA, Orphans' Court Will 13 (also National Archives, 11/59/109)

Note: the will was proved via Canterbury on 12 February 1577. John Hooker noted in his *Chronicle* that Prestwood died while serving as mayor on the last day of December. He also noted, in a long passage on him, that 'as his father and he were of like conditions, qualities and virtues in their lives so was one and the same grave their burial after their deaths' (Todd Gray, *The Chronicle of Exeter*, Exeter, 2005, 108). There was an Inquisition Post Mortem (National Archives, C142/176/27). An ancillary part of his inventory recorded his death on 30 December. Recognisances were entered into on 2 September 1577 regarding his children George and John, Katharine and Marie, Thomas & Susan (ECA, Book 141, folios 59 to 60 dorse).

[1] **In the name of God** Amen this Thertyneth Daye of December in the yeare of our lorde god 15C 76 and in the 19th yeare of the reigne of our moste Soveraigne Ladye Elizabeth by the grace of god of England Fraunce Irelande queene Defender of the ffaythe &c, I Thomas Prestwode of the Countye of The Cytye of Exon gent, beinge of good mynde perfyte rememberaunce praysed be unto thallmyghtye god do ordayne and macke this my laste will and Testament

in manner and fforme following. Firste, as tuchinge [my] solle which is hevenly ffirme and Immortalle I do comende the same unto [the] mercyfull hande of my all mightye and everlastinge lorde god the deare father of my only saviour creator and redeamer Jesus Criste havinge an assured hoppe that it hath pleased him of his gracious godnes to Electe and chuse in to the Everlastinge Lyffe and eternalle sallvation not by my owne worthynes and ryghtousnes but by the puryfying my solle with the most precyous bloude deathe and passyon of his deare sonne Christe Jesus to thende that I sinffull creatour myght appeare as ryghtous and Justeffyed in his syght throughe him unto whome be all honor and glory for ever Amen. And as touchinge my bodye which is Earthly fralle and mortalle I commende the same to the Earthe ffrom wenche yt came to be buryed in suche place as by the discrecyon of myne Executours shalle be thought moste convenyente. At the ffuneralles wheare of I will that some vertuous and godly Sermonde be had and made by some vertuous and learned mane to the prayse of thall myghty god, the avauncement of [the allmyghtye god – crossed through] his glory and everlastinge worde the Edyffynge of his congregacyon and atestestyment of myne undowted and assured faythe in the unfallable promysyes of god in his holly scrypture which sayde Sarmon I ryghtly will that yt be made by Mr Wolton, Mr Phyllpote or Mr Tonnesen or some one of them so that thire pleasure be to accomplyshe the same accordyngly and I geve for his peynes in that be hallfe tenne shillynges but and if the sayde Mr Wolton, Mr Phyllpote or Mr Tonnsen or any one of them may not convenyently be gotten and had thare unto I will that the sayde tenne shyllings be geven to some other Preacher that shall be appoynted by the discrecyon of myne Executours for the supplynge of that rome whome I woulde to be suche a person as shalbe *[2]* as shoulde by his preachering sette forthe to the true light of the gospel to the advancemente of the glory of Criste the uteer suppresyon of all papysts and superstytious doctrayne with ene exortacon to imbrace vertue and to Eschewe vice as apearteynethe. Item I will that all suche debtes and dutyes that I owe of ryght or of consyence to any manner of person or persons as shalle appeare Evidently by any manner of Specyallytye of myne of otherwise be well and truly contented and payde by myne Executers heare after names withoute any delay or contradiction And after my debtes payed and my funeralle Expenses parfourmed I will that all my goodes cattells and debtes shalle be devyded in to three Equalle Partes whereof I will that Mare my wiffe shall have one Equalle parte to her owne proper use in manner of her purpertye and reasonable parte to her apartaynynge of all my sayde goodes cattells and debtes accordinge to the laudable custome and order of the cytye of Exon and E [*sic*] the seconde Equalle parte of all my sayde goodes cattells and debtes I geve and bequethe unto Susan Katheren George John Mary Thomas and Elizabethe my children and to that chylde where of my wiffe shall happen to be conceyved by me at the tyme of my deces Equally to be devided among them and to be delivered unto all and every of them by severalle portions when and assone as they shall accomplyshe and come to ther lawfull ages of twenty and one yeares or els be marryed, And yf any of my sayde chylldren do deces be ffore suche tyme as he or the shalle accomplyshe ther sayde full ages and before that tyme be not marryed that then I bequethe the party [*sic*] or portyon of him or them so desessinge to the survivers of my sayde children to be delyvered unto them when they shalle accomplyshe there sayde ages or els be marryed and yf all my chilldren do deces as at godes good will and pleasure the do heare remayne before that they or any of them do accomplyshe the sayde full ages and before that tyme be not marryed then I bequethe all and singuler the sayde severalle partes and porcyons of my sayde children of and to my foresayde goodes cattells and debtes to and amongst all the children nowe lyvinge of the boydes of Rycharde Prestowde [*sic*] and Allice his late wiffe my sister to be payde and delyvered unto them and ether of them at lycke ages [as is – crossed through] and inlycke manner as is appointed to myne owne *[3]* chilldren and the survivours of of [*sic*] the sayde chilldren lycke wise to have the benyfyte therof, And touchinge the thirde equalle parte of all my sayde goodes cattells and debtes I will that yt shall remayne unto myne

Execatours ther with to perforeme my legacyes and bequests in this my present testament especyfyed and the residue ther of to be disposed by myne [by – crossed through] Executours to suche use as are [and – crossed through] or shall be in this my presente laste will and testament Expressed and declared, Item I geve and bequeth unto Rychard Pytes my kinsman the some of 40s in monye to be payd him within one halfe yeare after my desses and also so muche blacke clothe to macke him a cloke so far forthe as he render unto my Executours heare after names a Just true and honeste accompt of 54 quarters 1 bushel of rye which and wherewith he standeth charged his charges and reasonable paynes always allowed therein, Item I will and geve unto the wardens of the paryshe of St Styphens of Exon aforesayde and to their successours all that my estate right terme intereste which I have of and in the seller sytuate and beinge under the sayde paryshe churche and also in and to the plott of grounde adjoyninge thereunto which I do holde of them by lease which my seayde estate and terme I do surrender into the hands of the sayde wardens to thende the shall and may converte the same to the beste comodytye of the said parysheners and all so intocken and asknowledginge of my farther good will towards them I geve to the sayde parishe churche to be payde to the wardens for the tyme beinge six shillings eyght pence in monyes, Item I geve and bequethe unto Joyce Bowdon my kinswoman the wife of Rycharde Bowden so muche blacke clothe as will macke her agowne, Item I will and geve unto George Yalle gentellman yf he be lyvinge in parte recompence of his good will towardes me and myne one neste of cupes towne wise 3 acase under one cover parcel gyllte poz [sic] 45 ounces which I bought of Mr Pylle and allso a scarlett clocke lyned with taffeta sarsnet which late was my fathers and worren by him and by me for a robe upon a scarlet gowne to the use of Kateren his wiffe, Item I geve and bequethe the some of fowre poundes to be distributed after my deces to and emongeste the poore houshoulders and other poore people inhabytinge with in the sayde cytye of Exon [4] And suberbes of the same at theire howses and Inhabytances and not otherwise which sayde some of foure poundes I will to be payde by my Executours

unto the tresorur and counsels of the company and fellowshype of the merchantes adventeres in France inhabytinge within the sayde cityе and by them to be destrybuted at suche tyme or tymes as by [them – crossed through] ther good discresyons shall syme moste convenyente. Item I geve and bequethe to and amongst [to and – crossed through] the poore prisoners in all the prisons and gaylles of Exetter and within the walles of the same the some of 40s to be equally devided amongste them by the sayde tresorer and counsel before resyted. Item I geve and bequethe unto every one of my mayden sarvauntes that shall be in my howse in covenaunte sarvice at the tymme of my deces a casacke of blacke clothe and to every one of my mens sarvauntes a blacke cote and fyve shillinges in monnye over the besydes ther wages that shallbe dewe unto them at the tyme of my deces. Item I geve unto my mayde Anstes [at – crossed through] my sarvaunte at the day of her marryayge the some of twentye shillinges. Item I geve and bequethe unto the governer counsoule and fewllowshipe of the corportyon of the merchantes aforesayde the some of 40s in monye to be payde unto them by my Executours as aremembereraunce of my good and affection towards that holle company the residue of [my – crossed through] the sayde holle thirde parte and portion of all my goodes cattells and debtes after my debtes as aforesayde payde my funeralle expenses performed and all and singuler thes my foresayd leagasyes discharged and fullfylled I holly geve and bequethe unto the sayde Mary my wife Susan Kateren George John Mary Thomas and Elizabethe my sayde chylldren and to that chyllde wherof my wiffe shoulde happen to be conseyved by me at the tyme of my deses Equally to be devided amongste them and the partyes and portyons thereof to be delyvered unto my sayde chelldren and to the survivors of them according to suche order and fourme as is to before prescrybed and declared towchinge there owne preparty and portion to them geven and bequeathed which sayde [resydue – crossed through] resydences of my thirde part and portyon of all my goods cattells and debtes before geven and bequeathed unto my sayde chelldren Joyntely with my [5] sayde wyffe is for this

respecte and consyderacon that my sayde chylldren and every
of them shall quietly parmytte and suffer the sayde Mary my
wiffe to have the full use possession and occupatyon of all
that my mansyon howse wherin I now do dwell for and
duringe all suche terme and yeares as I have yt to come there
in so that the sayde Mary my wiffe do so lonnge lyve and
macke her habytacon and dwelling in and upon the sayde
mansyon house and not ells wheare & for the better surtye of
the accomplyshmente of my devise and meaning hearin on
the behallfe of my sayde wiffe my wil is that yf any of my
sayde children do or shall wilfully or willingly interrupte
disturbe or moleste my sayde wiffe or her quiet possessyon of
and in my sayde mansyon howse during so many yeares as I
have yt therin to come yf she so longe do lyve and macke her
habytacon and dwellinge in and upon the sayde mansyon
howse and not ellse wheare then the sayde chyllde or
chylldren which dothe or shall so interrupt disturbe or moleste
her quiet possessyon of and in the same shall lose the
benyfyte of his or ther part or portyon which shoulde or ought
come to him or them of and by reason of my foresayde
leagasye touchinge the seayde thirde parte of my sayde
goodes cattells and debtes and the same his or ther portyon
soloste by that meanes shall go and remayne to the only use
and behalf of my sayde wife and yf [yf – crossed through] yt
shall so fortune that all my sayde chilldren do deces as to
gods pleasure and will they stand and before and the
acclomplyshe ther sayde ages and before that tyme be no
marryed then the resydue of the sayde thirde part of all my
sayde goods cattels and debtes unto them geven and appointed
after my debtes payde my funeral exspenses parfourmed and
this my leagases aforesayde fullfylled I geve and bequethe
unto the poore people of the sayde cytye of Exetter and the
subberbes of the same to be distrybuted to and amongeste
them at all tyme and tymes when nyde shalle require by the
discrecyon of the treasorer and consulles be foredeclared and
expressed and further my very will desyre and Intentes is that
shortly [6] after my deces and all and singuler my wares stuff
of househoulde plate and all other my goodes what so ever the
be shall be praysed by foure sixe or eyght honeste and

indeferent persons to be named and sworen by the maior of
the sayde cyty and his bretheren for the tyme beinge and all
and singuler the portyons ther of apperteyninge to my sayde
children as well the second equall part of my sayd goodes
cattells and debtes as also my sayde leagases so to them geven
& bequeathed of the sayde thirde part Imediatly afte the
praysinge ther of to be ordered by the maior and his bretheren
according to the custome of the orphanage of the sayde cytye
And my mynde and Intent is that Mr William Strode my
father in lawe Mr John Bodleigh my brother Mr George Galle
Mr John Trobridge and Eustas Olyver my cousens and the
survivers of them shall have the keepinge governinge and
bringinge upp of my sayde chilldren during ther nonages with
all ther part and portyon unto them geven and bequeathed so
farforth as thorder of the orffanage of the sayde cytye be ther
in accomplyshed accordingly And I do macke and ordayne
the sayde Marye Prestowde my wife Mr William Strowde my
father in lawe Mr John Bodlygh my brother Mr George Galle
Mr John Trobridge and Eustas Olyver my cousens myne
Executours of this my presente laste will and testament to
suche only uses and Intentes as Is before expressed moste
hartely praying them and every of them as ther will aunswer
before the eternall god at the day of Judgement that they and
every of them will use ther faythefull indeavours to se the
same duly executed and performed in all things according to
the specyall truste and confidence which I have repozed in
them and I will and bequethe to every of the seyde executours
the some of 40*s* in monye and a blacke gowne and for the
more [and – crossed through] better & certayne testemony
amd veryfyinge that this is my laste will and teastament I the
foresayde Thomas Prestowd have heare unto subscrybed my
owne hand the sayde thirtenthe daye of December in the
nintenthe yeare of the raigne of our sovraige Ladye Queene
Elizabeth.

[7] Here after followeth the last will & Testament of me the
foresayd Thomas Prestwood the elder for and consinynge
the devysynge orderinge and disposinge of all my manners
lands tenements and heraydytaments which was by me made

syneed and sealed with myne owne hand & seall geven the 12th day of Desember in the 19th yeare of the raygne of our Soverayne Lady Quene Elyzabeth

First I the foresayde Thomas Prestowde having always aspecyall regarde and singuler respect to and for the advancement and preferment of Mary my wellbeloved wife with aconvenyent portyon of Joynture to be had and assured unto her in recompence of the dowry which she shoulde might or ought to have oute of all and singuler my manners lands tenements and herydytaments as allso for the preffermente of my chelldren and payment of suche debtes as ar by me owinge unto any person or persons do therfor will and geve by this my present laste will and testament all those my manners of Butterforde Vennyttyttborne and Tinnatre in the county of Devon with all ther right members & appurtenance and allso and all singuler my lands tents & herydytaments in Butterforde Northhuyshe Venetellborne Crediton Clawton Biggeton Carlewes Hempson Cantelowe Broadhempston Uggborough Hereforde Windbrooke Kelley Worfford Ermington and St Thomas Theappostell with all and in singuler theire appurtenance in the sayde County of Devon And allso all and singuler my messuages Lands tents and heridytaments with theapptenances in the countye of the Cyttye of Exon unto those persons that are appoynted to be myne Executours of & in my laste will and Testement of for and concernynge my goodes debts & cattals namely Marye my wiffe William Strode Esquire John Bodleigh my brother George Galle & John Trobridge Esquires & Eustas Olyver merchante and to ther heires and assignes forever to thonly uses consyderacons purposes and intents in this my present laste will & testament mentyoned expressed & declared that is to saye that the my foresayde Executours before named their heares & assignes shall from and after my deceasse receave tacke & yearly receyve one hundrethe marckes of Lawfull monye of England of the year rent revenues issues & profytts of the sayde manners of Butterforde Venytettborne & Tynnatre [8] with theire appurtenances and of all singuler the foresayde Landes Tents and Herydytaments with thappurtenance lyinge in the county of Devon to theonlye use

and behalffe of the fore sayde Mary my wiffe duringe her naturalle lyffe at the ffoure princypalle and moste usualle feastes and tearmes of the yeare by even portyons to be payde ffor the more better assuraunce sure payment and accomplyshment of annuitye acertayne annuall rent chardge of the like some of one hundrethe markes which was and is of late unto her grunted asured and convyed by good and suffycyent conveance in lawe ouwt of the fore sayde manners of Butterforde Venytettborne Teneatre and oute of [my – crossed through] land [sic] singuler other my foresayde messuages Landes tenaments and heridatents lyinge in the sayde countye of Devon and to the intent allso that my sayde Executours before named there yeares [sic] and assignes shall from and after my deses yearely receyve tacke levy and perceyve the other moyety [of – crossed through] or hallfefindealle of all my rents revenyes yssues and profytes of all and singuler my foresayde landes tenements and herydytamements with theappurtenance lyinge and beinge within the sayd countye of the sayde cytye of Exon to thonly use and behaffe of George Prestowd my sonne and heare apparramet untell he shall accomplishe his full ayge of 21 yeares for his better maintenance Education and fynding at schoole and for the increae of knowledge in good learninge and vertuous qualyties and to theintente allso that my sayde Executours before named with ther yeares and assignes shall from and after the tyme that Thomas Prestowde my sonne shall accompleshe his full ayge of 21 years yearely receyve tacke levy and perceyve foure poundes ayeare of the rentes revveneyes Isues and profyttes of all and singuler my fore sayde manners landes tenements and herydytaments with in the countye of Devon and of the one moyitie and hallfeindeale of my sayde landes tenyments and herydytaments with in the cytye of Exon to the use and behalffe of the foresayde Thomas Presowd my sonne duringe the terme of his naturall lyfe ffor his better mentenaunce and preferment in lyvinge and to thentent allso that myforesayde Executours beforenamed ther heares and assignes shall after my desses [9] receyve tacke and levy and perceyve the some of foure hondreth mackes lawfull mony of England oute of the rents

127

revenyes Issues and profytts of all and singuler the foresayde manners messuages Landes tenements and herydytaments with theappurtenannce lyinge in the sayde county of Devon and of the same moyitye and halfe dealle of my sayde landes tenements and herydytaments lyinge in the sayde countye of the sayde cytye of Exon for the more better advancement and preferment in marryayge of my fowre daughters that is so saye Susan Prestowde Kateren Prestowde Mary Prestowde and Elizabethe Prestowde Equally to be devided betwene theme that is to witte unto every one of them one hundrethe marckes to be payde unto them at thare dayes of marryages and yf it do so happen that any of my sayd foure daughters do deses this present lyfe before suche tyme as she or they be marryed that then my will and meaninge is that the part of him or them so decessinge shalle remayne and be to the reste of my sayde daughters then survivinge the same to be lycke wise payd and delyvered unto them at thare sayde dayes of marryages as is aforsayd and to thentent allso that my foresayde Executours ther heyres and assignes shall with in ashorte tyme after my deses as the may convenyently receyve tacke levy and perceyve the some of £40 lawfull monnye of Inglande oute of the rentes revenyes Issues and profyttes of all and singuler the foresayde manners landes tenements and herydytaments within the sayde contye of Devon and of the sayde moytie of my lands tenements and herydytaments lyinge in the sayde cyty of Exon and the same so longe by them levyed and receyved shall be delyvered & payed ever unto the governer counselles and company of the merchanntes adventerers of the sayde cytye of Exon to thentente to be by them converted and Imployed with in threeyeares next after the receate then of in and aboute the rectinge builldinge and edyffyinge of one convenyente howse or tenemente with in the foresayde cytye of Exon or subberbes of the same which shall *[10]* or may serve for an Almes house for fowre powre personnes to make their only habytacyon theryn which shallbe ffor the due performaunce and accomplyshmente of acertayne device and ordenaunce in that behalfe made lymytted and appointed by and in the laste will and testement of Allice Prestowd my late mother decessd. And I will that the sayde howse and tenement shall be scytuated erected and buillded in suche convenyent place within the sayde cyty or subberbes as by the sayde governour counsells and company of marchanntes adventerers shall be thought moste myte nessesary and convenyent and I will and geve full poore and autorytye to the maior of the sayde cytye for the tyme beinge or to his lyve tennents and to the fourge stewardes of the sayde cytye ffor the tyme beinge to have the fre Electyon and nomynacon from tyme to tyme for ever of the sayde fourge poore persons that shall be plased and appointed to inhabyte with in the sayde allmes howsses but my further will intente and meaninge is that yf the sayde governour counsulles and company of the marchanntes adventerers of Exon aforesayde before thende of the sayde three yeares next ensuinge the tyme that they shall have receyved the sayde some of £40 shall by ther good discretyons thincke yt a more requsyt or nessesary charetable acte to cause or procure the sayde monye to be Imployed in or upon the purches of a certayne small rente to be had graunted and assured unto the sayde corporation and company for the pupetuall mayntemaunce and contynuall relyffe of foure poore persons then by providinge exertinge and buildinge of the fore sayde howse or tenement for an allmes howsse that then the sayde corporation and compony shall have full poore and authorytye to converted and Inployew the sayde some of fourty poundes for and towwardes the purches of a parpetuall annuitye or small rente to the use before mensyoned in suche sorte as to ther discretions shall seame moste beste and convenyent accordynglye the sayde foure poore persons *[11]* to be nether the too [mentayned – crossed through] nominated and appointed by the sayde maior and foure stewwardes as is aforesayde and the sayde governor counsells and company of merchannts adventerers to render and acconpte unto my sayde executours at thende of the sayde thre yeares of for and consernynge the Imploymente of the sayde some of £40 and to thentent allso that my sayde Executours ther yeares *[sic]* and assignes or four of them of which the foresayde William Strowde my father in lawe and the fore sayde Mary my wiffe beinge then lyvinge shallbe alwayes twoo shall with in

ashorte tyme after my desses as the may convenyently macke two severall demysyes leases and grauntes unto some person or persons for terme of certyen lyves or terme of years of and for all those messuages Landes tenements and herydytaments called Combe lyinge and beinge in North Huis aforesayed and now beinge in the tenor or occupatyon of one Walter Volley or of his assynes and of and in all those messuages Landes tenements shyndle quarye gryste mylls and other herydytaments lyinge and beinge in Northe Huishe aforesayde which are in the tenur or occupacion of one Phylype Chullson or his assignes wher by and so as my sayde executours may levy receyte and tacke of and for the fynes in combes and casalltyes of the sayde laste recyted premises the some of £200 lawfull mony of Ingland for the discharge and payment of suche lawfull debtes and duties as I shall happe to owe and be Indebted at the tyme of my deces and my very will Intente and meaninge is that after suche tyme and assone as all and every the foresayde severall devices and payments be fore lymitted and appoynted shall or may be fully accomplyshed and performed that my sayde executours be fore named ther heares and assignes other then suche persons as shalbe the grauntes and leases of the sayde laste recyted premysses duringe suche severall tearmes as shall be to them assured or [12] granted shall from thence fforth stand and be seised of all and singuler the foresayd moyeties lands tenements and herydetaments lyinge in the sayd county of Devon and in the county of the sayd cyty of Exon to the use and be holfe of the foresayde George Prestowde my sonne and heire apparante and to his heires and assignes for ever provided never theles that yf the sayde George my sone his heyres or assignes or any other of my heares that shall happen to be [rea – crossed out] seised of the sayde manners and other the premises or any part or parcel thereof or any other person or persons by his or ther procurement manner or assent shall at any tyme heare after amove erecte expell or evict any of the teanaments farmours leases or occupyers of the sayde premyses or of any part or parcle ther of which they or any of them do holde cleame or Injoye by vertue of any demise graunte or lease made by my late ffather or by my sellfe ether by writtinge or with oute writtinge beinge entred or mencyoned in any of my bookes or rentalles except yt be by reason of the not performaunce of the covenaunce condysions or agrements of and for the same thinges so leased that then my will intent and meaninge is that my sayde executours before named ther heares and assignes shall stand and be seasede of the same landes tenements and herydytaments wher of any suche tenents & farmours leases occupyers of the sayde premyses shall fortune to be so mouved ejected expelled or evicted to the only use and behoufe of suche tenents farmour lesse or occupyer as shall so happen to be amoved ejected expeled or evicted for and duringe suche lycke estate terme and Intereste to all intentes and purposes as the same tennents farmour lease or occupyer had myght shulde or ought to have yf the [sayde – crossed through] same evictyon had not byne so hade or made [13] in wittnes and testymony that this is my laste will and testament I have heare unto sett my hande and sealle geven the sayde thirtenthe daye of December in the nyntenthe yeare of the raigne of our soverainge ladye Queene Elizabethe *Anno domini* 1576
By me Thomas Prestowde.

Memorandum that this was Signed Sealed and delyvered as the laste will and testament of the aforesayd Thomas Prestowde the daye and yeare laste above mentioned in the presence of thos persons whose names be heare subscrybed and dyvers others

John Strode
Per me Walter Helle
Nicolas Goodridge
John Denham

Memorandum that this coppy was truly examinned seene and pased by the verye last will and testament of the foresayd Thomas Prestowde & dothe concorde and agre with the same Verbatim writtinges thare unto thos persons whose names ar heare under

Witnessed by Phillypp Strode.

34B. INVENTORY OF THOMAS PRESTWOOD, 4 JANUARY 1577

ECA, Orphans' Court Inventory 24

The Inventory of all the goods & cattells of Mr Thomas Prestwood decessed the fourth of Januarie 1576 In the Nyntenth yere of the reigne of Queene Elizabethe praysed by Michell German Geffrey Thomas John Levermore & John Dorne sworne for the true assessment before William Trevett one of the aldermen of the said cittie

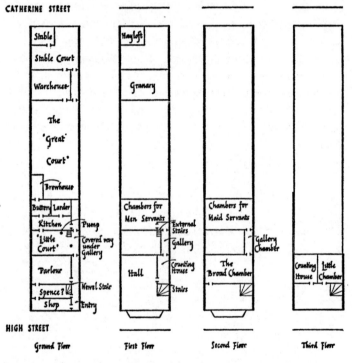

CATHERINE STREET

HIGH STREET

Ground Floor   First Floor   Second Floor   Third Floor

Fig. 17. W.G. Hoskins' reconstruction of the layout of rooms in Thomas Prestwood's house in St Stephen's parish, which combined evidence from his inventory (OC 24) with familiarity with the city's old buildings (Hoskins 1966, 91; *reproduced by courtesy of the University of London*).

[m. 1] Firstly In the Hall
One Joyned table borde with Cubberds 40*s*;
One litell Joyned borde 10*s*;
Three formes 2*s*;
One other Joyned borde with a cubberd 10*s*;
One Cubberd 40*s*;
One litell borde 12*d*;
Sixe quysshens 9*s*;
One pare of Andirons 6*s* 8*d*;
One Carpett 20*d*;
One Candelsticke 2*s*;
One backe of Iron in the Chimney 5*s*;
One lokinge glasse 2*s* 6*d*;
Item all the sealinge ther 15*s*;
Item the hangins and steyne clothers and the carde with three storries paynted 10*s*;
One doble brasen candelsticke 2*s* 6*d*;
One timber frame for arrowes 2*d*;
One deske for a booke 4*d*;
Crookes to hange mases and sords unto 6*d*;
One skrynne 6*d*;
Sum £7 18*s* 10*d*;

In the Parler
One foldinge table borde 30*s*;
One side table 16*d*;
One Cubberde 16*s* 8*d*;
One Cheayre 2*s*;
One dosen of Joyned stooles 16*s*;
Fowre litell stooles 2*s*;
Fyve litell foote stooles 6*d*;
One pare of tables 3*s* 4*d*;
One pare of andirons 6*s* 8*d*;
One pare of doggs to bare woode 6*d*;
One apple roster 6*d*;

Three paynted disshes 12*d*;
A courten cloth with the Iron 6*d*;
Fyghtene brassen Crookes to hang hats one 18*d*;
Sum £8 14*s*.

[m. 2] In the Spence
One Table borde 2*s* 6*d* one litell foldinge table borde 3*s* one
    longe cubberd 8*s* two formes 12*d* two stooles 20*d* – 16*s* 2*d*;
One Cheayre 16*d* fowre quysshens 2*s* A case with six knyves
    and two table knives 3*s* two snuffers 6*d* – 6*s* 10*d*;
One glassen bottell and one letheren bottell 6*d*;
A wyker flaskett 3*d* A playinge borde and a bowlinge alier
    6*d* – 9*d*;
A litell toster 2*d* two paynted borders 6*d* One Iron hoope to
    sett a basen upon 4*d* – 12*d*;
Sum 25*s* 3*d*.

In the Kechen
Two garnyshe of disshes
One dosen of fruyte disshes
One dosen of square podengers
One dosen of square sawsers
One dosen of pawridge disshes
Halfe a dosen of round podengers
Fowre dosen of platters
One dosen of podengers
Halfe a dosen of sawsers
One dosen of litell sawsers
Halfe a dosen of squarre pawridge dysshes
Three plates for pies
Tenne trancher plates
Fowre chargers
Two litell cruets for oyle
Fowre basens and one bole
One pery basen one custerd plate
One dosen of eare disshes
All which pewter contains in weight 442 lb after fyve skore to
    the hundred at 5*d* the pounde it amounteth unto £9 4*s* 2*d*;
One Cheyse wringe & a seltinge vate 2*s*;

Fig. 18. Nos 36–37 High Street: two of the last surviving merchant
houses of St Stephen's parish in the mid 20th-century, shortly before
their demolition (*courtesy of English Heritage*).

One fier panne 8*d* one pare of tongs 8*d* one pare of bellies 6*d*
    – 22*d*;
One carpett 13*s* 4*d* six quysshens 6*s* – 19*s* 4*d*;
One doble skable 20*d*;
Item all the sealinge ther £3 6*s* 8*d*;
Tenne glasses for drinke 2*s*;

Two tubbes one borde one ladell one torne One range one candelsticke of tynne 3s;

Seven Pannes of brasse both great & small 30s;

One Chaffendishe with a foote 5s;

Fowre Cawdrens 20s;

One longe cawdren at 20 lb in weighte 12s;

Two cawdrens of Iron 3s 4d;

Nyne Crockes both great and small one longe Crocke with his cover one brode skillett containing in weight 206 lb at 4d the pounde amounteth at £3 8s 8d;

Three skilletts 18d;

One Chaffer for water 8s;

Three dripinge pannes 5s;

Two viniger bottells 12d;

Seven spitts 10s;

Two chaffendisshes of Iron 12d;

One great drypinge panne 6s 8d;

One warmynge panne 3s 4d;

A great Cheste 20d;

Three gridirons 6s 8d;

Fyve brandises 5s;

Fyve crookes 3s 4d;

Three pare of cotterells 18d;

Three doggs to bare woode 2s 6d;

[m. 3] One litell andiron 12d;

Two Irons to Save the dripinge pannes 2s;

One fier peecke one fier panne one pare of toungs 3s 4d;

One pare of rackes 13s 4d;

One fryinge panne 8d;

One morter and pestell 4s;

One Iron barre in the Chimney 5s;

Two baken pannes and three salte tubbes 10s;

One dresser one pare of bellies 3s 4d;

One fallen borde 6s 8d one Iron Candelsticke 6d one round borde 3s 4d – 10s 6d;

Fyve choppen knyves two whetstones 20d;

Two fleshookes two musterd potts 8d;

Two stooles one stony morter a chest with baken two dripers two treyinge pestels and morter two lantrons 12d;

One buntinge hutche 8 meale barrels a mowsnappe fowre tubbes two ranges beinge olde one Iron pyle 8s;

Two Salte barrells with salte 3s 4d;

All the reste of the shelves and bords In the kechen 12d;

Sum £22 14s 2d.

In the larder by the Kechen

Fowre powderinge tubbes 5s;

Eyghte gallons of butter 20s;

One barrell to kepe verges in 12d;

One cubberd 12d;

Item shelves and bords and other trashe 2s 6d;

A Koope for pultrey 5s;

34s 6d.

In the backe Chamber over the larder

One olde woole bedde 3s 4d;

Item woole 5s;

One litell bell 6s 8d;

A coffer with candels 8s;

Two Chests to put fishe in 2s;

Item fethers 2s 6d;

Two cheyse rackes 2s;

A tubbe of girts 6d;

Sixe cheses a pare of woole cards 3s;

Thirteyne coples of milwill and linge 13s 4d;

Two litell sope barrells with sope 10s;

Glass broken and hole 10s;

A bout a quartren of hopes 6s 8d;

A litell panne 8d;

A whitte plate candelsticke 2d;

Item certeyne clowtinge lether 12d and three dosens of cresses for howses 4s 6d – 5s 6d;

Item bawtes showes and spures 6s 8d;

Two Iron plates 3s 4d;

Item olde timber with divers other old [m. 4] trashe in the same chamber 20s;

Sum £5 9s 4d.

In the litell Courte
A plompe of ledde 26s 8d;
A sestrone of ledde 20s;
A laver of tynne 8d;
A still of ledde 6s 8d;
Two piller stones of marble with a musterd myll of stoune 2s
    6d;
Eyghte longe pickes 16s;
£3 12s 6d.

In the Butterye
Three basons and yeores 7s 6d;
Two latten basens 2s 6d;
Fyghteyne candelstickes 20s;
Three litell olde candelstickes 16d;
Nyne flower potts 18d;
Two olde yeores of tynne 12d;
Three chamber potts 18d;
Two pottell potts 3s;
Two quarte potts 2s;
One pynte potte 10d;
Eyght Juggs litell and great of stoune 3s;
Three dosens of fruyte tranchers of timber 3s;
Six dosens of tranchers 12d;
Two letheren bottels 12d;
One candell case one litell stoole 3d;
The paynted borders and one shelve 3s 4d;
A chest to put crumes [?] in 4d;
Two barrers for drinke 12d;
Sum 54s 1d.

In the broode Chamber
One standinge bedsteede 53s 4d;
One truckell bedsteede 3s 4d;
One foldinge table borde 20s;
Two litell cubberds 2s 6d;
One presse 26s 8d;
One coverlet 13s 4d;
Three longe quysshens of vellet 30s;

Sixe square quysshes of vellet 30s;
Item a pare of silke curtens 20s;
Five great quysshes of tysshen 30s;
Sixe greene quysshens 6s;
One longe carpett and shorter Carpett £3;
Two olde coverletts 2s 6d;
One other carpett of Levant lyned 10s;
[m. 5] One cubberd cloth 16d;
One olde carpett one olde bolster 4s 4d;
One greate Coverlett £3 6s 8d;
Item a matteris and five courtens 23s 4d;
Item the sealinge and stories 46s 8d;
A blacke lether cheste 10s;
One other chest 4s;
One cheayre 4d;
Two doggs in the chimney 12d;
One other litell quysshen 8d;
Two formes 12d;
One pare of bellowes 6d;
One pare of fustian blanketts 6s 8d two coverletts 6s 8d – 13s
    4d;
Sum £24 10d.

In the litell Chamber in the gallery
One standinge bedsteede 26s 8d;
One cubberd with a cubberd cloth 2s;
One cheayre one quysshen 2s 6d;
The hangins and two courtens and the windowe clothers of
    redde saye and greene 6s 8d;
A matteris 3s;
One coverlet 5s;
A whitte Coverlet and a pare of blanketts 10s;
Sum 55s 10d.
In the gallerye
Two great chests 13s 4d;
Fyve Coffers 20s;
Fyve olde quysshens 3s;
Sum 36s 4d.

In the fore Chamber
One standinge bedsteede 26s 8d;
One truckell bedsteede 3s 4d;
One Presse 26s 8d;
One foldinge table borde 24s;
One forme 18d;
One great chest 26s 8d;
Fowre Coffers 26s 8d;
A litell foslett 12d;
Two doggs to bare woode 12d;
A fier panne 6d;
The hangins and courtens of the Chamber and windowe 26s
    8d;
A lute 6s 8d;
A coverlet 13s 4d;
A rugg 8s;
A pare of blanketts 6s 8d;
A coverlet for the truckell bed 2s 6d;
[m. 6] A rugg for the same 2s 6d;
A pare of blanketts for the same 3s 4d;
A matteris 5s;
Sum £10 12s 8d.

The napery
Item Sixe diaper clothers £4;
One litell frandged cloth of diaper 6s 8d;
A square cloth 5s;
Two cover panes 10s;
Fower diaper towels 26s 8d;
Sixe diaper towels 30s;
Two diaper towels 6s 8d;
Two olde diaper towels 2s;
One dosen and halfe of diaper napkens 18s;
Two dosen of litell napkens 10s;
Tenne frandged napkens 6s 8d;
One dosen and a leven of fyne napkens 23s;
Fyve dosen of napkens at 8s the dosen 40s;
One dosen & halfe of olde napkens 6s;
Thirtenne pare of olde woren shitts 44s;

One pare of Holland sheetts 20s;
Two other pare of lardge sheetts 24s;
Fowre pare of sheetts 26s 8d;
Fowrteynne pylloberes 35s;
Tenne olde pilloties 5s;
Eyghte Shyrts 26s 8d;
Fowre frendged cobberd clothers 6s;
Nyne table clothers 24s;
Six square clothers and cubberd clothes 9s;
Three longe towels 5s;
Six chamber towels 3s;
Fowr breakefast towels 2s 8d;
One dosen of canvas napkens frendged 7s;
A leven napkens 3s 4d;
Three dosen two napkens 9s 8d;
A leven Canvas table clothes 20s;
Fowre canvas towels 2s 8d;
Sixteyne course Napkens 4s;
A leven course hand towels 2s;
Twelve pare of olde sheets 33s 4d;
Sum £29 3s 8d.

In the Countinge house
One Iron Cheste 40s;
One other chest 3s 4d;
A countinge borde with shelves 4s;
Two Iron fawceletts 5s;
A quysshen 12d;
Item other tryfles as glasses and others 5s;
[m. 7] Sum 58s 4d.

In the maidens Chamber
Two bedsteedes 5s;
Two olde coverletts 3s 4d;
Two pare of blanketts 10s;
The hangins of the same chamber and one olde Cheste 2s;
Sum 20s 4d.

In the higher Chamber
One standinge bedsteede 40s;
One litell foldinge table borde 5s;
One coffer 3s 4d;
One Cheayre 12d;
One coverlett 6s 8d;
One redd rugg 6s 8d;
A pare of blanketts 5s;
The hangins 5s;
The portall 4s 4d;
Sum £3 17s.

In the Countinge house adioyninge to the same Chamber
A borde and the shelves 12d;
12d.

In the litell Chamber therby
One standinge bedsteede 13s 4d;
A matterice 4s;
A Coverlett 2s;
A rugg 2s;
A pare of blanketts 3s 4d;
The hangins 5s;
Two formes 4d;
Sum 30s.

In the men servants Chamber
Two bedsteedes 4s;
Two testers 5s;
One cubberde 6d;
One matterice 6d;
One coffer 6d;
A forme a coverlett a rugg and blanketts 3s 4d;
One olde coverlett mantell and blanketts 5s;
The hangins and Courten 2s;
Sum 20s 10d.

[m. 8] In the brisshinge Chamber

One borde one cheayre one litell truncke 3s 4d;
3s 4d.

The apparell
Item a newe blacke gowne faced with fawens and lyned with Calaber £8;
Item a skarlett gowne faced with fawens and lyned with Calaber £8;
Item a cloke of skarlett £3;
Two velvet tippetts 50s;
Item a newe blacke gowne faced with boudge and lyned with lambe £5;
Item an other blacke gowne faced with boudge 50s;
Item an olde blacke gowne 13s 4d;
Item one olde frise gowne 3s 4d;
Item a cloake of Kersie faced with tafita 40s;
Item a cassocke of damaske skallope frendged 40s;
Item a Jacket of velvet 30s;
Item a cassocke of blacke satten 13s 4d;
Item a cassocke of blacke Kersie both furred and frendged 30s;
Item a blacke coote to ride in 13s 4d;
Item a ridinge cloake with clapses of silver 15s;
Item a doblett of satten newe 33s 4d;
Item an olde satten doblett 10s;
Two other olde dobletts of silke 16s;
A petticoate of wite beyes 3s 4d;
Two other whitte petticoates 3s 4d;
A pare of buskens and a hoode 5s;
A buffe Jerken 8s;
Two other lether Jerkens 5s;
Two pare of blacke slyders 6s 8d;
A counter cloake 5s;
Two whitte pare of slyders 2s;
Two pare of rounde hose 6s 8d;
Three pare of stockens 5s;
Two pare of knytte hose 2s;
A frise Jerken 3s 4d;
Fyve cappes 8s;

Two velvet nightcappes 6s;
A dagger and a kniffe two waste girdels one of them velvett 6s;
Item a knytte calve of silke & a hatt 3s 4d;
Three brusshes and a lookinge glasse 2s;
A showinge horne of Iron 6d;
Item a cappe boxe with other litell boxes & trifles 2s;
Sum £46 10d.

[m. 9] The beddinge with bolsters
Item one bedd containing 112 lb and his bolster containing 35 lb – 147 lb;
Item one other bedd containing 84 lb and his bolster containing 14 – 98 lb;
Item one other bedd and his bolster containing 82 lb;
Item one other bedd containing 72 lb and his bolster containing 13 lb – 85 lb;
Item one other bedd containing 76 lb and his bolster containing 17 lb – 93 lb;
Item one other bedd containing 51 lb and his bolster containing 17 lb – 68 lb;
Item one other bedd containing 57 lb and his bolster containing 14 – 71 lb;
Item one other bedd containing 76 lb and his bolster containing 17 lb – 93 lb;
Item one other bedd containing 58 lb and his bolster containing 14 lb – 72 lb;
Item one other bedd containing 80 lb and his bolster containing 17 lb – 97 lb;
Item one other bedd containing 66 lb and his bolster containing 8 lb – 74 lb;
Item three other bolsters containing 43 lb;
The sum of the 11 beds & 14 bolsters in weighte 1023 pounds at fyve pence the pound it amounteth unto £21 6s 3d;
Item fowrtenth pillowes containing 64 lb at 8d the pounde 42s 8d;
Sum £23 8s 11d.

The noate of the armerye
Imprimis one Corselett 26s 8d;

Fyve pare of Almayn revetts 50s;
Two Jackes lyned with fustian wherof one plated 3s 4d;
One mourren headpece graven 5s;
One rounde skull 18d;
Two nyghtcappes of mele 2s 6d;
One Gantlett 2s;
Fyve mourrian headpeces 12s 6d;
Two base musketts 20s;
One Caliver 5s;
Two daggs 10s;
Two flaxes with twiche boxes 3s 4d;
One head pece for a horse man 5s;
Three shirre hooks 4s;
Two halberts one pollax 5s;
Two Gealings 3s;
Two sheves of arrowes 2s;
Two mouster bowes 3s 4d;
One targett and one buckler 5s;
One handbowe with fynne arrowes 10s;
Six armynge sords 9s;
Sixe daggers 6s;
One longe sowrde 5s;
One hanger 3s;
Two moulds for shote 4d;
[m. 10] A crosbowe with bender 10s;
A barrell of powder 4s;
Sum £10 16s 6d.

In the Countinge house by the hall with the bookes
Item two bibles one of Geneva makinge
Calvins booke
Turners Herball
Two bookes of service
One booke of the fall of princes
A bridgment of the statute
Halls Cronycells with divers other bookes of Latten frenche and englishe 53s 4d;
A table and sealings 20s;
A pyle of weights 6s 8d;

A pare of gold ballaunce 12*d*;
A pare of ballaunce and weights 20*d*;
A great weight of brasse 2*s*;
Item certeyne tables with olde Ier worke as knyves sawes keyes & other olde trashe 26*s* 8*d*;
Sum £5 11*s* 4*d*.

In the brewhouse
Three hogshilds 3*s*;
Three brewinge kyves 3*s*;
Fyve trendels 2*s* 6*d*;
Twelve barrells 8*s*;
One trendell 3*s* 4*d*;
One clensinge sive 4*d*;
One olde coverlett and carpett 2*d*;
Three litell kyves 18*d*;
One litell wasshinge tubbe 6*d*;
One furnyce 26*s* 8*d*;
Sum 49*s*.

In the warrehouse
One busshell and one pecke 12*d*;
Sixe vessells 4*s*;
Sixe halfe hundred weights 30*s*;
Two halfe quarters 2*s* 6*d*;
One fowre pound weight one two pound weight one pound weight and halfe pound 15*d*;

A beame and skalles 3*s* 4*d*;
Sum 42*s* 1*d*.

In the Shoppe
Two Chests 33*s* 4*d*;
Fowre dosen of Hoopes 3*s* 4*d*;
Sixe sealinge bords 2*s* 6*d*;
Two olde coffers 4*s*;
A bedsteed 2*s*;
The shelves and borders 3*s* 4*d*;
Fowre busshels of Hellinge pinnes 4*s*;

[m. 11] A portall sealings tyle and other olde timber sundry bords of walnot treye 20*s*;
Sum £3 12*s* 6*d*.

In the Corne Garnarde
Item Sondry timber of stoods and Resters 5*s*;
5*s*.

In the greate courte
One dosen of Hardwood 7*s*;
Item tooles of Ier as wedges and others 10*s*;
Item Coles to burne 20*d*;
Item divers keyes and other necessaries ther 2*s*;
Sum 20*s* 8*d*.

A noate of plate
Item a neste of gobletts doble gylte with his cover wayinge 86 ouncs quarter at 5*s* 2*d* the ounce – £22 5*s* 7½*d*;
Item a standinge cuppe doble gylte wayinge 33 ouncs at 5*s* 2*d* the ounce £8 10*s* 6*d*;
Item a salte with a cover doble gylte wayinge 33 ouncs at 5*s* 2*d* the ounce – £8 10*s* 6*d*;
Item a salte wayinge 34 ouncs quarter at 5*s* 4*d* the ounce – £9 2*s* 8*d*;
Item two litell whitte bolles wayinge 14 ouncs halfe at 4*s* 8*d* the ounce – £3 7*s* 8*d*;
Item a salte parcell gylte wayinge 13 ouncs 3 quarters at 4*s* 10*d* the ounce – £3 6*s* 4*d*;
Item a litell salte doble gylte wayinge 2 ouncs halfe at 5*s* 4*d* the ounce 13*s* 4*d*;
Item a goblet parcell gylte wayinge 16 ouncs at 4*s* 8*d* the ounce £3 14*s* 8*d*;
Item a ale cupp doble gylte wayinge 15 ouncs quarter and halfe quarter at 5*s* 4*d* the ounce – £4 2*s*;
Item a ale cupp dobell gylte wayinge 12 ouncs and halfe – £3 6*s* 8*d*;
Item a ale cupp with his cover doble gylte wayinge 11½ ouncs at 5*s* 4*d* – £3 1*s* 4*d*;

Item a ale cupp with his cover doble gylte wayinge 9 ouncs at
    5s 4d the ounce – 48s;

Item a castinge glasse wayinge 5 ouncs at 5s the ounce – 25s;

Item a toonn [?] with his cover p[arcel] gylte wayinge 45
    ouncs quarter at 5s 2d the ounce £11 13s;

Item a forke wayinge 1 ounce halfe quarter 6s;

Item two dosens of spones waienge 32 ouncs at 4s 6d – £7 4s;

Item two great Juggs waienge 15 ouncs at 5s the ounce – £3
    15s;

Item three litell cuppes of stone covered wayinge 9 ounces –
    36s 8d;

Item a braunche of silver 2s 6d;

[m. 12] Sum £98 11s 5d.

The corne in the Garnarde

Item of barlie malte 50 busshels by stricke which maketh
    corrante 33 busshels at 4s bushel – £6 12s;

Item of rye 30 busshels £4 10s;

Item of beanes 12 busshels 32s;

Item of pesons 8 busshels 21s 4d;

Sum £13 15s 4d.

In the Courte by the stable

Item a grindinge stone with trowe 3s;

Item the welbokett and cheyne 2s;

Item a hogg 10s;

Item divers olde timber with oves bords 30s;

Item divers stounes and other things in the same courte 3s 4d;

Sum 48s 4d.

In the stable and haye lofte

Item sondry timber in the same £3;

Item a nagg dappell graye 40s;

Item a white nagg 13s 4d;

Item a grey mare [illegible] 26s 8d;

Fowre saddels with ther furniture 15s;

Item certeyne olde timber without Westgate 10s;

Item the hay the laftes and timber ther £3;

Sum £11 5s.

In the barne and straw house

Item in beanes 20 busshells at 2s 4d bushel – 46s 8d;

Item in wheat 15 busshells at 3s 4d the bushel – 50s;

Item in barlie 30 busshels at 2s 6d bushel – £3 15s;

Item three busshels more of beanes 7s;

Two pykes a mattocke a showell a sherhooke a hatchet a axe a
    hooke six seves one pare of crowkes three rakes two vates
    5s;

Item a pare of harrowes 5s;

Item certeyne Rude 4s;

Item a Whelebarrowe a pare of doungpotts with other trashe
    18d;

Sum £9 14s 2d.

At St Johns

Item a myll to grinde Corne 10s;

Item a spowte 3s 4d other trashe under St Stephens Churche
    26s 8d – 30s;

Sum 40s.

[m. 13] Item fowre akers of woode standinge in Pynne Woode
    which coste ther £12;

£12.

In Butterforde

Item a bedsteede a truckell bedsteede two fether bedds two
    bolsters two coverletts two pare of blanketts and an olde
    pare of sheetes prec £4;

£4.

Item two tenements in St Marie Steppes for terme of certeyne
    yeres not yet ended valued in £3 6s 8d;

£3 6s 8d.

Item a tenement In Exilande late in the tenure of Richard
    Wyer [?] a terme not yet ended to the valewe of 40s;

£2.

Item all the glasse in the house wherin the saied Mr Thomas
    Prestwood dwelt £6 13s 4d;

£6 13s 4d.

Item the Lesse of the house wherin the said Mr Thomas Prestwood dwelt which is for certeyne yeres yet to comm valued in £60;

£60.

Item a lesse of seven peesses of ground with a barne contenynge by estimacion thirtye two akers for terme of certeyne yeres not yet ended is valued in £160;

£160.

For somuche as Mr Prestwood had in redy monye £25 8s;
£25 8s.

Certeyne debts which were dewe unto Mr Prestwoode
Ought to have of Mrs Champernowne £27;
Ought to have of Peter Villeys £3 16s 8d;
Ought to have of Mr Fowell 2s 6d;
Ought to have of Mr Walter Bogins 22d;
Ought to have of Mr Geffrye Thomas 4s 2d;
Ought to have of Hauckes 40s;
Ought to have of John Geale for nyne sheepe at 7s 6d – £3 7s 6d;
Rents received for Chrismas quarter £32 6s 11d;
£68 19s 7d;
John Lauarons awith 40s;
Sum £70 19s 7d.

Desperat debts which were owed unto Mr Prestwood
Ought to have of Willm Cholwell and John Wilcocks carriers 21s 9d;
Ought to have of Nicholas Pagett of Yarnsye 20s;
Ought to have of Willm Gibbes £3 6s 8d;
Ought to have of Richard Halse 10s;
[m. 14] Ought to have of John Bruton 6s;
Ought to have of Holland upon Hollawaye 6s 8d;
Ought to have of James Ketwaye 4s 11d;
Ought to have of Margerett Gilbert £1 16s 8d;
Ought to have of Mr Edward Yarde £2 3s 7d;

Ought to have of Thomas Burrell 2s 11d;
Ought to have of John Williams of Ugborough 10s 5d;
Ought to have of the Cittie of Exetter 3s 3d;
Ought to have for a rereges of rents 7s;
Ought to have of Nycholas Grenowe 6s 1d;
Ought to have of John Lauerence £2 [entry crossed through];
Ought to have of Roger Bidlacke 6s;
Ought to have of John Bawier 10s;
Ought to have of John Geale for three wethers 22s 6d;
Sum £14 4s 5d.

Mr Walter Hele oweth £180 for a lesse of two bargaines sold by the executors towards the payment of Mr Prestwoods debts – £180;
M[emorandum] to receive of Mr Hele £180 [entry crossed through];
Som total ys £904 15s 11d.

Such debts as were dewe by Mr Prestwoods tyme which hath benne paid since his death
Item paid unto Willm Warde tayler for makinge of certene apparell for Mr Prestwoode 26s 6d;
Unto Edmond Cooke the furrier 7s 4d;
Unto Geffry Thomas 13s 8d;
Unto John Thornynge for rent dewe to Mr Wadham for chrismas quarter 15s;
Unto Nicholas Robenson for his quarters wages dewe at chrismas 20s;
Unto Christopher Prater for his wages for chrismas quarter 9s 2d;
Unto Annisse Wilkens for 3 weckes worke 18d;
Unto Richard Harries for his wages dewe at chrismas 10s;
Unto Peter Govier for his worke for one weeke & halfe 21d;
Unto the parson of St Stephens for the domynicalls dewe at chrismas 13d;
Unto Richard Pitts and unto Markes to ride for phisisians 5s 6d;
Unto the bayliffe of Exiland for chrismas quarter 3s;

Unto Baskefill for potecary stuffe 9s;

Unto Anstice Goffe for fyve quarters wages dewe at chrismas 27s 6d;

[m. 15] Unto Grace Downinge my servant for her quarters wages dewe at chrismas 6s 8d;

To the clarke of St Stephens for his quarteledge 16d;

Unto Osborne for settinge of certene hares bonnes 3s;

Unto Miles Lambert for potecary stuffe 11s;

Unto Mr George Trobridge £3 for somuche was received of Mr Wolton – £3;

Unto the stewerd of Exiland 4d;

For Justment of the ground of St Davies 3s;

Unto the widowe Priggs 18d;

Unto Mr Cholwell for his fee dewe at michelmas for keppinge of his courts 5s;

Unto Hugh Wilston for debt dewe to him for divers parcells as did appeare by his booke £10 10s 2d;

Unto Twiggs for fuyghty dole [?] 12d;

Unto Willm Hunt for a peeche barrell 12d;

Unto Fursdon for timber for tuckinge milles 9s;

Unto Mr Olippland [?] for woode bought of him 21d;

Paid Ponsford for fuyghtie dole [?] 3s 4d;

Paid Bowden for makinge of a petticoate 12d;

Dewe to Mr Willm Stroode £18;

Dewe to Mr John Bodleigh £15 18s 6d;

Dewe to Mr George Gale £26 9s 5d;

Dewe to Mr Richard Bodleigh £33 6s 8d;

Dewe to Mr Nicholas Godtheridge £100;

Dewe to Mrs Alice Meere £8 16s 5d;

Dewe to Mr Pill £8 17s 6d;

Dewe to Peter Lapken £3 13s 2d;

Dewe to Mr Webb 4s 9d;

Dewe unto Richard Hardinge 50s for so much dewe to him by doctor Warrissas Pramperayns [? preparations] which Mr Prestwood promysed payment by his bill 50s;

Unto Mr Bodleigh for the garden for chrismas quarter 5s;

Unto my Lord of Bedford for the same garden dewe at chrismas 20d;

Unto Mr Borington for rente dewe at chrismas for Mr Prestwoods house 16s 8d;

Unto the Recever of this cittie for rent dewe unto him at chrismas out of Marks house 3s 4d;

To Richard Pitts for the collection of Mr Prestwoods rents in Exettr and the subberbes for chrismas quarter 3s 4d;

Sum £242 16s 6d.

Such charges as was bestowed at Mr Prestwoods funeralls

Unto German tayler for makinge of the childrens coates 3s;

[m. 16] Unto the ringers for ringinge of the knilles 10s 9d;

Unto Garrett Joyner for the chest 6s;

Unto the vicars to singe at the buriall 6s 4d;

Paid for a tumbe stone 13s 4d;

Paid for gravinge of the same tumbestone 9s;

Paid the masen for wallinge & stones and lime for the same tumbe 31s 6d;

Unto the praysers for praysinge of the goods and ther meat & drinke & for ther paines & unto Mr Gale Mr Trobridge Mr Oliver with the men attendinge upon the same for sondry daies 40s;

Unto Roger Bidlacke to goe to Mr German to fache the Inventorye 2s;

Paid by Mr Bodleigh for provinge of Mr Prestwoods will 40s;

Paid unto Mr Oliver the which he paid for to have a more longer tyme for bringinge in of the Inventory at London 2s;

Paid for one to ride to Honyton with letters 7d;

Paid for newe coppyinge of the hole will 2s 8d;

Paid for 10 yards of blacke cloth for the childrens gownes & coates £4;

Sum £12 7s 2d.

Such Legasies as are geven by Mr Prestwoods will the which are allredy paied

Unto Mr Oliver to be geven unto the poore £4;

Unto Mr Oliver to be geven to the prisoners 40s;

Unto Mr Philpotte for preachinge 10s;

Paid for the blackes for the gownes coats & a cloake £29;

Unto Richard Pitts 40*s*;

Unto the wardens of St Stephens 6*s* 8*d*;

For the toom of silver parcell gilt beinge geven unto Mr Gale £11 13*s* 10*d*;

For a cloake of skarlett beinge geven unto Mr Gale £3;

Unto the two mayden servants 10*s*;

Unto Anstice my servant at her marriage 20*s*;

Unto my three men servants 15*s*;

To the company of the merchaunts 40*s*;

To Sixe executors 40*s* a pece £12;

Sum £68 15*s* 6*d*.

ECA, Orphans' Court Inventory 24 [Item 2]

More Chargs dewe at the funeralls of the said Mr Prestwood 1576

Unto the widowe Priggs for a certaine rent dewe unto her for Chrismas quarter 18*d*;

Unto Hugh Wilson for certaine Warres bought of him by Mr Prestwoods tyme £10 10*s* 2*d*;

Unto Willm Hunt for a peeche barrell & for certaine peeche & rawsoune 12*d*;

Unto Fursdon of Ugborough for certaine timber which he bought for Mr Prestwood for the tuckinge milles at Ivy Bridge 9*s*;

Unto Mr Cholwell stewerd for his fee in kepinge of courtes dewe at michelmas 5*s*;

Unto Mr Clifflande for wood bought of him by Mr Prestwoods tyme 21*d*;

Unto Roger Bidlacke to geve unto Mr German to fache the Inventorie to be Ingrossed 2*s*;

Unto Bawden tayler for makinge of a petticoate of whitte beyes for Mr Prestwood 12*d*;

Paid in Mr Bodleigh accounts [?] for provinge of the will 40*s*.

ECA, Orphans' Court Inventory 24 [Item 3]

Thomas Prestwood

Funeralls

To Garret for the coffyn 6*s*;

To the syngyng men 6*s* 4*d*;

For a tombe stone 13*s* 4*d*

For stone & lyme 1*s* 2*d*

For the setting up 24*s* 4*d*

For graving the stone 9*s*

[For the last four entries] 53*s* 10*d*;

For ryngnyng the knell 10*s* 9*d*;

To syx chyldren for their blacks & 10 [?] yards £4;

For making of their garments 3*s*;

For a copye of the inventorye 2*s*;

For probat of the testament 40*s*

[For the last two entries] 42*s*;

For chardges of the praysers 40*s*;

To Mr Olyver for delayeng the inventorye 2*s*;

To one that caried [illegible] to Hurtes [?] 7*d*;

For new copiinge the will 2*s* 8*d*;

£12 7*s* 2*d*.

Debts

To Mr Webb 4*s* 9*d*;

To Richerd Harding 50*s*;

To Mr Bodley 5*s*;

To the [illegible] of Bidford 20*d*;

To the receaver of the citie 3*s* 4*d*;

To Burryngton 16*s* 8*d*;

To the wydowe Muggs [?] 18*d*;

To Rycherd Pytts 3*s* 4*d*;

Sum £216 9*s* 2*d*.

£242 17*s* 12*d*.

[Verso] Debtes dewe by the testator

To Willm Ward 26*s* 8*d*;

To the furryer 7s 4d;
To Mr Goffrey Thomas 13s 4d;
To John Thornyng 15s;
To Nychas Robynson 20s;
To Chrestiphor Prater 9s 2d;
To Agnes Wylkyns 18d;
To Richerd Harrys 10s;
To Peter Gover 21d;
To the parson of St Stephens 13d;
To Richerd Pytts 18d;
To Thoms Roberts 3s;
To Baskervyle 9s;
To Anastys Goff 27s 6d;
To Grace Downyng 6s 8d;
To the parishe clerke 16d;
To Richerd Osborne 3s;
To Myles Lambert 11s;
To Markes 4s;
To George Trobrydge £3;
To the steward of Exilond 4d;
To the proctor of St David 3s;
To wydowe Pryggs 18d;
To Hew Wylsonby [?] £10 10s 2d;
To Willm Hunt £12;
To Fursedon of Ugborough 9s;
To Mr Cholwell 5s;
To Mr Clyveland 21d;
To Bowdon 12d;
£23 5s 7d.

To Mr John Bodley £15 18s 6d;
To Mr Rycherd Bodleighe £33 6s 8d;
To Mrs Aliis Prestwode £8 16s 5d;
To Nychus Goodryg £100;
To Mr Gale £26 9s 5d;
To the queene for the 10th 3s 4d;
[Entry crossed through;]
To Mr Strowde £18;
To Jo Pyll £8 18s 6d;

To Peter Lapkyn £3 13s 2d.

ECA, Orphans' Court Inventory 24 [Item 4]

To Mr Webbe 4s 9d;
To Richerd Harding 50s;
To Mr Jo Bodlyghe for a quarters rent 5s;
To the Erle of Bedfford 20d;
To the receaver of the Citie 3s 4d;
To Burryngton for rent 16s 8d;
To Richerd Pytt 6s 4d;
Sum [blank].

Legacyes
To the preacher 10s;
To Richerd Pytt 40s;
To the parishe church 6s 8d;
To Mr Gale a trime of cupps [blank];
To Mrs Gale a clok £3;
To the poore £4;
To the prysoners 40s;
To Anastys Goghe 20s;
To the company of the merchaunts 40s;
To the 6 executors every of thym 40s – £12;
To his men servaunts 15s;
To the executors for there blackes £21 8s;
To Joys Bowdon a cassok 38s;
To Anastys Goff a cassok 28s;
To Grace Downyng a cassok 28s;
To John Dynham a coat 12s;
To John Harrys a coat 12s;
To Rycherd Harrys a cote 12s;
To Chrystopher Pratt 12s;
To Rycherd Pytts [a clok – crossed through] 20s;
[No sum.]

[Verso] Debtes dew & which the Testater dyd owe
To Willm Warde 26s 8d;
To the furrier 7s 4d;

To Geffrey Thomas 13s 4d;

To John Thornyng 15s;

To Nychus Robynson 20s;

To Chrystopher Prater 9s 2d;

To Agnes Wylkyns 18d;

To Richerd Harrys 10s;

To Peter Gover 21d;

To the parson of St Stephens 13d;

To Richerd Pytts 18d;

To Thomas Roberts 3s;

To Tho Baskervyle 9s;

To Anastis Goffe 27s 6d;

To Grace Downynge 6s 8d;

To the parishe clerk 16d;

To Richerd Osborne 3s;

To Myles Lambert 11s;

To Marks 4s;

To George Trobridge £3;

To the steward of Exilond 4d;

To the proctor of St David 3s;

To the wydowe Prygges 18d;

To Hew Wylsedon £10 10s 2d;

To Willm Hunt 12d;

To Fursedon of Ugborough 9s;

To Mr Cholwell 5s;

To Mr Clyveland 21d;

To Richerd Bowdon 12d;

£23 5s 7d.

To Mr Bodley £15 18s 6d;

To Mr Richerd Bodley £33 6s 8d;

To Mrs Aliis Prestwode £8 16s 5d;

To Nychus Godreg £100;

To Mr Gale £26 9s 5d;

To the Quene 3s 4d;

To Mr Strowde £18;

To John Pyll £8 18s 6d;

To Peter Lapkyn £3 13s 2d.

ECA, Orphans' Court Inventory 24 [Item 5]

[1] The Inventory of all the Goodds & Chatells of Thomas Prestwode late of the Citie of Excester who decessed the 30 of December 1576 and praysed by Mychaell Germyn Geffrey Thomas John Levermore & John Dorr

The pewter & other Kechen stuff [£18 6s 4d – crossed through] £22 13s 2d;

The larder 34s 6d;

The Chamber over the larder £5 9s 4d;

The lytle Courte £3 12s 6d;

The kychen £4 3s 6d [entry crossed through];

The spense 25s 3d;

The parlor £8 14s;

The Hall £7 18s 10d;

The buttrey 54s 1d;

The broade chamber £24 10d;

The lytle galerey chamber 55s 10d;

The forechaumber £10 12s 8d;

The Gallery 36s 4d;

The naperye £22 12s also £6 11s 8d – £29 3s 8d;

The compting howse 58s 4d;

The maydens chamber 20s 4d;

The higher chamber £3 18s;

The lytle chamber 30s;

The menns chamber 24s 2d;

The Apparell £46 10d;

The bedding £23 8s 11d;

The Armorye £10 16s 6d;

The compting howse £5 11s 4d;

The brewhowse 49s;

The warehowse 42s 1d;

The shopp £3 12s 6d;

The granerd 5s;

The greate Courte 20s 8d;

The plate £98 [12s 2½d – crossed through] 11s 5d;

The corne yn the granerd £13 15s 4d;

The Courte by the stable 48s 4d;

[2] The stable & hayloft & horses £11 5*s*;
The barne & strawe £9 14*s* 2*d*;
St John the garden & sellers & St Stephen 50*s*;
The wood at Pynnewod £12;
The beddyng at Butterfford £4;
The leases for yeres & the glasse wyndons of the howse £232;
In golde £9 3*s* 6*d*
In Whyt money £16;
In broken money 4*s* 6*d*
[Last three entries] £25 8*s*.

Debtes dew & recovered *viz* of Rycherd Pyts for opeter writs
    [?] £13 8*s* 9*d*;
Of John Goale for chap [?] £3 7*s* 6*d*;
Of Mrs Champernowne £27;
Of Nychus [illegible] 13*s* 4*d* [entry crossed through];
Of Mr Fowell 2*s* 6*d*;
Of Mr Booggyns 22*d*;
Of Mr Geffrey Thomas 4*s* 2*d*;
Of Richard Androwe for the rents of Butterford & Ugborow
    £10 10*s* 3*d*;
Of Peter Wyllys £3 16*s* 8*d*;
Of Hawkes 40*s*;
John Lawrens 40*s*;
[Illegible] £70 19*s* 7*d*;
Also receved by the executors for a fyne for certyn bargeyn
    sold to Walter Heale £180;
£557 12*s* 2*d*.

The rent £32 7*s*;
Desperat detts £14 4*s* 5*d*.

ECA, Orphans' Court Inventory 25

Thomas Prestwood

The Inventorie of all the goodds & chattels of Thomas
Prestwode late of the citie of Excester whoe decessed the
[blank].

[1] The Hall £7 18*s* 10*d*;
The parlor £8 14*s*;
The spense 25*s* 3*d*;
The Kychen & pewter £22 13*s* 2*d*;
The larder 34*s* 6*d*;
The Chamber over the larder £5 9*s* 4*d*;
The lytle Court £3 12*s* 6*d*;
The buttrey 54*s* 1*d*;
The broade Chaumber £24 10*d*;
The lytle gallery chamber 55*s* 10*d*;
The forechamber £10 12*s* 8*d*;
The gallerye 35*s* 4*d*;
The Napery £29 3*s* 8*d*;
The Comptyng howse 58*s* 4*d*;
The maydons chamber 20*s* 4*d*;
The higher chamber £3 18*s*;
The lytle chamber 30*s*;
The menns chamber 24*s* 2*d*;
The Apparell £46 10*d*;
The bedding £23 8*s* 11*d*;
The Armory £10 16*s* 6*d*;
The Comptyng howse £5 11*s* 4*d*;
The brewhowse 49*s*;
The warehowse 42*s* 1*d*;
The shop £3 12*s* 6*d*;
The granerd 5*s*;
The greate Courte 20*s* 8*d*;
The plate £98 11*s* 5*d*;
The corne yn the granerd £13 15*s* 4*d*;
The Courte by the stable 48*s* 4*d*;
The stable hayloft & horses £11 5*s*;
[2] The barne & strawe £9 14*s* 2*d*;
St Johns & the seller under St Stephens Churche 50*s*;
The wood at Pynnewood £12;
The beddyng at Butterfford £4;
The leasses & termes & the glasse wyndowes £232;
In golde £9 3*s* 6*d*
In whyt money £16;
In broken money 4*s* 6*d*

[Last three entries] £25 8s.

Debtes dewe for rents at Chrystmas £32 7s;
Mrs Champernowne oweth £27;
Peter Wyllys owethe £3 16s 8d;
John Geale owethe £3 7s 6d;
Mr Fowell owethe 2s 6d;
Walter Buggyns owethe 22d;
Geffry Thomas owethe 4s 2d;
[Blank] Hawkes owethe 40s;
John Lawrenc owethe 40s;
Also dew by Walter Heale for a fyne £180;
Debts dew by Willm Colwell & Jo Wylcocks 21s 9d;
Nychus Paget 20s;
Willm Gybbes £3 6s 8d;
Rycherd Hals oweth 10s;
John Bruton 6s;
John Holland 6s 8d;
James Ketway 4s 11d;
Margaret Gylbert 36s 8d;
Edward Yard 43s 7d;
Thomas Burell 2s 11d;
John Wyllms of Ugborough 10s 5d;
The Citie of Excester 3s 3d;
Arrerages of rents 7s;
Nychus Greneowe 6s 1d;
Roger Bydlak 6s;
John Bowyer 10s;
John Coyle 22s 6d;
Sum total of all the goods money plate & debtes [blank].

[3] Debtes which the testator dyd owe at the tyme of his dethe
To Willm Warde 26s 8d;
To the furrier 7s 4d;
To Mr Geffrey Thomas 13s 4d;
To John Thornyng 15s;
To Nychus Robynson 20s;
To Chrystopher Prater 9s 2d;
To Agnes Wylkyns 18d;

To Richerd Harvys 10s;
To Peter Gover 21d;
To the parson of St Stephens 13d;
To Richerd Pytts 18d;
To Thomas Roberts 3s;
To Thomas Baskervyle 9s;
To Anastys Goff 27s 6d;
To Grace Downyng 6s 8d;
To the parishe Clerke 16d;
To Rycherd Osborne 3s;
To Myles Lambert 11s;
To Markes 4s;
To George Trobrydge £3;
To the baylyff of Exylond 4d;
To the proctor of St David 3s;
To wydow Pryggs 18d;
To Hew Wylsoune £10 10s 2d;
To Willm Hunt 12d;
To Fursedon [?] of Ugborough 9s;
To Mr Chollwell 5s;
To Mr Cleveland 21d;
To Rycherd Bowdon 12d;
£23 5s 7d.

To Mr John Bodlye £15 18s 6d;
To Mr Richerd Bodley £33 6s 8d;
To Mrs Alis Prestwood £8 16s 6d;
To Mr Strowd £18;
To Nychus Goodrydge £100;
To Mr Gale £26 9s 5d;
To the Quene 3s 4d;
To John Pyll £8 18s 6d;
To Peter Lapkyn £3 13s 2d;
To Mr Webb 4s 9d;
To Richerd Harding 50s;
To Mr John Bodley for a quarters rent 5s;
To the Erle of Bedfford for rent 20d;
To the Recever of the Citie 3s 4d;
[4] To Burryngton for rent 16s 8d;

To Richerd Pytt 3s 4d;
Sum of the debts [blank].

Also the restethe yn debts desperat £14 4s 5d.

Fig. 19.   Thomas Prestwood's inventory of 1577 mentions payment
'To Garnet forhe coffyn 6s'. The Garrett or Garnett family built up a
thriving joinery business in the city in the period 1586–1619; they were
probably Dutch immigrants (Wells-Cole 1981, 8). This entry is the
earliest record of the family known so far. They have been associated
with an accomplished local style of furniture with a
distinctly continental appearance, such as the chest shown here
(*photo: courtesy of Marhamchurch Antiques*).

Funeralls
To Garnet for the coffyn 6s;
To the syngyng men 6s 4d;
For the tombe the stuffe workyng & setting 53s 10d;
For the Knolle 10s 9d;
To the 6 children for theire blacks £4;
For makyng the same 3s;
[Last six entries] £7 19s 11d;
The Copye of the Inventory 2s;
For probat of the testament 40s;

For copyenge of the same 2s 8d;
For delayeng to put yn the Inventory 2s;
For carieg of a letter 7d;
[Last five entries] 47s 4d;
Also for the chardges of the praysers 40s;
Sum £12 7s 2d.

Sum total of all the detts which the testator dyd owe of the
desperat detts & funeralls [blank];
So remains [blank].

Which sayde some of [blank] is to be devyded yn to three
equall partes *viz*
To the testator [blank];
To the wyff [blank];
To the 7 children [blank].

[5] Memorandum that of one third part being the testators
owne portion there ar to be deducted all the legacyes which ar
as folowethe
To the preacher 10s;
To Rycherd Pytts 40s;
To the parishe churche 6s 8d;
To Mr Gale £11 13s 10d;
To Mrs Gale £3;
To the poor £3;
To the prysoners 40s;
To Anastys Goff 20s;
To the company of the merrchants 40s;
To the 6 executors £12;
To his servants 15s;
£29 5s 6d.

To the executors for theire blacks £21 8s;
To Joyes Bowden a Cassoke 28s;
To Anastys Gogh a cassok 28s;
To Grace Downyng a cassok 28s;
To John Dyrham a cote 12s;
To John Harrys a cote 12s;

146

To Rycherd Harrys a cote 12*s*;
To Chrystopher Prat a cote 12*s*;
To Richerd Pytt a cloke 20*s*;
£29.

Sum total £48 5*s* 6*d*;
So remains [blank].

Which some of [blank] so remaynyng of the testaters 3rd parte is to be devyded yn to 8 equall [parts], *viz* to the wyff &

to 7 children that is to wete
To the wyff [blank];
To George Prestwode [blank];
To John Prestwode [blank];
To Thomas Prestwode [blank];
To Susan Prestwode [blank];
To Katherin Prestwode [blank];
To Mary Prestwode [blank];
To Elysabeth Prestwode [blank].

35A. WILL OF THOMAS BYRDE, TAILOR/DRAPER OF ST LAWRENCE'S PARISH, 17 JUNE 1577

ECA, Orphans' Court Will 19

Note: Recognisances were entered into on 17 August 1578 for Alice and Agnes, the daughters of Thomas 'Birde', Draper (ECA, Book 141, folio 62 dorse). Byrde was also described as a Tailor, or Merchant Tailor, in leases of the early 1570s (DRO, Z1/10/84 & Z1/36/1a-b).

In the name of God Amen on the 17th day of the month of June in the 19th year of the reign of Queen Elizabeth **I Thomas Byrde** of the Cittie and countie of Exon tailor, being sicke of bodie but of perfect remembrance thanks be geven to almightie god, doe macke and ordeyne this my laste wille & Testamente in manner and forme folowenge **first** I revoke all former willes and Testamentes whatsoever by me heretofore made& doe by these presente declare them and everie of them to be voyed and off none effecte, and this to stande and be had ffor my laste wille and Testamente, *Firstly*, I geve and bequeathe my soule to almightie god my heavenly father and my bodie to be buried. **Item** my wille and entente is that out of all my goods, & chattells which I have, may have or ought to have, my dettes shalbe firste deducted and satisfied. And then that which shall remayne of my goods after my dettes be dischardged and payde my wille is shalbe devided into three equall partes, whereof, the one parte I geve and bequeathe unto Grace my wife, and the other parte to my two Daughters Alice and Agnes equallie between them to be devided. And if anye of my daughters happen to dye before

they be marriadgeable, or shalbe married, then that porcion of ther so divided (yf anye happen to dye) shall remayne holie to the other sister then lyvenge. And the other thirde parte of my goods (as aforesaid) shalbe to the dischardgenge of my funerals, & the performinge of such legacies as hereafter I shall geve and bequeathe. Item that which shall remayne (my legacies paid & my funerals dischardged) I geve and bequeath unto Grace my wife, whome I make my hole executrix of this my laste will and Testamente. **Item** I doe make Mr Walter Dennys esquire, Mr Humfrye Carewe gent, Mr John Dimscombe of London merchant draper and John Ryder of the Cittie of Exon my overseers of this my said wille and Testament **In witnes** hereof I have sett my signe and seale, theis beinge witnesses the signe of Ric Hunte, Myles Lambarte

[A note follows that the will was proved in the Archdeaconary of Exeter on 29 June 1577.]

35B. INVENTORY OF THOMAS BYRDE, TAILOR/DRAPER OF ST LAWRENCE'S PARISH, 6 SEPTEMBER 1577

ECA, Orphans' Court Inventory 28

This ys the Inventorye of all the goods Chattalls and debts of Thomas Byrde late of the parishe of Saynte Lawrence within the Cittie and Countie of Exeter Deceased, **Praysed** by us John Levermore & Thomas Spycer merchants, William Hunte & Richard Cover, the 6th daye of September. **In the** yere of our Lord god 1577 **And in** the 19th yere of the raigne of our Soveraigne Ladie Elizabeth by the grace of god of England France and Ireland Quene defender of the ffaythe &c.
6 September 1577

[m. 1] **In** the Halle
Firstly the Sylinges with a Spence £3;
Item a longe table boorde 20s;
Item a fforme 2s;
Item a litle table boorde with a forme 3s 4d;
Item one Joyned stoole 8d;
Item one Iron barre in the Chymley 2 Cushions, & a payer of Andyrons 5s;
Sum £4 11s.

In the Parler
Firstly the Sylinges 33s 4d;
Item a Cobberd & a Cobbord clothe 13s 4d;
Item a Bason & a Eyver 3s 4d;
Item the hangings 3s 4d;
Item a table boorde 5s;
Item a fforme 16d;
Item 7 Cusshyons 4s 8d;
Item a Carpett 3s;
Item one Iron barre in the Chymley 16d;
Item a latten skonce for a Candell 12d;
Sum £3 9s 8d.

In the Gallerye
Firstly one Presse 10s;
Item a Cheste 4s;
Item one Corslett 20s;
Item one Pyke 12d;
Item one barre & a sheefe of arrowes 3s 4d;
Item 6 burdois skynnes 8s;
Sum 46s 4d.

In the Chamber over the Parlor
Firstly one standinge bedsteede with a trockell bed 30s;
Item 2 ffeather bedds & 2 bolsters 50s;
Item 4 pyllowes 10s;
Item one Redde Coverlett 5s;
[m. 2] **Item** one payer of Curteyns 10s;
Item one Presse 30s;
Item a Square boorde 3s 4d;
Item one Cheste 8s;
Item 3 payer of blancketts 20s;
Item 2 Coverletts 30s;
Item 3 Carpetts 30s;
Item 4 Cusshyons 16s;
Item 2 peeces of Saye £3;
Item 2 wyndowe clothes 2s 6d;
Item a Cassacke which lyethe at gage for 10s;
Item a Cloke bagge 3s 4d;
Item 2 Joyned stooles 12d;
Item a remlett of blacke Kersey 10s;
Sum £16 9s 2d.

In the Chamber over the Shoppe
Firstly one standinge bedsteede with a trockell bedd 16s;
Item a ffether bedd & a bolster 40s;
Item 2 pillowes 6s 8d;

Item a redde Coverlett 4*s*;
Item Curteynes 13*s* 4*d*;
Item the hangings of household makinge 26*s* 8*d*;
Item a glasse 3*s* 4*d*;
Item 2 Cusshyons 12*d*;
Item one Close stoole of roddes 2*s*;
Item one table boorde 10*s*;
Item one Coobborde 6*s* 8*d*;
Item a latten bason 2*s* 6*d*;
Item one forme 12*d*;
Item 4 Coffers 20*s*;
Item a Joyned doore & sylings 5*s*;
Item a plancke befoer the Chymley 6*d*;
Item a payer of Andyrons 12*d*;
Sum £7 19*s* 8*d*.

In Plate
Firstly 3 gobletts gilte weyenge 56 ounces at 5*s* 2*d* the ounce
   – £14 9*s* 4*d*;
Item 2 saltes parcell gilte, weyenge 14 ounces, at 4*s* 6*d* the
   ounce – £3 3*s*;
Item 19 sylver spoones weyenge 36 ouncs – £8 2*s*;
Item 4 Ale cuppes, covered and trymed with Sylver 53*s* 4*d*;
Item a cover of silver, with a litle cuppe of silver weyeng 2
   ouncs & halffe – 10*s*;
Item a golde ringe 26*s* 8*d*;
Sum £30 4*s* 8*d*.

In Lynnen
Firstly 8 payer of sheetes 53*s* 4*d*;
Item 7 payer of pillowe ties 16*s*;
Item a Callacowe sheete 6*s* 8*d*;
Item a towell for a bason 3*s* 4*d*;
Item a payer of ffustyan blancketts 10*s*;
Item 4 boorde napkyns 4*s*;
Item 3 towells 5*s*;
Item 7 boorde clothes 26*s* 8*d*;
Item 2 dossen of napkyns 10*s*;
Item 5 payer of household sheets 16*s* 8*d*;

Item 4 borde clothes for the keechen 5 hande towells, & one
   dossen of napkins of the same for the keechen 5*s*;
Item 2 glasses with a [blank] 3*s*;
Item a Testament, 5 sherts, and a waste cote 15*s*;
Sum £8 14*s* 8*d*.

[m. 3] **In** the Chamber over the woorkinge shoppe
Firstly one standinge bedsteede with a tester of Saye 15*s*;
Item one ffetherbedd 26*s* 8*d*;
Item one fflocke bedd 3*s* 4*d*;
Item one ffether bolster 2*s*;
Item 3 pillowes 3*s*;
Item a syde boorde 3*s* 4*d*;
Item 2 litle coffers 3*s* 4*d*;
Item water glasses, 2 Eyrynoles [?] & a redd Coverlett 5*s*;
Sum £3 20*d*.

In the mayds chamber
Firstly 2 bedde steeds 4*s*;
Item a ffether bedd, a bolster & a pillowe 26*s* 8*d*;
Item a payer of blancketts 3*s*;
Item a blewe Coverlett & a quylte 5*s*;
Item a fflocke bedd & 3 bolsters 6*s* 8*d*;
Item a rugge, a coverlett, & a quylte 3*s* 4*d*;
Item 2 litle Coffers 20*d*;
Item 2 Cusshions 8*d*;
Sum 51*s*.

In Apparell
Firstly 5 Clokes £5;
Item 4 gownes £3;
Item 3 Cotes 10*s*;
Item 2 Jerkyns 3*s* 4*d*;
Item 6 dubletts 13*s* 4*d*;
Item 4 payer of hose 6*s* 8*d*;
Item a Cloke bagge 5*s*;
Item 3 cappes 2*s*;
Item a hoode 16*d*;
Item 3 hattes 2*s*;

Item a velvett hatte 3*s* 4*d*;
Item a Jerkyn 2*s*;
Sum £10 9*s*.

In the meale Chamber, & in the Chamber over the keechen
Firstly a Candell mould a busshell, 4 tubbes, 2 bagges one
    dowe sheete, seeves & a ranger 6*s* 8*d*;
Item brome ffagotts 4*s*;
Sum 10*s* 8*d*.

In the Mylke Chamber
Firstly a stylle 2*s*;
Item a spynninge toorne, a thridde toorne basketts &
    fflasketts with other trashe 5*s*;
Item a payer of labells, & a hanger 12*d*;
Sum 8*s*.

In the servunts Chamber
Firstly a bedsteede with a trookell bedd 6*s* 8*d*;
Item 2 woolle beddes 10*s*;
Item a ffether bolster, with a fflocke bolster 4*s*;
Item halffe ynche boords 2*s*;
Item 3 Coverletts 5*s*;
Sum 27*s* 8*d*.

In the woorkinge shoppe
Firstly a shoppe boorde and a Presse 3*s* 4*d*;
Sum 3*s* 4*d*.

In the clothe shoppe
Firstly a shoppe boord & a presse 10*s*;
Item 2 Coffers 3*s*;
Item the shelves aboute the shoppe, 2 pressinge yrons, & 2
    payer of sheeres 3*s*;
Sum 16*s*.

[m. 4] **In** the Spence in the Halle
Firstly 9 platters 13*s*;

Item 7 podgers 8*s* 6*d*;
Item 6 ffrewte dishes 3*s* 4*d*;
Item 11 sawcers 3*s* 4*d*;
Item a pottle potte 12*d*;
Item 12 fflower pottes 2*s*;
Item 8 gallons of butter 18*s* 8*d*;
Sum 50*s*.

In the keetchen
Firstly a boorde & a forme 2*s* 6*d*;
Item a keidge & Shelves 2*s*;
Item 2 brandices 3*s* 4*d*;
Item 2 payer of potte hooks 12*d*;
Item 2 payer of potte hangings 20*d*;
Item 3 [blank] 12*d*;
Item a Toster 2*d*;
Item a gryddle 10*d*;
Item one barre in the Chymley 3*s* 4*d*;
Item 5 broches 3*s* 4*d*;
Item a payer of racks 5*s*;
Item a Chaffer of brasse 5*s*;
Item a payer of dogges 8*d*;
Item 2 goose pannes 12*d*;
Item a musterd mylle 6*d*;
Item 7 platters 6 podgers and 6 Sawcers 16*s*;
Item 6 eare disshes 18*d*;
Item 3 bassons 3*s*;
Item a pottle potte, a quarte potte & a pynte potte 5*s*;
Item 2 Krewetts a salte seller & 3 krewses 3*s*;
Item 4 pannes 22*s*;
Item 2 Cawdrens 5*s*;
Item a Warmynge panne 3*s*;
Item a brasen ladell 12*d*;
Item a Skomer 2*s*;
Item 7 candelsticks 5*s*;
Item 2 posnetts & 6 brasen potts 50*s*;
Item a ffleshe hooke 4*d*;
Item one yron potte 2*s* 6*d*;

Item a butter bolle, and a pestell & morter of woode 12*d*;

Item a pestle & morter 12*d*;

Item a Candell case 2*d*;

Item 3 Cusshens & a nolde carpett 2*s*;

Item a boorde 2*s*;

Item the Sylinge & shelves with a boorde & a forme 3*s* 4*d*;

Item one Chaffen dishe 8*d*;

Item a Chittell weyenge 44 poounds 22*s*;

Item a tynnen cuppe 6*d*;

Item bottells & other trashe 2*s* 6*d*;

Item skales, beame, & weightes with sheeres & other trashe 5*s*;

Sum £9 10*s* 10*d*.

In the Seller

Firstly 2 herdells & other trashe 3*s* 4*d*;

Item 16 tubbes & hogeshedds with a breewinge keeve 10*s*;

Sum 13*s* 4*d*.

In the Courte

Firstly a wrynge for cheese 2*s*;

Item 2 Stocks 8*d*;

Item 2 shovells & a hatchett 12*d*;

Item a lymbecke 12*d*;

Sum 4*s* 8*d*.

Firstly the glasse that is aboute the house with the lattyzes 40*s*;

Item their remayneth in the house of 2 sacks one olde Coverlett, a bedsteede, a boorde, a Coobbord, a benche & hanginges with a payer of bootes 13*s* 4*d*;

Sum 53*s* 4*d*.

In the woolle shoppe

Firstly 2 tubbes 6*d*;

Item one Coffer 12*d*;

Item 2 payer of stocke cards & frames 2*s*;

Item [blank] 6*d*;

Item certen broke yearne 5*s*;

Item 10 pounds of woolle 10*s*;

Sum 19*s*.

[*m. 5*] **Firstly** 2 payer of olde tressells at Este Gate 4*d*;

Item certen woode 30*s*;

Item certen tymber 26*s* 8*d*;

Item 2 coffers, a nolde pipe, stones & lathes 5*s*;

Sum £3 2*s*.

In the Stable

Firstly certen haye 20*s*;

Item Saddells with other stuffe 4*s*;

Item a pigge 10*s*;

Item 64 fleeches of wheate 50*s*;

Item a Mare 46*s* 8*d*;

Item 3 kee one heyffer & 2 Calves £9;

Item 2 pykes forkes & rakes 8*d*;

Item 25 kneeches of Stryke 20*d*;

Sum £15 13*s*.

In the Parler coobbord

Firstly 5 dossen of redd loope buttons 4*s*;

Item 4 cloke buttons 12*d*;

Item one dossen & halffe of loope buttons 15*d*;

Item 3 strings of Crewell for cloke baggs 18*d*;

Item certen byllament lace, and other lace of Silke 6*s* 8*d*;

Item in velvett gards, & other triffells 5*s*;

Sum 19*s* 5*d*.

Item the woolle Clothe in the shoppe as in a bill of parcells appearethe and rated as hit is solde £67 3*s* 6*d*;

Item all Chattells, and leases for terme of yeres yett enduringe preysed at £57;

Item the seconde best ffetherbedd with the bedsteede in the litle chamber performed with the seconde best of all things therunto belonginge, nowe remayninge in the custodie of Katheryne Rychardson wyddowe, the Executrix of the testament & last will of Thomas Rychardson, one of the Aldermen of the Cittie of Exeter late deceasid, geven &

bequethed by the saide Thomas Richardson in his said last will & Testament, unto the saide Thomas Byrde deceasid, by estymacon 53s 4d;

Sum £126 6s 10d.

Sum total of the goods and chattels aforesaid £255 14s 7d.

Debttes Sperate and desperate, dewe unto the sayde Testatour
Firstly Robert Michell gentleman 6s 8d;
Item Dorothie Chychester 2s 8d;
Item [blank] Vaysey 22s 1d;
Item Peter Rychardson 42s 1d;
Item Richard Chardon for Canvas 2s 6d;
Item Mr Bodleyghe 58s;
Item Mr Rowsewell 13s 2d;
Item Furneys the vytler 7s;
Item Mistres Hart 14s 6d;
Item Mistres Shilston for rente 4s;
Item [blank] Mortymer 7s 2d;
Item Robert Awstyn & [blank] Whiterowe £14;
Item Samuell Knight 6s;
Item Gyllyam Southmeade 5s 8d;
[m. 6] **Item** Thomas Hollacombe gentleman 31s 4d;
Item Lewes Larder gentleman 16s 2d;
Item Thomas Parrett 57s 2d;
Item Richard Witherton 4s 9d;
Item Hughe Pollard gentleman 50s 2½d;
Item Robert Carrowe 12s;
Item Gylbert German Clarke 20s 2d;
Item Gabryell Seyntclere gentleman £7 4s 5d;
Item Fraunces Yearde 28s 8d;
Item Rychard Gervice 2s 6d;
Item John Bentlowe 3s 4d;
Item Nicholas Waye 38s 2d;
Item William Colthurste 13s 4d;
Item [blank] Faryndon gentleman 36s 2d;
Item Michaell German gentleman 5s 4s ½d [sic];
Item [blank] Beare gentleman £6 13s 6d;
Item Ellice Graundeson 2s 10d;

Item [blank] Kethe 3s 8d;
Item William Hoopell gentleman £9 17s 10½d;
Item Phillippe Sydnam 17s 2½d;
Item Robert Carye the younger gentleman 38s 10½d;
Item John Courtney gentleman 7s 2d;
Item William Parker gentleman 27s 4d;
Item [blank] Gee 5s 6½d;
Item Mallacheus Mallett gentleman £11 18s 2½d;
Item Humphrey Buryes servaunte 18d;
Item John Carrowe 13s 7d;
Item Rychard Hutchens £3 19s 3d;
Item [blank] Garrett 2s 2d;
Item [blank] Garrett Mr Carewes servaunte 3s 3d;
Item [blank] Strobridge gentleman 8s 1d;
Item [blank] Collyford Mr Buryes servaunte 8s 10½d;
Item Henrie Dulynge gentleman 19s 10d;
Item Roger Mr Buries servaunte 8s 2d;
Item Phillippe Bigilston gentleman 14s;
Item William James gentleman 2s 4d;
Item [blank] Zooley the weaver 30s 3d;
Item [blank] Weeks of Weeke gentleman 50s;
Item Marcks Weeks gentleman £3 12s;
Item William Weeks gentleman 3s 7d;
Item Kyddell the Hellyer 2s 8½d;
Item Roger Weeks gentleman 7s 8½d;
Item Katheryne Rychardson wyddowe 54s 8d;
Item Mychaell Mallett gentleman 26s 8d;
Item Mistres Mallett 18s 2d;
Item Hughe Ackeland gentleman £7 14d;
Item John Ackeland gentleman 37s 4½d;
Item [blank] Prowse gentleman 6s 7d;
Item Mr Pollards Executors 33s 8d;
Item Rychard Burye gentleman 3s 7½d;
Item the Caryers Clarke at Northgate 18s 3d;
Item Edward Dennys gentleman £6;
Item Thomas Southwoode 7s;
Item Nicholas Beerye gentleman 7s 5½d;
Item Humphrey Burye gentleman 26s 2d;
Item [blank] Drake £4;

Item John Blewett gentleman 20*s*;
Item Venner 22*s*;
Item Parson Slade £4 2*s* 11*d*;
Item Anthonye Pollard gentleman £4 5*s* 6*d*;
Item Humfrey Carowe gentleman 53*s* 4*d*;
Item [blank] Carye gentleman £4 13*s* 4*d*;
Item Mistres Kenne 27*s* 6*d*;
Item [blank] Kroncke 11*s* 8*d*;
Item [blank] Lutley 11*s*;
Item Russell Mr Caries servaunte 9*s*;
Item John Ryche 2*s*;
Item Mr Blewett 36*s* 2*d*;
Item [blank] Sheperd 2*s*;
Item Mistres Kyrckehm 7*s* 4*d*;
Item for one elle of canvas 22*d*;
Item [blank] Pyne servaunte to Mr Tothill 14*s* 5*d*;
Item John Lownde 4*s* 2*d*;
Item [blank] Norbrooke deceasid 2*s* 8½*d*;
Item the olde Banckes 2*s* 9*d*;
[m. 7] **Item** Richard Bagott 18*s*;
Item John Davye 6*s*;
Item the wyddowe Vennycombe 4*s*;
Item Sir Ellyce Fylimer 19*s* 11*d*;
Item [blank] Styell 9*s*;
Item Edward Allyn 3*s* 4*d*;
Item Margarett Jervis 7*s*;
Item Johanne Burrell 5*s*;
Item John Brusheford 16*s* 1½*d*;
Item John Edwarde 20*d*;
Item Vaughon Tayler 19*s*;
Item Robert Morbed 8*s*;
Item Edward Clappon 15*s*;
Item Mr Whitefilde 3*s* 3*d*;
Item Harris of Plymouthe 6*s* 8*d*;
Item Thomas Sheperde 16*d*;
Item Furseman 16*s* 2*d*;
Item Sampson Lye 2*s* 6*d*;
Item Lippingcott 5*s*;
Item Burrell Sir Thomas Dennys servaunte 13*s*;

Item Tanner servaunte to the Erle of Bedford 14*s* 11*d*;
Item my Ladye Pollarde 8*s* 4*d*;
Item William Pye 15*s* 4*d*;
Item Stephen Herrynge 18*s*;
Item Anthonye Courtney gentleman 32*s* 3½*d*;
Item Edmonde Allyn 3*s* 4½*d*;
Item Hughe Pollerde gentleman 14*s* 11*d*;
Item Richard Prewsey 15*s* 2*d*;
Item John Knolles 21*d*;
Item George Comes 46*s* 2*d*;
Item [blank] Wyncott 6*s* 6*d*;
Item Mr Horwyll 6*s* 10*d*;
Item Bennett Fortescue gentleman 43*s*;
Item John Awtrey 7*s* 6*d*;
Item Thomas Harrys 3*s* 4*d*;
Item Edwarde Catlyn 36*s*;
Item William Powell & Elizabeth Powell 46*s* 8*d*;
Item Richard Sackefilde 20*s*;
Item Roger Dynhm 58*s*;
Item William Adams 9*s*;
Item more William Adams by bill *obligatorie* £8 14*s* 8*d*;
Item [blank] Luffe 40*s* 8*d*;
Item [blank] Walle 46*s* 8*d*;
Item Thomas Rychards 9*s* 4*d*;
Item William Parhoosse 28*s* 3*d*;
Item Gyllam Staplyn 10*s*;
Item Edward Thorne 2*s*;
Item Robert Mr Beryes servaunte 7*s* 4*d*;
Item Mr Makepowder 20*d*;
Item Mr Jerome Maye 2*s*;
Item Mr Thomas Drake 4*s* 7½*d*;
Item John Aprice 6*s*;
Item John Jones 2*s* 6*d*;
Item Peter Yearde 5*s*;
Item Mr Rawleighe 27*s* 5*d*;
Item [blank] Jennyngs 29*s* 6*d*;
Item Marcks with Mr Bampfild 18*s* 4*d*;
Item Robert Holbeame 2*s* 11*d*;
Item Andrewe Tremayne gentleman 20*s* 3½*d*;

Item [blank] Lyell 10*s* 2*d*;
Item Symon Lyell 22*s*;
Item [blank] Awstyn 9*s* 2*d*;
Item Edwarde Yearde gentleman 11*s* 7½*d*;
Item Gyrrens 11*s*;
Item John Warren of Wellington 12*s* 8*d*;
Item Phillippe Glover 4*s* 1*d*;
Item John Dyer 5*s* 10*d*;
Item John Woode 8*s*;
Item [blank] Parkyns 38*s* 7*d*;
Item Gyles Rowe 5*s* 1*d*;
Item Andrewe Cannyngton 18*s*;
Item Jennyngs Moore 3*s* 8*d*;
Item the olde Melburye 2*s* 7*d*;
Item Thomas Yearde gentleman 9*s*;
Item Gawyne Carewe Knighte 24*s* 4*d*;
Item Mistres Bolfilde 2*s*;
Item John Tothill for his servaunts debtt 4*s* 7½*d*;
Item Phillippe Cliffe 22½*d*;
Item John Shalme 2*s* 5*d*;
Item Mr Gyles 6*s* 6*d*;
Item Thomas James 50*s*;
[m. 8] Sum of all the foresaid debts £214 15*s* 8*d*;
Sum total of the foresaid inventory along with the foresaid debts £470 10*s* 3*d*.

Debttes which the saide Testator did owe, att the tyme of his lyffe and deathe
Firstly to Thomas Mallett gentleman £35 7*s*;
Item to John Dunscombe gentleman £84 14*s*;
Item to Walter Dennys gentleman £20;
Item to John Pylle £3;
Item to George Smythe £8 16*s* 7*d*;
Item to Walter Fyssher £4 13*s* 4*d*;
Item to Hughe Wylsdon £12;
Item to John Webbe gentleman £3 2*s* 5*d*;
Item to Nycholas Burye gentleman 53*s* 4*d*;
Item to [blank] Mayne £5 5*s* 8½*d*;
Item to Mr Mouncke 34*s*;

Item to [blank] Burnarde 11*s* 6*d*;
Item to Agnes [blank] 20*s*;
Item to Gill the weaver 10*s*;
Item to a nother weaver 10*s*;
Item to John Ryder 7*s* 6*d*;
Item to Thomas Greenewood 4*s* 6*d*;
Item for the makinge of haye 6*s*;
Item for Sande 8*d*;
Item to the Mayde for her quarters wages 5*s*;
Item to Mr Coles for rente 30*s*;
Item to John Ryche the Tooker 10*s*;
Item for mowinge of the meadowes 6*s*;
Item for a busshell of barley malte 4*s*;
Item to John Dyer for rente 20*d*;
Item to Katheryne Rychardson for rente 3*s* 4*d*;
Item to Roger Chardon for Justements 12*d*;
Item to Mr Yeo for domynicalls 13*d*;
Item to Mr Nicholas Martyn for rente 4*s*;
Item to Mistres Fyelde for lynclothe 7*s*;
Item to Mr Sampforde for rente 23*s* 4*d*;
Item to Robert Bachealler 33*s* 4*d*;
Item to Rychard Hunte 14*s*;
Item to Mr Sandye 26*s*;
Item to West for tythinge haye 3*s* 4*d*;
Item to him for mendynge the waye 12*d*;
Item to [blank] Gye the shoo maker 21*s* 6*d*;
Item to a mayde for 7 weeks service 2*s* 4*d*;
Item for reepynge & cuttynge of the wheate 6*s*;
Item for carryenge of the corne & haye 7*s*;
Item to Salter the dyer 10*s* 6*d*;
Sum of all suche debtts as the sayde testator did owe att the tyme of his deathe £191 13*s* 1½*d*.

Sum total of all the goodds & debts £470 10*s* 3*d*;
whereof the Testator did owe £191 13*s* 1½*d*;
also remaining yn desperat debts £142 18*s* 3*d*;
Sum £334 11*s* 4*d*;
So resteth clere £135 18*s* 11*d*.

36. INVENTORY OF WALTER JONES, VINTNER OF ST MARTIN'S PARISH, 24 FEBRUARY 1578

ECA, Orphans' Court Inventory 27

Note: Recognisances were entered into on 5 April 1578 for his son John and daughter Mary (ECA, Book 141, folios 61 & 62).

The Inventorie of the goodes Chattalls & Debtes of Walter Jones Of the parishe of St Martyns in the Cittie of Exeter deceased, presie By Mr John Webber, Mr Thomas Spicer, Mr Robarte Webber and William Greenewood the 24 of Ffebruary 1577

[1] In the Hall
Firstly the seeling of waynscot with Benchis £3;
Item a Longe Table borde with a fframe 5s;
Item a greene Carpet upon the same Borde 16d;
Item 2 Joynid ffoormes 4s;
Item a nother table Borde with a Cobbord in the same 5s;
Item a Greene Carpet upon the same Bord 20d;
Item 3 Joynid Stooles 2s 6d;
Item a Chaire 8d;
Item a dossen of Quosshins of Tapestrie old 12s;
Item an old Cobord with a Linimme [?] cloth with a ffrenge, & a Border of Steole woork 5s;
Item a Bason and yoer of tynne 4s;
Item a paire of candlestick of tynne 2s;
Item under the Cobord a wasshing Bason, a pottell pot, 2 Quart Pottes, & a pynte pot 8s;
Item a Litle folding Borde 6s 8d;
Item a Carpet upon the same 11d;
Item a Greene cloth in the wyndow 2s;
Item old Hanginges of Red say and greene with a Border of paintid Cloth above the seeling 2s;
Item 1 paire of andIrons with a paire of Tonges & a shovill 10s;
Item a paire of dogges 18d;
Item a Backe of Iron 4s;
Sum £6 18s 4d.

In the Parlor
Item an old Table Boord with a Cobord in the same 4s;

Item the seeling with Benchis 20s;
Item a ffoorme 12d;
Item a old Chaire 6d;
Item a Litle Spruce Chest 6s 8d;
Item an old carpet upon the boord 2s;
[1v.] Item a Joynyd Presse 26s 8d;
Item a Joynyd Cobbord 5s;
Item a Joynyd Bedsteed 30s;
Item a ffether Bed with a bolster 40s;

Fig.20. The vintner Walter Jones' house was in St Martin's parish, most of whose properties lay in the block of properties between the High Street and Cathedral Close, shown in the foreground of the Hedegeland model of Exeter (*photo: D. Garner, courtesy of Exeter City Museums*).

Item a paire of Blankets 10s;
Item a Coverlet of tapastrie 20s;
Item a Joynid Troockle Bedd 3s 4d;
Item a fether bed with a Bolster 20s;
Item a paire of Blankets 6s 8d;
Item 2 Coverlets 8s;

Item Curteynes of Red say and Greene abowt the high Bedd
    13s 4d;
Item a Cloth upon the Cubbord 2s;
Item a Greene cloth in the wyndow 2s;
Item hangins of Red say and greene with a Border of Payntid
    cloth above the seeling 2s 6d;
Item 2 Joynid stooles with Quosshins & another Litle one 3s
    4d;
Item a Bason and yoer upon the Cubord of Tinne 2s 6d;
Item a greate Chardger of tynne 18d;
Item a old Curtayn of Bockram in the wyndow with a Iron
    rodd 2s;
Item an old paintid Cloth under the wyndow with old frenge
    12d;
Item one andyron [entry crossed through];
Item a payre of dogges;
Item a paire of Tonges, and a fyer Shovell;
[Last two entries] 2s;
Item 6 Greene Quosshins old 2s;
Item Quosshins of Qilt Lether 12d;
Item a Candelstick with a buckes hedd & a Lokinge Glasse 16d;
Item a barr in the Chymney 8d;
Sum 12s 6d [sic].

In the utter Chamber
Item an old Bed steede with an old Testor 18d;
Item a fether Bed with a bolster of ffethers 13s 4d;
Item a paire of Blanckets;
Item coverlet of Liftes;
[Last two entries] 2s;
Item a nother old Bed steede with a tester 16d;
Item fflock Bed with a bolster 4s;

Item a paire of Blanckets;
Item a Coverlet of Redd;
[Last two entries] 4s;
Item an old Chest & a candell fo [?] Cofer 2s 6d;
Item old paintid Clothes 2d;
Item 2 old Swoordes rustie;
Item an old Bill;
[Last two entries] 3s 4d;
Item 2 old Boordes 8d;
Sum 32s 10d.

[2] In the midle Chamber
Item a standing Bedstede with a old Testar of Red say &
    greene 8s;
Item 2 ffether Bedes & a Bolster 46s 8d;
Item a whit Rugg 10s;
Item a Coverlet of Tapestrie 12s;
Item 3 Corteins of Calecow, cloth & Iron roddes to the same 3s;
Item the Hangins of paintid cloths with a litle table 6s 8d;
Item 9 pilowes of ffethers 20s;
Item 2 old chairs 5s;
Item 2 old Bordes, 1 rownd and a nother Square 2s 6d;
Item an old Chest 16d;
Item a Litle Quoasshin of old damask 6d;
Item a paire of old and Irons with a bad paire of dogges, & a
    Litle paire of Tonges 2s;
Item a brushe to brusshe away the Cobbwebbes 1d;
Item a Close Chaire made of yardes 16d;
Sum £5 19s 1d.

In the Inner Chamber
Item a carved Bedsteede with a testor of Red saye & yelow 6s;
Item a fether bed with a bolster 26s 8d;
Item a paire of Blanckets 6s;
Item a Coverlet of Tapistrie 5s;
Item a Trockle Bedd, with a fether Bed & a bolster of fethers,
    a paire of Blanckets & a Bad coverlet 25s;
Item the payntid Clothes 2s 6d;
Item a paire of dogges 12d;

a

b

c

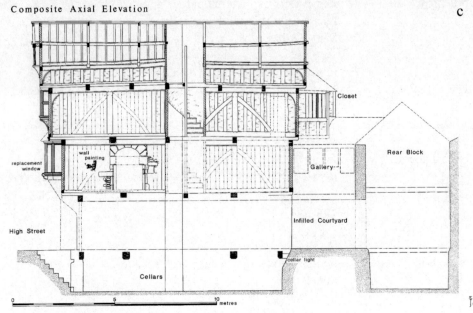

Composite Axial Elevation

Closet

Rear Block

Gallery

replacement window

wall painting

Infilled Courtyard

High Street

cellar light

Cellars

0   5   10 metres

Fig. 21. Several of the St Martin's parish houses survive, the most complete being Nos 41–2 High Street, built in 1564. (a). The street frontage; (b) The rear courtyard; (c). This section through No. 41 shows the main block of the house on the street frontage, with a kitchen at the rear of the property and a small courtyard between. This was probably a common house type in the city centre (c – *drawn by John Thorp; © Exeter Archaeology*).

Item 3 forsletts & a Litle chest 4s;
Sum £3 16s 2d.

In the presse which standith in the Parlor
Item 5 Corteines of [blank] with the valance of red & greene
  mockade frendgid 46s 8d;
Item 3 Quoosshins of nedle woork 15s;
Item 6 Quoosshins & one Longe quoosshin of Greene & black
  tuft mockado 13s 4d;
Item a Coverlet of Tapistrie 53s 4d;
Item 2 Carpets of Tapistrie 16s 8d;
Item 3 Carpets of black & greene Cruell 20s;
Sum £8 5s.

Apparell
Item a Gowne of Browne blew facid with Bowge with a lace
  abowt the same gowne £4;
Item a nother gowne with a standinge Color facid with Bowge
  26s 8d;
Item a Cloke of Browne Blew 26s 8d;
Item a Cloke of Ratts Colowr 10s;
[2v.] Item a Jerkin of Browne blew with a billement Lace a
  bowt hit 15s;
Item a satyn dublet 33s 4d;
Item a nother Jerkin of cloth 4s;
Item a Dublet of Rasshe 5s;
Item a dublet of chaungeable taffata & a paire of Bodyes of
  mynsyn [?] taffata 6s 8d;
Item a paire of Sliders of purple & 2 paire of stockinges of the
  same 10s;
Item 2 wast dublets one of Keryse [kersey] & a nother of
  Canvas 2s;
Item 2 Cappes 5s;
Sum £11 4s 4d.

Napery
Item 8 peare of sheetes of dowles & morlers cloth £5 6s 8d;
Item 12 paire of Canvas shetes £6;
Item a paire of fustian blankets 13s 4d;

Item 20 pilloties £4;
Item 2 diaper Borde clothes & 5 diaper Towells £3 10s;
Item 7 Bordclothes 53s 4d;
Item 6 Canvas Borde clothes 20s;
Item 3 frengd Towells & 12 other Towells 28s;
Item a dossen of other towells 16s;
Item ½ a dossen of hande towells 5s;
Item a dossen of diaper napkins 18s;
Item a dossen & ½ of fyne holand napkins ffrendgid 27s;
Item a dossen of napkings of canvas ffrengid 16s;
Item 2 dossen of Canvas napkins Playne 20s;
Item 6 Shirtes 40s;
Item 2 Cobbord Clothes 2s 6d;
Sum £31 15s 10d.

In the Low hall
Item the Seeling 33s 4d;
Item payntid Clothes above the Seeling 2s;
Item 2 Table Bordes 6s 8d;
Item 2 fformes 2s 6d;
Item a Litle Cobbord 2s;
Item a Litle barr of Iron in the Chimney 4d;
Item a Litle paire of dogges 12d;
Sum 47s 10d.

In the Litle parlor with in the Low hall
Item a Table Boord 2 Benchis & a old Chaire & a litle peece
  of Seeling 5s;
Sum 5s.

[3] In the Spying howse
Item 2 Table Bordes, 2 bench 4 ffoormes a pece of seeling & a
  litle paintid cloth 10s;
Sum 10s.

In the Litle studye
Item 3 shelves a Powdring Tubb a stoole 2s 6d;
Sum 2s 6d.

In the Kytchin

Item in pewter vessell 140 pownd at 6*d* the pownd £3 10*s*;

Item 11 Candellsticks 3 chafyndiss[hes] & a scomer containing 24 lb – 16*s*;

Item 3 Brasse pannes, 6 Cawdrons & 2 Skilletts containing 56 lb at 8*d* – 37*s* 4*d*;

Item 3 Brasse pottes containing 78 lb at 6*d* – 39*s*;

Item 3 other brasse pottes containing 70 lb at 6*d* – 35*s*;

Item 1 Brasse pott & a broken pot 2 possnets & a chafer containing 56 lb at 4*d* the Pownd 18*s* 8*d*;

Item a Paire of Rackes of Iron, a barr of Iron 13*s* 4*d*;

Item 2 dogges of Iroune 1 fflatte barre of Iroune 2 gredierounes & A brandis 4 pote hangeings 4 pott Croucks A pere of tonges & A ffiershube 6*s*;

Item 6 brotches 5*s*;

Item 4 gousepannes of Iroune & 2 ffrienge pannes 6*s* 8*d*;

Item A Settell of Juned seling A Cowpe & 3 shillffes with A olde Cheare & A dressing borde A buckie toube [?] & 2 Cowles A Chappine bord & 6 Toubbes 8*s*;

Sum £12 15*s*.

In the chamber over the Kitchin

Item an old Chest and ½ a hundreth of talow in the same 13*s* 4*d*;

Item old emptye Cask, woode and other Trasshe 2*s*;

Sum 15*s* 4*d*.

[3v.] Plate

Item 1 Goblet 1 boll of silver 1 Ale cupp with a Cover 2 Saltes with one Cover of Silver and Doble gilte wainge 53 ozces & a halfe at 5*s* 4*d* – £15 2*s* 8*d*;

Item 4 Goblets of Silver percell gilt waying 57 onces at 4*s* 4*d* the unce – £12 7*s*;

Item one Cupp with a Cover for Bere, a fflat Peace parcell gilt a dossen & halfe of spoones with Gilt knoppes & a cover with the mowith of a bere Cupp wayng 50 unces at 4*s* 4*d* – £10 16*s* 8*d*;

Item 1 Stone pott garnished with silver with the Cover neck & ffoote 26*s* 8*d*;

Sum £39 13*s*.

Item in monay £20;

Sum £20.

In the Shopp

Item in Cloth to the valew of £135 – £135;

Item [2 Chestes – crossed through] 1 Cheste 12*s*;

Item 3 shelves with the payntid Borders 4*s*;

Sum £135 16*s*.

Item the Glasse with the Casementes in Bothe howses £8;

Sum £8.

Leases

Item the Lease of the Litle howse in the Fore Streete wherof there is to Com 43 yere £30;

Item the Lease of the Howse at the Broadgate wherof there is to come 35 yere £70;

Sum £100.

[4] Debtes

Item in debtes we fynd by his booke to be owyng £107 13*s* 4*d*;

Wherof we do thinck we that there may be recovered £66 13*s* 4*d* [entry crossed through];

[Illegible] oweth £26 13*s* 4*d*;

And for the rest we do Judge to be desperate debts which a mowntith to the some £53 6*s* 8*d* [entry crossed through];

Also Sir John Gylbert Richard [illegible] John Smith & Mr Martyn £16 13*s* 4*d*;

Sum £66 13*s* 4*d* [entry crossed through];

Sum of debtes sperate & desperate £151 5*s*;

Sum of the desperat debts £53 6*s* 8*d* [entry crossed through].

In the Hall in the Litle Howse in the Fore Streete

Item the Seeling, & the Bedsteade in the same 53*s* 4*d*;

Item a fether Bede & a bolster 46s 8d;
Item a paire of Blanckets and a Coverlet 18s;
Item 4 Curteines of Saye & the paintid Clothes abowte the
    howse, & a paintid tester 6s 8d;
Item a framid table Borde & a Joynid forme 10s;
Item a Carpet 4s;
Item a Litle Cofer 2s;
Sum 7s 8d.

In the Kytchin in the said howse
Item 1 andyron & 2 dogges 18d;
Item a ffletch & halfe of bakon 5s;
Item a old chest & a old chaire 8d;
Item meale tubbes [illegible superscipt] and other old trasshe
    2s;
Sum 9s 2d.
In the fore chamber in the same Howse
Item a Joynid Bedsteede and Seeling 26s 8d;
Item a fflock Bedd & bolster 5s;
Item a Coverlet & a Quilt and A payre of blanckets 6s 8d;
Item a fforme 8d;
Item a Calyver, a moryan with flaske [?] & tooche Boox 13s
    4d;
Item a paire of allmayne Rivets a Black Bill & a Swoord &
    dagger 20s;
Sum £3 12s 4d.

[4v.] In the Back chamber
Item 2 old Baskets with 8 lb of wooll 4s;
Item a turne, a paire of stock Cardes & a paire of Hand
    Cardes and a Hurdle 3s;
Sum 7s.

In the Stable and Cowrt in St Martyns Lane
Item a wood Reeke 30s;
Item Empty Caske £3;
Sum £4 10s.

In the Stable and gardyn in St Powles Lane
Item 2 Emptie Kaskes a old Cheste, an old Sadell and a
    showell & other trasshe 6s 8d;
Item a Reeke of woode 46s 8d;
Sum 53s 4d.

['Wyne' crossed through] in the seller at the Brodegat & other
    stuffe
Item 11 Buttes of Seck [entry crossed through];
Item 3 Pipes Bastard [entry crossed through];
Item a virkin of Tainte [entry crossed through];
Item 5 Tonne of gaskoyne wyne [entry crossed through];
Item a Tonne of vineger [entry crossed through];
Item a Tonne of emptie Caske 4s;
Item an allandrie [?] a brode basket, a Racke & 2 cheses 5s;
Item 6 Quarters pottes and 6 pintes, 2 peny potts of Tinne
    10s;
Item 2 galons of Butter 5s;
Sum 24s.

[5] Wynes In the Seller at the Broade Gate
Item 11 Buttes of Secke £82 10s;
Item 3 Pipes of Bastard £28;
Item 1 virkin of Taint 40s;
Item 5 Tonne of gaskoyne wyne £60;
Item 1 Tonne of vyneger £4;
Sum £176 10s.

In John Raphes Seller at Opsam
Item 36 Buttes of seck £270;
Item 7 hogshedd gaskoyne wyne £21;
Sum £291.

Item Richard Roes Seller at Opsam
Item 21 Buttes of seck £157 10s;
Item 3 hogsheds gaskoyne wyne £9;
Sum £166 10s.

In a Seller in the Rack Lane
Item 4 Tonne Gaskoyne wyne £48;
Sum £48.

Sum Total £1,162 7s 1d [entry crossed through];
Sum Total £1,223 13s 9d.

Sir Jo Gilbort oweth £3 10s;
Richard Corbyn oweth £10 10s;
John Smythe of Clyst oweth 33s 4d;
So £1,239 7s 1d.

Desperate detts £72 19s 10d.

37. WILL OF JULIAN GUNSTONE, WIDOW OF ST PAUL'S PARISH, 15 JUNE 1578

ECA, Orphans' Court Will 21

Note: A note follows that the will was proved on 19 July 1578 in the Archdeaconry of Exeter. The registers for the parish of St Paul were heavily damaged during the blitz of Exeter in 1942 but an earlier transcription, published by the Devon & Cornwall Record Society in 1933, recorded the burial of 'Gulean Gunstone' on 20 June 1578. Recognisances were entered into on 4 September 1570 regarding Johan, John, Peter and Richard, the children of Nicholas Gunstone (ECA, Book 141, Folio 24).

In the name of god amen the 15th daye of June In the yere of our lord god 1578 and the 20th yere of the Raygne of our Soveraygne lady Elysabethe by the grace of god of England Frannce & Ireland queene deffender of the ffaythe &c I Julean Gunstone of the paryshe of Sayntte Pawles within the cytty & countye of Exceter wydoe beyng sicke of bodye butt perfett of remembranse thanckes be geven unto god, do make & ordeyne thys my presentt testamentt and laste wyll In manner and forme folowyng fyrste I geve & bequeathe my soule to almighty god and my body to the earth, also I geve & bequethe 20s to the pore people to be dystrybutted whereas moste nede shalbe also I geve & bequethe to the paryshe clarke 3s 4d, also I geve and bequethe to Jone my syster my fryse cassacke a red pettycote & 2 smockes, also I geve & bequethe to Petter Gustone my sonne my beste cassack to make hym a cloke, also I geve & bequethe to Humfrye Keymers wyfe my Russett Cassacke, the residye of all my goods moveable & nonmoveable nott before geven nor bequethed I geve bequethe unto Petter Gunstone my sonne and to Alse Whytteare the daughter of Henry Whyttreare whome I do ordeyne & make my trewe and lawfull executors of all my godds nott geven nor bequeathed equally to be devyded betwyne them, also I do ordeine my trusty frynds Thomas Jorden and Wyllyam Hewes to be my overseers to see thys my laste wyll and testament Justly & trulye to be performed and they to have 3s 4d a pece of them for ther paynes.

38A. WILL OF WILLIAM CHAPPELL, MERCHANT & ALDERMAN OF ST PETROCK'S PARISH, 3 FEBRUARY 1579

National Archives, PROB 11/62/47

Note: The will was proved on 1 February 1580. The register for the parish of St Petrock recorded the burial of 'Mr William Chapple' on 10 December 1579. John Hooker noted in his *Chronicle* that Chapple died whilst serving as mayor in the beginning of December. Hooker also noted that 'he was well bent to the good of the common wealth but death so shortened his course that he had not the time to yield the fruits of his government nor to do that good which he was determined to have done' (Todd Gray, *The Chronicle of Exeter*, 2005, 110-111). Recognisances were entered into on 20 January 1580 for Richard, Nicholas and Elizabeth the children of William Chapell, Alderman (ECA, Book 141, Folios 76, 77, 78).

[1] **In the name of god amen** The Thirde daie of Februarie in the yeare of oure lorde god A Thowsand five hundred Seaventie and eighte, And in the one and Twentie yeare of the Raigne of oure Sovereigne ladie Elizabeth by the grace of god Quene of England Fraunce and Ireland Defender of the Faithe &c I William Chappell of the parishe of St Petroke within the Cittie of Exeter Marchaunte, In good and perfecte mynde and remembrance Thankes be geven to Allmightie god, doe revoke Adnichilate and make voide all former Testaments willes and legacies by me hearetofore made and geven. And doe make and ordaine this my laste will and Testamente in maner and forme followinge. First I bequeathe my Sowle to Allmightie god my maker Savioure and redemer, and my bodie to be buried as it shall be thoughte good by my Executors and overseers. And as touchinge my leace and Terme of yeares in and to the Moietie and halfendele of the manor of Iddesley with all his rightes, members and appurtenances in the Countie of Devon, my will and mynd is that Thomas Hele gentleman John Hassarde of Lyme Regis and my brother Thomas Chaple and my Cosen John Chapell of Exeter, marchauntes shall have the whole use ordre and governmente therof, And also take the whole yssues and profetts therof, untill Thomas Chapell my eldest soune shall accomplishe the full age of Twentie six yeares if the saide Thomas my soune shall so longe live. And if he die before he shall accomplishe his saide full aige of Twentie six yeares Then untill suche tyme as he or they that shalbe my nexte heire or heires or one of them shall accomplishe the Age of Twentie six years. And my minde is that the saide Thomas Hele John Hassard Thomas Chapell my brother and John Chapell, shall Assigne over and Convey all the whole Terme and Intereste of the saide Lease to the saide Thomas my eldeste soune or to suche as shalbe my nexte heire or heires whensoever they or anie of them shall accomplishe the age of six and Twentie yeares. And my will and intente further is

That the saide Thomas Hele John Hassarde Thomas Chapell my brother and John Chapell shall converte the ysseues and profettes of the saide lease to the use and comoditie of the saide Thomas Chapell my soune duringe the tyme they shall have the same, And if he die then to the use of my nexte heire or heires allowinge themselves reasonable for theire expenses as my speciall truste is in them. Item I give and bequeathe unto the saide Thomas Chapell my soune, All my estate and Terme of yeares which I have in the fowrthe parte of all those landes and Tenements in the parishe of Brodecliste nowe or late in the tenure occupacon or possession of [blank] Germaine widow or [of - crossed out] hir Assignes which I had of the graunte of Anthonie Copleston gentleman and all maner of Obligacons and writinges which I have concerninge the same. Item my will is that my executors shall give and deliver to the use of the poore one hundred markes of lawfull money of England to be distributed by the discretion of the Maior and Aldermen of the Cittie of Exeter or the moste parte of them, and of the saide Anthonie Copleston, Thomas Hele and of the rest of the saide persons to whom I have bequeathed my saide lease of Iddesley. Item I will and bequeathe to everie of my daughters Grace and Elizabeth Three Hundred markes of lawfull money of Englande and to everie of them a Tankarde of silver gilte to be paide and delivered to them at ther daies of mariage or at ther full age of Twentie and one yeares which shall firste happne, to be paide by my executors in full Satisfaccon of all ther porcon which they maye demaunde or Challenge for ther childres parte or otherwise of all my goodes and Cattelles. And if either of them die before they be maried or accomplishe the age of Twentie one yeares Then hir parte that diethe shall remaine amonges all my children equallie to be devided amongeste them. Item I will and devise unto Richard Chapell my soune, All my landes and Tenements with thappurtenances called Manston in the parishe of Sydburie in the Countie of Devon.

To have and to holde to the saide Richarde and to the heires males of his bodie lawfullie begotten. And for default of suche issue the remainder therof unto the saide Thomas Chapell my eldeste soune and to the heires males of his bodie lawfullie begotten and for defaulte of such issue the remainder therof to Nicholas Chapell my youngeste soune and to the heires males of his bodie lawfullie begotten. And for defaulte of suche issue the remainder therof to the righte heires of me the saide William Chapell for ever. Item I will and devise to the saide Nicholas Chapell my yongeste soune All my Capitall house landes and tenements called Winslade and all other my landes and tenements with thappurtenances in the parishe of St George Cliste *alias* Cliste Barnefeilde in the countie of Devon And all my landes & tenements with the appurtenances called Larkebeare in the parishe of St Leonardes in the saide countie of Devon nowe in the Tenure of Roberte Edmondes or his Assignes, To have and to holde to the saide Nicholas and to the heires males of his bodie lawfullie begotten, And for defaulte of such isshewe the remainder therof to the saide Thomas Chapell my oldeste soune and to the heires males of his bodie lawfullie begotten And for defaulte of suche isshew the remainder therof to the saide Richarde my soune and to the heires males of his bodie lawfullie begotten And for defaulte of such yssue the remainder therof to the righte heires of me the saide Wiliam Chapell for ever. Item I will and devise unto Cristian my wyfe All my *[2]* Capitall messuage and Tenement with the Appurtenances called Brockwill in the parishe of Brodecliste aforesaide and all other my landes and Tenements Meadowes leasnes pastures and hereditamentes whatsover which I the saide William [obscured] manurance or occupacon in the saide parishe of Brodecliffe. Item I give graunte and devise to the saide Cristian my wife one Anuitie or yearlie rente of Twentie poundes of lawfull money of Englande goinge oute of all my landes, Tenements and hereditaments in the Countie of Devon which by this my laste will and Testamente shalbe devised to the saide Thomas Chapell my soune or which shall discende from me to the saide Thomas my soune or to my heires To have and to holde the saide Capitall messuage

landes Tenements medowes leasnes pastures and hereditamentes Together with the saide Annuitie or yearelie rente of Twentie poundes to the saide Cristian for Terme of hir naturall life in recompence of all hir dower to hir belonginge of anie and all my manors landes Tenementes and hereditamentes, The saide Annuitie or yearlie rente of Twentie poundes to be paide at the foure moste usuall termes of the yeare, That is to witte at the feastes of the Annuntiacon of oure blessed ladie Marie the virgine, The nativitie of St John Baptiste St Mychaell tharchangell and the birthe of oure lord by even porcons, the firste Terme of paymente therof to begine at that feaste of the feastes aforesaide which shall firste happen after my decease, And that if the saide Annuitie or yearelie rente of Twentie poundes be behinde in parte or in the whole by the space of eighte daies nexte after anie of the feastes afforesaide in which it oughte to be paide, That then it shalbe lawfull to the saide Cristian and hir Assignes into All and singuler the foresaide landes Tenementes and hereditamentes with thappurtenances hearafter devised to the saide Thomas my soune And also into all my landes and tenementes which shall discende from me to the saide Thomas or to my heires to enter and distraine. And the distresse so ther taken from thence to drive carie awaie and ympounde and in a pound to detaigne untill of the foresaid rente so beinge behynde with the arrearages of the same if anie be unto the saide Cristian be fullie satisfied and paide. Item I will and give to everie of my saide sounes Richarde and Nicholas Twoe hundred poundes of lawfull money of England in full Satisfacon of all ther porcons of all my goodes and Cattelles, the saide somes to be paide them by the discretion of my overseers. Item I give to everie of my saide sounes A Goblette of Silver doble gilte and to everie of them six of my beste silver spoones. Item I give and bequeathe also unto my saide soune Richarde the lease of the land in Sothinhay percell of the Mawdlyn. And my will further is that if anie of my sounes or daughters die before they come to theire full age or be maried, That then the porcion of him or hir so dienge to them above geven or bequeathed shalbe equallie devided amonges the reste of my children livinge.

Item I will and devise to my Brother Anthonie Chapell for Terme of his life one Annuitie or yearelie rente of fourtie Shillinges of lawfull money to be paide at the foresaid fouer most usuall Termes of the yeare by even porcons, And that if the said Annuitie or yearlie rente be behinde in parte or in the whole after anie of the feastes aforesaide in which it ought to be paide, That then it shalbe lawfull to the saide Anthonie Chapell and his Assignes into all and singuler my landes and tenementes hearafter in theis presentes devised to the saide Thomas my soune to entre and distraine, and the distresse to detaine untill he be therof fullie satisfied and paid. Item I will and devise to Thomas Chapell afforesaide my soune all my landes tenementes and hereditamentes not before devised nor bequeathed together with the revercon of all the landes and tenementes before to my wife devised, To have and to hold to the saide Thomas Chapell my soune and to the heires of his bodie lawfullie begotten, And for defaulte of such ysshewe to the saide Richard my seconde soune and to [the] heires males of his bodye lawfullie begotten, And for defaulte of suche yssue the remander therof to the saide Nicholas my youngeste soune and to the heires males of his bodie lawfullie begotten. And for defaulte of suche ysshewe the remainder therof to the righte heires of me the saide Will[ia]m Chapell for ever. Item for my parte of the advowson for Iddesley beinge Fosters graunte which my Brother Thomas haithe in truste, my will is that my said soune Thomas shall have the disposicon of the same. Item I will and devise to everie of my brother Thomas children five markes, and to everie of my saide Cosen John Chapells children fourtie shillinge and to everie of my Brother George his sounes Twentie shillings and to everie of my Brother Anthonies children Twentie shillinges. And to everie of my servauntes at the tyme of my deathe Twentie shillinges. The residewe of all my goodes and chattelles not geven nor bequeathed I give and bequeathe to the saide Cristian my wyfe whom I make my sole executrix of this, my laste will and Testamente. And also I make the saide Thomas Hele *[3]* Anthonye Copleston, my Brother Thomas Chapell and my Cosen John Chapell Overseers of this my laste will and testamente, And to everie of them for ther paines therin

to be taken I give fourtie shillinges or a blacke Gowne. In witnes whearof to theis presentes I have subscribed my name and putte my Seale beinge witnesses therunto those whose names are underwritten. By me William Chapell, *Witnessed by me* Thomas Hele *by me Anthony* Copleston.

A codicell annexed to the laste will and Testamente of me William Chapell nowe Maior of the Cittie of Exeter maide the Seconde daie of December in the Twoe and Twentithe yeare of the Raigne of oure Soveraige ladie Quene Elizabethe and Added to my saide Laste will and Testamente to theis presentes Annexed as followethe:

I William Chapell Maior of the Cittie of Exeter beinge of perfecte remembrance thankes be geven unto allmightie god allthoughe somwhat seicke in bodie. And callinge to mynd that the tyme of mannes deathe is onelie knowen to the moste higheste have therfore perused a will and Testamente by me hearetofore made and to theis presentes annexed, And finding therin somwhat contayned which I did mislike, I have therfore this presente daie of Decembre in the yeare abovesaide firste altered the saide will to theis presentes annexed and revoked that parte therof onelie whearby I had made and willed or ordained my soune Thomas to be ioyncte executor of my saide will and Testamente with Christian my wife and have therby made and ordained the saide Christian my wife to be my hole and sole executrix accordinge as by the saide my will and testamente so altered appeareth. And further I doe by this my Coddicill make and ordaine the said Christian my hoolle and sole executrix of the saide will and Testamente to theis presentes annexed and of all other thinges in this my Codicill to the saide Testamente annexed contayned. And in consideracon therof I doe by this my Codicell to my saide will annexed give unto the saide Thomas my soune All the Lease and Terme which I have to come in and to the Shefe of Brodecliffe in the Countie of Devon and unto everie parte and percell therof. And also I give unto the saide Thomas my soune my neste of Gilte Bowles which I laste boughte and Twoe hundred poundes of lawfull money of Englande to be paide him by my saide executrix Provided that if I in my life tyme do not Sealle unto William Beare a leace for my Tenement called Haie and Claie in Brodecliffe whearby his fine beinge agreed to be one hundred and fourtie poundes maie be payable to my executrix That then ther shalbe paide to my soune Thomas but one Hundred pounds of the said legacie of Two Hundred poundes. Item I further notifie and declare that my will minde and intente is That the Hundred Markes which by my saide laste will to this my Codicill annexed I have geven to the poore and have appoincted no tyme for the paimente therof, That the same shalbe paide by my saide Executrix at suche tyme as unto my overseers named and appoincted in the saide Will and Testamente to theis presentes annexed shalbe thoughte mete. Item I further give unto Roberte Chapell soune of my brother Anthonie

Chapell the some of Six poundes Thirteine shillinges foure pence to be paide him by my saide executrix at suche tyme as it shalbe thoughte good by my said overseers. Item lastelie my intente and meaninge is that all thinges nowe remayninge and beinge in my saide will and Testamente to theise presentes annexed as the same is altered or changed as afforesaide shall stande remaine and be in full force And the same I doe pronounce to be my verie laste will and Testamente in suche maner and forme as the same now is. In witnes wheareof to this presente Codicell I have Subscribed my name and put to my Seale the daie and yeare above in this presente Codicell menconed By me William Chapell, *Witnessed by Anthony* Copleston By me Thomas Chapell By me John Chapell *Sign of George* Chapell.

38B. INVENTORY OF WILLIAM CHAPELL, MERCHANT & ALDERMAN OF ST PETROCK'S PARISH, 18 JANUARY 1580

ECA, Orphans' Court Inventory 28A

Note: there are two copies in roll form of this inventory which are entitled 'The Inventorye of all the goodes, Chattells & debts late belonginge unto Mr William Chappell one of the Aldermen of the Cittie of Exon decessed and praised by Henry Ellacot, John Webb, Robarte Webber, and William Grenewoode the 18th daie of Januarye in the twoo and twentieth yeare of the raigne of our soveraigne ladie Elizabeth by the grace of God Quene of England Ffrance and Irlande defender of the ffaithe &c 1579'.

[1v.] The some of all the goodds of Mr William Chaple comprysed yn his Inventorye and is £2,369 4s 2d; £2359 4s 2d *[sic]*.

Whereof for funeralls & other chardges £104 10s 3d; Also for doubtfful debts £113; Sum £217 10s 3d; So remains £2,151 13s 11d.

Which some of £2,151 13s 11d being devyded yn to three equall partes there and to everie part as folowethe
To the wyff for her 3rd part £717 4s 7d;
To the executrix for his 3rd part £717 4s 7d;
To Thomas Chaple £143 8s 11d;

To Richard Chaple £143 8s 11d;
To Nychus Chaple £143 8s 11d;
To Grace Chaple £143 8s 11d;
To Elizabeth Chaple £143 8s 11d;
[Sum of the five childrens' portions] £717 4s 7d;
Sum £2,151 13s 11d.

Legacyes geven to the chydren
To every of theym yn monye £200 – £1,000;
To Thomas Chaple a nest of bolls £18 9d;
To Richerd & Nichus 2 guilt goblets £10 4s;
To theym one dossen of spones £6 13s 9d;
To the too daughters 2 tankerds guilt £40 10s;
Sum £1,046 8s 6d.

By my accompte it apperethe that there is geven yn legacies more then the 3rd part for the orphangs amounts £329 4s 11d.

[2] The Inventorie of all the goodes chatells and debtes Late belonging unto Mr William Chapell one of the aldermen of the Cittie of Exeter deceased and Prasid by Henry Ellacot, John Webb, Robart Webber and William Grenewoode, the 18th daie of Januarie 1579 [1580]

In the Hall
In the Sealinge and benchis £4 10s;
Item a Joynid Coborde 26s 8d;
Item a Joynid table Borde;
Item a sware table to Joyne with the Longe table Borde;
[Last 2 entries] £3;
Item a Litle Jonid Borde with a Coborde in the same 6s 8d;
Item a Joined forme, and 6 Joyned Stoles 8s;
Item 2 litle stooles with quoshins on them and one Litle Joned Stole 6s 8d;
Item one greate Chaire wrought with needle woorke 10s;
Item a litle Chaire coverid with mockado 2s 6d;
Item 2 Tables with paintid stories 10s;
Item the Glasse with 3 Casmentes 20s;
Item a Coortyne of Redd & greene saye, with narow hanginges of the same with paintid Borders 8s;
Item 8 Quosshins wroght with blew and yelow upon Redd fflaming 20s;
Item 6 Quosshins of black & greene 2s;
Item a long Carpet & a short of venis [Venetian] worck, a litle carpet of dounts and a old Carpet & 2 litle old ones 13s 4d;
Item a paire of Andirons with a paire of Tonges, a fier shovill & a Pike 17s;
Item a Litle Paire of dogges a litle ffier shovill & an Iron barr 3s 4d;
Item Irons wroght to hange the Swordes, hattes & maces 3s 4d;
Item a Comptinge Chest 30s;
Item a Basen & yewer, & 2 yeuer potts 4 bolls of tynne, a Jack & a basen with the Irons to the same 16s;
£16 18s 6d.

In the Rome withowt the Hall
Item a Table Boord with a Joyned ffoorme 3s 4d;
Item a old Chaire Coverid with greene cloth & a Joynid Stoole 20d;
Item an old Carpete, & old staynid Clothes & 2 Shellves 3s 4d;
Item a old Portall with a new lattis 3s 4d;
11s 8d.
In the Buttrey
Item an allmery, 3 Shelves and a Joynid ffoorme, and a litle Stoole 26s 8d;
Item the Buttrey, 12 platters 12 Sawcers, 2 aple disshis more 6 platters, 6 potingers 6 saucers, 2 salet disshis, 6 potage disshes wainge 80 lb – 48s 6d;
Item 6 paire of Candlesticks & a Chafyndisshe 24s;

Item 3 potell pottes, 2 yewer pottes 2 fflower potts, 2 Chamber pottes & 2 litle saltes of Tynne 18s;
£5 17s 2d.

[2v.] In the Chamber over the Hall
Item a Joynid Bedsteede, & a trockle Bede steede 53s 4d;
Item a Joynid Coborde 6s;
Item a Joynid table Boorde and 4 Joynid Stoles 20s;
Item a litle Joynid Chayre wroghte with needle woorck with Cruell 10s;
Item 4 Spruce [?] Chestes £4;
Item 2 Barred Chestes of flanders making 20s;
Item 3 litle Joyned chestes 5s;
Item 2 Joned boxes, & 3 litle ffosletts 5s;
Item Glasse in the wyndowes 20s;
Item the hanginges of the Chamber of payntid Canvas of the Storie of Josephe, and Cortaine of Redd And Greene say before the wyndow 50s;
Item 5 Coortaynes of Redd and Greene mockade, with a ffrenge of Redd, and Greene abowt the Bedd £3 6s 8d;
Item a ffether bed, 2 bolsters and 2 Pillowes £5 6s 8d;
Item a Coverlet of Tapistrie containing 18 Elles £3 6s 8d;

Item one paire of wollen Blanckets & 2 fflaunders Rugges 33*s* 4*d*;

Item Curteins for a bedd [with a ffrenge – crossed through] of Taffata sarremet of Blew and yelow, with a ffrenge of silk of the same Cooloor £5;

Item a new Coveringe for a chaire of neeld woorke with Cruell and silk & ffrengid with silks, and 4 gilt Knoppes £3 6*s* 8*d*;

Item one Covering of a stoole wroght with Cruell and Silke, with a ffrenge of silk, and one Covering of cruell with a ffrenge of Cruell 13*s* 4*d*;

Item a Carpet of dornex 2*s* 6*d*;

Item a Paire of andyrons & a little paire of doggs 10*s*;

Item a dossen of Box trenchers gilt 6*s* 8*d*;

£37 1*s* 10*d*.

Naperie in the same Chamber

Item 4 paire of fyne dowles sheetes 40*s*;

Item 3 paire of shetes of morlers cloth 40*s*;

Item 2 paire of sheetes of Holland 53*s* 4*d*;

Item 19 pillow ties of Holland wherof 10 of them be wrowght £4;

Item 2 Table clothes of damask woorke containing 13 yardes £7;

Item 2 table clothes of dyaper £3 6*s* 8*d*;

Item 2 table Clothes of morles cloth 20*s*;

Item 2 table Clothes of lyne Canvas 10*s*;

Item 3 Towells of damaske worke £3 10*s*;

Item 4 Towells of dyaper £3;

Item 4 Towells of morleis Cloth to Cover the Table 30*s*;

Item 10 Towells wrowght £10;

Item 7 Towells wroght & playne 40*s*;

Item 4 drinking Clothes 3 of Black worke & one of damaske 26*s* 8*d*;

Item a dossen & halfe of napkinges of Black woorke 26*s* 8*d*;

[3] Item 1 dossen and halfe of diaper napkins and 2 old napkins 26*s* 8*d*;

Item 2 dossen and 9 napkins of damask woorke £8 5*s*;

Item 3 dossen of napkins of morleis cloth wherof 2 dossen were wroght £3;

Item 11 napkins of ffyne Canvas 13*s* 4*d*;

Item 12 Cobord Clothes, wherof 5 be wroght £7;

Item 6 Towells for the Jacke and 6 Jack Clothes and 6 clothes to hang over the dore, and 6 Shelve clothes £3 16*s*;

Item 6 yardes of wroght work & frenge to set abowt a Coborde 33*s* 4*d*;

Item 10 Shirtes £5;

£75 17*s* 8*d*.

In the midle Chamber

Item a Joned bedsteede, and a troocke Bedsteede 33*s* 4*d*;

Item a Presse 20*s*;

Item a folding Borde with a Cobord in the same 13*s* 4*d*;

Item 2 danske Chestes, wherof one was a litle one 10*s*;

Item the Glasse in the same chamber 7*s*;

Item the Payntid Hanginges of Canvas 15*s*;

Item a Carpet of dornax and 2 wyndow cloth of greene say with a ffrenge 2*s* 6*d*;

Item the Coortaynes of the Bed of greene saye 20*s*;

Item 2 ffether Beddes, 3 Bolsters & 2 pillows of ffethers £6 13*s* 4*d*;

Item 2 paire of Blankets 1 rugge and a Quylt & a mattresse 40*s*;

Item 2 Coverlets of Tapestrie wherof one is 18 Elles 53*s* 4*d*;

Item a litle paire of dogges & a litle paire of Tonges 16*d*;

Item a Close Chaire, and a Litle Stoole 5*s*;

£17 14*s* 2*d*.

In the maides Chamber

Item a Bedsted Joyned Bedstede and a Trocle Bedd steede 10*s*;

Item 2 fflock Beddes a paire of Blanckets a Rugg & a Coverlet & 2 Bolsters of fflocks & one of fethers & a Testor Payntid with a pece of Payntid cloth payntid [sic] & a window Cloth of greene saie 40*s*;

Item the Glasse in the same chamber 5*s*;

Item a Joyned Chest & a little Joind Stoole 8*s*;

£3 3*s*.

Naperi in the same Chamber

Item 12 paire of Canvas sheetes £4;

Item 8 paire of dowles sheetes £4;

Item 12 pillow tyes 24s;

Item 13 Table Clothes £4;

[3v.] Item 3 Short table Clothes for the Kitchin 4s;

Item 10 dossen of table nappkins £3 6s 8d;

Item 2 dossen of Towells 26s 8d;

Item 6 drincking Clothes wherof 3 be wrought 17s;

Item 8 hande Towells for the kytchen 8 [sic] and 12 canvas
   clothes for the Kitchin 3s 4d;

£19 1s 8d.

In the fore Hall

Item a Table Boorde 53s 4d;

Item a ffoorme & 6 Stooles 13s 4d;

Item the Seelinge of the same hall 7s;

Item a Plat Cobord or a side table 20s;

Item a Spruce Chest 40s;

Item a litle paire of dogges 16d;

Item the Glasse 40s;

£15 8s.

Apparell

Item a Gowne of Scarlet ffacid with ffoynes & ffurred with
   squerells a Scarlet cloke, with a velet tipet £16;

Item a Gowne of Browne blew with a welt of velet & facid
   with ffoynes £4;

Item a Gowne of Browne blew with a welt of velet & facid
   with Booge 53s 4d;

Item a Gowne of Browne Blew with a welt of velet & facid
   with satyn 53s 4d;

Item a old Gowne of Browne blew with a Lace of Silk & facid
   with Boge 20s;

Item a old Gowne of Browne blew and facid with damask 16s;

Item a Cassack of damask gardid with velet & set with
   ffrenge £4 6s 8d;

Item a nother Cassack of damask gardid with velet & frengid
   £3;

Item a old Cassack of damask & a old Cassack of woolsteede
   10s;

Item a Cote of Cloth xvis

Item a dooblet of Satyn & a paire of Bodyes of Satyn 20s;

Item a paire of hose 10s;

Item a old Cloke 12s;

Item 2 Cappes 6s 8d;

Item 2 velet night cappes, and a paire of gloves 6s;

£37 10s.

In the fore chamber

Item a Joyned Presse 53s 4d;

Item 2 Bedstedes Joyned & a trockell Bedsteede & 2 old
   testors painted 13s 4d;

Item a Brusshing Borde 12d;

Item a flaunders Chest Barred and 2 old Chestes 26s 8d;

Item a fether bedd a bolster and a pillow of fethers 26s 8d;

Item 3 fflock beddes with 3 bolsters 20s;

Item 2 paire of blanckets & 3 Quiltes 20s;

Item the glasse in the same chamber 15s;

[4] in the same chamber

Item 2 Peces of Redd & greene Saye £4 13s 4d;

Item a Carpet of Tapestrie £5;

Item a nother Carpet of tapistrie 53s 4d;

Item a square turkie Carpet 10s;

Item 2 Longe Carpets and one short of Cruell & wooll 46s 8d;

Item a Coverlet of Arras £6;

Item 5 wyndo Clothes 6s 8d;

Item 6 Cusshins of arras unmade £6 13s 4d;

Item a dossen of Quosshins of nedle woorke £6;

Item halfe a dossen of quosshins of Tapestrie 53s 4d;

Item a dossen of Greene Quooshins 12s;

£45 4s 8d.

napery in the same chamber

Item 5 paire of dowles sheetes & 3 paire of Canvas sheetes £3;

Item 12 Boorde clothes £3;

Item 5 dossen of table napkins 40s;

Item 2 hande Towells wroght with Blew 2s 8d;

£8 2s 8d.

In the highest chambre

Item a Brusshinge Borde 6*d*;

Item 2 old Chestes 3*s* 4*d*;

Item 2 Costletts 53*s* 4*d*;

Item a paire of allmayne Rivets 10*s*;

Item 2 boes & 2 sheves of arroes & 2 Billes 8*s*;

Item 2 Calivers with one moryon & a Scull 2 flasks & toch boxe 26*s* 8*d*;

Item a paire of Iron dogges 2*s*;

Item the Glasse [in the Kychin – crossed through] 22*s*;

Item a paire of Bootes & 1 barels [*sic*] and 2 litle Barells with fethers and an old Cap of steele places 5*s*;

£6 10*s* 10*d*.

Pewter in the same chambre

Item 6 dossen of disshes 3 dossen of Sawcers, 6 podage disshes, a voyder, & a boll of tine waiing a hundreth 86 lb – £5;

more 3 dossen and 4 plates a bason & yeor & 12 fflower pottes 26*s* 8*d*;

£6 6*s* 8*d*.

more in the Buttrie

Item 2 Quarte pottes, 3 pynte potts & halfe a pynt pot 6*s* 8*d*;

Item a perfume pott, & a latyn Candelestick to hange against the wall 5*s*;

Item 5 stone pottes 2*s*;

Item 4 dossen of trenchers 8*d*;

14*s* 4*d*.

[5] In the Kitchen

Item 8 Cawdrons containing 63 lb at 7*d* – 36*s* 9*d*;

Item one great panne containing 14 lb at 9*d* – 9*s* 9*d*;

Item a coper Cawdron containing 17 lb [at] 10*d* – 14*s* 1*d*;

Item 5 brasse pottes containing 146 lb [at] 4½*d* – 54*s* 9*d*;

Item 3 Chafers of brasse containing 26 lb [illegible] – 10*s* 10*d*;

Item a posnet of brasse containing 8½ lb [at] 4½*d* – 3*s* 2*d*;

Item 3 Ladells of Brasse & 2 scomers of Brasse containing 4½ lb – 2*s*;

Item 2 Litle Scillets containing 3 lb – 2*s*;

Item a litle Cawdron containing 2 pownde;

Item a Lattyn Bocket containing 5 lb;

[Last 2 entries] 4*s* 8*d*;

Item a warmyng panne & a Colander containing 7 lb – 5*s*;

Item a Chafyndisshe 2*s* 6*d*;

Item 8 Candellstickes 5*s*;

£7 10*s* 7*d*.

Item 2 dossen of & halfe of platter 1 dossen of Sawcers 6 potage disshes, 6 plates, 5 other od disshes, 2 Basons, a voyder containing 88 lb at 6*d* – 44*s*.

[Item a paire of Rackes containing 44 lb – crossed through];

Item 3 drippinge pannes containing 28 lb – 6*s*;

Item a dripping panne of white plate 6*d*;

Item 4 Iron cawdrons containing 84 lb – 10*s*;

Item a morter of brasse and a pestell of Iron 2*s* 6*d*;

Item 7 Spittes of Iron containing 39 lb – 8*s*;

Item 2 Iron crocks containing 44 lb – 5*s*;

Item a paire of Rackes and dogges of Iron containing 52 lb – 10*s* 10*d*;

Item 4 hangins, 4 pot crookes 2 fflesshe Hookes a ffier pike of Iron, a brandize, a paire of Tonges, a fyer pan, a toster containing 48 lb – 10*s*;

Item 3 gredirons containing 15 lb – 3*s*;

Item a barr of Iron, & an Iron to set before the pannes 3*s* 4*d*;

Item 2 dressing Boordes 6*s* 8*d*;

Item a Coope for Capons 3*s* 4*d*;

Item a hogshed with salte 2 powdring Tubbes, & 4 other tubbes & 3 stooles, & shelves 3*s* 6*d*;

Item 2 Chopping Knyves 8*d*;

Item 6 treene platters with other disshes of woode 12*d*;

Item Sestorne of Ledd 40*s*;

Item 3 Bockets 6*d*;

Item 2 Canstikes of white plate 4*d*;

£7 19*s* 2*d*.

In the seller

Item a berer for drinck 2*s*;

Item 6 Coastes 6s 8d;

Item 4 tressells, 2 plancks 4 Boordes 3s;

Item 4 wasshing tubbes, a powdring tubbe a Coole a Lanttern 3 bolles a musterd mill & other trasshe 6s 8d;

Item a dossen of woode 8s;

£1 6s 4d.

[5] Plate

at 6s 6d the unc

Item 3 doble Gilt Bolls tochid and graven containing 55 onces & halfe £18 9d;

at 6s the onc

Item 3 Gilt Goblets dooble gilt tochid containing 51 unces – £15 6s;

at 6s once

Item 1 Gilte Goblet dooble gilt tochid containing 16 unces and halfe £4 19s;

at 6s once

Item 3 Gilt Tanckers dooble gilt tochid containing 57 oncs & half £17 5s;

at 6s once

Item one ale Cupp with a Cover doble gilt & tochid containing 13 oncs & quarte £3 19s 6d;

at 5s 6d

Item one Salt of silver with a Cover doble gilt tochid containing 18 Oncs & half £6 9s 3d;

at 6s onc

Item 1 trenchor salt doble gilt containing 2 oncs quartor and farthinge gold waight 13s 10d;

at 5s once

Item 1 Salte of silver with a Cover doble gilt, containing 9 uncs & halfe, tochid 47s 6d;

at 5s once

Item 3 Goblets parcell gilt tochid, containing 68 oncs & half £12 2s 6d;

at 4s 10d onc

Item one ale Cupp with a cover parcell gilt tochid, containing 11 owncs & halfe 56s 7d;

at 5s 2d once

Item 2 trencher plates parcell Gilt tochid containing 10 unces 51s 8d;

at 5s once

Item 13 Spones of silver with postells [apostles] parcell gilt tochid containing 26 oncs 3 Quarters £6 13s 9d;

at 4s 10d Onc

Item 12 Silver Spoones parcell gilt tochid, containyn 17 oncs halfe & halfe quarter £4 5s 2d;

at 4s 8d onc

Item 9 Spones of Silver parcell Gilt containing 10 onces halfe and halfe Quarter 49s 7d;

at 5s once

Item 5 stone Cuppes garnisshid and Gilt, Contayning by Estymation 34 onces £8 10s;

at 4s 8d

Item one stone Cupp with a cover and the mowith garnishid with whit Silver by Estimacion 3 unces & halfe 16s 4d;

£109 5s 5d.

Item a Case of Knives 6s 8d.

Leases

Item a Lease of a Stable and a Garden in the parisshe of St Pancrace in Exeter £20.

[5v.] In the Shopp

Item a Joyned Chest 20s;

Item 4 lb of colord peceing [?] threde 6s 8d;

Item 4 Shelves & shelfe clothis and a Lattis 5s;

Item a fflaunders beame and Scales 6s 8d;

Item 1 hundreth & quarter of Iron waightes 10s;

Item 1 hundreth Lack 3 lb of Ledd waights at 10s;

Item 3 lb of Brazen waights 2s;

Item 2 paire of Ballance 3s 4d;

£3 8s 8d.

In Thomas Chapells back Howse

Item 14 Bagges of clome containing 31 C 2 quarters & 4 lb at 22s the C – £34 13s 10d;

Item half a Case of glasse 10s;
£34 13s 10d;
10s.

In the Stable
Item a Geldinge and a nagge £7 10s;
Item a Sadell and a Bridell with that belonges therto 5s;
Item the Haye in the lofte 10s;
Item a old portall, a litle Ladder & 2 olde hogsheds & a seame
    stone and an old dore 3s;
Item a nother old Sadle & a bridell 5s;
£8 8s;
5s.

in the owithowse
Item 5 old hogesheds & a pipe 12 old peeces of Tymbre, with
    one Longe pece, with other old Peces 13s 4d.

in the entrie
Item 2 old Cages for capons 10s;
Item a Litle peeke, and a donge pik 6d;

In the garden
Item a Bocket and a chaine for a well 2s 6d;
£1 6s 4d.

debtes
[Item of Thomas Perye of Glocester by a bill £13 – crossed
    through];
Item there is to receve of Wm Beare of Broade Cliste for the
    ffyne of a Bargayne [£100 – crossed through] 40s;
Item of Wm Germyn of the same parissh for a ffyne £20;
Item Davie Baggewell owith upon an accompte from Morlen
    [?] that Thomas Chapell must pay 34 ffrancks;
Mr Knight upon an obligacion £100;
[Sum crossed through and illegible].

[6] debtes due by specialties
Phillip Yarde & John Illecombe £62 10s;

Henrie Ellis by Bill £22 16s;
Thomas Ellis by Bill £30 8s;
Richard Tom'she [?] and John Sampford £25;
Robert Webber by Bill £11 4s 2d;
Thomas Herle and Walter Herle £110;

Sir [Gilbert – crossed through] Humfre Gilbert and Sir John
    Gilbert £110;
Philipp and Vincent Moore £11 10s;
John Marshall and his Soune £7 in tynne;
Henrie Borowgh by obligacon £30;
Item for rent by him £20;
Thomas Pais £7 10s;
[Thomas Weare £4 10s – crossed through];
Robert Austen £20;
[Nicholas Spicer £60 – crossed through];
Mr John Farindon £10;
Bolt and Webbe £10;
Tusserd of Brodeclist 10s;
Owen Cook £19;
Thomas Chapell £46 3s 10d;
Thomas Trubervill £35;
Agnes Coyle £30;
Mr Chauncelor £100;
Thomas Dare & John Davye of Stock Lande £20;
Mighell Beare 10s;
Sum £1,029 19s 6d.

Item in monay £191 10s.

in adventures a Brode
Item Nicholas Spicer £60;
Item Robart Vynton £30;
John Hayward In the Iles £34;
Thomas Ellis in Spayne £321 19s;
John Barstable £33;
Sum £478 19s.

debtes dowtful
Thomas Perye of Glocester £13;
Mr Knight £100.

ECA, Orphans' Court Inventory 28A [Roll; 2 copies]
Note *mm. 1–6* are copies of flat inventory.

[m. 6] The Inventorye of all the goods Cattalls, Chattells
& debts late belonginge unto the said William Chappell
decessed at his Berton of Brockwill within the parishe
of Broadecliste in the Countie of Devon, and praised by
William Beare, Reymonde Medlande Edward Ratcliffe,
and Robert Dalley the [blank] daie of [blank] in the 22nd
yeare of the raigne of or soveraigne ladie Elizabeth by
the grace of God Quene of Englande France & Irlande
defendor of the ffaiethe &c 1579

In the Hall
Item a framed tabell borde with one leaf 2 formes a plank that
standeth for a benche a litell square tabell with a tressell, a
Cubborde a ioyned Cheare a frame stolle 2 litell Cheares, 2
litell foote stooles 20*s*;
Item a paire of dogges a litell tablett by the spewringe a latten
Candelstick 12 litell grene Quishions 10*s*;
Item the barr of the Chymney, 11 foote of glasse with 2
casements one Carpett that lieth uppon the borde & a longe
foote stoole before the windowe 12*s*;
Sum [blank].

In the Parlor
Item a framed borde with a leaffe a ioyned forme a benche &
a Carpett on the tabell 16*s*;
Item a standinge bedd with a truckell bedd a litell ioyned
Cheare a litell shelff with 2 litell tressells to laie cloaks or
hatts on and a longe foote stoole before the bedd 40*s*;
Item a paire of tabells & a litell Chest 3*s* 4*d*;
Item a ffetherbedd, 2 fether bolsters a Coverlett of tapestrie a
paire of blancketts 5 Courtens of redd and grene saie with
the frame about the bedd £4;

[m. 7] Item 12 foote of glasse with three casements & 32
yeards of stayned cloth 15*s*;
Sum [blank].

In the Chamber over the Parlor
Item a standinge bedd & a truckell bedd, a presse, a Chest 2
litell shelffs, 4 tressells, a Standinge Cheare a litell stolle 2
longe foote stolles by the bedd & a close cheare of welgars
[?] £3 13*s* 4*d*;
Item 17 foote of glasse with 2 casements 8*s*;
Item a ffetherbedd, 2 fetherbolsters 4 ffether pillowes a whit
quilte, a paire of blancketts 2 Courtens of redd and grene
saye, the frame aboute the bedd & one stayned cloth before
the windowe £4;
Item in the presse 6 quishens 3 shelf clothes of redd & grene
saye, one of redd clothe for the same shelf 2 yeards of
painted clothe a hatt and a Cappe a brush & a paire of
doggs 20*s*;
Sum [blank].

In the maides Chamber
Item a beddsteede & a truckell bedd, a brushinge borde a litell
square borde to laie clothes on and twoo olde Chests 9*s*;
Item 2 flockbeddes, 2 flock bolsters a redd Coverlett & a
paire of blanckets 13*s* 4*d*;
Item a ffetherbedd in the truckelbeddstede a fether bolster a
paire of blancketts, a Coverlett, and a quilt 30*s*;
Item 13 foote of glace & 2 casements 6*s*;
Sum [blank].

In the Chamber over the Kitchen
Item a standinge bed with a tester a truckell bedd a brushing
borde with 2 tressells & a olde fforme 13*s* 4*d*;
Item a ffether bedd 2 flock bolster[s] a Coverlett, a paire of
blancketts a flock bedd and a flock bolster with a Coverlett
30*s*;
Item 23 foote of glasse with 2 Casements 10*s*;
Sum [blank].

In waters [? Walter's] Chamber
Item a beddstede with a truckellbedd a hamper 2 duste bedds 2 dust bolsters a whit Coverlett, 2 paire of blancketts a olde quilte a olde blewe mantell, a yearde of Lettis 16*s*;
Sum [blank].

In the Chese Chamber
Item 4 bords to laie Cheses on, 2 olde hampers to putt woll on 3*s* 4*d*;
Item 2 Chese racks 40 cheses & 2 tressells 30*s*;
Item 2 barrells to kepe gearts 2 gallonds of stame [?], a paire of olde weights 30 lb of ledden weights 7*s*;
Item 17 lb of woll, a litell stoole, a yearde of lattis & 5 lb of course russet yearne 23*s*;
Sum [blank].
In the spence
Item 2 selten vessells & a salte barrell 2*s*;
Item 3 gallonds of Butter 7*s*;
Item a pottell of Honye 2*s*;
Item a hoxehedd and a barrell 2*s*;
Item 3 litell glasses to kepe water a goblett to put beer on & a brandize 4*s*;
Item 2 foote of lattis of the windowe & 2 litell shelves 4*d*;
Sum [blank].

In the Buttrey
Item 12 platters, 12 podgers, 12 sawcers, 12 potage dishes 30*s*;
Item 12 litell sawcers & 12 flower potts 6*s*;
Item 6 platters, 8 podgers, 3 bassens one boll 2 litell tynen cuppes and 3 salte sellers 14*s*;
In the hall 3 standinge plates one litell Ewer pott a litell tynen pott 6*s* 8*d*;
Item in the Buttrey 4 candelsticks 7 stoninge Cuppes with Covers and without Cover and 2 Chamber potts 6*s* 8*d*;
Item 2 litell brasen flower potts, a Chaffen dishe & a morter and pestell of Copper 3*s*;
Item 6 silver spones 20*s*;
Item 4 dossen of trenchers, 12 smale trenchers, 4 litell glasses and twoo [blank] glasses 20*d*;

Item a Amarey a forme, 7 shelves with painted clothes a hamper 2 brishes to swepe the howse withall 8*s* 8*d*;
Item 3 foote and halfe of glasse 18*d*;
Item a sacke & a latte skomer 6*d*;
Item 7 drincking glasses 2*s* 6*d*;
Sum [blank].

In Lynnynge
Item in Mrs Chamber 3 paire of sheits 20*s*;

Item 2 Cubborde clothes a presse clothe & 4 paire of pillibears 13*s* 4*d*;
Item 3 dossen of napkings & 4 tabell clothes 20*s*;
Item 2 drinckinge clothes a wollen clothe 3 kearchers 6 towells 6*s* 8*d*;
Item in the maids chamber in the chest, 8 paire of Canvas sheits 2 longe course tabell clothes and 6 borde clothes 29*s*;
Item 3 towells 5 hande towells 8 chese clothes & 3 dishe clothes 4*s*;
Item in the parlor a litell cheste a paire of dowlis sheits 3 tabell clothes 3 dossen of napkings a rolinge towell 6 wrought pilloties 3 plaine pilloties a drinckinge cloth 2 Cubborde clothes 2 towells for the bason 2 Jack clothes a dore cloth a cloth frenged £3 6*s* 8*d*;
[*m. 8*] Sum [blank].

In the Kitchen
Item 2 greate plancks with feet and a fourme, a litell Coupe for Capons and 6 shelfes 2 stoles & a stock 2 piles for the oven 3*s*;
Item a paire of teekes & doggs 3 hangings for the Crocks 3 pott howkes a fleshe Crowk & a ladell 10*s*;
Item the barr of the Chymney 2 brandizes a greddell a toster and 4 spitts of Iron 13*s* 4*d*;
Item 4 Iron Cawdrons 2 Iron Crocks 13*s* 4*d*;
Item 2 brassen Crocks 10*s*;
Item 2 Iron drepinge pannes 3 latten dreepinge pannes a skemer and a drepinge ladell 4*s*;

Item 2 greate Brasen pannes 3 litell brassen Caudrons a skillett 2 Choppinge knives and a shridding kniff 43s 4d;

Item a Cowle 7 bucketts 3 washinge boles 8 treing dishes a paire of billis 5s;

Item a paire of tonges a pik a fier panne, a hower glasse & 4 litell lade bolles 3s 4d;

Item 10 fleches of Bacon 40s;

Item a paire of Sheares, 6 foote of glasse & a stoninge Cuppe 2s 6d;

Sum [blank].

In the milke howse

Item a brak 5 shelves, a plank a lanterne, a musterde mill 7 Chese vates and a selter 4 tankers, a gratter and a letherne Bottell 8s 4d;

Item 12 litell brasen pannes £3;

Item 7 gallonde Crocks of earth 5 earther pichers 3 pancrocks 2 Clomen Chaffers a Candell Moull of Clome a pippercorne a frienge panne of Iron, 6 basketts in the entry a Coupe for Capons 3s;

Sum [blank].

In the malte howse

Item 2 olde hoxeheds a uten vate, a greate Cowle 2 Chese wrings and other trashe 10s;

Item 8 sacks of malte, weet and drie, made and unmade 40s;

Item 6 boushells of Barley malte 10s;

Sum [blank].

In the Brewehowse

Item 16 coasts for beare 2 trendells 14 keves & vates & mollen borde 2 Jeves 2 Hucmucks a greate black baskett 2 trucks to beare vats with all a tunner and a ranger 2 sacks 10 seaves and semetts [?] 40s;

Item 2 malte sacks, 8 baggs a dawe sheite and 2 breade clothes 10s;

Item a ffurnys £3;

Item a pik a Colerack a ladder by the brewhowse wall and a grendinge stone 5s;

Sum [blank].

The Cattell

Item 6 labor Oxen and 2 fatt oxen £19;

Item 8 keene and 10 yonge cattell £26 6s 8d;

Item 2 labouringe guildings £4;

Item a mare and a Colte 53s 4d;

Item 66 shepe yonge and olde £10;

Item 7 piggs and a varren [?] sowe 46s 8d;

Sum [blank].

In the Stabell

Item 2 pack saddels, 2 paire of Crowks 2 pair of panniers with that belonges therunto 9s;

Sum [blank].

Towles to the howse

Item 3 Iron wadgs 3 sawes, one Iron barr a pickas 2 showles 2 mattocks 2 howkes a ax 2 dunge picks & 4 Corne picks 13s 4d;

Item a paire of Whiles and a butt with a litell slide to drawe tymber 40s;

Item 59 sawed bords & plancks 20s;

Item 3 beames for a sowle a paire of whells a paire of hames [?] & tresses a payr of Harrowes a Sheare & Culter for a sowle 10s;

Sum [blank].

Leasses Corne in the grounde & Barne, Tymber woode and other things as ffolloweth

Item one lease for certaine yeares yet enduring of three Acres of meadowe in Wishe Meadow praised at £20;

Item 4 acrees of Corne in the grounde 33s 4d;

Item 9 okes at Cliste St George 45s;

Item 6 okes more at Carswill 10s;

Item one ok at Haye and Claye with certaine woode made at Brockwill 12s;

Item 3 okes at South Whimple 6s 8d;

Item 6 dossen of wood in a rick at Clist St George by
    estimacon 24*s*;
Item the donge at Brockwill 20*s*;
Item 2 mowes of Corne and Corne in the Barne £33 6*s* 8*d*;
Item Haye at Brockwill £4;
Item tymber unwrought 20*s*;
[m. 8v.] Item woode and ffurse 33*s* 4*d*;
Item the pultrey 6*s* 8*d*;
Item a while barrow with all other trash about the howse 6*s*
    8*d*;
Sum [blank].

Sum total [blank].

Of which some [blank] Chappell wiefe and Executrix of the
said William Chappell desireth to be allowed as hereafter
ffolloweth

For funeralls *viz* his Buriall and other chargs
Firstly she asketh allowans for the blacks £64 9*s*;
Item delivered unto the poore £4;
Item paid for the Chest 5*s*.

39A. ADMINISTRATION OF WILLIAM TRIVETT, ALDERMAN, 15 MAY 1579

National Archives PROB 11/61/537
Note: Tryvet was named as a parishioner of St Mary Major in 1564 (DRO, 51/1/6/5). William 'Trevett' died in London and
administration of his estate was granted to his widow Johan on 17 May 1579 and the will was proved in November of that year.
Recognisances were entered into on 31 December 1580 for Trevett's son Peter (ECA, Book 141, folio 69 dorse).

In the name of God Amen Willyam Trivett late of the Cittie
of Exon Alderman deceased whils he lived *viz* the ffiftenth
Daye of Maye *Anno Domini* 1579, beinge sick in body but of
verie good and perfecte mynde and remembraunce, before
diverse honest persons, did make and declare his last will
and testament *nuncupative* [orally] in manner and forme in
effecte as followeth. *Viz* the saide William Trivett, beinge
demanded howe he wolde leave his wife, answered that he
wolde leave her aswell provided for, and in as good case, as he
other husbande did leave her, and better. And beinge further
asked whether it were his mynde that his saide wife shoulde
be his executrix he sayde yea. Item he beinge also demanded

what he woolde geve his daughter Marcella Trivett, which
was then onely unmaried, he made answeare and saide that he
gave her asmuch as every othere of his Daughters had yf his
goods woolde so farre reache. The premisses were spoken and
don in effecte, as is above declared in pure and hearinge of
Thomas Gee, Thomas Spicer, Thomas Edwardes and others.
Note: It is alleged that Joanna failed to produce the will but
William Drury states that he has seen it and that William
Trivett was of sound mind. William Drury undertakes
that he will see that Joanna Trivet produces the will in the
Prerogative Court of Canterbury in London on 18 May 1580
in the presence of William Saye, Notary Public.

39B. INVENTORY OF WILLIAM TRYVET, ALDERMAN, 4 JUNE 1579

ECA, Orphans' Court Inventory 28B

[1] **An Inventory** of all and singuler the gooddes and cattalls of William Tryvet, late one of the Alderman of the citie of Exeter decessed Taken and had [by – crossed through] the 4th daye of June 1579 in the one and twentie yere of the reigne of our sovereigne ladie Queene Elizabeth By John Jones Goldsmyth, Richarde Newman, Thomas Spicer, and Myles Lambert: Who were sworne before Me Richarde Prowze maior Mr John Blackaller one of the Justices of the saide citie and others for the trewe praysement of the same

In the Haule
Fyrst 6 cusshinges of greene cloth and 6 carpetts of the same 10*s*;
Item a turkey karpet £5 5*s* [? part crossed through];
Item a Cobarde 16*s*;
Item 2 litle side bordes 10*s*;
Item a ioyned table borde and a ioyned forme 20*s*;
Item a backe of Iron in the chymney 2*s* 8*d*;
Item a Bason and an ewer of tyn, a cobberde cloth, a pepper box, an erthen dyshe and a glasse 6*s* 8*d*;
Item 3 brusshes for clothes 6*d*;
Item the glasse in the wyndowe 12*s*;
Item the Seeling of waynescot £4;
Sum [£12 2*s* 10*d* – crossed through] £8 2*s* 10*d*.

In the Shopp
Item in druggs apoticarie ware, a Shopp chest Two Stills, with their appurtenancs certen balanses and waightes & morters and pestells, and other necessaries apperteyning to the saide Shopp and science of apoticarye £65 12*s* 8*d*;
Sum £65 12*s* 8*d*.

[1v.] **In the higher parlor**
Item the Seling of wynscot and paynted clothes and a plancke and a frame 45*s*;

Item a clok bagg and three cortyns of See and a chere of strawe 8*s*;
Item 3 chests 6*s* 8*d*;
Item a basket & a knyff of wodd to tak upp a table 8*d*;
Item a dozen of ffyne trenchers paynted 10*s*;
Item the glasse in the wyndowe 12*s*;
Item 3 hangings of greene & redd sea 13*s* 4*d*;
Item an Irishe rugg 2*s* 6*d*;
[Sum £4 2*s* 4*d* – crossed through] Sum £4 18*s* 2*d*.

In the lowe parler
Item the Seeling of waynscot £4;
Item the glasse in the wyndowes 25*s*;
Item 2 cortyns for the wyndowes 5*s*;
Item a byble & a booke of common prayer 13*s* 4*d*;
Sum £6 3*s* 4*d*.

In the newe chamber
Item a ffaier Bedstede £5;
Item 5 taffata cortyns frenged with silk to put about the said bedd £3 10*s*;
Item a counter borde with a lock and a kaye 5*s*;
Item a paior of Andirons a paier of tonges and a ffier Shovell 8*s*;
Item 3 ioyned stoles 3*s*;
Item the glasse in the wyndowes 20*s*;
Item the Seeling about the said chamber £4;
Item a faier coverlet, and a wrought coffyn of sylk £4 6*s* 8*d*;
Sum £17 12*s* 8*d*.

In the chamber over the lytel style
Item 4 [?] corsletts with their ffurniture and one almon ryvet with his ffurniture [superscript: these cosletts be my lady Tayllors] 33*s* 4*d*;
Item a Calyver with his furniture 10*s*;

Item an Avindy [?] a coberde one pece of olde seling one olde planck and 2 ioyned stoles 3 chese vates & one trene platter 14*s*;

Item fower pounde of candles 12*d*;

Sum 58*s* 4*d*.

[2] **In the two chambers** over the higher parler

Item a presse, a beddstede and a troklebedd 25*s*;

Item a ffether bedd, a bolster, a pillowe a coverlet, 2 blancketts 33*s* 4*d*;

Item 6 wrought cusshines of one sorte, and 6 of an other sorte 26*s* 8*d*;

Item 5 other cusshains 2*s* 6*d*;

Item a litle paynted cloth of the prodigall sone 2*d*;

Item a bedstede 2*s* 6*d*;

Item 2 ffetherbeddes 2 bolsters, 3 pillowes, a paier of blancketts, one paire of shetes, and an olde coverlet 33*s* 4*d*;

Item a Chese racke, and certen olde paynted clothes, a chest, an olde mantell a coffyne, and a valence and frenge for a bedd stede 3*s* 4*d*;

[Item a litle truncke 16*d* – crossed through];

Sum £6 8*s* 2*d*.

In the woll chamber

Item 20 pounde of blacke woll and 20 pounde of lam tawe 33*s* 4*d*;

Item 2 pounde of white yarne 2*s* 8*d*;

Item 2 ioyned stoles a marking hamer ten olde hampers and other trashe 16*d*;

Item an olde bedstede, two tornes, two bordes a stole, and a pounde of browne threede 5*s* 4*d*;

Item for scales & weightes 6*s*;

Sum £2 8*s* 8*d*.

In the higher lofte

Item 18 lynges, and 8 mylwyls 15*s* 4*d*;

Item 116 cople of Newland ffyshe 10*s*;

Item 2 olde coffers 2 olde maundes & other trashe 12*d*;

Sum £1 6*s* 4*d*.

In the Styll chamber and in the Boyes chamber

Item 3 ffetherbeddes 3 bolsters 2 coverletts one paier of blancketts 2 olde testers 2 borde bedstedes, one trokle bedd, one olde coffer, one stole of strawe, 2 planckes, and one hanging borde 26*s* 8*d*;

Sum 26*s* 8*d*.

[2v.] **In the gallery**

Item the Seeling and 2 shelves 10*s* 6*d*;

Item the Glasse and 4 casements 12*s*;

Sum £1 2*s* 6*d*.

In the Kytchyn

Item in brasse candlestickes wayng 16 pounde 10*s*;

Item a Copper Kettell and brasse pannes waying 51 pounde at 8*d* the pounde 34*s*;

Item [3 brasse Crockes – crossed through] an olde pan which Thomasine Shorte claymeth waying 28 pounde [blank];

Item 3 brasse crockes waying 71 pounde at [8*d* – crossed through] 4*d* the pounde 23*s* 8*d*;

Item in Iron spitts, drypyng panns and other Iron stuffe waying [16 pounde – crossed through] 86 pounde at 3*d* the pounde 21*s* 6*d*;

Item a bealnce and Scales and 213 pounde in wayghtes 18*s*;

Item the Seeling, an olde borde, 4 shelves a ioyned stole, a forme and other trasshe 24*s*;

Item a Sinker of ledd 13*s* 4*d*;

Item 3 chopping knives two boketts a tubb, and other trifells 2*s* 4*d*;

Item the glasse in the wyndowes 2*s*;

Item an Iron barr in the Chymney 2*s* 6*d*;

Item a litle caldron 16*d*;

Sum £7 [11*s* 4*d* – crossed through] 12*s* 8*d*.

In pewter vessell

Item in pewter vessell 11 score pownde at 6*d* the pounde £5 10*s*;

Item in pewter potts and candlesticks 28 pounde at 6*d* the pounde 14*s*;

Sum £6 4*s*.

Napery

Item 10 fayer towells 40*s*;

Item 2 diaper bordeclothes, and two dozen of diaper napkyns 26*s* 8*d*;

Item 4 dozen and 4 table napkyns 18*s*;

Item 5 bordeclothes 20*s*;

Item 4 litle bordeclothes for a side borde 4*s*;

Item 6 other bordeclothes 16*s*;

Item 5 dozen and 8 table napkyns 26*s* 8*d*;

Item 2 hande towells 6*s* 8*d*;

Item 15 yardes of Normandy canvas 26*s* 8*d*;

Item 7 paier of sheetes and one sheet good & bad 33*s* 4*d*;

Item 4 cubberd clothes and a bredd napkyn 10*s*;

Item 7 pilloweties 14*s*;

Item 3 yardes 3 quarters of cresse 2*s* 6*d*;

Sum £12 4*s* 6*d*.

[3] **His apparell**

Item 3 cassacks of silke garded with velvet £5;

Item 3 satten dubletts: 2 of them new slyved, and one olde and done 36*s* 8*d*;

Item one paier of Gaskyns of sylk grograyne, and an other paier of other [sylke – crossed through] grograyne garded with vellet 30*s*;

Item one paier of stockyns 2*s* 6*d*;

Item 2 cotes one Jerkyn 2 cassackes and one olde lether Jerkyn 22*s*;

Item 7 yardes of redd carsey 18*s* 8*d*;

Item a skarlet gowne with a clok of scarlet and a typpet of velvet £10;

Item 2 black gownes furred with lambe and facid with ffoynes, and welted with vellet £8;

Item an other black gowne faced with satten, and welted with vellet £5;

Item an other black gowne faced with satten and welted with vellet 40*s*;

Item a black gowne faced with budge and lyned with lambe with a welte of vellet 30*s*;

Item an olde russet gowne 10*s*;

Item a shorte clok with slyves 10*s*;

Item 8 shyrtes 25*s* 4*d*;

Item 3 rounde capps and two vellet nyght capps and one of satten 6*s* 8*d*;

Item 4 handekarches 8*s*;

Item a vellet powche and a skarf 5*s*;

Item 2 paier of newe shewes, and one payer of pantafells 3*s* 2*d*;

Item a fflannyn peticote 2*s* 4*d*;

Item 2 paier of bootes and one paier of shewes 6*s* 8*d*;

Item 2 trusses 12*d*;

Item one olde gowne of blacke 13*s* 4*d*;

Item 3 golde ringes, being a turkes, a synet and a Jemye waying 3 quarters of an ownce £5;

Sum £44 11*s* 4*d*.

In the Brewhowse

Item a Bottome of a ffornes 20*s*;

Item certen brewing vessells, and 2 olde hoggeshedds and a capons coupe 10*s*;

[Item 3 rackes of Iron, a spade and a chopping knyffe 14*s* – crossed through; superscript: these be my lo: Tayllors];

Item 45 baggs of alame waying 206 pounde a pece: at 22*s* the hundred amounts to £101 13*s* 7*d*;

Sum £103 3*s* 8*d*.

[3v.] **In the Seller**

Item certen Barrells tubbs and trasshe 20*s*;

Item a bashynge tubb 5*s*;

Item the wood in the Seller and the churche yarde 16*s*;

Item in bacon 10*s*;

Item 2 litle reryng piggs 8*s*;

Sum [54*s* – crossed through] 59*s*.

Certen Sheepe and **stuff** which was upon the ground at
  Duryherde

Item 72 old Shepe: whereof some are yeues: which yeues with
  their lamb are accompted but one Sheepe at 4*s* 8*d* a pece –
  £16;

Item a gelding named Moggridge 26*s* 8*d*;

Item a baye nagg £5;

Item 3 kyene a hefer and a sire [?] £8 6*s*;

Item three acres and a half of Barley Otes and beanes nowe in
  the grownde at Duryherd 53*s* 4*d*;

Sum £33 6*s*.

Plate and redy money

Item a bason and euer of silver gylt waying 78 Onnces at 5*s*
  6*d* the Once – £21 9*s*;

Item an nest of gobletts with a cover gylt waying 72½ ounces
  at 6*s* the ounce – £21 15*s*;

Item a next of gobletts parcell gylt waying 45 ounces at 5*s* the
  ounce – £11 5*s*;

Item a gylt Goblet waying 15 ounces 5*s* 6*d* the ounce – £4 2*s*
  6*d*;

Item a sylver salte doble gylt waying 13 ounces quarter as
  [*sic*] 5*s* 2*d* the ounce – £3 8*s* 5½*d*;

Item 11 sylver spones [doble gylt – crossed through] with
  maydens heddes waying 12 ounces quarter at 4*s* 8*d* the
  ounce – 57*s* 2*d*;

Item a litle trencher salt gylt waying 1 ounce quarter and half
  quarter at 7*s* 4*d* the ownce – 10*s* 1*d*;

Item a cover and amonts of sylver for a stone cupp waying 3
  ounces as [*sic*] 4*s* 4*d* the ounce 14*s*;

Item 2 ale cupps with covers mouts [mouths] and feet gylt
  waying by estimacion 10 ounces at 5*s* the ounce – 50*s*;

Item in redye money £7 10*s*;

[Sum crossed through].

[4] Item a Sawcer of sylver parcell gylte conteyning 6 ounz
  quarter [and] half at 4*s* 10*d* the ownce – 30*s* 10*d*;

Item a portygne of golde £3 6*s* 8*d*;

Sum £80 17*s* 8½*d*.

Leases

Item a Lease from the maior Bailiffes and commynaltie of
  the citie of Exeter of a tenement orcharde and meadowe in
  Saint Davys called Shoren Hedge £10;

Item an other lease of the maior bailiffs and comminaltie of
  three tenementes without the West Gat wherein Andrewe
  Mory & others doo dwell £16;

Item an other lease of a stable and garden in Exlande by theim
  graunted £8;

Item an other lease by theim graunted of a Stable curtiledg
  and gardens without West Gat of Exeter £7 10*s*;

Item a lease of a howse garden & orcharde of the graunte of
  the Mawdlyn without the Sowithgat of Exeter £8 10*s*;

Item an other lease wherein William Holder dwelleth of a
  tenement without Westgat of Exeter of the graunt of the
  maior bayliffs and cominaltie of Exeter £7 10*s*;

Item a garden of the saide graunt being sometyme a wyde
  pec of grounde neare the waulis of the citie of Exeter in the
  parrish of Saint Paule 26*s* 8*d*;

Item a lease of the tenement wherein the testator dwelt in
  Exeter for certen yeres yet to come after the decesse of
  Johane his wyff £40;

Item a lease of a barne in Sowithing Haye taken of Hockridge
  20*s*;

Sum £99 16*s* 8*d*.

[4v.] **Debtez** sperat and desperate

Item Mr Richarde Hals oweth by his bill £5 2*s*;

Item Mr Duckingfelde oweth by his bill £5;

Item Humfry Stofford [?] oweth by his bill £10;

The right honorable therle of Bedford oweth by bill £40;

Thomas More oweth by bill 30*s*;

John Wylls of Exmister Robert Smyth & Alice Roberts of
  Exmister oweth by bill 4*s*;

Humfry Stofford above named oweth by an other byll £10 5*s*
  4*d*;

Gilbert Mole of Budleigh oweth by bill 3*s* 4*d*;

John Wyks oweth by bok 11*s* 4*d*;

Fraunces Fulford oweth by bok 11*s* 4*d*;

Harry Wheler oweth by obligacion £25;

The right honorable the ladye Tayleboyes oweth by bill £20;

Item ther is £40 delivered out by the saide William Tryvet with his two sones Walter, and Petter Tryvet being put apprentizes that is to saye to ether of their maisters £20 – £40;

Debtes in the Shopp to be answered at daies by Thomas Edwardes & Humfrye Stofford £20;

Item venter to Naples by Richarde Colshurst £12 10s;

The Citie oweth for John Lante the yonger out of his orphane portion 53s 4d;

Roger Allye 27s 4d;

Lewes Argent £4;

Mr Walters £4;

Thomas Germyn brother [?] £3 16s;

Humfry Stofford oweth £5;

Richard Davy [?] of Huldentry [?] oweth £26 13s 4d;

Sum £238 7s 4d;

Sum total £729 15s 6½d.

[5] debtes which the sayde Testater dyd owe at the tyme of his deth

To the executrix of Mr Kastle £6 15s 2d;

To William Budgell 25s 2d;

To Mr Thomas Martyn 52s 2½d;

To Mr Ellycot 47s 6d;

To Thomas Sawnders 12s 3d;

To Laurens Soldome 15s 3d;

To Alexander Mayne 58s 4d;

To Hew Wylesdoune £3 3s 9d;

To Mr Westgrove of London £18 12s 1d;

To Mr Burcher of London £19;

To Mr Northecot £8;

To John Ketchell £10 16s 8d;

To Mr Olyver 11s 8d;

To Richerd Whyting 20s;

To John Pyll [?] £4;

To Chrystyan Tryvet 25s;

To Thomas Geffrey for caridge of dong 21s 3d;

To Mr John Tremayne £80;

To Eustice [?] Quicke for lyme & clothe 8s;

To the house of correction 40s;

To John Barret upon a rem' [?] 16s;

To William Greenewode 26s;

To Thomas Grenewode 26s 4d;

To John Sampford 23s 4d;

To John Arscot of Hollesworthie £30;

To Peter Wills upon an obligation £40;

To Skynner & others for grasse 13s 2d;

To hym for oyle 12s;

To Jeremy Helyerd 32s 10d;

To Thomas Edwards £3 6s 8d;

To Humfrey Stofford 53s 4d;

To theym both for the freedomes ffees 26s;

To the Quenes Gaole 5s 4d;

To the Citie for trayning of soylders 5s;

To Mr Levormore 27s 10d;

To Mr Jones goldesmythe 39s 8d;

To John Ford [?] for teaching Peter & Walter 10s;

To Thomas Marshall £26 13s 4d;

To Pyrwell [?] for a wryte [illegible];

To the Recevor of the Citie for 1 quarter rent 25s;

To Mrs Blackaller for [illegible] rent 30s;

To Gover for the rent of the house at the lytle style & yn St Martyns parishe 28s 4d;

To the Taylors for the rent 20s;

To the vycars for rent 10d;

To Isaak for Mr Aylworthes rent 23s 4d;

Sum £289 21½d.

Funeralls

To Tho Spycer for blacks [?] £21 15s 9d;

for his buryall at London £12 7s 2d;

for chardgs of the houshold £9 2s 8d;

for the probat of the testament & for the admynestration 35s;

for engrossing the Inventary 26s 8d;

To the prayser 20s;

for a stone to be layde upon the grave £3 13s 4d;
Sum £51 7d.

[5v.] debtes desperat
William Dukingfeld oweth £5;
Gylbert Moll oweth 3s 4d;
Fruncys Fullfford oweth 11s 4d;
The lady Taylboys oweth £20;
Lewes Argenton oweth £4;
Robert Allyn oweth 27s 4d;
Richerd Berry of Halberton oweth £26 13s 4d;
Sum £57 15s 4d;
Sum total £397 17s 8½d;
So remains £331 11s 10d.

which some of £331 11s 10½d is to be devided yn to three
    equall parts viz
To the wyff £119 4s 1½d;
To the Executrix £119 4s 1½d;
To Marrella £39 14s 8½d;
To Peter £39 14s 8½d;
To Walter £39 14s 8½d;
[For the children's portions] £119 4s 1½d;
Sum £357 12s 4½d.

[On a loose leaf of paper:]
The 8th of November 1579
The whole gooddes comprysed yn Mr Tryvets inventory
    amount to £701 10s 4½d;
whereof paied for legacyes debts funeralls & debts desperat
    £314 14s 6½d;
So remains £386 15s 10½d.

whiche being devyded yn to 2 partes there groweth to every
    part viz
To Mrs Tryvet £193 7s 11¼d;
To Marrell Tryvet £64 9s 3¾d;
To Peter Tryvet £64 9s 3¾d;
To Walter Tryvet £64 9s 3¾d;

[For the children's portions] £193 7s 11¼d;
Sum £386 15s 10½d.

but being devyded yn to three parts then ther amount to every
    part as foloweth viz
To the wyff £128 18s 7½d;
To the Admynestratryx £128 18s 7½d;
To Marrella £42 19s 6½d;
To Walter 42 19s 6½d;
To William [sic] 42 19s 6½d;
[For the children's portions] £128 18s 7½d;
Sum £386 15s 10½d.
After this dyvysyon made there was demanded £3 13s 4d
    for a stone graven and layed upon Mr Tryvet and this said
    allowed ther amount to every portion as foloweth

the 11 of November 1579
The whole goodds amount to £701 10s 4½d;
whereof payed for debts [legacyes – crossed through]
    funeralls and debts desperat £318 7s 10½d;
So remains £383 2s 6d;
whiche some being devyded yn to too parts ther groweth to
    every part as foloweth
To the wyff £191 11s 3d;
To Marrella £63 17s 1d;
To Walter £63 17s 1d;
To Peter £63 17s 1d;
[For the children's portions] £191 11s 3d.

but if the devysion be to be made yn to 3 parts then there
    groweth every part as foloweth
To the wyff £127 14s 2d;
To the Admynestratrix £127 14s 2d;
To Marrell £42 11s 4¾d;
To Walter £42 11s 4¾d;
To Peter £42 11s 4¾d;
[For the children's portions] £127 14s 2d.

40. INVENTORY OF MICHAEL FRIGGENS, OF HOLY TRINITY PARISH, 6 APRIL 1582

ECA, Orphans' Court Inventory 28E

Heere followeetth an Inventory of all the goods and debs of Michell Friggens Late of the parishe of St Trinitie decessed praised by Sylvester West William German, Gilbert Penington John Knight and John Clavell the sixthe daie of Aprell *in the year* 1582

[1] Firstly 6 Silver spoungs 36s 10d;
Item a table bord and a forme 6s;
Item a Cobbord 7s;
Item an other Cobbord 3s 4d;
Item a round Table 16d;
Item a Chaire and 3 stools 18d;
Item a tyninge Quart 12d;
Item a tyninge Pint 8d;
Item sixe flower potts and a salt of Tynne 2s 6d;
Item platters poudingers & sawsers 16s;
Item 6 Candlestiks 3s 4d;
Item 3 old Cicocks and a posnet 12s;
Item an old pan 3s 4d;
Item a dreeping pan 3d;
Item a Bill 6d;
Item a featherbed with a bolster and 2 pillowes 23s;
Item a Coverled 6s;
Item 4 paire of sheetes 20s;
Item an old paire of shetes 2s;
Item an old sheete more 4d;
Item a paire of blanketts 4s;
Item 2 pillowe tyes 2s;
Item a bed steade 5s;
Item an old borde 18d;
Item an old forme & an old coffer 6d;
Item 6 table napkins 18d;
Item an old Cobbard clothe 4d;
Item 2 old bord clothes 12d;
Item a steane [? stained] cloth 12d;

Item an old bord & forme, more 16d;
Item 6 old Cusshins 18d;
Item an old matters & bolster 5s;
Item a flock bed bolster and bedstead 6s;
Item a great chest 10s;
Item 2 ladders 18d;
Item an old grindingstone and a whetstone 3d;
Item a sallatt [?] 10d;
Item an old bunting hutch 6d;
Item 2 skeuers [?] 8d;
Item 3 solves 12d;
Item 2 pecs of old tymber 8d;
Item an old gowne 5s;
Item a womans kertle 13s 4d;
Item an apron 12d;
Item an old Kearcher 4d;
[1v.] Item a powch & dagger 8d;
Item his tooles & old Iron 27s 9d;
Item an old Coverled 16d;
Item an other Coffer 20d;
Item 2 old bedsteads with their teasters 6s 8d;
Item 3 Coffers more 3s 8d;
Item an other flock bed with the bolster 6s;
Item the tymber £14;
Item 6 roolers 2s;
Item a Carpet 20d;
Item a broche Crooks eyrons & a griddell 2s 10d;
Item a brassen crock 10s;
Item 3 Cawdrons 9s;
Item a skillet 16d;
Item a frieing pan 8d;
Item a paire of blanketts 6s 8d;
Item a womans partelett 12d;
Item a bord cloth & a towell 3s 4d;
Item a trocle bed 5s;

Item a flock bed bolster Coverled and a blankett 12*s*;

Item an old bedstede 4 stooles and old painted clothes 3*s*;

Item glasse 5*s*;

Item a quilt 5*s*;

Item a chest 2*s* 8*d*;

Item a range 8*d*;

Item a powdring Tubb 6*d*;

Item 2 dawe Tubbs 6*d*;

Item shelves & old tymber in the spence 20*d*;

Item a Coole 4*d*;

Item 3 old Tubbs 10*d*;

Item a fier pike and 2 pepkins 4*d*;

Item a powdering pott 3*d*;

Item a grindingstone 2*s* 8*d*;

Item his apparell 35*s* 6*d*;

Item a womans kertell 3*s* 4*d*;

Item a lanterne & a washe kitell 6*d*;

Item a Compas & a pricker 6*d*;

Item a chaffeing dishe 18*d*;

Item a pece of leather 12*d*;

Item the lease of a garden £6 13*s* 4*d*;

Item in readie money £6;

Item Mr Barcombe oweth £7;

Item 2 barsketts 4*d*;

Item an litle old bruinge tub 6*d*.

[2] depts awed by the saide Mihill

To William Dudeney £4 20*d*;

To John Knight 4*s* 3*d*;

To John Clavell and John Wilcocks 6*s*.

41. WILL OF JOHN HUTCHINS, MERCHANT, 22 JUNE 1582

Orphans' Court Will 22 (and National Archives, 11/64/481)

Note: The will was proved via Canterbury on 8 November 1582. One difference between the two versions is that the Canterbury copy notes that Hutchins' daughters should not marry a man of 'evil' name. The witnesses were John Tozer, William Hillinge, Mathewe Ezen and Robert Slowman. Recognisances were entered into on 21 October 1583 for his children Rose and Mary (ECA, Book 141, folio 81 dorse).

In the name of god Amen the 22th daye of June *in the year* 1582 I John Hutchins of the Cyttie of Exter marchant being wke of bodye & yet perfite of remembrance thankes be to god do make this my laste will & testament in maner & forme fellweyng first I bequeth my sowle unto the almythtye god my only saviour & redemer [& my – crossed through] Item I geve & bequeth to the wardens of the parishe of Saynt Olaves to the use of the churche there 6*s* 8*d* & 20*s* to the power peopell to be destributed by my lovinge wyffe Rose Hutchins & my bodye to be buried in such place as it shall please my executrix item I geve & bequethe unto my daughter Alys Hutchings the some of one hundred markes of lawfull money of England & one ffetherbedd performyd when she shall accomplish the ayge of 21 yeres or be espowsed. Item I geve & bequeth unto my daughters Rose & Marye Hutchins the revertions of towe tenementes with the apprutenances liyng in Stockley Pomery nowe in the severall tenures of Gerome Payne & Thomas Bende that they thre shallbe named in the grantes in manner following that is to saye my sayd wyffe my daughters Rose & Marye one Bonde my sayd wyffe my daughters Mary & Rose [& Marye – crossed through] provided alwayes that yf my sayd daughter Als do marrye with a person of Ill name & creditt & so reputed adidged & taken by my sayd wyffe then the sayd Als shall have only £40 & the [resydue – crossed through] resydewe of the resited legacye before to her assigned shallbe equally devided emongest my other daughters that shall accomplishe the sayd ayge or be married as aforsayd that my will & mynd is that the portion of those that do decesse shall remeyne unto them that shall happen to survyve & overlive Also I geve & bequethe unto my sonne Robert Hutchins the messuage tenement & curtlage where I now dwell & inhabitt so that he suffer my sayd wyffe quietly to inioye the same during her natturall lyffe she yelding bearing paying & paying all such rentes reperations & services as is to be yelded boren payd & done for the same Item I geve & bequethe unto my son Morris Hutchins my lease & tearme of years which I have to come of & in one messuage with theapurtenaces now in the tenure & occupatione of Agnes Lyghe in the sayd Cyttye of Exter widowe Item I geve unto my sonne John Hutchins my lease & tearme of yeres which I have yet to come of & in one messuage without the Weast Gate of the Cittie of Exter now in the tenure of Henery Deymand hatter Item I gyve & bequethe unto my sonne

Nicolas Hutchins my lease & tearme of yeres yet to come of & in one messuage now in the tenure or occupation of

Christopher Hawke of the sayde Cittie Cowke Item I gyve & bequethe unto my servant [servitnd – crossed through] John Rowe 20s and 20s to my servant Johane Ruge in consideratione of ther good service Also wheras I have receyved A fine of my tenent Robert Slomane for a tenement in Venotary my full mynde & intent is that my sayd wyffe doe within a convenient tyme next after my decesse make an estate unto the sayd Robert Slomane Margaret his wyfe & Thomas ther sonne for terme of ther lives & the longest liver of them the newe messuage only excepted according as I am bounde to doe the residew of all goodds not geven nor bequethed I geve & bequethe unto my sayd wyffe whome I make my sole executrixe of this my last will & testament And I appoynte for my overseers of this my last will & testament my brother in lawe John Levermore marchant & John Tozer gentelman whome I beseche to doe ther Indever for the best performance hereof In witnes whereof I have set my hand geven the daye & yere first above written.

42. WILL OF ROGER CURTIS, OF HOLY TRINITY PARISH, 14 DECEMBER 1582

ECA, Orphans' Court Will 23

1582

In the name of God Amen the 14th daye of December and In the yere of our lorde god 1582 I Roger Courtise dwellinge in the parishe of the Holy Trinitie in Exeter beinge whole of mynde and In perfect remembrannce thankes be unto god do make this my last will and Testamente In manner and fourme followeinge first I bequeathe my soule unto almightye god my body to be buried in the churcharde of St Peters by my wiffe **Also** I geve and bequeathe unto John Courttise 26s 8d **Also** I geve and bequeathe unto John Courtise 26s 8d Also I geve and bequeath unto Wilmote Courtise 26s 8d Also my will is that none of these children above named shall have this mony paide unto them beffore they come unto the aige of 21 yeres or marriageable and if any of them do dye before the come unto the aige of 21 yeres or mariageable that then his or her

parte that so dyeth shall remayne unto them that be alyffe. **Also** my will is that Jone Courtise shall have the lease of my house that I nowe dwell in duringe the tearme of the yeares which are to come And if she chaunce ffor to dye before the Tearmes be expired that then my will is that the termes that remayne shall go unto John Courtise & Wilmost Courtise Jointly. And if it chance that the saide John and Wilmot ffor to dye bothe that then my will is that the Tearmes that shall Remaine shall to unto Roger Courtise my brothers sonne. **Also** I geven and bequeathe unto Jone Hill my servant my wiffes Second Smoke a peticote next the best & a kirchiffe next the best **Also** I geve and bequeathe unto John Courtise and to Jone Courtise and unto Wilmot Courtise Six pewter vessells a pece **Also** I geve to Alce Horrell a smoke and a kirchiffe **Also** I geve unto the poor of the parishe 3s 4d Also

to everye goddchilde 4d pence a pece **Also** the resedewe
of my goods cattells and debts the which is not geven nor
bequethed my detts & legacies paid, I geve and bequeathe
unto my Brother John Courtise And to George Searell whome
I do ordaine and mak my whole and sole Executors they to
see me honestlie brought In earth my debts and legacies paide

and the Residewe to bestowe for the wealthe of my soule **Also**
I do ordayne and make to be my rewlers of this my last will
and Testament to see hit well and truely done and performed
Thomas Nicoles and John Blackemore and they to have ffor
thier paynes 2s apece Wittnesse hereunto is Sir Thomas
Tuckey parson Thomas Nicoles John Blackmore with others.

43. INVENTORY OF WILLIAM JEFFORD, OF ST LAWRENCE'S PARISH, 22 FEBRUARY 1583

ECA, Orphans' Court Inventory 30

The trew inventorie of they goods and cattell of William
Jefford of St Lawrauns within the Cittie of Exon praysed by
Nicholas Stockman and John Gye the 22 of February 1582
and in the 25 year of the reaigne of Elizabeth the queens
Majastie that nowe is

[1] *Firstly* one framebord one Joyne forme 6s 8d;
Mor one standing beadstead one truckell beadstead and two
    flockbeads performed 20s;
Mor one badd flockbead 2s;
Mor one pece of howshold russett 8s;
His apparell 10s;
Mor certaine lynyn 8s;
Mor 6 Coffers 3s 4d;
Mor 12 platters 3 podingers 8 sawsers 5 tynyn potts 7s;
Mor 4 Candlstickes 2 Crockes 2 pans 2 Caldrons and one
    skillett 23s;
Mor *C* half of Tallowe 41s [?];
Other Trashe 6s 8d;
Sum is £6 14s 8d.

Mor 4 Colts £5 6s 8d;
Mor one geldin and 2 keen £3 13s 4d;
Mor 96 hoggots and 2 piggs £11 19s 2d;
Sum is £20 19s 2d.

Debts sperat
Firstly Nicholas Stockman £5 4s 8d;
John Gye 31s 4d;
Mor John Tocker 3li;
John Furnys £6 5s 8d;
Harrie Humfrie £3 1s;
Mor John Jefford £15;
Richard Jefford £9;
Richard Turner 20s;
Thomas Esworthey 14s 2d [entry crossed through];
William Hutchin 7s 10d;
Mor £5 13s 4d;
Mor Davie the Tailer 10s;
Clarke of Stoke 13s [entry crossed through];
Nicholas Gryawnie [?] 17s;
Richard Denis 8s;
Mor John Heard 6s 8d;
Christopher Furnoye 14d;
Mor Robert Carew 4 marks [entry crossed through];
Sum is £56 14s 10d.

Debts desperate
Richard Hussine 10s;
Firstly Gabrell Sinckler 46s;
John Saunders £4 19s;
Mor Lucas Carrow 2s;
John Clement 3s;

Mor chardges in lawe 10s;
Mor William Bowdon 23d;
Evyns of Nertherex 40s;
Mor Wills the Carrior 14s;
Sum is £10 10s.

The whole sum cometh to £93 8s 8d.

In witnes this to be trew we Nicholas Stockman and John Gye have here unto putt owr hands.

N h S by me John Gye *per me* Samuele Knyght *script*.

Exhibited through the administration on the 26th day of March in the year 1583 to be true etc Jaspar Bridgeman registrar.

The whole goodds comprised yn this inventory amounts to
   £93 8s 8d;
Whereof paid
For funeralls 6s 8d;
For the admynestracon 12s;
For debtes which the Testator dyd owe £16 12s 7d;
For desperat debts £14 17s 7d;
£32 8s 7d;
So remaineth £61.
To the wiff for her porcion £20 6s 8d;
To her being admynestratrix £20 6s 8d;
To John Gifford £6 15s 7d;
To Philyp Gifford £6 15s 7d;
To [Mary – crossed through] Margaret Gifford £6 15s 7d;
[For the children's portions] £20 6s 9d;
£61 1d.

44. INVENTORY OF JOHN DYNHAM, WEAVER OF ST PAUL'S PARISH, 13 MAY 1583

ECA, Orphans' Court Inventory 31

Note: The register of the parish of St Paul was burnt during the Second World War but an earlier transcript, published by the Devon & Cornwall Record Society in 1933, noted the burial of 'John Denham' on 4 April 1583. Recognisances were entered into on 19 July 1583 for his children Mary and Christian (ECA, Book 141, Folio 80 dorse).

An Inventorie of the goods of John Dynham late of the parishe of St Pawles in the Cytie of Exeter weaver decessed praised the thirtenth daye of Maye in the 25 yeerre of the reygne of our sovereigne lady Elizabeth by the grace of god quene of England Fraunce and Ireland defender of the fayth &c by John Tucker Thomas Jordane and Edmond Coke as hereafter foloweth

[m. 1] In the hall
Firstly the table borde forme & benche 6s 8d;
Item one newe Cubberde with a presse to the same & a
   Cubberd cloth uppon it 26s 8d;
Item one olde Cubberd 5s;

Item one Chest and an olde Coffer 13s 4d;
Item two Chaires & a stoole 20d;
Item a bedsteed and a paynted tester to the same 4s;
Item fyve Cushens & a matt uppon the benche 12d;
Item the paynted Cloathes about the hall 3s;
Item a fether bed a dust bed a fether bolster a flock bolster a
   fether pyllowe and a peare of blancketts 20s;
Item two bowes a sheafe of Arrowes & a blackbyll 4s;
27s 8d [?].

In the Chamber
Item three bedsteedes and three paynted testers to them and
   the paynted cloathes about the Chamber 10s;

Item a fether bedd a flock bed a fether bolster & a flock
   bolster a fether pyllowe a blanckett a sheete and a Coverlett
   of Tapistry Worke 20s;
Item a flock bed two dust beds a fether bolster two litle fether
   pyllowes a peare of blancketts a Coverlett a flock bolster &
   two olde Coverletts 19s 4d;
Item foure Coffers and a shippe Coffer 8s;
[m. 2] Item a litle olde borde and two hampers 14d;
Item a peece of Clowte leather 16d;
£3 10d.

In the Chamber over the shoppe
Item a table borde a benche two olde formes & a Carpett 5s;
Item a bedsteed and an olde Coverlett 2s 6d;
Item a paynted Cloth 2s;
9s 6d.
In the two shoppes
Item three loomes and two queele tournes 53s 4d;
Item two sleas and harneys & three sets of staves 6s 8d;
Item a litle table borde foure tubbes and a standerd two
   stooles two bucketts a Cradle olde paynted Clothes and
   other olde trashe 54s;
£3 4s.

In the garden
Item a heape of stones 8d;
8d.

In the out Chamber
Item two bedsteedes a flock bed A Dust bed and two olde
   Coverletts & a bolster 5s;
5s.

In the out Shoppe
Item A Warpinge tree a Baggle [?] a plancke a turne a hamer
   a hand Sawe a peare of pynsers and other olde trashe 3s 4d;
3s 4d.

In the Stable & over the stable
Item the Woode over the stable and A Grynding Stone in the
   Stable 6s;
6s.

[m. 3] In the Kytchen
Item a table borde a benche a forme & a ioyned stoole 2s 6d;
Item an olde Cubberd a bearer to sett barrells over two shelfes
   and a lether bottell 20d;
Item a Cage for poultrye and two shelfes over it 12d;
Item a Spytt a goose pan a frying pan two gredirons a peare
   of tonges three pott hanginges three pott Crockes and other
   olde Iron 6s;
Item 12 Pewter platters and a pewter bason 12 pewter
   poddingers 8 Sawsers & 5 tynne spoones 20s;
Item six brasse potts and three Posnetts 33s 4d;
Item foure brasse pannes & a litle Cawdren 13s 4d;
Item two pottell potts of tynne three quarte potts of tynne
   three pynte potts of tynne & fyve flower potts of tynne 4s;
Item seven Candlesticks a bason of brasse two Chafing dishes
   & a litle salte of tynne 4s 8d;
£3 16s 6d.

Item three score and two poundes of yarne £5 8s 4d;
Item two peare of slyders and a peare of stockens 6s 8d;
Item one Jerkyne 3s;
Item one dublett 8s;
Item two Cloakes 38s;
Item two Gownes 33s 4d;
Item a peare of Dowles sheets & one [of] Canvas sheets 10s;
Item two peare of Canvas sheets 4s;
Item two Canvas borde Cloathes 3s 4d;
Item three sherts & 6 bands 6s 8d;
Item one yarde of fyne Canvas 2s 6d;
[m. 4] Item 4 yards of Iyrishe Canvas 14d;
Item one Dyaper borde napkyn and six Canvas napkyns 2s;
Item 2 Pyllowebeeres 12d;
Item three drinckyng glasses and 2 Cupps 8d;
Item three peere of gloves 6d;

Item in monye £4 1s;
£23 10s 2d.

Pawnes

Item one Cassock 2 Kyrtles of sylke & a Coverlett lyeth for
    40s;
Item two platters and a sawser of Pewter lyeth for 12d;
Item one brasse pott lyeth for sixe shillinges – 6s;
Item two peare of sheets lyeth for 10s;
Item a peece of olde Damaske lyeth for 2s;
Item halfe a dosen of sylver spoones lyeth for 33s 4d;
Item one sylver spoone lyeth for 3s;
Item one Goblett and a Cover to it of sylver double gilded
    lyeth for £7;
Item half a dosen of sylver spoones lyeth for 10s;
£12 5s 4d.

Debts

[m. 5] Item Nycholas Grenoe oweth 26s 8d;
Mr Symon Knyght oweth £3;
Wylliam Knolles oweth 26s 8d;
Dumas [?] Gyll wydowe oweth 20s;
Thomas Edbury of Tuton [?] in the parishe of Credyton oweth
    £4 10s;
Mr Nicholas Marten oweth £35;
£46 3s 4d.

A revewe made the 18 of Maye folowyng

Item an Iron shuvell & an olde garden rake 8d;
Item a bundell of leastes 4d;
Item Chirekoole 6d;
Item lyme £4;
Item an olde rack & an olde plancke for a [illegible] 2d;
Item 4 olde Costs & an olde Cowle 8d;
Item a Conye hutche 4d;
Item 2 bushels of Rye & half a bushell of meale 5s;
Item a hatt & a Cappe 20d;
Item a playing tables & an olde breade grater 8d;
Item a Carpett 20d;

Item a litle brasse morter & a pestell of Iron 12d;
Item an olde mantell 4d;
Item a Rathe [?] 4d;
Sum £90 13s 8d.

[Signature of] Edmond Cock [signs of] Thomas Jorden John
    Tucker.

Exhibited and executed the 24th day of the month of May in
    the year 1583 and a correct record witnessed by me Jaspar
    Bridgeman Registrar.

ECA, Orphans' Court Inventory 31 [Item 2]

The accomptes of Ursula Denham of suche monye and
chardges as she the said Ursula for the dethe of her late
dicessed husband John Denham and uppon him and his
housholde as well in the tyme of his sicknes as sythence his
deathe writen the 13 daye of July *in the year 1583 in the reign
of Queen Elizabeth ...* as followeth

Firstly paid to Hughe Armestronge tucker for dressinge of 14
    kersies at 17d a peice Some 19s 10d;
Item paid to George Smythe for rent for the laste lady quarter
    7s 6d;
Item paid to Wills the brewar for halfe a Barrell of Ale 3s;
Item paid to Mamell tayler for drinke 3s 8d;
Item paide to doctor Narcnessus for Phizick 5s;
Item to John Heale thappotycary for potycary Stuffe for Him
    5s;
Item paide for a Shrewde for him 4s;
Item for the funerall dynner 13s;
Item paid to Mr Bearde the preacher for a Sermon at his
    Buryall 4s;
Item for 4 dosen of Bread gyven to the poore 4s;
Item paid for provinge the wyll 8s;
Item paid to the Stonynge the Scryvener for writing the
    Inventory 6s 8d;
Item to the Curatt and to the clarke for the buryall 12d;

Item paid to the 2 women that kepte ym in his syckenes 2s;

Item the Scryver for writing this and Mudfords inventory 12d;

Item more the greate chardges laide out about him and in his housholde in the tyme of his Sycknes not yett called to remembrance 5s;

Item to the praisers of the goods 5s;

The totall of the Somes knowen particuled above sett downe £4 12s 8d.

ECA, Orphans' Court Inventory 31 [Item 3]

The goodds & chattels of John Dynneham decessid amount to £80 13s 4d;

Whereof for his funeralls 13s 4d;

So resteth £80.

Which £80 beinge devided yn to 3 equall parts there groweth to every parte £26 13s 4d;

Viz to the wyff £26 13s 4d;

To the executrix £26 13s 4d;

To Christyan £13 6s 8d;

To Mary £13 6s 8d;

[For the children's portions] £26 13s 4d.

Out of the executrix parte there is to be abated for legacyes

Viz to Christyan Dynneham £20;

To Mary Dynneham £20;

To Thomas Modiford £8;

To John Dynneham 2s;

To Nychus Dynneham 20s;

£49 2s.

So he hathe geven yn legacys more then his therd parte dothe growe and amount unto £22 9s;

By which rekenynge every legatary losethe yn every pounde [blank].

So then there is dew to Chrystyan for her legacy [blank];

To her for her orphanege £13 6s 8d;

To Mary for her legacy [blank];

To her for her orphanege £13 6s 8d.

ECA, Orphans' Court Inventory 31 [Item 4]

1583 The Inventory of the goodds & Chatles of John Dynneham late of the Citie of Excester decessed

The whole goodds amount to £79 16s 8d;

Whereof to be allowed for debts & funeralls £4 12s 8d;

So remaineth £75 4s.

Which is to be devided yn to 3 equall parts viz

To the weff for her parte £25 16d;

To the executrex for performnc of the will £25 16d;

To Mary Dynneham £12 10s 8d;

To Christyan Dynnham £12 10s 8d;

[For the children's portions] £25 16d;

Sum £75 4s.

Memorandum that the Testator gave yn legacyes £69 2s which must be paied with £25 16d which is the Testators parte and then every legatory is to have of every pound but 10s 2¾d;

By which accompte is Dew to every of the children as foloweth

Mary Dynnham of £20 is to have £10 5s 8½d;

And of her childs portion £12 10s 8d;

£22 15½d.

Christyan Dynhm of £20 is to have £10 5s 8½d;

for her childs porton £12 10s 8d;

£22 15s 4d.

45A. WILL OF NICHOLAS GLANFILDE, BAKER OF HOLY TRINITY PARISH, 25 JUNE 1583

ECA, Orphans' Court Will 25

In the Name of God Amen The 25 daye of June 1583 And in the 25th yeare of the raigne of our soveraigne Ladie Elizabethe by the grace of god of Englande Fraunce and Irelande Quene Defender of the faithe &c I Nicholas Glandfilde of the parishe of the Holie Trinitie in the Countie and Cittie of Exceter Baker beinge sicke of bodie neverthelesse thankes be unto Almightie god hole and perfecte of memorie and mynde ordayne and make my testamente Declaringe herein my laste will in manner and forme followinge That is to saie ffirst I Comende my soule unto Almightie god my maker and onlie redeemer and my bodie to be buried in Christian buriall where it shall please my Executor hereunder in this my presente will named Item I geve to the poore sicke people in the Mawdlyn to everie of them 4d a pece Item I geve and bequeathe to John Glanfilde my soune £20 Item I geve and bequeathe to Judithe my daughter twentie poundes to be paide to either of them at suche tyme as they shall accomplishe and be of the full aidge of twentie and one yeares And if my daughter be married before that daie Then she to have her saide £20 at the daie of her saide marriadge And if either of my saide children happen to die before he or she be of the full aidge of 21 yeares or that my daughter be married as aforesaide Then his or her portion to remayne to the Survivor of them and if bothe of my saide Children die before they shall accomplishe the saide aidge of 21 yeares or that my saide daughter be married then theire portions to them geven as aforesaide to be and remayne to Alea my wief Item I geve and bequeathe to my brother Harrie all my clothes aswell lynnen as wollen belonginge to my bodie savinge my beste Cloake And also to him 40s in money Item I geve to everie of my godchildren 4d apeice Item I geve to John Horwell my Apprentice 6s 8d The Residewe of all my goodes and cattells not geven nor bequeathed I geve and bequeathe to the saide Alea my wife whome I make and ordayne my full and whole Executor of this my laste will and Testamente And I make and ordayne John Gayne my fatherinlawe and Silfester Weste Overseers to see this my laste will and Testamente executed and I geve to either of them for their paynes to be taken in that behalfe 3s 4d In wittnes whereof I have hereunto sette my signe and Seale geven the daie and yere firste above writen in the presence of the saide John Geyne Silfester Weste Harrie Glandfelde and Thomas Clarke scriptor hereunder writen signed John Weste signed Silfester Weste Henrie Glandfilde Thomas Clerke

[*dorse*] Robert Bachelor £3 6s 8d;
Godesland of Dodescombe 40s;
Luscombe of Exmynster 10s;
Gere of Alfyngton 4s;
Andrew of Exon 4s;
Jo: Wilcokes 44s 2d;
Jo: West 5s 5d ¼;
Rob[ert] Talman 6d;
Wydow Smalridge 6d;
Her soune 6d;
The vicar of Dunsford 10s;
Kingswell of Dunscomb 10s 3d;
Leighe of Morton 18d;
Sowden of Powderham 8d;
Robert Vyntey of Exmouth 35s;
Tapley of Dawlish 18d.

[Enclosure] Dettes desperate
Roberte Bacheller oweth £3 6s 8d;
More payd for charges for inlawe;
The said Bacheller £3 13s;
Roses Gotham allowed & John Colle 20s;
Godestand of Dodcombesley 40s;
Richard Dollygrave of Dawlyshe 40s;
John Wilcockes 44s;

John Willes of Exmyster 30*s*;

David Wylles 20*s*;

Lucombe of Exminster 10*s*;

Garrett of Alfyton 4*s*;

Andrew of Exon 4*s*;

Stevyn Hollie 4*s*;

John Weste 5*s* 6*d*¼;

Pringe 3*s*;

John Marten of Bearstowe 6*s* 8*d*;

William Willes of Morton 13*s* 4*d*;

Wollcott of Alfyton 18*d*;

Wyddowe Whitehed 14*d*;

Wyddow Durninge of Dawlyshe 8*s* 4*d*;

Wotton of St Thomas 4*s*;

Mylles Bowive clarke 10*s*;

Humfry Collepriste 4*s*;

Robarte Tallman of Donnforde 6*d*;

Widdo Smalridge 6*d*;

Her sonne 6*d*;

The vicker of Donnsforde 9*s*;

Kingwill of Doneham 18*d*;

Will Lygger of Moreton 18*d*;

Sowdon of Powderham 8*s*;

Robarte Wyntton of Exminster 33*s*;

Tyshops Tapley of Dawlysh 18*d*;

Foster of Kenton 8*s* 10*d*;

John Fyllmore for a horsse 33;

Gorge Courteney Richard Peppryll hathe lefte to pay £5 10*s*.

Paid unto Mr Bygleston for Myllys Glanfyllds detts £3;

Sum £3.

Jude[th] Glanfylde came unto me

Item for 2 gownes;

Item 4 peticoates;

Item 2 wastecotes;

Item 2 smockes;

Item 6 peare of hosse;

Item 8 peare of shoes;

Item 5 [??];

Item 5 partlets;

Item 6 aprons;

Item 2 hattes;

Item for here table for 3 yeares & a ½;

Item for her scowlinge.

John Glanfyld was with me halfe ayeare

Item for his scowlinge;

[item for his apperell – crossed through];

Item 2 doubletts;

Item 1 yearbeyn;

Item 1 peare of breaches;

Item 2 peare of showes;

Item 2 hattes;

Item 4 bandes;

Item for a shrowde;

Item for his buryall;

Item for his table;

Payd for entryinge of my Surtyes.

45B. INVENTORY OF NICHOLAS GLANFILDE, BAKER OF HOLY TRINITY PARISH, 17 JULY 1583

ECA, Orphans' Court Inventory 33

Note: Will 25 enclosure appears to be part of this inventory and not that of Roger Curtis with which it has been listed. A summary copy of this inventory exists in ECA, Book 141, folios 95-6. It also has details of the administration of the estate including the recognisance regarding John and Judith, the children of Nicholas.

The **Inventorie** of all & singular the goodes cattalls chattalls debtes Implyments which late were Nicholas Glanfeilde of the countie of the cittie of Exon Baker decessed taken and praised by George Glubbe John Marshall John Blackmoore & George Searle the 17th daie of Julie in the 25th yeare of the raigne of our Soveraigne Ladie Elizabeth &c

[1] In the Hall
Firstly one ioyned Cubborde with a presse in the same
    praised at 30s;
Item [three – crossed through] one Brasen Crocke 13s 4d;
Item three Brasen Crocks 14s;
Item a Bason and Ewer 3s 4d;
Item 56 lb of pewter vessell at 5d the pounde 23s 4d;
More 8 lb of pewter 2s;
Item a morter and a pestell 20d;
Item three latten Chaundlers 2s;
Item 5 stone Cuppes 8d;
Item a dossen of trenchers 2d;
Item trow fformes 2s;
Item a litell borde and a stoole 6d;
Sum £4 13s.

In the Parlor
Item a ffetherbedd with a bolster and pillowe of ffethers 36s;
Item a paire of blancketts 10s;
Item a truckelbedstede a flock bedd, a paire of blancketts a
    bolster and twoo Quishins 6s;
Item one andiron & 3 pott Crocks 2s 6d;
Item a bord a fforme & a olde Cubborde 3s 4d;
Item a olde Coffer a Chere & a stool 3s 4d;
Item a Cheare 3d;
Item a blacke bill 10d;
Sum £3 2s 3d.
[1v.] **In** the Chamber over the Hall
Item one Bedstede 3s 4d;
Item a flaske and tichebox 2 skayners & a Chaine for a dogg
    18d;

Item a bedd and a bolster 13s 4d;
Item a olde Coverlett 3s 4d;
Sum 21s 6d.

In the Chamber over the Shopp
Item a bedd a bolster & a Coverlett 18s;
Item a beddstede one bedd 2 bolsters and twoo Coverletts 28s;
Item 2 Coffers 18d;
Item a Coverlett 46s 8d;
Item a Clock 33s 4d;
Sum £6 7s 6d.

In the Shoppe
Item 2 olde Coffers & a hoxhedd 16d;
Sum 16d.

In the Buttrey
Item a turne and a lanterne 12d;
Sum 12d.

In the Kitchen
Item twoo brasen pannes 8s;
Item twoo bruches a Chaffing dishe a frienge panne, a skillett
    a drepinge panne, a drepinge ladell & a Cawdron 4s 4d;
Item 3 tubbes, twoo barrells & 2 salte tubbes 4s 8d;
Item 8 earthen potts 2d;
Sum 17s 2d.

[2] In the bakehowse
Item 4 sacks of meale £3 4s;
Item 8 boushells of Branne 3s 4d;
Item a Coffer and poales 12d;
Item 4 newe sacks 8s;
Item 6 sacks 6s;
Item 7 sacks 16d;
Item 2 plancks and a brak 4s 8d;
Item 5 boushells & half of wheat at 2s 8d the boushell 14s 8d;
Item peeles a pek & other poles 8d;

Item 3 boushells of malt 4s 6d;

Item three Bunters 6d;

Sum £5 8s 8d.

Lynnen

Item 4 paire & one sheite 13s 4d;

Item twoo bordeclothes one Towell & a Cubborde clothe 4s;

Item twoo pillowes 2s;

Sum 19s 4d.

Plate

Item 2 Cuppes covered with silver £3 6s;

Item one silver salt and a dossen of silver spones containing 16 uncs at 4s 4d per unce £3 9s 4d;

Sum £5 [sic] 15s 4d.

In the Back Chamber

Item a olde borde a fourme and a olde forselett 8d;

Sum 8d.

[2v.] In the Stable

Item a horsse a pack sadde[l] & a heckeney saddell 18s;

Item a paire of panniers & a hoxehed 18d;

Item 10 pecs of tymber 2s;

Sum 21s 6d.

In the back Court

Item a sowe & 4 piggs 36s;

Item Broomes 3s;

Item a woodevyne 33s 4d;

Item a cock and 2 hennes 12d;

Sum £3 13s 4d.

Sum total [of the goods] £33 17s 7d.

Good debts

Firstly Mr Drak of Topsham aweth for bisky £15;

Gilberte Dicher aweth for bisky £7 2s;

Thomas Browne of Exmouth aweth for bisky 44s 6d;

Walter Rawley of Exmouth for bisky 35s;

Roberte Vynten of Exmouth aweth for 4 C of bisky at 9s C – 36s;

Jesper Logis of Topsham for bisky 33s 2d;

Widowe Weste of Weare for bread 4s 6d;

John Clerk of Dunsforde for bread 30s;

John Browne of Dunsforde for bread 3s;

Robert Taleman of Dunsforde for bread 6d;

Widowe Smalerudge of Dunsforde for breade 6d;

More her soune aweth for bread 6d;

The Vicar of Dunsforde for bread 60s;

William Goreman for bread 53s 10d;

Goselande of Doddescomblegh aweth 40s;

John Clark of Kistow for bread 15s;

Kingwill of Doccombe for bread 18d;

Willm Ligar of Morton for bread 18d;

[3] Garrett of Alphington for bread 53s;

Lucombe of Exmister for breade 10s;

Sowdon of Powderham for bread 8s;

Richard Collins Cutler aweth 24s;

Preston of Kenton for bread 4s;

Clet[illegible] of Gosforde for bread 2s 6d;

[Illegible] for Tapley of Dawlish for bread 18d;

Androwe of Exon for bread 4s;

John Crowne aweth 15s;

Stephen Hole aweth 2s 2d;

Anthonie P[illegible] aweth 4s 6d;

Mr Langeford aweth 10s;

William Snowe aweth 18s;

William Webber aweth 16s 6d;

William Berrie aweth 3s 4d [margin: payd by And(rew?) Berye];

John Weste aweth 5s 5½d;

Robert Mounstephen aweth 14s;

Pringe aweth 3s;

Phillipp Gilden aweth by bill £31;

Roberte Bachelor aweth by bill £3 6s 8d;

George Courtenay, Richard Peperell & Anthonie Peperell awe £9 15s;

John Ryman [?] & William Cloade awe 55*s*;
Sum £89 8*s* 1½*d*.

The totall some of the goods & good debts amount at £123 5*s*
   8½*d*.

Debts desperate
Firstly to Yeo of Dunsforde aweth 3*s* 9*d*;
Soper of Dunsford for bread 20*d*;
John Martyn of Kistow aweth 6*s* 8*d*;
William Wills of Morton for bread 13*s* 4*d*;
Wolcott of Alphington for bread 18*d*;
John Wills of Exmester for bread 30*s*;
Foster of Kenton for bread 8*s* 6*d*;
Widowe Whithead aweth 14*s*;
Widowe Marshall of Kenton aweth 30*s*;
Widowe Duringe of Dawilish aweth 8*s* 6*d*;

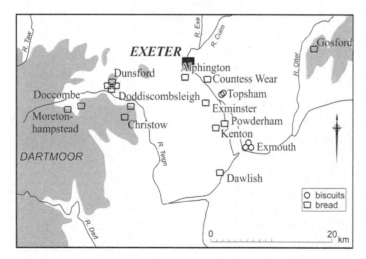

Fig. 22. The pattern of debts owed to the Exeter baker Nicholas
Glanfield on his death in 1583 (OC 33). The debtors for bread fall
into two groups – one around the Exe Estuary, the other extending
westward to the Teign Valley and towards Dartmoor. Those owing for
biscuits came solely from the ports of Topsham and Exmouth; they
were presumably ship's biscuits
(*graphic: T. Ives, Exeter Archaeology*).

Richard Dallegrave of Dawlish aweth 40*s*;
Wotton of St Thomas parish aweth 4*s*;
William Carewe 4*s* 6*d*;
John Felows for a horsse £3 6*s* 8*d*;
David Wills aweth 20*s*;
Miles Barrowe clerk aweth 10*s*;
Humfry Collipresse aweth 4*s*;
Richard Pope aweth 40*s*;
John Wilcocks aweth 44*s* 10*d*;
[3v.] Mark Palmers aweth 10*s*;
Thomas Upham & Thomas Hearde awe by a bande £20 for
payment of £10 wherof £5 is paid so rest to paie £5;
Roger Gotham and John Cole awe by bill 20*s*;
Sum £23 17*s* 11*d*.

Debts awinge by ye Testator
Firstly to John Geane £6 18*s*;
To John Trewman of Crediton £4 10*s*;
To John Morris for wood 14*s*;
To Richard Addis for malt 9*s*;
To Henry Glanfeilde £3 2*s*;
To William Mathew 50*s*;
To my Lorde for rent 23*s* 4*d*;
More to hime for rent 6*s* 8*d*;
Sum £19 13*s*.

Funeralls
Wherof the Executrix Craveth allowans for funeralls 30*s*;
Sum 30*s*.

**Summary Inventory of Nicholas Glanfilde, 17 July 1583
ECA Book 141**

[97v.] (95v.) Nicholas Glandfylde
The Inventorey of the Goodes & chattells of Nicholas
Glandffilde late of the Cittie of Excester lately decessed
praysed by George Glubb John Marshall John Blackmore and
Geordge Serell uppon theire othes the 17th of Julye *in the 25th
year of Queen Elizabeth* 1583

The Halle £4 13s;

The parlor £3 2s 3d;

The chamber over the Halle 21s 6d;

The chamber over the Shoppe £6 6s 6d;

The Shopp 16d;

The Butterey 12d;

The kytchen 17s 2d;

The Bake house £5 8s 8d;

The lynnen 19s 4d;

The plate £6 15s 4d;

The backe chamber 8d;

The stabell 21s 6d;

The backe Courte £3 13s 4d;

The Debtes £88 8s 1½d;

The Debtes Desperat £23 17s 11d;

Sum £147 3s 7½d.

Whereof yn Debtes which the Testator did awe £19 13s;

Also in Desperate Debtes £23 17s 11d;

Also for funeralles 30s;

Sum £45 11d.

So remeineth £102 2s 8½d;

Which *[98] (96)* which some of £102 2s 8d *[sic]* is to bee devyded in to 3 equall partes and then theire amounteth to every parte £34 10¾d.

Viz.

To the wife for her 3th parte £34 10¾d;

To John Glandffeelde & Judeth Glandfylde £34 10¾d;

To the executrix for the performaunce of the wille £34 10¾d;

Sum £102 2s 8¾d.

Memorandum that theire is geven in legacys first [to] the Mawdlyn 2s 8d;

To John Glandfilde the Testators soune £20;

To Judeth his daughter £20;

To Henry Glandfilde the Testators brother 40s;

To John Horwell 6s 8d;

Sum £42 9s 4d.

Which some of £42 9s 4d muste bee payde with the Testators parte which [amounts] to £34 10¾d and so there is loste in every pounde of the legacye 6s 9½d *[sic]* and every legacie is to receve for every pounde geven in legacye bute 16s 2½d by which Accompte every Childe or Orphane of the Testator is to have as followeth

To John Glandfylde and Judeth Glandfylde for theire Orphanage every of them £17 5¼d - £34 10¾d *[sic]*;

To them of £40 geven in legacies or every of them £16 4s 2d - £32 8s 4d;

So dewe to the Orphanes £66 9s 2¾d.

46. INVENTORYOF JOHN MUDDYFORD, 13 JULY 1583

ECA, Orphans' Court Inventory 32

This Inventory [of – crossed through] Indented taken the 13 daye of July 1583 *in the 25th year of the reign of Queen Elizabeth* of the goods and chattels that were the goodes of John Muddyford some tyme the husbande of Ursula Denham of the Citie of Exon widow by John Tucker cordwayner and Thomas Jordaine wever as foloweth

The Hale

Firstly a Benche 6d;

Item an olde cowbarde 5s;

Item an olde coffer 3s;

Item a Chare & stoole 14d;

Item a Bedsted a paynted Tester to the same 4s;

Item 5 cushens and a matt upon the benche 12*d*;
Item the painted clothes about the hall 3*s*;
Item a fetherbed a duste bed a fether bolster a flock bolster a
    fether pilow a peare of Blanketts 20*s*;
Item one Bowe a sheeffe of arrowes and a blacke bill 3*s*.

In the Chamber
Item 3 bedstedes 3 painted Testers to them and the painted
    clothes about the chamber 10*s* 8*d*;
Item a fetherbedd a flocke bedd a fether Bolster a flocke
    bolster a fether pylowe a Blanckett and a Sheete 15*s*;
Item a flocke bedd 2 duste bedds a fether bolster 2 litle fether
    pylowes a coverlett a flock bolster and 2 olde coverletts 15*s*
    4*d*;
Item 3 coffers and a Shippe coffer 6*s*;
Item a litle olde Bord and 2 hampers 14*d*.

In the chambre over the Shoppe
Item a table borde a Benche 2 olde formes and a carpett 5*s*;
Item one olde Coverlett 2*s*.

In the Shoppe
Item a litle table borde 4 Tubbes a Standerd 2 Stooles and olde
    painted clothes and other olde trashe 3*s* 6*d*.

In the Garden
Item a Heape of Stoons 8*d*.

In the oute chambr
Item 2 Bedstedes a flock bed a dust bedd and 2 olde coverletts
    and a bolster 5*s*.

In the oute Shoopp
Item a plancke a Towrne a haver a hande sawe a pare of
    pynsis and olde trashe 20*d*.

In the Stable
Item a Gryndinge Stoone and 2 Roles and a great shed of
    tymber 12*d*.
In the Kychen
Item a Table bord a Benche A fforme and a Joynyd Stoole 2*s*
    6*d*;
Item an olde Cowbarde a Bearer a Salt Barrells uppon two
    shelves and a lether Bottle 20*d*;
Item a Cage for poultrye and 2 Shelves over ytt 12*d*;
Item a Spytt a goose panne a ffryenge panne 1 grydyrons a
    pare of Tongs 3 pott hangyngs 3 pott crookes and other
    olde Iron 5*s* 6*d*;
Item 8 pewter platters a pewter basen 12 pewter podgers 6
    sawcers and 5 tynne spones 16*s* 8*d*;
Item 6 brasse potts and 3 posnetts 27*s* 4*d*;
Item 4 brasse panns and a litle Cawdron 13*s* 4*d*;
Item 2 pottle potts of Tynn 3 quarte potts of Tynn 2 pynt potts
    of Tynn and 2 flowre pots of Tynn 3*s* 2*d*;
Item 7 Candlesticks a basen of brasse 2 chafyndyshes and a
    litle salte of tynn 4*s* 8*d*;
Item one gowne of broodclothe 10*s*;
Item a pare of dowlas sheetes and one canvas sheete 10*s*;
Item 2 pare of canvas sheets 4*s*;
Item 2 Canvas Bordclothes 3*s* 4*d*;
Item 2 pyllobers 12*d*;
Item 2 Stoone Cupps and one drynkinge glasse 6*d*;
Item one Iron Shovell and one olde garden rake 8*d*;
Item an olde Racke and an olde planke for a manger 2*d*;
Item 4 olde costes and an olde Cowle 8*d*;
Item a Conye Hutche 4*d*;
Item a peare of playenge tables and an olde bread grater 8*d*;
Item a litle Brasse morter and a pestle of Iron 12*d*;
Item an olde mantle 4*d*;
Sum total £10 16*s* 8*d*.

47. WILL OF NICHOLAS GRENOWE, BARBER OF ST DAVID'S PARISH, 17 JANUARY 1584

Orphans Court Will 24
Note: The will has been partly devoured by vermin.

In the name of God amen I Nicholas Grenowe of St Davids in the countie of the Cittie Barber of good mynde & perfecte remembraunce thanks be unto almightie god in the 17th daie of January *in the year* 1583 *in the twenty-seventh year of our gracious queen Elizabeth* do make and ordeyne this laste will and testament in manner and fourme followinge That is to saie ffirste I geve and bequeath my soule to almightie god my Creater and maker, besechinge himm of his everlastinge goodnes for his sone my savior & redeemer Jesus Christe sake to receave the same, and my bodie to be buryed in the earth Item my lease of my groundes called Bradley and Yeilder Hall Parke after the death of Katheryne Grenowe my mother I geve with the same groundes to Thomas Grenowe my sonne duringe the terme that then shalbe to come of the said lease in the same, But my said mother duringe her lease to enjoye the same lease and groundes Item more to the said Thomas my sonne I geve my Tenement and one acrer of grounde with the lease of the same, which I bought of Mr Pollerde lienge and beinge in Otterie St Marie in the countie of Devon. And to the said Thomas my sonne I do also geve all my lands and tenements that I holde of William Filmore and are lienge and beinge in the parishe of Ottery St Marie in the Countie of Devon aforesaid with the conveyaunces concerninge the same, and to the same Thomas my sonne I geve my twoo great Iron Andirons in the kitchen, my second Brasen Crocke, and twentie six shillings eight pence of lawfull money of England to hime to be paid and delivered at his aige of one and twentie years. All which premises to my said sonne geven I do will and ordeyne that my Executrix and overseers of this my laste will and testament together do oversee & use to the most advantage [of – crossed through] and profitt of my said sonne , untill it shalbe to himm paid and delivered as aforesaid. Item the obligation that I have under the handes and seales of Thomas Coppe and Thomas

Coppe [*sic*] in the which they stande bounde to me in twentie poundes for the payment of tenne pounds as in the same appeareth I geve and bequeath unto Marie my daughter and to John Furse equally betwene them to be devided when it is or shalbe recorded. Item to Elizabeth my daughter I geve and bequeath that my own ffetherbedd furnished and that one standinge beddsteede which nowe & be in my litle Chamber with my cubberd and tabelborde nowe standinge in my heigher hall. And to the same Elizabeth my daughter I do also geve and bequeth three poundes of lawfull money of Englande and my presse that standeth in one of John Furnace Shoppes and my beste Brasen Crocke. All which premisses to my said daughter Elizabeth geven shalbe to her paid and delivered at her aige of sixetene yeares or daie of marreage which firste shall happen and my will is that myne Executrix and myne Overseers togeither shall see the same used to the best advantage of the said Elizabeth my daughter untill it shalbe to her dewe to be paid and delivered as aforsaid. Item to Marie my daughter I geve and bequeath my ffethbedd and bolster with the standinge bedsteede tabell borde and forme nowe standinge and beinge in the Chamber wherein I nowe lye. And to the said Marie my daughter I do also geve and bequeath three poundes ... of Englande and my thirde great Brasen Crocke all which premisses to the said Marie my daughter ... and delivered at her aige of sixetene yeares or daie of marriage which shall first happen ... my said Executrix and overseers together do use the same premisses or cause the same to be us... advantage of the said Marye my daughter untill it shalbe dewe to her to be paid and delivered ... Richarde my wiefe I geve and bequeath one Shoppe, twoo Chambers and one stable p ... dwell in St Davids aforesaid and whare next the Eastgate of the Cittie of Ex[eter] ... holde unto her for and during the terme yet to come of the lease of my house where it is ... geve and graunte to that John Furnace my

Tenant shall holde my twoo shoppes that ... me parcell of my said house wherein I nowe dwell for and duringe the whole terme yet to co ... said house where it is parcell, so that he the said John Furnace do and shall year ... terme so it is to come yeilde and paie trulie to the said Executrix of this my last will ... testament ... yerlie rente of three poundes of lawfull money of Englande for the same quarterly by even ... during ... terme to come as aforesaid otherwyse the twoo shoppes clearlie to be and remayne to thonlie ... duringe the saide terme. Item I do farther will and grante that Harrye Reynoldes my Tenant duringe the terme that shalbe to come of the leas of this my house wherein I nowe dwell after the determynacon & expiracon of the lease by me to him graunted concerning certaine parcells of the same house shall or maye have a ... holde all and singuler the chambers roomes and other the premiss to the said Henry by me the said lease granted So that he the said Harrie shall and will yeilde and paye for the same to my said Executrix the Annuall or yerlie [dorse] rent of ffouer poundes of lawfull money of Englande yearlie duringe the said terme so then to come by over porcons quarterly accordinge to my trewe meaninge otherwyse all the said premisses after the expiracon of my lease and grante to the said Harrie made concerninge the same Clearlie to be and remayne to myne Executrix during the saide terme so then to

come. Item to Richarde my wief I do geve and bequeath my best brasen Crocke. Item to Katheryne my mother I geve £5 of lawfull money of Englande Item to my unckell John ... owe of Oterye I geve £5 of lawfull money of Englande Item to my three sisters I geve 12 ... Item to Nicholas Babbe I geve 12d. Item to John Babbe I geve 12d provided alwaies and ... will ... said somme happen to die before he shalbe of the aige of 21 yeares or my daughters ... or age of 16 yeres a peece the legacie or leagices of him her or them, so dieng be ... childe or children then livinge equally emongest them to be devided. Item all the ... Debts Chattells and demandes whatsover not before geven nor otherwise by ... Testament [deposed – crossed through] dispersed my debts, legacies & funerall paid and disclosed I e ... to Richarde my wief whom I mak and ordeyne to be my sole and onlie execut' ... last will and testament. And the overseers of this my last will and Testa ... Charitable desier and appointe to be Thomas Elworthie and John Furnace ... Overseight and Charitable paynes herein to be taken I do geve to them my s ... my own tabelborde that is nowe standinge in one of John Furnaces shoppes wittene ... my laste will and testament the persons and is named Tho: Elworthie Christopher Halstaff ... Batten, John Furman and John Martin with others.

48. INVENTORY OF ANTHONY ROBYNS, OF ST JOHN'S BOW PARISH, 28 SEPTEMBER 1584

ECA, Orphans' Court Inventory 34

Note: Recognisances were entered into on 11 May 1585 for Philip, Robert, Alice and Margery, the children of Anthony 'Roberts' (ECA, Book 141, Folio 85. See also Folio 150).

The Inventorye of the goods & chattelles of Anthonye Robynes dessessed of the parishe of St Johns bow of the Citye of Exon the 28th of September 1584

Firstly in the backer chamber 16 yeards of paynted clothes at 4d the yeard 5s 4d;

Mor one old bord standinge upon a frame with one old forme 2s;

In the mydell chamber a bedsted wythe a fylled tester & a trockell bed at 20s;

Mor one sellinge bord standinge upon a frame with 6 Joyned stolles one forme and one old bynche 15s;

Mor one old close stoll & a lytell stoll and one old bedstead at 4s;

Mor one fether bed 3 bolsters 5 pelowes containing 127 lb att 5d the pound – £2 12s 11d;

Mor one fether bed & one bolster containing 72 lb att 5d the pound – £1 10s;

Mor one old flocke bed containing 38 lb at 2d lb – 6s 4d;

Mor 5 canvas bedtyes & 2 bolsters at 3s 4d;

Mor 2 yernynge coverletts at 6s 8d;

Mor 3 old yernynge coverletts at 2s;

Mor 3 pere of old blancketts at 10s;

Mor one doblet of taffata with a lase 20s;

Mor one doblet of dyid canvas at 5s;

Mor one cloke of brode clothe at 26s 8d;

Mor one gowne with a lase faced with boudge £2 10s;

Mor one old gowne faced with lame 23s 4d;

Mor one old cloke att 6s 8d;

Mor one old wosterd Jaquet with owt Slyves at 4s;

Mor 2 old wastcotts at 12d;

Mor one old fryse cot withowt slyves 2s;

Mor one old doblet of Rashe at 3s 4d;

Mor one old frise gowne & a Kassacke of fryse faced with Lame 10s;

Mor one pere of botthose of whyt Kersye & a pere of yeringe stockens 5s;

Mor 3 nyght capes of Sattyne good & bad at 5s;

Mor one Rowne cappe at 2s 6d;

Mor 2 hatts at 2s 8d;

Mor 2 quyshins of Lyse unfylled 1s;

Mor one old bearinge blanckett and one old gryne carpett at 2s;

3 pere of canvas shytts at 16s 8d;

Mor 1 old pere of dowlas shitts at 2s 6d;

Mor 1 pere of canvas shitts at 1s 4d;

Mor 6 pelotyes at 4s;

Mor one dozen of dowlas napkens at 5s;

Mor 6 napkens of canvas 18d;

Mor 6 old canvas napkens at 6d;

Mor 3 handcarchers at 6d;

Mor 3 tableclothes of canvas 3s;

Mor one pere of Lynynge Slyders and a pere of Lynynge hosse & a pere of socks 12d;

Mor 3 old sherts at 5s;

Mor 5 sherts bands & 3 pere of hand Koffs 5s;

Mor 2 hand towells at 6d;

Mor 2 cobordclothes at 2s;

Mor in platters poddingers Sassers flower potts copes with one goblett & one candelstycke of tyne containing 52 lb att 5d the pound – 21s 8d;

Mor 2 crocks one possenett containing 38 lb at 4d the pound – 12s 8d;

Mor 2 old drypinge panes of platt 6d;

Mor 3 candelle stycks of brase 2s;

Mor one old catherne & a skellett 2s;

Mor one ffryinge panne 6d;

Mor one broche one pott hanginge one pot hock one gredell one pere of an Irons one brandyse with other things belonginge to the Kychen containing 46 lb att 1½d the pound – 5s 9d;

[2] Mor for a pewer Salte gylted which lyethe in pawne in £2;

In the fore chamber 2 old bedsteds 2s 6d;

Mor one Rowne bord standinge upon a frame 18d;

Mor 3 old coffers at 2s;

Mor one old tressell bord at 6d;

Mor one canvas tester paynted 6d;

Mor one Lockinge glase 6d;

Mor one hand barskett 4d;

In the gallerye & stable in wod & colles 13s 4d;

Mor 5 tubbes & one peck 3s;

Mor one lader 6d;

Mor 3 corse & a coull 2s 6d;

Mor one mosterd myll 12d;

Mor one chyse Rack with other trashe 18d;

Mor in the hall 6 tynnynge spones 3d;

Mor 6 stonynge copes 12d;

Mor 3 drynckinge glasses 6d;

Mor 5 old cheres Lytell & great 18d;

Mor 4 yeards of whyt Kersyes at 2s – 8s;

Mor 2 pere of Slyders & one old gyrken 5s 6d;

Mor one barskett & a lytell boll 3d;

Mor one cradell 6d;

Mor a handflaskett 3d;

Mor one pere of bellowes 2d;

Mor 2 mylwell fyshes 8d;

Mor one towell of narowe clothe 12d;

Mor a dowe clothe of canvas 12d;

Mor a synge herdell & a lattes 6d;

Mor 2 cornne bagges 16d;

Mor 2 brushes 12d;

Mor in cornne 3s 4d;

Mor in the shope 88 yeards of canvas att 8½d the yeard – £3 2s 4d;

Mor 25 yeards of canvas of 9½d the yeard – 19s 9½d;

Mor 2 newe smocks of canvas 3s 4d;

Mor one shert band of dowlas 8d;

Mor one pere of wolcards 12d;

Mor 4 dozen trenchers 12d;

Mor 11 dozen Lether poynts 10d;

Mor in Best thryd 6s;

Mor one deske 20d;

Mor 5 combs with 4 boxes 6d;

Mor 2 Knyves 1d;

Mor one case of boxes 2s;

Mor in takell 3d;

Mor halffe a pound of starche 2d;

Mor 9 lether pursses 4d;

Mor in p'ingsetye [?] 18d;

Mor halffe a grose of thryde bottons 4d;

Mor 6 lb of black Sope with the barell 18d;

Mor one pere of skalles 2s 6d;

Mor in black Inkell 3d;

Mor one dozen of Lether lase 1d;

Mor one pound of brase wyghts at 18d;

Mor one pere of Small ballences 12d;

Mor one pere of sheres 2d;

Mor one Slyken stoune 4d;

Mor a cheste 5s;

Mor the shelffs with the bordes 16d;

Mor 2 old prime bagges 4d;

Mor one salt tubbe at 6d;

Mor one wylowe to put hopes in 6d;

Mor one pound wayght of led 1d;

Mor 3 Lytell bands for chyldron 6d;

Mor 31 yeards of Inderlyngs at 10s;

Mor 4 yeards ½ quarter of Red mockado at 7s 6d;

Mor 61 yeards of dowlas 13d yeard £3 1s 1d;

Mor 48 yeards of dowlas at 11d the yeard £2 3s;

Mor 64 yeards ½ of narow treger at 8½d – £2 5s 8d;

Mor one elle holand at 6s 4d;

Mor 7 elles ½ of holand at 5s 2d thell £1 18s 9d;

Mor one ell holand at 4s 8d;

Mor in 2 Remletts 14 ells ¼ of holand at 4s – £2 17s;

Mor 27 elles holand at 2s 8d thell £3 12s;

Mor in Remletts 2 yeards of hollmes fustyn 2s 6d;

[3] Mor 3 quarter of hambrowclothe at 6d;

Mor in Hoppes 8d;

Mor in holand wrapes of tragor & canvas 20d;

Mor in Redye monye the some 26s 8d;

Mor the lease of the howse £18;

Sum £69 17½d.

Deapts speratt & desperatt as foloweth

Firstly by here shope bock £5 8s 11d;

Mor by a band upon Thomas Esworthy William Esworthey & Jno Wylles £15;

Mor by Humffrye Martyne £3;

Sum £23 8s 11d.

Sum total £92 10s 4½d.

Deapts due by here as folowethe

Firstly to Mr John Howell £14 10s 2d;

Mor to Richard Bevyse £9;

Mor to Mrs Alse Swyt wydow £10 17s;

Mor to the wydow Trelewe 8s;

Mor to a woman that kept him in his syknes 5s;

Mor to John Welles the hosser for & in consyderacyon of his paynes in hope to Receve his helthe 5s;

Mor due to Johane Romley the syster of the sayd Anthony desseased £3.

The Whole some of the Inventory amount to £92 10s 4½d;
Whereof funeralls 13s 4d;
For detts which the testator dyd ow £38 5s 2d;
For desperate debts £8 8s 11d;
Sum £47 7s 5d.

So remaineth £44 2s 11½d.

Whereof
To the wiff for her 3rd part £14 14s 4d;
To the executrix to performe the will £14 14s 4d;
To the 3 orphans for their orphaneg £14 14s 4d;
Sum £44 2s 11½d.

Memorandum there is geven yn legacye £26 which is to be payd onely out of the testators which is onely £14 14s 4d and then their is lost yn evry pound 8s 4d and so every legatary is to have of every pound bequethed but 11s 8d and then every orphane is to have as foloweth [blank].

[3v.] [31 October] 1587
The debts of Anthony Roberts [*sic*] decessed
By the shop book £5 8s 11d;
Esseworthe oweth £15;
Humfry Martyn £3;
Jo[hn] Hopkyns £12;
Edw[ard] Polyn £15;
Roger Davy £10;
Geyllye of Inpham [?] 40s;
Andrews of Rockebeare 40s;
Alis Robyns of Exmyster 20s;
Henry Taylor of Pynne 8s;
£65 16s 11d.

Legacys
To Philyp Robyns a gowne priced at 50s Item a doblet price at 20s – £3 10s;
To Philip Alys & Mary at the mareg of their mother £20;
To the poore 20 [illegible];
To Robert Robyns [a gowne price – crossed through] 23s 4d;
To Roger Davy & George Drew 6s 8d;
£26;
Which some of £26 is to be payed with £14 14s 4d and so every legatory loseth yn every 20s – 8s 8d.

To Philip Roberts for his orphanege £4 18s 1½d;
To him of his legacye of £6 13s 4d – £3 15s 7d;
To him of his legacy of £3 10s – 39s 8d;
£10 13s 4½d.

To Alys Roberts for her orphanege £4 18s 1½d;
To her of her legacy of 20 nobles – £3 15s 7d;
£8 13s 8½d.

To Margaret for her orphaneg £4 18s 1½d;
To her for her legacy of 20 nobles – £3 15s 7d;
£8 13s 8½d.

ECA, Orphans' Court Inventory 34 [Item 2]

Monie laid out since my husbands death
Firstly paid to Mr Robarte Ellecot for a barne in Southinghaye that he tooke of him 28s 4d;
Item paid to John Podger for a peice of grasse that he tooke of him which yeelded us not a pennie 40s;
Item paid to William Bale for his charges & pains bestowed aboute my husband 20s;
Item for the buriall and for charges in his sicknes 30s;
Item for provinge his will 12s 4d;
Item for charges in my sicknes, and paid to them that did for me in the same 26s 8d;
Item for charges bestowed on my 2 children in theire sicknes, wherof the one had a greate impostrane in his arme 6s 8d;

Fig. 23. Three inventories (OC 34, 40A, 48) make reference to the Dayment family of masons; Gregory Hunt's inventory of 1592 records John Deament's home 'without Southgate'. Both Richard and John Deament worked on the building of the new portico of Exeter Guildhall in 1592–4 and on the city wall; John has also been identified as the maker of a number of grand local tombs including that of Sir John Acland's monument in Broad Clyst church, probably erected *c.* 1613–14, shown here (Wells-Cole 1981, 11–12; Blaylock 1990, 141–2; Stoyle 2003, 145–57; *photo: G. Young*).

Item paid to Priggs for horsmeat 6*s*;
Item paid for a stabell that he tooke 2*s*;
Item paid to John Deament the mason 20*s*;
Item paid to Heithfill the baker 20*s*;
Item paid for reparacons about my house 5*s* 4*d*;
Also my horse is dead of late beinge prised upon the will;
Some is £10 15*s* 6*d*.

ECA, Orphans' Court Inventory 34 [Item 3]

The dets that Farnandy Callender hath receved uppon sartayn bands and byls whych was of the dets of Anthony Robyns late desessed
Item John Happkyns also Gybs hath receved £12;
And of on[e] Edward Pallen of Fenton £15;

And of on[e] Roger Davey of St Sydwyles £10;
And of on[e] Thomas Esworthey of Exon £13;
And of he that ys lord of hys hous £3;
And of Gelley of Hucksom [?] 40*s*;
And of on[e] Aandros of Rakbear 40*s*;
And of on[e] Alys Robyns of Exmister 20*s*;
And of on[e] of Brod Clest £3;
The hoele Som ys £61.

ECA, Orphans' Court Inventory 34 [Item 4]

Mony which Rawling Mallock of Axmister & Robert Robens do charge Fardynando Callender with all as exewtre to Anthony Robens of Exceter decessed
Firstly they charg him with £3 8*s*, which is left out of the Inventory;
Item with £24 19*s* receyved from Thomas Eswourthy whereof he hath put in the Inventory butt £15;
Item whearas Anthony Robens by his testament gave unto Phillip his soun one howse wherein he lat dwelt, they charg the said Fardynando with the rent of the said howse ever sythens the decesse of Margery Robens wife of the said Anthony;
Item they Charg him with £3 which her doth with hold from Johane Runilith [?] being dewe dett by Anthony Robens as may appear uppon the Inventory;
Item they stand bond in the some of £20 to Mr Hooker with condycon to pay unto him £10 & interest for the same, not withstanding they do sythens charg themselves with the keeping of the said Phillip, which bond they pray to bee redrest.

ECA, Orphans' Court Inventory 34 [Item 5]

[verso] Anthony Robyns desperat debtes
Harry Tayler 26*s*;
John Gregory of Stocke 4*s* 3½*d*;
Peter Warren of Stocke 7*s* 10½*d*;
John Gannerley 1*s* 6*d*;

Elizabeth Norley 8s;
Nycholas Jacobe 3s 2d;
Goumid [?] Weleys 2s 6d;
William Bruer 3s 4d;
John Lovis 1s 8d;
A man of Rockbere 5d;
Bronewyll of Alphynton 2s 2d;
John Crues 10d;
A woman of Kenton 2s 3d;
Margaret Walis 2s 8½d;
Thomas Hunte 1s 6d;
John Hosyers wyffe 1s 11d;
Florens Waye 9d;
One Arthure of Chydley 1s 2d;
Stephen Ford 4s 10d;
Mary Jarman 5d;
Thomas Welis 1s 1½d;
Gommyrd [?] Ford 8d;
Ammys Lawerans 2s 3d;
James Helyer 3s 4d;
Gommyr Willes 2s 6d;
Anthony Tayler 9s;
Elizabeth Woodcok 2s 7¾d;
Johan Hayne 2s;
William Hopen for a peare of wolcards 1s 4d.

ECA, Orphans' Court Inventory 34 [Item 6]

[verso] Lewes Robert debitors
[1] Umpounded
John Fyshe; John Maynard; Thomas Wylson; Fraunces
Walker; Richard Wetherton; Mr Thomas Harrys; Peter
Gonestone; Edward Flud tayler.

Dischardgd
Roger [Sadler – crossed through] Selby sadler.

Hathe [rest illegible]
Thomas Grenewodd £5 19s 9d; William Chaffe.

Pleaded a release at the comon law
Robert Prowse; Edward Jermyn; John Anthonye.
Reffered to Mr Hert whether it be paid or not
John Ellicot tayler; Mr John Tosyer he is yn suet at the law;
Sinckler; Edward Webber late servaunte to Hugh Wylsden;
Vallentyne Tidberye carryor; Seprian Nedle; Thomas
Suthwodd tucker; Richerd Duck; William Stone; Robert
Dunscombe; Mr John Hoyle; William Prowse servaunt to
Mr Nycholas Martyn; Jerom Hillyar goldsmyte; John Bande
tucker; Richerd Master and John Butcher; Harry Payne; John
Prowse; Richerd Hardinge; Christopher West; Mr Collyn
preacher; John Downe; John Chalyce.

[2] Promyseth payment
John Stansby 10s; Mr Lewys Bagbier; Harry Smyt; Harry
Smyt for John Butler; Thomas Sandy; Myles Lambert; William
Yard; William Payne; Thomas Blackeller; John Trewman;
Thomas Sampson; Mr William Martyn; Richerd Smarrage; Mr
Denyse; Gylbert Dodd alias Lymbrey; John Elacot; Mr John
Levermore; Bartholmewe Thorne; John Twiggs; John Keridge.

Dischardged
Mr Bigglestone; John Spurwaye.

49. INVENTORY OF WILLIAM DODDRIDGE, OF EXE ISLAND, 7 MAY 1586

ECA, Orphans' Court Inventory 35

Note: Recognisances were entered into on 30 October 1587 for John, William, Florence, Margaret, Christopher and Thomasine, the children of William 'Doddridge' (ECA, Book 141, Folio 92 dorse).

The Inventory of the goodes & cattalls late of William Dodderudge of Exiland in the countie of the Citty of Exon deceased praised by Jerome Harmon Richard Meyne & Nicholas Evans the 7th dae of Maie 1586

[1] In the Hall
Firstly one Tabell borde 26s 8d;
Item one Presse with A Cubbord 26s 8d;
Item 6 Joyned stooles 6s;
Item one little Borde with Two fformes 5s;
Item one Settell 5s;
Item one little Chaire 4d;
Sum £3 9s 8d.

In the Chamber over the Parlor
Firstly one Cubbord 6s 8d;
Sum 6s 8d.

In the middle Chamber
Firstly one Bedsteede 13s 4d;
Item one Presse with a deske upon it 30s;
Item one fflockbed 23s 4d;
Item one Sweete Cheste 30s;
Item the Seelinge with the Benches 30s;
Item two Gownes £5;
Item two Clokes £3;
Item two paire of black brodecloth breeches 6s 8d;
Item one Spruse Lether Jerkyn and a doublett 6s 8d;
Item 16 yardes of new white Cloth 21s 4d;
Item 3 yardes of new Blew Cloth 6s;
Item one bed Tye 10s;
Item two Coverletts & a Carpett £6;
Sum £22 17s 4d.

The Pewter
Firstly 17 Platters great 17s;
Item 6 small Platters 5s;
Item 17 Pottingers 8s 6d;
Item two dosen of Sawsers 8s;

Item 6 Candlesticks 10s;
Item one Morter one Pessell & a Chaffing dishe 2s;
Item 2 Quarts & Pyntes and 4 fflowerpotts 6s;
Item one Bason & Ewer 1s 6d;
Sum 59s.

The Naprie
Firstly 10 paire of sheetes whereof 8 paire of Canvas one paire of dowlesse and one paire of Hoolland £3;
Item two dosen of Canvas Bordnapkins 12s;
Item 4 Bordecloths of Canvas & one of dowlesse 8s;
[2] Item 4 Pilleties 6s;
Item 3 Cubbord Cloths 5s;
Item 6 hande Towells 12d;
Item one Coffer 16d;
Sum £4 13s 4d.

In the Maides Chamber
Firstly one Corselett and an Aloman Ryvett 26s 8d;
Item one Calyver with a Hedpeece 10s;
Item one littell Settle 2s 6d;
Item one old Bedsteede 12d;
Item one fflock bed one Bolster of flocks one Blankett, one Coverlett and one olde Mantell 9s;
Sum 69s 2d.

In one other Chamber
Firstly one fflockbed one fflock bolster 2 father pillowes 2 Blanketts 2 Coverletts & the bedsteede 30s;
Item one other fflockbed one fflock bolster 1 blankett 2 Coverletts & the beed steed 20s;
Item one Truckell bedsteede one flock bed one Bolster 1 Blankett & 2 Coverletts 26s 8d;
Item one fflockbed one fflock bolster 2 Coverletts & 1 Blankett 20s;
Item 2 fflock Bolsters 3s 4d;
Item 2 bords & a fforme 12d;
Item 1 paire of playinge Tables 16d;
Sum £5 2s 4d.

In the Kitchen
Firstly two Pans & two Cauldrons 33s 4d;
Item 4 brasen Crocks 1 Possenet & 1 Skillett 40s;
Item 3 driping Pans 1 frying Pann 1 ladell & 2 Skeemers 6s 8d;
Item 3 Andyrons 2 doggs, 3 Crooks 2 Pott crooks 3 Broches 1 Toster and one Gridyron 13s;
Sum £4 13s.

In the Bruyng house
Firstly one greate ffurnys £6;
Item one little ffurnys 26s;
Item 2 Messhen Keeves 20s 8d;
Item 5 overlade Keeves 33s;
Item 23 Cooling Trendells 26s 8d;
Item 1 Coole Vate 6s 8d;
Item 1 Torner [?] & 1 Reering Keeve 3s;
Item 64 half Barrells £3;
Item 25 half dosens & 2 dosens 13s 4d;
Item 2 Standes 18d;
Item other Implements belonging to A Brewing house 2s;
Sum £15 12s 10d.
[3] In the Chamber over the brewhouse
Firstly one dosen of hard Woode 9s;
Sum 9s.

In the Garner
Firstly Sacks & half of Row Malte £4 4s;
Item 6 Sacks of Barly Malt £5 8s;

Sum £9 12s.
In the Courte
Firstly 16 Piggs £6;
Sum £6.

Debts sperat £18 12s 6d;
Other debts sperat £38;
Debts desperat £12 8s.

The Plate
One goblet gilted £7;
One goblet parcell gilted £3;
1 salte gilted £4;
2 stonyng Cupps Covered with sylver £4;
1 other stonyng Cupp gilted 50s;
11 Spoones 50s;
Sum £23.

There is other bad ymplements about the house amount at 10s;
Sum 10s.

The lease of the house for the widdowes life £8;
The revercon thereof for John her soune £4;
Sum £12.

Sum total £182 14s 10d.

[Signed] N E RM Jerome Harmon.

50. INVENTORY OF GILBERT LYMBERYE, HATTER, 2 JUNE 1586

ECA, Orphans' Court Inventory 36
Note: the register of the parish of St Paul was heavily damaged during the Exeter Blitz of 1942 but an earlier transcript published by the Devon & Cornwall Record Society in 1933 recorded the burial of Gylbert Lymbery on 10 May 1586.

The Inventori taken the second daye of June in the yere of our Lord god 1586 of all such goods, cattells, redye money, plate, dett, and howshold stuff as weare late in the possession of one Gilbert Lymbery of Exceter hatter deceased praysed and sett downe by John Spurwaye of Excet merchant & John Dode, and John Garrett of the same Citty Hatter praysers theire unto appointed according to the order and custom of the said Cittye *viz* 1586

[m. 1] *Firstly* syx weomenns hats lynded with spaynish Taffata att 4s 8d the peece 28s;

Item one dozen of weomenn hatts lynded with elbrode Taffata att 3s 10d the peece £2 6s;

Item 14 hats lyned with spaynish Taffata for menn att 3s 6d a peece £2 9s;

Item one dozen and half of hatts for menn lyned with elbrode Taffata att 2s a peece £1 16s;

Item 19 hatts lyned for menn att 2s 8d the peece £2 11s 8d;

Item 2 dozen of hatts lyned for menn att 2s 4d the peece £2 16s;

Item 18 estridg ffeelts lyned with Sassnett att 16d the peece £1 4s;

Item fyve littell Narrow felts lyned with vellett for men att 4s 6d the peece £1 2s 6d;

Item three ffelts of the midell syse lyned with Vellett att 4s 6d a peece 13s 6d;

Item one dossen and Syx ffelts fased, eidged for weomenn att 2s 4d a peece £2 2s;

Item ffourtenne brod weomens feelts eidged and ffased att 22s the dozen £1 6s 8d;

Item eight weomenns feelts fased after the rat of 26s the dozen 16s 8d;

Item 2 dozen & eight hatts of the middell syses, fased and eidged for menn att 21s the dozen £2 16s;

Item Syx ffeelts for weomen untrymed after the rat of 22s the dozen 11s;

Item 6 feelts of the middell syses for weomenn untrymed att 16s the dozen 8s;

Item 7 felts of the middell syse faced att 19s the dozen 11s 1d;

Item 8 braide feelts faced and eidged att 19s the dozen 12s 8d;

Item 2 dozen of menns feelts untrymed att 18s the dozen £1 16s;

Item Syx dozen and two hatts of smale hatts untrymed for menn att 15s the dozen £4 12s 6d;

Item three braide spaynish felts after the rate of 16s the dozen 4s;

Item 2 dozen of smale ffeelts untrymed after the rat of 9s the dozen 18s;

Item 3 estridg ffeelts for weomenn eidged, faced, and bounded after the rat of 24s the dozen 6s;

Item 13 estridg feelts eidged faced, and bounded att 20s the dozen 21s 8d;

Item 15 estridg ffelts faced, & bonded at 15s the dozen 18s 9d;

Item fyve littell Narrow feelts faced and eidged att the rat of 15s the dozen 6s 8d;

Item 17 estridge feelts untrymed att the rat of 10s the dozen 14s 2d;

Item 2 dozen and three feelts of course estridg feelts eidged and banded att 9s the dozen 20s 3d;

Item Syx course ffeelts eidged and banded att 8s the dozen 4s;

Item eight course feelts eidged and banded att 6s 6d the dozen 4s 4d;

Item 6 graye feelts eidged and banded att 15s the dozen 7s 6d;

Item 15 childers feelts faced, eidged and banded att 12s the dozen 15s;

Item 6 childeren hatts trymed att 12s the dozen 6s;

Item 11 boyes hatts trymed att 10s the dozen 9s 2d;

Item 2 dozen and Syx childeren feelts trymed att 7s the dozen 17s 6d;

Item 13 childeren hatts trymmed att 16s the dozen 17s 4d;

Item 2 cullered ffeelts eidged and faced att 2s 8d the peece 5s 4d;

Item 4 cullered ffeelts att 2s 6d a peec 10s;

Item 10 cullered feelts att 2s a peece 20s;

Item 13 course coullered childerens feelts untrymed att 4s the dozen 4s 4d;

Item 11 graye childeren hatts untrymed att 6s the dozen 5s 6d;

Item 4 coullered ffeelts lyned and unbonded after the rat of 3s 6d a peece 14s;

Item 4 coullered hatts lyned and banded att 4s the peece 16s;

[m. 2] Item one coullered ffelt, faced and banded 6s;

Item one coullered feltt untrymed 2s 4d;

Item 4 yeards and 3 quarters of Tawny [Taffat – crossed through] Sypars att 2s 6d the yeard 11s 10½d;

Item 5 yeards and quarter of black sipars att 20d the yeard 8s 2d;

Item one lardge vellett hatt banded 32s;

Item ffyve steeched hatts of Taffata att 8s the peece £2;

Item ffyve Taffata hatts playted att 6s 8d a peece 33s 4d;

Item 6 black feelts lyned att 32s the dozen 16s – 16s;

Item 6 feelts feelts lyned through att 10s the dozen 20s;

Item Syx smale felts lyned att 28s dozen 37s 4d;

Item 6 course feelts lyned att 22s the dozen 11s;

Item 6 Narrow feelts faced att 6s 8d a peece 34s;

Item 6 smal feelts eidged with vellett att 3s 10d a peece 23s;

Item 6 lardge hatts faced with vellett att 6s 8d a peece £2;

Item 8 brayde coullered feelts att 40s the dozen 26s 8d;

Item 6 coullered ffeelts att 30s the dozen 15s;

Item 15 coullered gerrells hatts att 18s the dozen 22s 6d;

Item 12 coullered hatts for boyes att 21s the dozen 21s;

Item 5 childerens hatts att 2s a peece 10s;

Item 2 brayed taffata hatts for menn att 3s 4d the peece 6s 8d;

Item 5 feelts lyned att 3s 4d a peece 16s 8d;

Item 9 course feelts banded att 20s the dozen 15s;

Item 15 course feelts banded att 8s the dozen 10s;

Item eight course feelts att 7s dozen 4s 8d;

Item 15 course feelts att 15s the dozen 18s 9d;

Item 21 weomens hatts eidged and faced att 25s the dozen £2 3s 9d;

Item 3 Estridge ffeelts faced for weomen eidged and faced att 22s the dozen 5s 6d;

Item 17 feelts faced and banded att 26s the dozen 36s 10d;

Item tenn feelts untrymed att 15s the dozen 12s 6d;

Item one dossen feelts for weomen lyned att 4s 6d a peece £2 14s;

Item 12 feelts lyned for weomen att 3s 8d the peece £2 4s;

Item 11 estridge feelts lyned with sarsenett and bands of 24s the dozen 22s;

Item one half block lyned and banded att 5s 4d – 5s 4d;

Item one half block faced and banded att 3s – 3s;

Item one dozen childerens feelts att 14s the dozen 14s;

Item 7 feelts for boyes att 12s the dozen 7s;

Item 15 childerens hatts att 9s the dozen 11s 3d;

Item three dossen of Childerens feelts att 6s the dozen 18s;

Item syx black childeren feelts att 8s the dozen 4s;

Item 8 course breaythed childerens felts att 4s the dozen 2s 8d;

Item Tenn breaythed cullered feelts faced and banded att 31s the dozen 26s;

Item 7 gerrells hatts cullered att 16s the dozen 9s 4d;

Item 6 feelts cullered untrymmed att 20s the dozen 10s;

Item 4 weomens feelts cullered untrymmed att 24s the dozen 8s;

Item 2 coullered feelts uneiged att 4s the peece 8s;

Item 4 coulered feelts [faced – crossed through], lyned and banded att 4s 8d the peece 18s 8d;

Item one dozen coullered feelts for weomen lyned and eidged att 4s 8d a peec £2 16s;

Item 8 coullered feelts lyned and eidged for weomen £2 1s 4d;

Item 2 coullered feelts lyned for menn with vellett att 7s the peece 14s;

Item one coullered feelt for a womann lyned with vellett pryse 11s;

Item one black feelt for a womann lyned with vellett with out band 10s;

[m. 3] Item 2 black feelts eidged with gold with out band att 5s the peece 10s;

Item one breaythed coullered fillt 3s 4d;

Item one coullered filt eaten with mothes 1s;

Item one dozen and half covering hatts att 6s the dozen 9s;

Item one golden band wrought uppon vellett 8s – 8s;

Item one golden band 6s;

Item 3 smal golden bands att 4s – 4s;

Item 20 copper bands att 6s the dozen 10s;

Item one copper band att 4s the dozen 5s;

Item 18 course smale copper bands att 20d the dozen 2s 6d;

Item one dozen of Round bands of silck att 8s the dozen 8s;

Item 13 round silck bands att 6s the dozen 6s 6d;

Item three round bands of silck att 3s the peece 3s;

Item 6 roles of Sypers att 4*s* the dozen 2*s*;

Item 6 round bands for weomen att 7*s* the dozen 3*s* 6*d*;

Item 2 dozen and half of arnoll bands att 8*d* the dozen 20*d*;

Item 22 course feathers for childerens hatts att 8*d* the dozen 14*d*;

Item 16 childeren feathers att 20*d* the dozen 2*s* 3½*d*;

Item 3 vellett nightcapes att 3*s* 6*d* [the – crossed through] a peece 10*s* 6*d*;

Item 2 Sattenn Nightcappes att 22*d* the peece 3*s* 8*d*;

Item one silck nightcapp pryse 3*s* 4*d* – 3*s* 4*d*;

Item 2 knytt cappes of renell att 14*d* the peece 2*s* 4*d*;

Item 4 worsted cappes att 8*d* the peces 2*s* 8*d*;

Item 2 fyne cappes att 3*s* 4*d* a peece 6*s* 8*d*;

Item 8 cappes att 22*s* the dozen 14*s* 8*d*;

Item 6 cappes att 12*s* the dozen 6*s*;

Item 8 cappes att 10*s* the dozen 6*s* 8*d*;

Item 7 course gerdells att 2*d* a peece 14*d*;

Item one dozen of black boxses att 20*d* dozen 20*d*;

Item 3 bryshes att 8*d* a peece 2*s*;

Item 5 cappes att 5½*d* a peece 2*s* 3½*d*;

Item 15 playen Sipars bands att 15*s* the dossen 18*s* 9*d*;

Item 2 dozen playen Sypars bands att 11*s* the dozen 22*s*;

Item 2 dozen of playen Sipars bands halfe breade att 7*s* 6*d* a dozen 15*s*;

Item 2 dozen of currell Sipars bands att 7*s* 6*d* a dozen 15*s*;

Item 9 currelld bands att 1*s* a peece 9*s*;

Item 11 whole breads sypars bands currell att 15*s* a dozen 13*s* 9*d*;

Item 6 dozen and half of smale Sipars bands att 5*s* the dozen 30*s*;

Item 6 whole breads bands of cullered silck Sipars att 2*s* 4*d* a peece 14*s*;

Item 5 half breades of cullered sipars att 13*d* the peece 5*s* 5*d*;

Item 5 half breads of Silck sypars att 11*d* the peece 4*s* 7*d*;

Item 4 yards of leven Taffata att 11*d* the yeard 5*s* 8*d*;

Item a fewe peecs of cullered Taffata 12*d*;

Item one yeard and half of Spanysh Taffata att 4*s* the yeard 7*s*;

Item a fewe peecs of black Taffata 3*s*;

Item 14 thousand bugells 2*s* 6*d*;

Item 2 steayes 6*d*;

Item one ounc and one quarter of gold att 5*s* the ounce 6*s* 3*d*;

Item 10 yards of welten vellett 20*d*;

Item 3 dozen of crowne leaves of vellett att 3*s* the dozen 9*s*;

Item a fewe peecs of vellett prysed att 3*s* 4*d*;

Item 4 ouz of spaynish silck 16*d*;

Item 7 ouncs London silck att 10*d* the ounce 5*s* 10*d*;

Item 6 ouncs and half of cullen att 4*d* an ounc 2*s* 2*d*;

Item 2 ouz of copper att 6*d* the ounc 12*d*;

[m. 4] Item a fewe Remletts of Sipars prise 2*s* 6*d*;

Item 2 breaythed pouches att 16*d* a peece 2*s* 8*d*;

Item 6 yeards of lace 1*s*;

Item one clu [?] of silck 4*d*;

Item 4 reames of cap paper att 2*s* a reame 8*s*;

Item 3 pear of Sysers pryse 16*d*;

Item 10 lb of led at 1*d* the pound 10*d*;

Item one peare of old weights pryse 10*d*;

Item one pear of Scalls and weights 16*d*;

Item 3 glasses pryse 6*s*;

Item 9 quyers of strong cappaper 2*s*;

Item one littell box a standich and a litell baskett 3*s*;

Item 2 stalclothes with a penticcloth a latteic and 8 blocks 6*s* 8*d*;

Item fyve studs 10*d* – 10*d*;

Item 15 yeards of Narrow peaynted clothes about the shopp att 1*d* a yeard 15*d*;

Item all the presses, with the furnytur about the shopp and thereunto belonging £3;

Item a littell sea cheast for the shopp 2*s* 6*d*;

Item 4 Monnmouth cappes att 2*s* 4*d* a pec 9*s* 4*d*;

Item 4 lichfeeld cappes trymmed att 20*d* a peec 6*s* 8*d*;

Item 6 course lichfyld cappes untrymed att 10*s* the [peece – crossed through] dozen 5*s*;

Item 4 Night cappes knytt of cruell att 14*d* the peece 4*s* 8*d*;

Item 4 wounsted cappes att 11*d* the peece 3*s* 8*d*;

Item 28 yeards of Sypars att 2*d* the yeard 28*s*;

Item 22 bands for hatts 12*s*;

Item 13 half breads of currelled sipars att 8*s* the dozen 8*s* 8*d*;

Item 13 playen Sipars bands att 8*s* the dozen 8*s* 8*d*;

Item tenn Sypars bands 10s;
Item 6 bands att 20d a peese 10s;
Item 4 bands att 13d a peece 4s 4d;
Item 6 Sypars roles att 9s the dozen 4s 6d;
Item 4 bands att 3d a peece 12d;
Item 12 bands att 7s the dozen 7s;
Item one Square pole feelt 18d;
Item 34 yeards of curreled sipars att 17d the yeard £2 8s 2d;
Item 26 yeards of cullered Sypars att 17d the yeard £1 16s 10d;
Item 23 yeards and half of smuth sypars att 16d the yeard 31s 8d;
Item 14 yeards of curreled sipars att 14d the yeard 16s 4d;
Item 2 yeards of smith sipers att 14d the yeard 2s 4d;
Item 28 yeards of cullered sypars att 12d the yeard 28s;
Item 27 yeards of curreled Sypars att 12d the yeard 27s;
Item 18 yeards of currelled sypars att 12d the yeard 18s;
Item 28 yeards of cullered sypa[rs] att 7d the yeard 16s 4d;
Item 32 yeards of smouth sypars att 7d the yerd 18s 8d;
Item 32 yeards of smouth sypars att 7d the yeard 18s 8d;
Item 29 yeards and 3 quarter of Sypars att 5½d the yeard 13s 3½d;
Item 36 yeards of Sypars att 5½d the yeard 16s 6d;
Item 33 yeards of sipars att 5½d the yeard 15s 1½d;
Item 29 yeards of Sypars att 5½d the yeard 13s 3½d;
Item 9 eells and a quarter of changabell Taffata att 11s 6d the ell £5 6s 3d;
Item 2 ell & 3 quarts of Taffata att 9s the ell £1 4s 9d;
Item one yeard and half & half a quarter of black vellett att 15s the yeard 24s 1½d;
Item 13 yeards of spaynish Taffata att 4s 8d the yeard £3 8d;
Item 2 dozen and Syx covering feelts att 6s the dozen 15s;
Item the glase in the wyndowes 5s;
[No sum.]

Howshold Stufe & apparrell
[m. 5] Firstly 4 Joyned stooles and 3 other stols and 2 chars stooles and one littell stoole 5s;
Item one prese in the Hale pryse 23s 4d;
Item 6 greene cusshens att 4 penc a peece 2s;

Item 2 littell carpetts 5s;
Item 2 yeards russett Kersye att 2s 4d the yeard 4s 8d;
Item one Jerken leayde with lace 10s;
Item one dublett of Raysh 6s;
Item one dublett of dyed canvas 3s;
Item 3 peair of bryches & 3 peair of stockens 18s;
Item one black Cloke 33s 4d;
Item one russett clock 15s;
Item one woren capp 1s;
Item 2 Wastcotts 4s;
Item 3 sherts and seven bands 8s;
Item one peair of sheets of dowlish 10s;
Item 2 peair of canvas sheets 11s;
Item 2 peair of littell canvas sheets 6s 8d;
Item 4 pillowtyes 4s;
Item one cubbord cloth 2s;
Item 2 canvas bord clothes 6s 8d;
Item 2 course bord clothes of canvas 2s;
Item 20 bord Napkens pryse 5s;
Item 8 hand towells course 2s;
Item one olde torren booke of marters 8s;
Item one Bibell 10s;
Item 10 littell books 3s;
Item 2 doges for the Hall chymny of Eeron 16d;
Item 20 yeards of paynted cloth 5s;
Item the Stayned clothes in the chamber 6s 8d;
Item one Joyned bedsteed with a truckelbed in the chamber 20s;
Item one littell squar tabell bord 2s 6d;
Item one chest 6s;
Item one coffer 5s;
Item 2 littell doggs of Ieron 1s;
Item one close cheare 1s 8d;
Item one pear of blanketts 12s;
Item 3 fether pillowes 5s;
Item one fflockbeead & bolster 2 blanketts and one old scryde coverlett pric 6s 8d – 6s 8d;
Item one fether beed one fether bolster one peair of blanketts & 2 old quilts 30s;

209

Item a flock bead and a flock bolster & a Thrummed coverlett 13s 4d;

Item one dust beead & bolster 2s 6d;

Item a playen bedsteed 4s;

Item 2 course coverletts 8s;

Item one Shopp Chest 6s 8d;

Item one long chest 2s;

Item 2 old [coverletts – crossed through] coffers 16d;

Item one old sword 3s 4d;

Item 2 bryshes att 6d a peece 12d;

Item 6 ynch bords 14d;

Item 2 flaskeets 8d;

Item 2 dawetubes 4d;

Item 7 peeair of old happers great and smal 7s;

Item wood about 5 seames att 8d the seame 3s 4d;

Item one Caidge 16d;

Item 2 pyks one evell, a colrake a hachett, and a horscombe 2s;

Item 3 lings 4 gerses 2 hearclosts one hallter 4s 6d;

Item 2 pack saddells & one old hackney saddell & a brydell 10s;

Item 2 peair of Tressells 4d;

Item Haye in the lafte 8s;

Item pools for a staninge 6d;

Item 3 old tylts one black cloth one old forshewe & 4 old packen clothes 8s;

Item 4 old buckerham clothes 2s 6d;

Item half a peece of weab & old rods 8d;

Item a short tabelbord 2s;

Item one old chapping stock and shelves about the kichen & 8 yeards of matt 2s;

Item one Almerye 2s 6d;

Item one powdering tubb 8d;

Item two costs 12d;

Item 2 old catherens 4s;

Item 2 brase potts one Skillett and scimmer & a frying pann 10s;

[m. 6] Item one peair of AndIerons a shoule a peair of tonges a pott hanginge & 2 crocks, a grediron, a fleshock & 2 spitts 10s;

Item one covering baskett a certayn erthen potts and cuppes & tryen boles with a hallf dozen of spounes 20d;

Item 7 candelsticks whereof one latten 6s;

Item one Basen and Eawer of peawter 2s;

Item half a dozen of yeardishes 2s;

Item 2 salts and one tyning bole 2s;

Item one Whytt peawter pott 2s;

Item half a dozen of spounes & one copper spoune 8d;

Item 10 platters 7s;

Item 6 poddengers 3s 4d;

Item 14 sawcers 4s;

Item 7 poole of old peawter 2s 4d;

Item one peair of snaffers 2d;

Item 2 vennes dishes 12d;

Item 4 drinking glasses 10d;

Item 4 dozen of trenchers 12d.

Plate

Firstly 2 Silver cuppes gylded with a cover weayinge 48 ounces att 5s the ounce £12.

Morrey [sic]

Item in redye mony £17 17s 7d.

Leases

Item one lease of the shopp in the Highstreat for 10 yeres yett to com wourth no more then the rent [blank].

Sperat detts dewe to the Testator

Sperat detts in the whole amounteth to £23 12s 2d.

Desperat detts uppon his book

Item desperat detts dewe uppon his book £15 14s 5d.

The whole some of this Inventory besydes the desperat detts cometh to £228 11s 3d;

And with the desperat dett this Inventorye commeth to £244 5s 8d.

51A. WILL OF JOAN REDWOOD, WIDOW OF ST KERRIAN'S PARISH, 18 MAY 1587

ECA, Orphans' Court Will 27

Note: a note follows in Latin that the will was proved in the Archdeaconry of Exeter on 23 June 1587. The register of the parish of St Kerrian recorded the burial of 'Jone Redwoode wydowe' on 28 May 1587. Recognisances were entered into on 8 October 1588 for Susanne and Nicholas, the children of John Redwoode, Baker and his wife Joan (ECA, Book 141, folio 97).

In the name of God Amen, the 18th daye of Maie in the yere of our lorde god 1587 I Joane Redwoode of Exeter widowe beinge sicke of bodie but thankes be unto god of good and perfecte memorie do make this my laste will and testamente in manner and forme followinge ffirste I geve and bequethe my soule into the handes of Almightie god my maker and to his sonne Christe my redeemer, and my bodie to be buried in the Churcheyearde of St Peters. Item I geve unto the poore people of this cittie 30s to be geven unto them in breade at the Discretion of my Executor. Item I geve unto my sonne Robarte Redwoode of the Cittie of Bristowe my beste salte seller of silver guylte desiringe him to be good and carefull for the reste of his brother and sisters as my truste is in him that he will doe. Item I geve unto my sonne Richarde one fetherbed perfourmed with one coverlette one peare of sheets one peare of blanketts one bolster and one pillowe. And unto everie one of the reste of my children not before named I geve the like bedd perfourmed. Item I geve unto Matthewe Downe my servante one flockebedd with one peare of blanketts and one coverlette. Item I geve unto Elizabethe my daughter my beste gowne of clothe and one wostedd gowne and my best petticoate And unto Susanna my daughter five petticoates and two [petticoates crossed through] cassockes, more I geve unto Elizabeth my beste coverlett and to Susanna my best carpette and my beste bordclothe of diaper and the rest of my wearinge lynninge to be divided betwixte my two daughters and the residewe of my householde lynnings to be devided amongest my children. Item to Elizabeth I geve one peare of curtens and unto Susanna one peare of curtens. Item I geve unto Nicholas my sonne £20 of lawfull money to be paide him by my Executor And unto Richard my sonne £7 and unto Hewe my sonne £6 and unto Lawrence my sonne £6 And unto Elizabeth my daughter £6 13s 4d And unto Susanna my daughter £6 13s 4d. And more unto Elizabeth my daughter I geve one brasen crocke one brewen chissell one cauldren. And unto Susanna my greate crocke and one panne and unto Richarde one crocke And unto Lawrence one crocke and unto Hughe one crocke more unto Lawrence one greate panne. All the Residewe of my lands goodes and chattells my Debtes funeralls and legacies beinge paid I geve and bequeathe unto my sonne John Redwoode whom I make and ordayne my whole Executor And I ordayne and appoynte for Overseeers of this my will and testamente Edmond Coke and John Sampforde and for their paynes I geve unto them 6s 8d apeice. I wittnes this to be of truthe I have hereunto putte my signe geven the daye and yere above writen witnes John Sampforde Anne Sampforde my will is that Elizabethe my daughter shall have for her parte the bedd and bedsteede in the parlor one bolster and two pillowes and that bedsteede with bed bolster pillowes in the litle Chamber nexte to the windowe I geve unto Susanna. Lawrence is to have one flockbedd of the beste besides the firste geven unto him Hughe is to have the middell bedd and bedsteede, more to Elizabethe my presse in the Chamber and boxe, and the cheste in the parlor to Susan. To Elizabethe my greate borde in the halle. To Lawrence the borde in the parlor and forme and to Hughe the carpitte. To Elizabethe the Cubbarde in the parlor. My will is that if any of my children do dye before they come to theire full yeres or be married that then theire partes to be devided emongeste the reste.

51B. INVENTORY OF JOAN REDWOOD, WIDOW OF ST KERRIAN'S PARISH, 21 SEPTEMBER 1587

ECA, Orphans' Court Inventory 37

The Inventorye of all and singuler the goods Chatells & debtes of Joane Redwoode widowe late of the parishe of St Kerian within the cittye of Exceter deceassed taken & praised by Thomas Jordene Roger Speere & John Toocker of Exceter aforesaid the 21th daye of September in the yere of the Raigne of our sovereign Ladye Elyzabethe by the grace of god of England France & Ireland Queene defender of the faith &c which praised were sworn.

[m. 1] In the Haull
Firstly a Cubbord 7s;
Item a foledinge tableborde & a fourm 12s;
Item another tableborde & a fourm 6s 8d;
Item the seelinge of wayscot with the binches & the portole 26s 8d;
Item the hangings of sea with borders staynd & a litle staynd clothe 6s 8d;
Item 2 ioyned stooles & 2 chayrs 20d;
Item a carpett & a dosen cusshins of greene 3s;
Item a bason and year 2s;
Item a platter & 8 flowerpotts 2s;
Item 4 candlesticks of brasse & a tinning salt 4s;
Item a cubbord clothe 6d;
Item a olde bible 2s 6d;
Item a Iron barr in the chimney and a payre of Iron dogges 4s;
Item a Carpett of dornex 4s;
Some £4 2s 8d.

In the Buttery within the Haull
Item 27 platters of Pewter 22s 6d;
Item 20 pongers of Pewter 10s 10d;
Item 6 porrishe dishes 2s;
Item 19 sausers & a olde ponger 4s 4d;
Item 7 plates of pewter 2s 4d;

Item a charger & a litle bason & a bole & 3 olde porishe dishes of pewter 3s 4d;
Item 2 pottle potts 2 quartepotts & 2 pynte potts of Powter 7s;
Item 2 Water potts a pynt & a half pynte 3s;
Item a latten bason & a yore 3s;
Item 4 chafinge dishes 4s 6d;
Item 10 candlesticks of brasse 7s;
Item a olde coffer & certayn shelves & litle borders of staynd clothe 20d;
Some £3 11s 6d.

In the Parler
Item a Cubbord 3s 4d;
Item a folding table & a fourm 6s 8d;
Item a dansck Chest 10s;
Item 3 olde coffers 3s 4d;
Item a bedstede & a trockle bedstede with ye Tester 12s;
Item 2 fetherbeds 53s 4d;
Item a bolster & 2 pillowes of fethers 6s 8d;
Item a coverlet & a payer of blankets 6s;
[m. 2] Item the seelinge of waynscot with the binches 10s;
Item the staynd hangings 20d;
Item a barr in the chimney 16d;
Item a pewter bason & 2 flower pots & a salt of pewter 20d;
Item a dosen of trenchers paynted 8d;
Item 2 brushes 8d;
Item a hand sawe a payr of pincers & other olde trashe 2s;
Some £5 19s 4d.

In the fore chamber
Item a standinge bed & a truckle bed stede 5s;
Item a longhe bedstede 12d;
Item 2 fetherbeds 30s;
Item 5 bolesters of fethers & 2 pillows 8s;

Item 2 flock beds 8s;

Item 4 olde blanckets 3s;

Item 3 olde coverlets a rugg & a olde mantle 5s;

Item a presse & a olde cubberd 8s;

Item a olde tableborde 16d;

Item 2 olde chests 2s;

Item a chear stoole 6d;

Item the staynd hangings & the olde curtings for the windowe & a olde cushing 4s;

Item a coverlet of tapestreworck 30s;

Item 5 curtayns of seagrene 7s;

Item 2 remnants of housholdecloth being 9 yards & half 10s;

Item a coverlet 3s;

Item 3 litle bells over the haule 2s 6d;

Some £6 8s 4d.

In the litle chamber

Item 2 olde bedstedes 20d;

Item 2 flockbeds 6s 8d;

Item 2 bolsters of fethers 2s 6d;

Item 2 olde coverlets & a olde rugge a ratten mantle & 2 blankets 3s;

Item a olde chest a olde tableborde 3s;

Item 2 payr of Almen rivets 2 bills & other trashe 12s;

Item the staynd hangings & a staynd teaster of a bed 2s 6d;

Some 31s 4d.

In the gallerey chamber

Item 2 olde bedstedes with teasters 5s 6d;

Item a olde featherbed & a olde bolster 10s;

Item a olde coverlet & 2 olde blankets & 2 olde ruggs 3s 4d;

Item a staynd hangings 20d;

Item a olde chest 12d;

Item a fetherbed a bolster a payr of blankets 13s 4d;

Item a coverlet 2s 6d;

Item a tableborde 3 dosen of tranchers 2s;

Some 39s 4d.

[m. 3] In the back chamber

Item 2 ioynd bedstedes with teasters 10s;

Item a fetherbed 33s 4d;

Item 3 bolsters & 4 pillows of fethers 10s;

Item a coverlet & a quilt 2 olde blankets & 2 olde ruggs 6s 8d;

Item a olde table borde & a olde Stoole 12d;

Item a coverlet 10s;

Some £3 11s.

In the brandlaft

Item 20 bushell of brand 6s 8d;

Item a tubb with a range a candle mould & 4 oven stocks 4s 4d;

Item a hogshed a coffer & a musterd mill 2s;

Item a peke & a Awter nett 10s;

Item 4 dosen of quarters timbre with other trashe 6s 8d;

Some 28s 8d.

In the shoppe

Item 2 chests to putt bred in 6s 8d;

Item 2 thousand of biskey £8;

Item a tubb a hogshed a olde borde 3 baskets & other trashe 2s 4d;

Item 16 sacks & a pece of sackcloth 20s;

Item 10 lb of lamtow 15 lb of melly woll 6 lb of course russet 16 lb of white woll 26s [6d – crossed through];

Some £11 5s.

In the seller

Item 3 hogsheds 5s;

Item 11 half barels 7s;

Item 6 half dosens 3s;

Item 6 bruige keves 12s;

Item 4 traindels a range & a tunner 4s 2d;

Item a powdring tubb & 2 boles 3s;

Item 2 hogsheds of beare 18s;

Some 52s 2d.

In the daackhouse
Item a baode trendell & a trowe to make bred & range &
   certayne other trumpery 3s;
Some 3s.

In the entrye
Item a beam a skale with the ropes 2s;
Item a great chest 16d;
Item 6 hogsheds a tubb & a bushle & half barrell & a Cowle
   4s;
Some 7s 4d.

In the bakehouse
Item 2 bunting hutches 5s;
Item 2 trawes 3 bordes pertaineng to them 10s;
Item 2 brakes & a couch borde 3s;
Item 6 piles & a streaner 8d;
Item 3 pecks with a salt box 12d;
Item a dow keve 2 graters & a peck 8d;
Item a payr of ballance with ledden weights 2s 2d;
Item certayn sargers 2s;
[m. 4] Item a pann 4s;
Item 3 sacks of wheatmeall & beanflower 50s;
Item 2 bushels of wheat 8s;
Item half a sack of malt 4s;
Item 2 shovells a oven stopper & other trumpery 16d;
Some £4 11s 10d.

In the Citchinn
Item a great brasse crock 12s;
Item 2 lesser crocks 12s;
Item a broken crock 2 litle crocks & 3 skillets 11s;
Item a brasse morter & a pessell 20d;
Item a great pann & 4 cauldrens 14s;
Item 2 litle panns with steales a skomer & another olde pann
   3s;
Item 3 dreping panns 6d;
Item 3 broches 3s;
Item 6 pothangings 3 Iron crocks a gridiron a fyrepan & a

payr of doggs 6s;
Item a friengpann & a grape of Iron 3s 4d;
Item a payr of Iron doggs 2 Iron barrs & a Andire 6s 4d;
Item 4 tubbs 4 buckets & a bole 18d;
Item a borde 8d;
Item the shelfes & other trumpery 20d;
Item a brassepann 4s;
Item Kitchingstuffe 2s;
Item 2 bottels 8d;
Some £4 3s 4d.

In the Backside & stable
Item a bucket & a roap & chayne 2s;
Item certayne olde stone 2s;
Item 5 trusse of haye £4;
Item the dunge 5s;
Item racks & mangers 2s;
Item a bruinge chittle 10s;
Item 2 sowes & a pigg 20s;
Item 3 capons a cock & a hen 20d;
Item certayne olde bordes 2 ratten tubbs & other trashe 20d;
Some £6 4s 4d.

In Southenhaybarn
Item in cornn rude & strowe £20;
Some £20.

Item in napery
Item 2 olde diaper bordeclothes 10s;
Item 2 bordeclothes of dowles & a olde diaper towell 6s 8d;
Item 4 canvas bordclothes 4s 8d;
Item 2 dosen of bordenapkins 7s;
Item 12 pilloties 12s;
[m. 5] Item 5 payr of shetes of dowles and hulland 33s 4d;
Item 5 payr of cressecloth & canvas 20s;
Item 4 payr of canvas shetes & a old shete 15s;
Item 6 bordetowels 12s;
Item 5 other towels 18d;
Item a cubberd cloth 2s;

Item 2 handtowels 4*d*;
Some £6 4*s* 6*d*.

In plate
Item 2 stoancupps with 2 covers & 2 footes of silver all gillt
£3 3*s* 4*d*;
Item 9 silver spoones wayeng 10 ounces 40*s*;
Item a salltt all gillt 3 ounces £4;
Item a goblet & a tunner parcell gilt at 4*s* 6*d* the ounce waieng
25 ounces £5 12*s* 6*d*;
Some £14 15*s* 10*d*.

Item a carpett 6*s* 8*d*;
Some 6*s* 8*d*.

Her aparell
Item a gowne of browne blew £3;
Item a wostead gowne 20*s*;
Item a peticoat 16*s*;

Item a gowne of buffing £3;
Item a clothe gowne 20*s*;
Item 2 peticoats 16*s*;
Item another peticoat 16*s*;
Item a taffetoe hatt 5*s*;
Item a feltt hatt 2*s* 6*d*;
Item a taffetoe Apron 18*d*;
Item another new hatt 6*s*;
Item 12 partlets 20*s*;
Item 4 dowlis aprons 3*s* 4*d*;
Item 4 canvas aprons 12*d*;
Item 16 karchers of hullond 20*s*;
Item 10 kearchers of Callecow 5*s*;
Item other trumpery 12*d*;
Item a desck in the parler 9*s* 4*d*;
Some £14 2*s* 8*d*.

Debts spirat & dispirat dew to her £50;
Some the hole £163 8*s* 10*d*.

52A. WILL OF JOHN FOLLETT, MERCHANT, 8 JANUARY 1588

ECA, Orphans' Court Will 26

Note: Recognisances were entered into on 3 October 1590 for Margaret the daughter of John Fallott (ECA, Book 141, Folio 113) and son John on 1 October 1591 (ECA, Book 141, Folios 134–135).

In the name of God Amen The eight daye of January 1587 and in the Thirteth yere of the Raigne of our soveraigne Ladye Queene Elizabeth I **John Fallett** of the cittye & countye of Exeter the Elder marchant sicklye in bodye butt perfect of mynde, the lorde be praised doe make & ordayne this my testament & last will in manner and forme folowynge **Fyrst** I bequeathe my sowle to Almightye god my onlye Savyor hopinge by hym to be saved, and my bodye to the Christyn buryall in the Churche yarde of St Peter in Exeter so neere to Agnes Fallett my lovynge wiefe decessed as may be **Item** I geve & bequeatheto the poore of the parishe of St Olave in Exeter 2*s* 6*d* Item I geeve & bequeathe to my sonne John Fallett All my seelynge in the hall of the howse wheare I dwell with a Table borde, a side Table borde Six stooles, a Roan chayre In the chamber withn the hall a bedsteade a cupbord with stayned clothes In the Chamber over the hall my seelynge & Presse In the kytchen a Table borde Cupbord Shelfes stayned Clothes a forme a peare of Iron Racks In the Shopp Two Chests Shelves & Bordes one Roan chest covered with lether my gold Ringe wherwithall I seale one spoone of Silver my litle Byble, my Beame Skales Leade weights the glasse in the wyndowes of the howse wherein I nowe dwell & My ffurnace in the kytchen **Item** I geeve & bequeathe to Hanry Fallett my sonne one Ale cupp garnyshed with silver and doble gilte A chest of walnutt in the Gallery Thirtye Pownds of lawfull money of England one Spoone of Silver & a golde Rynge **Item** I geve & bequeathe to Elizabeth Fallett my daughter my salte of slver doble gilte my greate Iland chest in the chamber within the Hall, a silver spoone one Holland sheete stytched & laced, a Bolster cloth of holland stytched & laced, Three Pillowe [tyes – crossed through] beares of holland stytched & laced & frynged, one Rynge of gold with a Rubye in itt And Thirtye Pounds of lawfull monye of England **Item** I geeve & bequeathe to Anne Fallett my daughter, my best goblett of silver doble gilte, a spoon of silver, a holland sheete stytched & laced, A bolster clothes of Holland stytched & laced, Three Pillowe [tye – crossed through] beres of holland stytched laced & frynged, a golde Rynge which was her mother's Maryage Ringe my vennys cheste in the chamber within the hall and Thirtye Pounds of lawfull monye of England **Item** I geve & bequeathe to Margarett Fallett my daughter my goblett of silver ungilted a silver sppon the fee symple of one close called Redd Downe within the mannor of Taunton Deane in the Countye of Somersett to have & to holde the said close with theappurtenances to the said Margarett her heres & Assignes forevermore after the decesse of mee the said John Fallett and Margye nowe my wiefe **Also** I geeve and bequeathe to the said Margarett Fallett my daughter Tenne Pownds of lawfull money of England **The residue** of all my goods & Chatells nott geven nor bequeathed my debts paid and funerall [dischar

– crossed through] discharged And legacies distributed I geeve & bequeathe to Margerye my wiefe whome I doe make sole Executrix of this my present Testament & last will and she to see my bodye decentlye broughte to the grave **And** for my Overseers I do ordayne & appoynt my Brother in lawe John Ley of Lyme Regis in the countye of Dorsett Maryner and also my Brother in lawe Raphe Cope of the parishe of Collyton in the countye of Devon Bowcher And doe geeve unto them for theire paynes takynge in that behalfe Tenne shillyngs a peece. **Moreover** I geeve & bequeathe to my sonne Henry Fallett my greate Byble my great Brasse crook which was my greate Grandfather's my grandfather's, my ffather's and now myne **Fynally** I geve & bequeathe to my Twoo daughters Elizabeth and Anne All the lynen in one walnutt chest standynge in the Gallerye sometyme pertaynynge to theare mother decessed One kerchiff for a Childe a Jack clothe frynged bothe of hollad A bearynge sheete with a Pawne of Stamell with Twoo laces & frynged with silke All equallye betwene the said [Anne – crossed through] Elizabeth & Anne to be devyded And yf eyther of theym dye, then the other survyvinge shall enioye the same wholye **In witnesse** whereof I have hereunto putt my hand & seile the daye & yere above written in the presence of thease whose names are subscribed

By me John Fallet

[Signed] *William* Notar.

52B. INVENTORY OF JOHN FOLLETT, MERCHANT, 20 AUGUST 1589

ECA, Orphans' Court Inventory 40A

Note: 40b and 40c are copies of this inventory which are also rolls and a summary copy exists in ECA, Book 142, Folio 30. It provides further details on the administration of the estate.

The Inventorye of all the goods & Cattalls and Debts late belonginge unto John Follett of the cytie of Exon merchant decessed praysed by Richard Dorchester Walter Horsey and Paule Triggs the 20th daye of August in the one and Thirtyth yere of the Raigne of our soverigne ladye Elizabeth bye the grace of god quene of England France & Ireland Defender of the faythe &c

[m. 1] In the Shopp

Normundye Canvas

One peece of Normundye Canvas Contayninge 22 elles 2 quarters & half at 16*d* per elle amonts unto 30*s*;

One pece of Normundye Canvas Containing 28 elles & one quarter at 16*d* per elle Amonts unto 37*s* 7*d*;

One pece of Normundye Canvas Containing 28 elles at 16*d* per elle 37*s* 4*d*;

Foure remlets Containing 24 elles 2 quarters & half of Normundye Canvas at 16*d* per elle 32*s* 8*d*;

2 Remlets Containing 14 elles & 3 quarters at 16[*d*] the elle amonts unto 19*s* 5*d*;

Vytrye Canvas

3 yeardes & 3 quarters of fyne Vytry Canvas at 11*d* per yerde 3*s* 5*d*;

42 yerds of vitry Canvas in two peces [of Vitry Canvas – crossed through] at 12*d* the yarde 42*s*;

20 nyne yerdes & 2 quarters of Vitrye Canvas in 4 peces at 15*d* per yarde 29*s* 6*d*;

Seventye one yerds & two quarters of Vitrie canvas at 12*d* per yerd monts to the Some of £3 11*s* 6*d*;

Seventyne yerdes of good vytrye Canvas in two peces at 10*d* the yerd 14*s* 2*d*;

Thirty eight yardes & 3 quarters of vytrye Canvas of the same goodnise [at – crossed through] in two pecs at 10*d* the yerd 32*s* 4*d*;

14 yardes & one quarter of the same vytrye Canvas in Remlets at 10*d* the yerd 11*s* 10*d*;

Seventye yerds [quarters – crossed through] of vytrye Canvas at 10*d* the yerde amonts to the some £2 18*s* 4*d*;

5 yerdes & 3 quarters of vytrie Canvas at 9*d* the yard 4*s* 4*d*;

14 yerdes & on quarter of vytrye Canvas at 7*d* the yarde 8*s* 4*d*;

[m. 2] 6 yerdes & half of fyne Canvas at 18*d* per yarde 9*s* 2½*d*;

11 yardes of Dowles at 11½*d* by the yerde 12*s*;

27 yerdes & half of Dowles at 11½*d* the yarde 26*s* 4*d*;

30 nyne yards of Dowles at 11½*d* the yarde 27*s* 5*d*;

8 yards & one quarter of Dowlese at 11½*d* the yard 7*s* 2½*d*;

33 yardes of Tregare in a Remlett at 9*d* the yard 24*s* 9*d*;

68 yardes of better tregar at 9½*d* the yarde 54*s* 10*d*;

3 yerds & half of fyne Dowlese at 11*d* the yerde 3*s* 6*d*;

6 yards & half of Callacowe at 9*d* the yerde 4*s* 10½*d*;

14 yardes & one quarter of Calacow at 14*d* the yarde 16*s* 7½*d*;

14 yerds & half of hamborowe Clothe at 8*d* the yerde 9*s* 8*d*;

15 yards of white fustyn geanes at 15*d* the yarde 18*s* 9*d*;

5 elles one quarter & one half quarter of holland at 3*s* 4*d* the elle amonts unto the some of 17*s* 8*d*;

8 elles and half of holland at 2*s* 8*d* the elle 22*s* 8*d*;

5 elles & half of Course holland 8*s* 3*d*;

One elle half & half quarter of holland at 2*s* 4*d* the elle 3*s* 9*d*;

4 elles and half of fyne holland at 6*s* the elle 27*s*;

Two elles of holland at 2*s* 4*d* the elle 4*s* 8*d*;

3 elles & one quarter of holland at 22*d* the elle 5*s* 10*d*;

One elle and one quarter of holland at 17*d* the [yarde – crossed through] elle 1*s* 9*d*;

3 elles & one quarter of browne holland at 2*s* 8*d* the elle 8*s* 8*d*;

11 yards on quarter of Rucett geane fustin at 9½*d* the yard 8*s* 11*d*;

5 yards & half of durance at 2*s* 4*d* the yard 12*s* 10*d*;

6 yards & one quarter of red quilts at 13*d* the yard 6*s* 9*d*;

4 sattacocks at 10*s* a pece 40*s*;

5 yard & half of Canvas at 6*d* the yerd 2*s* 9*d*;

11 yerdes & 1 quarter of russett geane fustyn at 9½*d* the yerde 8*s* 11*d* [entry crossed through];

5 yards & halfe of durance at 2*s* 4*d* the yerd 12*s* 11*d* [entry crossed through];

6 yerds & one quarter of rede vylletts at 13*d* the yarde 6*s* 9*d* [entry crossed through];

Half a yerde & half a quarter of colerd Canvas at 2*s* the yerde 1*s* 3*d* [entry crossed through];

[m. 3] 6 lytell shetts for Children at 1*s* a pece 6*s*;

9 plene bandes for Children at 3*d* a pece 2*s* 3*d*;

1 yarde and halfe of sacke Clothe at 14*d* the yerd 1*s* 9*d*;

In pynes 8*s* – 8*s*;

For browne threde 1*s*;

For 9 oncs & half of fine threade at 12*d* the once 9*s* 6*d*;

2 dossen and half of Themells [at 10*d* the dossen 2*s* 1*d* – crossed through] 10*d*;

4 yardes of bone lace at 9*d* the yarde 3*s*;

10 lb 5 yardes of bone lace at 4*d* the yarde 15*s*;

14 yardes of ode lace at [2*s* 4*d* the yarde – crossed through] 2*s* 4*d*;

For Nyldes 8*d*;

One dossen and 3 payer of wolle cards at 16*s*;

For Wycke yerne 12*d*;

For [blank] and 2 botles at 12*d* [blank];

For leather purses & lace 14*d*;

For half a pownde of blacke thred and thre girdells 16*d*;

For frame lace 18*d* & fleex 3 quarter at 6*d* the yerd 2*s*;

For a pownd & half of Whyt Inkell at 2*d* the yard 2*s* 6*d*;

For A sherte and other necessares 3*s*;

For buttons threade 3 dosen 3*s*;

For 48 lb of stirch at 4*d* the pownd 16*s* 8*d*;

For 5 lb & half of Annys seede at 6*d* the lb 2*s* 9*d*;

For 50 powndes of figgs & Reasons at 2½*d* the pownde 8*s* 4*d*;

For 2 oncs and half of saffron & one half quarter at 3*s*;

For 2 payer of ballance at 2*s* 6*d* & 2 pound troye weight 4*s* 6*d*;

For 10 lb of sope at 2*s* 6*d* and half a bushell of Musterdsead 12*d* – 3*s* 6*d*;

In Monye taken £18 2*d*.

[Desperat Debts – crossed through]

Item A boxe and a danske Chest 2*s* 6*d*;

For threde in the same Cheste 3*s*;

For A nest of smale boxes at 1*s* 8*d*;

For a glaced Deske 2*s* 6*d*;

For 2 faier Chests in the Shoppe 20*s*;

For 7 olde barrells in the Shope 2*s* 4*d*;

For the shelf clothers in the Shoppe 3*s* 4*d*;

For Debts in the Shoppe that is owinge £1 6*s* 2*d*;

The Sume of the Shoppe is £59 12*s* 7*d*.

Item for 11 *C* 3 quarters 18 lb of brasell wood at London praysed in £5.

[m. 4] In the Halle

Firstly for 44 yardes of sellinge att 20*d* the yarde £3 13*s* 8*d*;

For a fayer table bourd at 26*s* 8*d*;

For half a dossen of Joyne stooells 6*s*;

For 2 Joyned Chares at 6*s* 8*d*;

For a syde bourd in the same at 3*s* 4*d*;

For half a dossen of Cushines at 12*s*;

For two Carpetts at 17*s* 4*d*;

For A Bibell 10*s*;

For 2 Courtynes with the Iron Rades 5*s*;

For A lokinge glasse 12*d*;

For a Holberne with the 2 Croocks at 5*s*;

For a maye a Litle one 1*s* 6*d*;

For 41 foot of glasse in the Halle 20*s*.

In the next Chamber within the halle

Item a faire bedstede with the trocle bede £2 3*s* 4*d*;

For a feather bede with two bolsters and two pellowes of feathers & to little flocke beds 6 klanketts a Coverlet & Courtyne to yt £3;

For a flock bede on bolster one Pillow & a paire of blanketts at 13*s* 4*d*;

For a Joyned Chest at 40*s*;

For A siprys Chest 40*s*;

For a Cobborde 13*s* 4*d*;

For a payer of AndIrons with the furnitur lyttle Doggs and Byllose 11*s*;

For stene Clothers in the same at 20*s*;

For a whyt Chare of rades at 18*d*;

For the glasse in the same rome at 6*s* 8*d*.

A Chamber within the same Rome

For A bedsteede & a trokle bede at 8*s*;

For 2 flockebedes and 2 bolsters and 3 feather Pellowes 20*s*;

For a rougge & a quilte to the same bede 6*s*;

For 2 Chests in the same at 5*s*;

For stene Clothers in the same Rome 4*s*;

Item in a Cheste of his in Monye 30*s*;

Forsaid tents [?] that Awnsere the Padsle [?] 20*s*.

In the hier fore Chamber

Item a feather bede a bolster a flocke bede & a bolster £4;

For a Coverlett of tapistrye with klankets to yte 30s;

For Cortings in five peces with the frenge to yt 13s 4d;

For a prese in the same Chamber 26s 8d;

For a Chere in the same 4s;

For sellinge in the same 15s;

For 4 pelowes and one of flocks 10s;

For the glase in the same Chamber window 13s 4d.

[m. 5] In ane Iner Chamber

Item for a bedstede 14s;

For a feather bede a bolster & a payer of blankets with a Coverlett 50s;

For a broken bedstede 3s 4d;

For a frame to make Lace 2s 6d;

For a damiske Chest 10 Creses for a house 6s 4d;

For a Corslett and almon Ryvets performed 43s 4d;

For a muskett a sheffe of Arowes & 2 hed pecs at 20s;

For a table borde in the gallerye 8s;

For a Chest in the same at 13s 4d;

For a bedstede at Richard Wheatons 13s 4d.

The Chamber within the gallerye Caled a backe Chamber

Item for a prese in the same Chamber at 4s;

For a saddle & a payer of boots with other necessaryes in the Chamber 10s;

For the glase in these Chambers 3s 4d;

Item his best Coverlett praysed in £3.

For the Lynninge of the same howse

Item 11 table nattkins corse 3s 10 table naptkins at 4d pece 4s 8d;

Item 19 Course table nattkyns at 3s & 6 towells [table nattkines – crossed through] at 4d a peece 6s 4d;

2 fyne bordclothers and 2 Cou[r]se with 1 towell at 6s 8d;

7 payer of shets out of one Chest of ordinary 30s;

6 pylotyes ordinarye at 8s;

5 bands with 6 payer of Ruffs & 6 handarners at 6s;

3 sherts at 8s;

3 payer of Shets 2 payer of tregare & one payer of Canvas at 8s a payer 24s;

2 payer of shets one of Dowlese and thother of Morles Clothe 23s 4d;

One payer of Cheld bed shetts & a payer of half shetts of holland 33s 4d;

5 half shets for Childbede at 4s;

One Wraught towelle at 10s;

2 towells the one of Diaper & the other white at 8s;

One beringe shette & one kercher for a child at 20s;

6 pylotyes of holland at 30s;

3 pylatyes of Course holland at 10s;

Two pylaties of Calacowe at 3s;

One dossen of [fine – crossed through] table nattkyns of fine Canvas at 12s;

One dossen of table nattkyns of Dowlese at 6s;

One dossen of diaper nattkines franged at 13s 4d;

One dossen & half of plene Diaper at 10s;

Two Diaper table Clothers at 23s 4d;

Two table Clothers & one longe towell at 13s 4d;

One square table Clothe at 3s 4d;

One hande towell franged 12d;

In borderes for a Cobbart Clothers 3s 4d;

One fine wraught hand Carcher 2s 6d.

[m. 6] The parell of John Follets bodye

Item his best gowne at £3 10s;

For his next best gowne at 20s 10d;

For the Worst gowne 10s;

For his best Cloake 26s 8d;

For his rydinge Clocke 5s;

Item for his Coat a satten dublet & a fustyn doubtlet 13s 4d;

Item his Leather Jercyne & ane old tafatey Doublett 6s 8d;

Item his 2 payer of hosse 6s 8d;

Item his 2 payer of nether stocks at 3s 4d;

Item his other old Apparell as breches and Doublets at 2s 4d;

Item his hatt & Cappe at 4s;

Item his two brisses at 2s.

Item a goblett & a salt doble gilt at 23 onces at 6*s* & 6*d* the once amonts to £6 6*s* 6*d*;

Item a goblett & 3 spones of sylver 11 onces at 4*s* 8*d* bye the once amonts unto 41*s* 4*d*;

Item a fayer stone Cupp Coverde with silver doble gilte 44*s*.

The Puter Vessell in the Kitchin

Item the Pewter vessell wayeth 1 *C* & 1 quarter £3 10*s* 1*d*;

Item a bason & ever [3*s* – crossed through] 5*s* 4*d* with a quart & a pinte pote 2*s* at 5*s* 4*d*;

Item a salte & two Cuppes of tyne at 1*s* 2*d*;

Item 2 goblets of tyne & a lytle bottell at 18*s* [?];

Item a payer of tyne Cansticks at 11*d* [?];

Item 3 brase Candlesticks at 6*s* 8*d*;

Item 9 lb 3 four peces with a great tyne bottle [at 4 lb – crossed through] 3*s*;

Item a Laver of tyne and a Chamber poott 2*s*;

Item a payer of brase Candlesticks at 3*s*;

Item a bede pane 2*s*;

Item a table borde in the Kitchine at 5*s*;

Item the sellinge with the benche in the Kitchine 13*s* 4*d*;

Item one Amerye in the kitchyn with the Cuppes [?] 3*s* 4*d*;

Item in brase vessell with Cawdrons & other things as with 2 Chafyn dishes & skillets 51 lb at 6*d* the lb – 20*s* 6*d*;

Item more 2 Crocks 1 Chafer & one skyllet 59 lb [illegible];

Mor the stene Clothers in the Kitchine 3*s* 4*d*;

More the fernies in the said Kytchyne 20*s*;

More for a skryne with Rades a pece of selinge and other trasse 10*s*;

In 5 weights 2 rings wayinge 2 *C* quarters & 14 lb the beme & scales at 19*s* 10*d*;

More in 3 croks wayinge 43 lb at 4*d* the lb – 14*s* 4*d*;

Mor in trone [?] stuf & with broches & [illegible] 100 lb at 2*d* – 20*s*;

More for wood in the sealer & other placs 20*s*;

More for necessaryes in the seller with bruinge vessells 13*s* 4*d*;

More for ane Iron bare in the kytchine 3*s* 4*d*;

Mor for the glace in the kytchine 8*s*;

More for 2 hoggs at the gardene 10*s*;

Item in the Cowntinge house a table bord with other trashe praysed yne 3*s* 4*d*;

Item for Rent dewe for Mydsomer quarter Clere of Chargs which the widowe dothe Receiv £4 3*s* 3*d*.

[m. 6v.] Desperat Debts upon John Follets bouk

The goodwief Gibbins Awith [blank];

Richard Ellerye Awith [blank];

Thomas John Stansbyes man Awith [blank];

John Comyn Awith [blank];

Christopher Biniamen [blank];

Hugh Cutfords wief of Ken Awith [blank];

John Sidnam of Westgat Awith [blank];

Walter Newton Awith [blank];

Edward Holl of Chagford Awith [blank];

Richard John Stabacks man Awith [blank];

William Follett Awith [blank];

Nicholas Wheller Awith [blank];

William Pecke Awith [blank];

The goodwief Drevers Daughter Awith [blank];

[Blank] Pollyn Awith [blank];

John Pecke Awith [blank];

Henry Sotheron Awith [blank];

William Knolls the sergiant Awith [blank];

The goodwiff Somerton Awith [blank];

The goodwief Weare of Honiton Clist Awith [blank];

John Blackemoore of Honiton Awith [blank];

Henry Benett awith [blank];

Mother Lansford awith [blank];

Mrs Norman without Westgat Awith [blank];

William Hooker Awith [blank];

Henry Maunder Awith [blank];

John Inglond awith [blank];

William Bruer Awith [blank];

William [blank] Awith [blank];

Mother Whytlye Awith [blank];

Thomas [blank] Awith [blank];

Mr Peeter of Bony Awith [blank];

Mr Hert Awith [blank];

William Newton Awith [blank];

Mr Foweracres Awith [blank];

John Morish awith [blank];

Thomas [blank] Awith [blank];

William Cawly Awith [blank];

Thomas Terry Awith [blank];

Mrs [blank] Awith [blank];

Richard Deamond the mason Awith [blank];

Jane Dabrene Awith [blank];

Thomas Smyth of Exmister awith [blank];

Richard Wichalse of Dawlish Awith [blank];

Axe of Awtrye Awith [blank];

Moor due by Caley the rest remayninge also [blank];

Nicholas Lampery Awith in An other bouke [blank];

William Waltham of Weymouth Awith mee [blank];

Mr Thomas Martin Awith me [blank];

Thomas [blank] of Chard awith [blank];

Valentine Tooker Awith me as by Accompt Appears [blank];

[m. 5v.] My brother Warring awith [blank];

Humfrye Powle awith [blank];

John Hooll of Chagford awith [blank];

Roger Tucker of Ilmister awith [blank];

William Newton awith [blank];

William Follet of Coliton for A Cubord & a table borde [blank];

Thomas [blank] of Chagford Awith [blank];

Barretred Peter Awith [blank];

William [blank] Awith [blank];

Ames Adicott awith [blank];

John Beard awith for 25 lb of wexe [blank];

John Dolton Awith [blank];

Jane Dabryne awith for two beds [blank];

Mr Dies awith [blank];

Mr Sotheron Awith in a nother place [blank];

John Tickell awith [blank];

Andra Southye awith upon a band [blank];

Robert [blank] awith by his byll [blank];

John Cruse of Cruse hese awith by a band [blank];

Thomas Marton of [blank] the yonger [blank];

John Cutifford & Hugh by a obligacon doe awe [blank].

In Debts Accompted good Debts [blank];

In Debts Accompted Desperat [blank].

John Follett awith as ffolowith

Firstly to the Citie for Mr Periams Money £16 13s 4d;

Item to Nicholas Austin of London £7 18s.

Dewe to Jese Olaborow by Mr Follett [blank];

Due unto John Trosse [blank];

Due to Mr Marsh of Exmister for fright [blank];

Due by John Follett to Mr Gravett of Totnis the some of [blank];

Due to his motherlaw Mrs Sweet for sterch [blank];

Due to Richard Russell of London [blank];

More due to Fawtry a French man for Normundy Canvas [blank].

53. INVENTORY OF THOMAS JEWELL, 19 APRIL 1588

ECA, Orphans' Court Inventory 39

An Inventory of certen Goods prised by Jasper Horsey Jo: Withicombe Richard Barnes & William Gince the 19th of April 1588 in the howse of Thomas Jewell without Thestgate of the Citty of Exeter

[1] In thutter Courte

Item an olde hogsed a Cowle a tubbe an olde hutche & other olde stuffe 6s;

Item a smale grindinge stone 12d;

Item thone skale of a paire of brasen ballance 8*d*;
Item he tolde us of a hogge which we did not see; but by his
reporte worthe 13*s* 4*d*;
21*s*.

In the Middle Courte
Item certen bordes a Rack & Maunger a ladder & other olde
stuffe 3*s* 4*d*.

In the Stables
Item 2 Racks 2 maungers certen bordes & an olde forme 5*s*
4*d*.

In the Garnar
Item an olde hogsed & an other olde tubbe to measure malt
8*d*.
In the Brewhowse & the lafte over the same
Item 2 bad hogseds a tiere & a garden Rake 2*s* 8*d*;
Item 36 smale vessels for Ale 12*s*;
Item 22 half barrells very bad 11*s*;
Item 4 Botefates 5*s*;
Item 18 Trendles very bad 4*s* 6*d*;
Item 4 smale Kives 20*s*;
Item 2 greate Kives 20*s*;
Item 2 touners 5 bucketts a shovell & other trash 3*s* 2*d*;
Item 2 clensinge Ringes 4*d*;
Item a greate furnes very bad with an olde bottom of brasse
20*s*;
Item a lesser furnes with a copper bottom 23*s* 4*d*;
Item a Coulefate 6*s*;
Item 2 olde shutes & certen olde maltebags 2*s* 2*d*;
£6 10*s* 1*d*.

In thinner Courte
Item a Mustard Mill 6*d*;
Item the welbuckett & the Rope 12*d*;
Item a coupe & other olde trash 12*d*;
2*s* 6*d*.

In the Kitchen
Item 2 olde Cupbords a table borde 2 formes a bench & olde
stoles 13*s* 4*d*;
Item a bad Calliver performed 10*s*;
Item thiron stuffe 12*s* 6*d*;
Item the pewter vessell 31*s* 1*d*;
Item the brasse 17*s* 6*d*;
Item the potts & crokes 26*s* 8*d*;
Item the Candle sticks & chafing dish 5*s*;
£5 16*s* 1*d*.

In the Alehowse
Item berers for Ale & other trash 3*s* 4*d*.

In a lowe chamber
Item an olde bedstade a flock bed & bolsters and a coverlet
11*s* 4*d*;
Item one other Coverlet a frise gowne a pilowe and a bolster
3*s* 4*d*;
14*s* 8*d*.

In a spence within the Halle
Item an olde coffer & the shelffs 12*d*.

In the Halle
Item the selinge & benches aboute the Halle 20*s*;
Item 2 table bords 2 formes & a settell 20*s*.

In the littell chamber at Starehed
Item a borde a forme & a Bedstede 5*s*;
Item 2 fflockbeds a bolster & a pillowe an olde gowne &
Cussions 25*s*;
£3 10*s*.

In the fforechamber
A Borde a carpet a bench & 2 formes 6*s* 8*d*;
Item 2 troklebeds 2 bedstades & a portall 16*s*;
Item 7 paire of olde ragged shetes 14*s*;

Item 7 pilloties 7 tablenapkens 3 borde clothes all olde stuff & vorne out 5s;
Item a fflockbed 2 olde coverlets and 8 olde blankets 16s 8d;
Item 2 ffetherbeds bolsters & pillowes 52s;
£5 10s 4d.

In the middle chamber
Item 2 bedstedes a troklebedstede a table borde & a forme 6s 8d;
Item a fflockbed a dustbed a bolster 2 olde heard coverletts 6s 8d;
13s 4d.

In the Newe chamber
Item a bedstede a troklebed a borde a benche a forme & a chaire 13s 4d;

Item a fflockbed a bolster & a coverlet 6s 8d;
20s.

In the Cockelafts
Item olde bed stades & other trashe 5s.

Item a little Rome at Starehed
Item certen tooles olde Iron & other trash 3s 4d.
In a chamber over the kitchen
Item an olde borde an olde chest 2 olde Bedstedes 5s.
In plat
Item 5 smale silver spones 12s 6d;
Sum total £26 17s 7d.

[Signed] Jasper Horsey;
William Grice.

54. WILL OF JOHN YOUNGE, OF ST STEPHEN'S PARISH, 12 JULY 1588

ECA, Orphans' Court Will 28 (also National Archives, PROB 11/73/79)
Note: the will was proved via Canterbury on 12 November 1588.

In the name of God Amen, The 12th day of July *in the year* 1588 And in the 30th yere of the Raigne of our soveraigne Ladye Elizabeth the Queenes Majesty that now is John Younge of the parish of Saint Stevens in the Cittie & Countie of Exeter lyinge sicke in his bedd but beinge of perfecte memorye did make and declare his last will and testament nuncupative in effecte as followeth, first he gave unto Bridgett his wife the lease of his howse and all the rest of his goods exceptinge two fetherbedds performed which he gave and bequethed unto his two daughters Theossila and Marye. Also he gave willed and bequethed unto the said Theossila his daughter and to her heires for ever his free land lyinge in Bridgewater and then delivered the writinges therof into her handes in possession. Also he gave unto his sonne Ciprian and to his daugher Agnes 12d a peece. And he appoynted the foresaid Bridgett his wife the whole Executrix of all his goods & detts whatsoever wittnesses present at the declaringe herof Emanuell Driver Johan the wife of Peter Risedon & Johan the wife of John Pitford with others.

Proved by Master James Riddlestone surrogate of the Lord Bishop of Exeter on 17 September 1588 and the inventory was exhibited in the sum of £43 19s 7d.

55A. WILL OF RICHARD MAUDITT, MERCHANT, 11 AUGUST 1589

ECA, Book 142, folios 38–9

Note: The will was found by Reverend J. F. Chanter in 1917 in the North Tower of Exeter Cathedral. It was amongst the papers of the Archdeaconry of Exeter but was not listed in the Calendars of the Probate Office. Brief notes were made by Olive Moger which are housed in the Devon Heritage Centre. On 14 February 1593 recognisances were entered into regarding Richard, Isaac, Rebecca, Wilmot and Abraham, the children of Richard Mawdytt, Merchant (ECA, Book 141, folios 157–158).

[38] **In the name of God Amen** the Elventh day of August in the yere of our Lord god 1589 I Richard Mawdytt of the City and County of Exeter merchante havinge my perfitt mynde and memory I geve god thanks and this by the helpe of god do make my last will and Testament in manner and forme followynge. First I bequeathe my soule unto Almighty god Jesus Christ my savior & my body to the grasse unto the pleasure of almighty god. Thes is to understand the house that I now dwell in is to my soune Ottes provided alwaye that my wife Mary that now is shall dwell and abyde therein for Fyve yeres after my deathe as the writing will appere that my wyfe hathe payenge to Otes as the writing dothe appeare for the terme of Fyve yeres fully to be completed and ended. **Now** I geve to my soune Otes after the Fyve yeres beinge full ended the Table borde in the Hall and all the seelinge benches Joyninge to the same seelinge that is at the higher ende of the Hall borde and the seelinge of the buttery in the Hall upon Condycon Otes shall geve to his mother Twenty shillings of money for the seelinge of the Buttery. And the grounde that is at St Thomas parishe beyonde Exbridge that I hold of Mr Robert Courteney it dothe pertayne to Otes after my deathe. And my lande at Powdram it is to Otes and to his heires for ever lawfully begotten & to be begotten. And for defaulte of suche Issue that then to the use & behoufe of the right heires of the sayd Richard Mawditt for ever. All the writings therof is in the skebett in my Countynge house and this I pray god make him his servante & to geve him Joy therof to gods will and pleasure. **And** to my soune John he shall have the bargayne at Henssam in the parishe of Launsell in Cornewall by Stratton duringe his lyfe I bofte yt for him god geve hym Joye therof. And after John yt dothe remayne to my soune

George during his lyfe the writings therof is in the skibbett in my Countynge house in a littell boxe lett them be delivered to my sounes John & George the *[38v.]* one parre is in Latten and the other in Englyshe I pray god geve them Joie therof. And to my soune Richard and to my soune Isacke I will that they bothe together shall have the use & the occupacon of my peece of grounde that [I] have without the Eastgate of the City of Exeter by Hed Will Meadow duringe the terme of my leasse yf they bothe so longe shall lyve The Lords Rente to be payd quarterly and the over plus of the money to be equally devided betwixte the foresaid Richard & Isacke & to him that longest lyveth of them bothe the grounde to remayne duringe my terme as the writinge dothe appere. The writings be in the skebbett of my Countinge house. And yf Richard & Isacke do dye within the yeres of my terme Then my soune George & Abraham shall have the use & occupacon of the foresaid peece of ground above named payenge the Lords Rente And the money of the Rest to be to George and Abraham & to be equally devided betwixt bothe & he that longest lyvethe of them bothe to keepe the whole grounde during my lease yf he lyve so longe. And yf they bothe dye George and Abraham Then I would that my wyfe should have the use and occupacon of the foresayd grounde above named duringe my lease And do geve yt to whom shee liste duringe my terme of my lease and thus god send them Joye therof that shall have yt longe to lyve to the pleasure of god. And my soune Abraham shall have after the deathe of his mother the grounde that his mother hathe now here Joynter therin And after Abraham *[39]* yt dothe remayne to my daughter Wilmott as the writings will appere. And also the garden that I have at Freeren Haye I wyll that my wyfe shall have the use and occupacon therof duringe her lyfe and after her unto my daughter Rebecca yf Otes and John so longe do lyve after the deathe of my wyfe and my daughter Rebecca then to remayne to my soune Otes & John my soune as the writings therof will appere. And also I give and bequethe to my daughter Marye Twenty poundes of money I saye £20. And to my daughter Wilmott I geve & bequeathe here fyftene poundes of money & my best Salte wayenge 16 ounces valued in fyve poundes 16d the whole some is £20 16d. And to my daughter Rebecca I geve & bequeathe her Fiftene poundes of money and a goblett wayenge 14 ounces and halfe lacke 4d valued in £4 6s 8d so the whole is to Rebecca my daughter £19 6s 8d. And to my soune George I geve & bequeathe him in money Eighte poundes I say £8. And to my soune Abraham I geve and bequeathe 40s and the bargen after his mother I saye Forty shillings. And to Richarde & Isacke they shall have the grounde at Eastgat In hande after my deathe god geve them Joye therof. And to my wyfe I [geve – crossed out] make her my full & whole Executrixe of all my goods and to dispose yt as shee seeth good. And for my overseers to see this my will performed I geve unto every one of them Fyve shillings The which I will desyre my Cosen George Isacke And my Cosen

Brunton in the Close. And thus the lord geve me grace that I may be his servante and that god will take me into his mercye when soever god shall take me out of this world and that I may take my sickenes pacyently that god dothe laye on me and the blessinge of god be *[39v.]* with all Amen. And so this is my last will & Testament **In witnes** of trothe I have written this with my owne hande and have here unto put my name to be of trothe yeven the day and yere within written.
Richard Mawdytt
And moreover wheras I saye my daughter Wilmett shall have £15 I geve her now £20 of money besydes the salte, and also whereas I bequeathe to my daughter Rebecca within written £15 I do geve the goblett as is within written, and also the money that my soune Georges master had with George I do geve yt and bequeath yt unto my soune George besydes the Eight poundes that ys within written. And for the Twenty poundes I gave to my daughter Mary shee ys alredy payde therof when shee was maryed. And this ys my will god geve them grace to be the servaunts of god, and to my soune John I geve him 40s of money and there unto to be of trothe I have here put to hande to be of trothe & my name
By me Richard Mawdytt.

55B. INVENTORY OF RICHARD MAUDITT, MERCHANT, 17 JANUARY 1593

ECA, Orphans' Court Inventory 53
Note: the register of the parish of St Mary Arches recorded the burial of 'Richard Mawditt' on 13 December 1592. A summary copy of this inventory exists in ECA, Book 142, Folio 40 and provides brief details of the administration of the estate.

The Inventorie of all the goodes & Chattalls of Richard Maudytt late of the City of Exon merchant decessed taken and praysed by John Hackwill Walter Horsey Paule Triggs & Sewell Betty the sevententh day of January in the ffyve & Thirtyth yere of the Raigne of our Soveraigne Lady Elizabeth by the grace of god Quene of Englande Fraunce & Ireland defender of the ffaythe &c

[m. 1] His Apparell
Firstly a blacke clothe gowne with a welte of velvett and faced withe budge & lyned with lambe £3 6s 8d;
Item 2 other gownes of Clothe furred 50s;
Item a Casacke of Chamlett with a billymente lace 20s;
Item a Clothe Jerken with a lace 15s;
Item a blacke clothe Cloake lyned with saye 35s;
Item an olde Rydinge Cloake 8s;
Item a payre of Clothe breeches with lace 13s 4d;

Item an olde gowne 2*s*;
Item two olde dublets faced with satten 6*s* 8*d*;
Item two Cappes 3*s*;
Item 2 payre of stockins 2*s* 6*d*;
Item a ponado garnyshed with silver 6*s* 8*d*;
Sum £11 8*s* 10*d*.

The plate
Firstly one goblett & one bolle parcell gilte wayghinge 28
   ounces & halfe at 4*s* 10*d* the ounce £6 17*s* 9*d*;
Item 12 spoones wayghinge 17 ounces & halfe at 4*s* 4*d* the
   ounce £3 15*s* 10*d*;
Item 2 stone cuppes garnyshed with silver & gilte worthe by
   estimacon £4;
Item one salte parcell gilte wayenge 16 ouncs at 4*s* 8*d* the
   ounce £3 14*s* 8*d*;
Item a littell golde ringe worthe 6*s*;
Sum £18 14*s* 3*d*.

In the parlor
Item a walnutt Table borde 53*s* 4*d*;
Item 6 Joyned stooles & a forme 8*s*;
Item a walnut Cheare with a backe 3*s* 4*d*;
Item a bedstede 20*s*;
Item 3 Curtens & vallance of mockado 30*s*;
Item 2 olde feather bedds & 2 bolsters £3;
Item one Tapestrye Coverlett lyned with canvas 46*s* 8*d*;
Item 2 Carpetts of dornex 15*s*;
Item 2 olde cussions of needleworke 6*s*;
Item 6 gilte Cussions of leather stufte with flockes 12*s*;
Item 9 other Cussions very olde 10*s*;
Item one Ilande Chest with a locke and kaye 40*s*;
Item a Cubborde 25*s*;
Item a Coffer of elmen bordes 3*s* 4*d*;
Item an Iron backe or barre in the Chymney & 2 dogges 6*s* 8*d*;
Item the seelinge in the parlor with the portall & planchinge
   £3;
Item the glasse in the wyndowes of the parlor with the
   casements 15*s*;

Item a lookinge glasse 12*d*;
Item one olde byble & 3 other bookes 6*s* 8*d*;
Item a Cubbord clothe a bason and Ewer & 3 tynne Cuppes &
   2 flower potts of tynne 8*s*;
Sum £21 10*s*.

In the Hall
Item a table borde of wenscott a forme one Joyned stoole with
   an Iron barre 16*s* 8*d*;
Item the seelinge 3 settells a seeled buttery at 30*s*;
Item the stayned Clothe with a lyttell Ilande table 5*s*;
Item a branche of candlestickes of latten that hangeth in the
   hall 5*s*;
Item a payre of almenryvetts with 3 bylles & 2 poll axes 10*s*;
Item a Callyver performed with all his furnyture 15*s*;
Item a sworde & dagger a woode knyfe two olde bucklers a
   shefe of arrowes a pyke and 2 hay pykes 6*s* 8*d*;
Item 112 lb of pewter vessell at 4½*d* the pounde 42*s*;
Item 15 lb of latten Candlesticks at 6*d* the pounde 7*s* 6*d*;
Sum £6 17*s* 10*d*.

In the Chamber over the parlor
Item 2 bedsteeds and 2 trockell bedds 33*s* 4*d*;
Item 2 feather bedds 4 bolsters and 8 feather pyllowes £4 4*s*;
Item one littell flocke bed & 2 littell bolsters 10*s*;
Item one olde Tapestrye Coverlett 10*s*;
Item 3 yarnynge Coverletts & 3 payre of blancketts 36*s* 8*d*;
Item a payre of Curtens & 4 olde carpets 6*s* 8*d*;
Item one littell olde table borde & 2 olde formes 4*s*;
Item one olde presse 2 olde cheares 3 littell olde syde bordes
   10*s*;
Item the glasse in the wyndowes and the stayned Clothes 6*s*
   8*d*;
Sum £10 16*d*.

In the Chamber over the Kitchen
Item an olde bedsted and an old trockell bed with olde
   curtens 10*s*;
Item one feather bed 2 bolsters and one flocke bed 46*s* 8*d*;

Item one Rugge & one yarninge Coverlet 10s;

Item 7 olde coffers & one olde syde borde one olde presse and an olde Cheare 15s;

Item the glasse in the wyndowes with the Casements 2s 8d;

Item 4 payre of Canvas sheetes & 5 payre of olde sheetes 40s;

Item 2 payre of fyne canvas sheetes & one payre of Callacowe 24s;

Item 3 payre of olde sheets 7s;

Item 3 borde clothes & 2 Towells of Rone Clothe 33s 4d;

Item 5 course table Clothes of canvas 13s 4d;

Item 9 pyllowtyes & 8 olde pyllowtyes 26s 8d;

Item 3 drinkinge clothes & one cubborde Clothe 6s 8d;

Item 3 dosen of table napkins & 7 hand Towells 20s;

Item 2 shirtes & 4 bands 6s 8d;

Sum £13 2s.

[m. 2] **In the** maydens Chamber

Item one olde bedstede & one olde trocle bedde 5s;

Item one feather bed 2 bolsters & one flocke bed 20s;

Sum 25s.

In the Kitchen

Item one bed pan 2s;

Item in pannes & cawdrens 50 lb at 6d the pounde 25s;

Item in crocke mettall 140 lb at 4d the pounde 46s 8d;

Item a barre of Iron in the Chymney 2s 6d;

Item a fryenge pan very olde 6d;

Item in spytes, pothookes Rackes and other Iron wayenge 160 lb – 20s;

Item an Almerye the shelves a mouldinge table one musterd mill 3 littell booles 3 Barells and a Combe with other triffells 10s;

Item 6 seames fire woode 14 bushells of salte 10s;

Item 4 bruynge Tubbes and other small tubbes with other olde trashe in the backe Romes 5s;

Sum £6 20d.

In the shoppe

Item 190 yardes and halfe of vittery Canvas at 10d the yarde £8 2s 11d;

Item 15 yardes of stoupe [?] Canvas at 8½d the yard 17s 8d;

Item 19 yards of enderlyns at 4d the yarde 4s 8d;

Item 62 yards of dowles at 12d the yard £3 2s;

Item 10 yards of Holland at 4s the yard 40s;

Item 13 yards and halfe of Holland at 2s the yarde 31s 6d;

Item 5 yardes of course Holland at 20d the yarde 8s 4d;

Item 5 yardes and three quarters of Normondy at 20d the yarde 9s 6d;

Item 6 yardes of Scottishe clothe at 8d the yarde 4s;

Item 3 yardes of course Holland at 20d the yarde 5s;

Item 2 Reames of writinge paper at 4s the reame 8s;

Item one pound of frame lace made with Threde 2s;

Item 4 yardes and halfe of Course Canvas of Cane 2s 8d;

Item 3 yards of Britten Clothe at 8d the yarde 2s;

Item 3 yardes and thre quarters of Kunter [?] clothe at 6d the yarde 22d;

Item one dosen of playenge Cardes 3s;

Item 2 payre of wolle cardes at 14d the payr 2s 4d;

Item 13 lb & halfe of graynes at 8d the pound 9s;

Item 12 lb of pepper at 2s 6d the pound 30s;

Item 2 lb of Synamon at 3s the pounde 6s;

Item halfe a pounde of Mace at 5s;

Item 3 lb of Cloves at 4s the pounde 12s;

Item one quarter of a hundred of prunes 5s 6d;

Item 3 lb of Annest seedes at 6d the pounde 18d;

Item 2 lb of Almonts at 10d the pounde 20d;

Item one pounde of Rice 3d;

Item 12 lb of Currants at 4d the pounde 4s;

Item 4 lb of waxe at 9d the pounde 3s;

Item 9 barrells of Tryakell at 3d the barrell 2s 3d;

Item one virken of London sope 13s 4d;

Item halfe a bushell of white salte 20d;

Item 100 lb and halfe of Castell sope at 56s the hundred £4 4s;

Item sixe hundred of lathes at 4d the 100 2s;

Item the Cheste in the shoppe 20s;

Item the shelves and stayned Clothes about the shoppe 3s 4d;

Item 4 payre of ballons at 2s the payre 8s;

Item a beame & scales with one hundred and halfe of lead waights 16s 8d;

Item 2 tressells & 4 bords with 2 olde bords 5*s*;
Sum £30 19*d*.

Good debts
Item Otes Mawdyt oweth as by the booke of accompte
  appeerethe £4 7*s* 4*d*;
Item Mr Humfry Cooke of Ottery St Mary oweth as by the
  booke appeereth 6*s*;
Item Nicholas Wytchalse of Powderam oweth by booke 26*s*
  6*d*;
Item Mathew Germyn oweth 40*s*;
Item the wydow Ducke of Hevitre oweth 8*s* 3*d*;
Item Josephe Bartlett oweth by booke 2*s*;
Item Welthen Shoulder owethe 2*s* 10*d*;
Item Robert Isburne oweth 8*s* 6*d*;
John Gupwell servant to Walter Horsey is to yelde an accompt
  for 9 Crownes of the soune delivered to be imployed in
  Brest 54*s*;
Item Othes Mawdytt oweth upon two severall bandes £30;
Item Michaell Saunders & George Isacke do owe by their
  bande £20;
Item Katheren the late wyfe unto John Cotten of Wodbury
  & now the wyfe of Richard Huswyfe of Alfenton oweth
  £6 13*s* 4*d* to be payd one moneth next & imedyatly after
  the death of one Johan Holwell *alias* Hoppen of Woodbury
  wydow as by a band appeareth £6 13*s* 4*d*;
Item Thomas Slowman of Sampford Courtney oweth by his
  bande £4;
Item there are in the hands of William Bruer 24 peeces of
  Kerseys which cost at the first Raw £30 2*s* 6*d*;
Item in redy money £40 wherof there is owynge for wares
  bofte [bought] £8 17*s* 4*d* as by the bylls of parcells doth
  appeere So there resteth good & the debtes payd £31 2*s* 8*d*;
Item the lease of a pece of grounde in the tenure of Mr
  Dreaton lyenge in St Sydwills parishe wherin are about 45
  yeres yet to com which lease we esteme to be worthe £30;
[m. 2v.] Item for the lease of a garden in Frerenhay holden of
  the City for 80 yeres yf three lyves so longe lyve worthe £3
  6*s* 8*d*;

Sum £167 7*d*.

Desperate debtes
Item Thomas Westcott owethe for wares delivered 16*s* 4*d*;
Item Thomas Ryse owethe 6*s* 6*d*;
Item Richard Shute of Whymple 6*s* 2*d*;
Item Elizabeth Hunte at Southege 10*s* 3*d*;
Item John Marshall of Honiton Clist 10*s*;
Item John Saunders owethe 13*s* 7*d*;
John Burnell without Estgate owethe 5*s* 4*d*;
Item John Hellyar & John Wynes *alias* Cove do owe for mony
  lonte them 13*s* 4*d*;
Item William Pope of Brodeclyst owethe 2*s*;
Item the parishe Church of St Mary Arches oweth for mony
  lonte 17*s*;
Item John Row of St Thomas parishe oweth 18*s*;
Item Henry Whitrow oweth 29*s*;
Item Hercules Deble owethe 21*s* 8*d*;
Item the goodwyfe Shilson oweth 9*s* 2*d*;
Item Richaurd Markes wydow oweth 17*s* 4*d*;
Item Symon Gryffitts wydow of Tanton £5 11*s*;
Item John Hellyar owethe for mony lonte him 6*s* 6*d*;
Item Robert Cadew of Exmouth owethe for wares delivered
  him 12*s* 9*d*;
Item Richard Jervys the boucher oweth for wares delivered at
  sundry tymes 14*s* 7*d*;
Item Mary Rider at Westgate oweth for wares delivered 4*s* 4*d*;
Item the wydow Bynnam owethe 3*s* 9*d*;
Item Humfry Wheaton owethe for mony monye lonte hym 2*s*
  6*d*;
Item Symon Webber owethe for mony lonte & for wares
  delivered as by byll & booke appereth £6 10*s* 2*d*;
Item the wydow Gifford in the Boucherow 23*s* 5*d*;
Item the good wyfe Juell without Est Gate oweth 38*s* 9*d*;
Item Walter Skynner oweth 17*s* 9*d*;
Item David the Tucker at Exbridge ende 8*s*;
Item Dor[o]thy the Laundres oweth 6*s* 6*d*;
Item Robert Prouze Taylor oweth 18*s* 4*d*;
Item John Levermore of Exmyster owethe 10*s* 6*d*;

John Cottons wyddow Catheren owethe for wares 6*s* 10*d*;

Item Anthony Pouleman of Alfenton 6*s*;

Item Mary the wyfe of Triggs the Taylor without Eastegate 4*s* 1*d*;

Nicholas Good of Kingsweare oweth 4*s*;

Oxenbere of Exmouth Smyth owethe for wares delivered him 4*s* 2*d*;

Item John Tucker Bruer oweth for mony lont him at sundry tymes and for wares delivered him £15 8*d*;

Thomas Mydwynter oweth as by a note of his hand appeares £8 17*s*;

Item John Cotton of Wodbery oweth by his band £13 6*s* 8*d* wherof is receaved at sundry tymes £7 6*s* 8*d* so restethe due £6;

Item William Penten oweth by his byll £6 2*s* 6*d*;

Item John Peryman oweth by his l[ette]re 40*s*;

Sum £69 9*s* 9*d*.

Sum total £355 13*s* 10*d*.

56A. WILL OF THOMAS CHAPPELL, MAYOR AND MERCHANT, 22 AUGUST 1589

National Archives, PROB 11/75/273

Note: An extract exists in ECA, Book 142, Folios 15–17. Recognisances were entered into for Thomas, Ambrose, Richard, Christopher, Nicholas, Elizabeth and Katherine the children of Thomas Chappell on 25 September 1590 (ECA, Book 141, Folios 104–111, also see Folios 167–168).

[1] **In the name of god amen** the twoe and twentithe daye of Auguste in the yere of oure Lord god a thousande Fyve hundred eightie nyne and in the one and thirtithe yere of the raigne of oure soveraigne Ladie Elizabethe by the grace of god of Englande France and Irelande Quene defender of the faithe &c. I Thomas Chapell Maior of the Cittie of Exceter marchaunte beinge of good and perfect remembraunce thanckes be to Allmightie god do make and ordeyne this my laste will and testamente in manner and forme Folowinge. Firste and principallye I bequeathe my soule to Allmightie god and my body to the christian burriall wheresoever yt shall please god to visit me. Item I geve amongeste the poore people of the cittye of Exceter Fyve poundes of lawfull money of Englande to be distributed at the discrecon of my overseers hereafter named & Appoynted. Item I give and bequeathe unto the Maior Bayliffes and Cominaltie of the cittie of Exceter the full somme of Thirtie poundes of lawfull money of Englande to be paied within three yeres next after my Deathe that ys to saye yearely in the twentithe daye of June

the somme of tenne poundes untill the full Somme of thirtie poundes be paied uppon condicon and of truste that they the saied Mayor Bayliffes and Cominaltie of the saied cittie then for the tyme beinge the governoure and treasorer of the marchaunts of the sayed cittie then for the tyme beinge the Master and Master wardens of the companye of the taylors then for the tyme beinge which shalbe assembled at the counsaile chamber of the sayed cittie by reason of the laste will and Devyse of Johan Tuckeffeilde late wife of John Tuckeffeilde late Alderman of [the - crossed out] saied Cittie deceased. And uppon the receipt of every of the saied sommes of tenne poundes my will ys that the same shalbe by them the saied Maior and Receyvor Governoure and Treasorer Master and Master Wardens put into a *[2]* certeyne cheste togeather with suche moneys as shalbe by them receyved the saied daye by reason of the saied will of the saied Johane Tuckefeilde there to remayne untill the twentie daye of Julie then Folowinge which twentie daye of Julie my will ys that the saied Maior and Receyvor governoure & Treasurer Master and Master Warden shall delyver fourthe the saied severall Sommes of tenne pounde as yt shall [come - crossed out] yerelie come unto suche twoo Inhabitants of the saied Cittie and Freemen of the same as to them or the moste parte of them shall seame moste meete *viz.* to everye of them fyve poundes to have and use the same for the space of three yeres unto the twentithe of June then next folowynge, and then in the saied twentithe of June to delyver and repaye the same Somme so to them Delivered unto the saied Maior and Receyvor Governoure and tresorer Master and Master warden betweene suche howers and uppon suche good Sewerties as they shall devyse and to paye onlye the like Fees for the makinge of the [same - crossed out] Assurance and to that same Clerke as by the Will of the saied Johane Tuckeffeilde ys devised. And my will and mynde ys that the saied severall sommes of tenne pounde after the repaymente therof as aforesaied in the saied twentie daye of Julie then next folowinge shalbe Delyvered and put fourthe agayne to twoe other Inhabitaants and Free men of the saied cittie to have the same unto them for the like tyme and in like manner. And that the same shalbe as aforesaied receyved repaied and Delyvered fourthe for ever from tyme to tyme as aforesaied accordinge to the late will and devyse of the saied Johane Tuckfeilde to twoe inhabitaunts and free men of the saied cittie. The whiche I do desire the saied Maior Bailiffes and Cominaltie to see to be performed as they have a care for the mayntenaunce of the good estate of the cittie. Item I give to my soune John Chapell my beste Saulte, two litle Bowles of Silver guilte twoe silver spoones and one Hundred and Fiftie poundes of lawfull money of Englande. Item I give unto William Chapell my Soune one silver tankarde guilte twoe silver spoones and one Hundred and Fiftie poundes of Lawfull money of Englande. Item I give to George Chapell my soune a goblet of silver parcell gilte twoe silver spoones and one Hundred and Fiftie poundes of lawfull money of Englande. Item I give to Nicholas Chapell my soune one goblet of silver twoe silver spoones and one Hundred and Fiftie poundes of lawfull money of Englande. Item I give unto Ambrose Chapell my soune One goblet of silver parcell guilte

twoe silver spoones and one Hundred poundes of lawfull money of England. Item I give unto Christofer Chapell my Soune one silver tankarde parcell guilte twoe silver spoones and one Hundred and Fiftie pounds of lawfull money of England. Item I give unto Elizabeth Chapell my daughter One silver Bowle guilte twoe silver spoones and one Hundred and Fiftie poundes of lawfull money of Englande. Item I give to Katherine Capell [*sic*] my daughter One silver Bowle guilted and twoe silver spoones and one Hundred and Fiftie poundes of lawfull money of Englande. Item I give unto Johane Bagewell my daughter one silver bowle gilted and twoe silver spoones. All whiche sommes of money and plate before by me given and bequeathed to be Delyvered them or any of them when they shall come to the age of twentie and Fower yeres or before at the discretion of theire mother and my Overseers, in full contentacon of all and every theire legacyes bequeathes childes parte and portion of my goodes to them or any of them apperteyninge or belonginge [or apperteyninge – crossed out] by reason or force of the custome of the foresaied Cittie of Exeter. And if yt happen that any of my children to dye before they shall accomplishe the age of twentie and Fower yeres or before any of this my bequeste be delyvered unto them that then my will and mynde ys that the parte and portion of every or any of them so deceasinge shalbe and remayne to and amongeste the residue of my children that shalbe then lyvinge by equall portions to be devyded. Item I remitt to Davie Bagewell my soune in Lawe twentie poundes of lawfull money of England which he oweth me. Item I give unto the saied Davie Bagewell thirtie poundes of lawfull money of England. Item I give unto the foresaied Davie Bagewell['s] children called William Bagewell and Precilla Bagewell and to every of them the Somme of three poundes six shillinges and eighte pence a pece of lawfull money of England. Item I give to every of my Servauntes that shalbe with me dwellinge at the houre of my deathe tenne shillinges a peece of good and lawfull money of Englande. Item I give to Brother Chapell my brother Anthony his soune twentie shillinges of lawfull money of Englande. Item I give unto my cosen Joane Chapell my maide Fyve markes of lawfull money of England. Item to give to [3] Edward Chapell my brother Anthony Chapells soune twentie shillinges of lawfull money of England. Item I give unto Humfrey Chapell soune unto Edward Chapell when he shall come to be of the age of one and twentie yeres the somme of twentie shillinges of lawfull money of Englande. Item I give unto William Brewer twentie shillinges of Lawfull money of Englande. Item I give unto my Brother George Chapell Fower poundes of lawfull money of Englande. Item I give to my Brother George Chapell['s] twoe Sounes twentie shillinges a peece of lawfull money of Englande. Item I give unto Anthonye Chapell the soune of Thomas Chapell the Somme of twentie shillinges of lawfull money of Englande. Item I give and bequeathe to every of my godchildren twoe shillinges a peece. Item I give and bequeathe to the poore people of Alphington twentie shillinges of lawfull money of Englande. Allso, my will, minde and intente ys that Thomasine my wife shall duringe her naturall life have houlde and enioye all that gardeine of myne lyinge nere the Highe Streete of the foresaied Cittie of Exeter which I latelye purchased of one Henry Paramore deceased. Provided allwayes and my will intente and meaninge ys that yf any of my saied children do or shall at any tyme or tymes hereafter demaunde or require to have any parte or porcon of my goodes or chattells beinge in me at the tyme of my deathe or before by reason of the custome of the cittie of Exeter otherwise to apperteyne or belonge to them or either of them by reason of theire his or her childes parte and porcon of my goodes or chattells or otherwise yf any of my saied children shall or doe happen uppon the tender or offer of theire his or her Legaceys refuse to make to my saide Executrix a sufficiente Release and Dischardge of theire his or her parte or portion of my saied goodes to them hym or her belonginge for theire his or her childes parte but clayming by force of the saied custome of the cittie of Exeter, That then all and every gifte Legaceys and bequeathes to them hym and her devised willed or bequeathed so denyinge or refusinge shalbe utterlie frustrate voide and of none effecte as yf them hym or her so deneyinge or refusinge had never ben named or mencyoned in this my testamente. The residue of all my goodes, chattells, moveable and unmoveable not given nor bequeathed my debtes legaceys and Funeralls paied I freelie give and bequeathe unto the foresaied Thomasine my wife whome I make and ordeyne my full and whole Executrix of this my present laste will and testamente. And she to order and dispose the same as to her wisdome shalbe thoughte moste meete and conveniente. And for my Overseers I make and ordeyne Mr John Davye Nicholas Spicer my cosen John Chapell and my cosen Thomas Chapell and for the better accomplishment of this my laste will and testamente according to thintente and true meaninge thereof I give to every of my Overseers for theire paynes takinge herein the somme of twentie shillinges a peece of lawfull money of Englande. In witnesse wherof I the saied Thomas Chapell have hereunto subscribed my hande and set my Seale the daye and yere above written in the presence of those whose names ar hereunder written Thomas Chapell John Chapell the elder *by me Thomas* Chapell. Memorandum the sixte daye of September *in the year* a thousande Fyve hundred eightie nyne Whereas I have devised and bequeathed to my soune John Chapell one Hundred and Fiftie poundes amongest other thinges as aforesaied forasmuche as I have nowe latelie paied to the saied John my Soune one Hundred and twentie poundes of lawfull englishe money I will that the residue therof beinge thirtie poundes shalbe onlie paied to my saied soune John and no more money therof any thinge in my saied testamente to the contrarye notwithstandinge &c. Thomas Chapell To his wief Th[omasine] Chapell Memorandum the nynthe of Januarye: my will and mynde ys that my Executrix shall give unto Sixetene poore people eache of them one blacke gowne of Cotton Thomas Chapell. Tho: Chapell.

56B. INVENTORY OF THOMAS CHAPPELL, MAYOR AND MERCHANT, 16 JUNE 1590

ECA, Orphans' Court Inventory 43

The Inventorie of all the goods and Chattells of Mr Thomas Chappell of the Citie of Exon merchant deceased praysed by us Richard Jurden Edwarde Langdon John Spurwaye & John Aplyn the Sixteenth daye of June in the Two and Thirtieth yere of the Raigne of our soveraigne Ladie Elizabeth by the grace of god Queene of England Ffraunce and Irelande defender of the faith &c

[m. 1] In the parlor
Firstly a longe table borde with Six Joynedstooles at 40s;
Item 2 side table bordes 2 Cheares and 2 low stooles 12s;
Item 2 greene Couborde Clothes and 6 greene Cuishings 18s;
Item one Bason and Ewer 3s 4d;
Item 8 Canapes upon the Coubord 1s;
Item the seelinge with the Couborde £3 9s;
Item one payre of danske tables 1s 6d;
Item for bands to the Coubord in the parlor 20s;
Sum £8 4s 10d.

In the halle
Firstly one longe Tableborde with Six Joyne stooles £2;
Item one plat Couborde & one side bord 15s;
Item 2 Carpets one Couborde Cloth 6 toughe mockadow Cuishings £1 6s 8d;
Item one greene standinge Cheare and one littell Cheare 10s;
Item one peare of andirons with shovell & tonges with the backe of Chimney and doggs £1 2s;
Item 5 picktures one Tabellment and one Carde 10s;
Item the seelinge and binches with a standinge borde £1 13s 4d;
Item 2 rangers of Iron for mases 2s;
Item one olde bibell 6s 8d;
Item one Cronickell 6s 8d;
Item 3 service bookes & one booke of sickman Saule 6s 8d;
Sum £8 19s.

In the buttery
Firstly one Amery and 2 shilves 13s 4d;
Item 3 greate Jugges one Joyne stoole one tubbe one case of knifes & two Tabell knifes and one olde hamper 12s;
Item 6 doosen of Trenchers and 4 doosen of Round trenchers 3s;
[m. 2] Item 4 drinkinge Glases 1s 4d;
Item 294 lb of pewter at 5½d by the pounde amounteth to £6 14s;
Item 4 Tinninge Candlestickes 5s;
Item one pottell pott 4 quartes and 2 pyntes 13s 4d;
Item 4 greate Candlestickes of brasse 12s;
Item 8 Small Candlestickes of brasse with one Chafindishe 10s;
Item 3 Chamber potts 2s;
Sum £10 6s.

In the Kitchinge
Firstly one bruinge ffurnes £3;
Item one greate Cawdren £1;
Item one greate olde pan 10s;
Item 4 Cawdrens of brasse 13s 4d;
Item 3 skilletts of brasse 13s 4d;
Item one bed pan 1 scoomer & 2 ladells of brasse 5s;
Item one great brasse Crocke and 2 littell Crockes;
One posnett one skillett & one Chaffer of brasse;
[Last two entries] £1 13s 4d;
Item 3 Iron Chetells & 2 Iron Crockes 17s;
Item 2 ffryenge pannes 4s;
Item 9 spitts £1;
Item 2 greate dripinge panes of Iron 8s;
Item 2 payre of Rayckes £2;
Item one fyre peeke and shovell & tongs & 4 Iron doggs to beare the woode and one Ire for the pan 6s 8d;
Item 5 peare of pott hangings 7 pott Crookes 12s;

Item 2 fleshe hookes 2 Tosters 2 greedells & one old
  Chafindishe 4s;
Item 3 Chopinge knives and 2 littell knyves 1s 6d;
Item 2 bordes and A Capen Cage 10s;
Item one Settell one Cheare and one Joyne stoole 3s 4d;
Item Sixe shelves and one Choppinge borde 3 Cowells 6
  buckets 2 watringe Tubbs 7s;
Item one Trowe of stone 2 littell stooles and 2 olde dripinge
  pannes 4s 6d;
Item one Cawdren one brandise and one littell brasen Ewer 6s
  8d;
Sum £14 19s 8d.

In the pasterhouse
Firstly one Coubord 6s 8d;
Item one pastinge borde & 2 other bordes with 3 shellves 10s;
[m. 3] Item 5 voyders for paste & 2 pyles 1s 4d;
Item 2 shridinge knyfes 2s;
Item 2 littell woodinge Tubbes 2 littell boules one ladinge
  bole and 3 treeinge platters 2s 6d;
Item 3 littell Serges one seeve one pecke one Gratter one
  lantren and other things as panes and potts with other
  earthinge vessell 5s;
Sum 27s 6d.

In the parler chamber
Firstly one standinge bedsteede and one Trouckell bed £2;
Item one Tabell borde and 3 formes £1;
Item one spruese Cheste £1 10s;
Item on littell Sipres Cheste 13s 4d;
Item 3 Couffers 6s 8d;
Item one Case of draweres 5s;
Item 2 Cheares 6s 8d;
Item one littell Hamper and one littell flaskett 1s;
Item one fyre pann one shovell and one payre of dogges 1s
  8d;
Item the olde hanging of the Chamber and 4 Courtinges of the
  windowes 13s 4d;
Sum £6 17s 8d.

In the Chamber over the parlor
Firstly one ffeather bed & bolster and one matres £3 10s;
Item 2 pillowes and one payre of blankettes 15s;
Item one Coverlet of Tapestre £3 6s 8d;
Item the Courtings to the bed £1 10s;
Item one ffeather bed in the Troukell bed £1 10s;
Item one Rouge for the Troukellbed 5s;
Item the Courtings for the wyndow and greene Clothes for the
  same with the grene of the Cheste 16s;
Item one scarlett goune with the Robe and Tipitt £16;
Item one blacke gowne faste with bouge and welted with
  velvett £6;
Item one blacke gowne of ffowens garded with velvett £8;
Item one blacke gowne faste with satten and welted with ye
  same £6 13s 4d;
Item one olde gowne welted with velvett £2;
Item one olde night gowne 5s;
Item one night gowne 13s 4d;
[m. 4] Item one dameske Cayssocke £1 6s 8d;
Item on Taffatye Jackett faste with velvett £1 4s;
Item one Grogaren Jackett 13s 4d;
Item one doublett of Satten £2;
Item 2 other satten doublets £1 10s;
Item one blacke Cloake faste with fuge red satten £2;
Item one payre of breeches with drawers 10s;
Item 3 Round Cappes and 3 night Cappes 8s;
Item 2 Hattes 5s;
Item 3 payre of Round breeches 3 payre of galley breeches
  with other olde apparrell £3;
Item one ffurde Caysecke 13s 4d;
Item one gowne of Rashe faste with bouge £2 10s;
Sum £67 9s.

In the Chamber next to the parler Chamber
Firstly one standinge bed steed with tester 5s;
Item one fflocke bed with a boulster & a Coverlett 6s 8d;
Item one Coubord with the Cloth 10s;
Item one bason and Ewer with glasses 8s;
Item 2 stooles Covered and a Table borde 8s;

Item one Hamper one baskett and one pille of wights with
    ballens 6s 8d;
Sum 44s 4d.

In the Gallery
Firstly one standinge presse £1;
Item one Spruse Chest 10s;
Item one halfe dousen of Cuishings of Tapestree £1;
Item one halfe doosen of fflannen Cuishings wrought 12s;
Item 3 Carpets of Tapestrye £3;
Item one halfe doosen of greene Cuishinges 5s;
Item 4 Carpets for side Tabells £1;
Item 2 Carpets for plate Tables 6s 8d;
Item 2 Coverletts £1 13s 4d;
Item one muskett & 2 Calivers with their furniture £3 6s 8d;
Sum £12 13s 8d.

In the Chamber over the Kitchinge
[m. 5] Firstly one standinge bed steed with A Trouckell bed
    13s 4d;
Item 2 ffeather beds one boulster & 2 pillowes £3 6s 8d;
Item the Coverlets & blanketts £1 6s 8d;
Item 3 greene Courtings 6s 6d;
Item 2 Seay Chestes 6s;
Item one wecker stoole and one Hamper and one peare of
    Belles 1s 6d;
Item the steine Cloth £1;
Item one bedsteede 3s 4d;
Sum £7 4s.

In the Chamber over the paysteri
Firstly one bed steed and one Trouckelbed 6s 8d;
Item one Course ffeather bed and A boulster with a flocke
    bed and boulster £1;
Item 2 Coverletts and 2 peyre of blanketts with one white
    Ruge 10s;
Item 2 Chestes one Couffer and one Hamper 6s;
Item one bed steede a fflocke bed and one payre of blanketts
    and one Ruge £1;

Sum £3 2s 8d.

In the brishinge Chamber
Firstly one brishinge borde one littell brishe one stoole and
    one littell Cheste 6s;
Item one peece of steene Cloth 3s;
Sum 9s.

In the fore Chamber
Firstly one bedsteed and one Trouckell bed £1;
Item 2 ffeather beds 2 boulsters and 2 maters £5;
Item 2 payre of blanketts 3 Ruges & 2 pillowes £2 10s;
Item 5 Courtings for the bed & two Courtings for the window
    one greene Carpet [and one spruse Cheste – crossed
    through] 16s;
Item one spruse Cheste £1;
Item one Cipres [spruse – crossed through] Cheste £1;
Item 2 other Chestes & one littell Couffer £1;
Item one side Tabell borde 2 Joyne stooles one low stoole &
    one hamper 7s;
Item 6 Cuishings of Tapestrye £3;
[m. 6] Item 2 greene Cuishings wraught 10s;
Item 4 Cuishings of neeld worke 16s;
Item 2 longe Cuishings for A window £1;
Item one shovell one payre of tongs one payre of doggs one
    littell payre of billes & one wicker Cheare with the backe of
    the Chimney 7s;
Item the seelinge £1 2s;
Item the steyne Clothes 13s 9d;
Sum £20 1s 9d.

In the lafte
Firstly one bed steed 1s 6d;
Item 4 pillowes 8s;
Item 7 Course pillows & A boulster 10s;
Item one Skryne one willey 3 foote stooles & one Candell
    couffer with one frame 8s;
Item one payre of ballens 4s;
Item one Tabell borde and a forme 16s;

Item 2 olde Chestes 4 hodgsheads with 4 flaskets & one olde
   borde 7s;
Item one Coslett & 2 Almon Rivetts £1 16s 8d;
Item one Stille and one Racke 9s;
[Sum £5 2d – crossed through.]

In the same lafte
Item one olde Croocke 2s;
Item one bed steede one flocke bed 5s;
Item 3 Cases of Glasse £1;
Item one Cheste for ffishe 2 Tubs for meale & one Torne 5s;
Item one bage of feathers & one Stone bow £1;
Sum £7 12s 2d.

In the Shoppe
Firstly 2 ffardels of Canvas £33;
Item 5 peeces of Treager beinge 1 ffardell £26 13s 4d;
Item 20 peeces of medreneckes £20;
Item the Shope Cheste 8s;
Item the shelves & bourders 5s;
Item one hodgshead one pecke and one Cheare 2s;
Item one markinge hamer and one payre of sheares 16d;
Sum £80 9s 8d.

In the ware house
[m. 7] Firstly 27 baggs of Red Allome weighinge 100 lb at £1
   3s 4d the C – £58 6s 8d;
Item 11 baggs weighinge 22 C at £1 6s 8d the C – £29 6s 8d;
Item 11 baggs and halfe of Currants weighinge 39 C at 32s the
   C – £62 6s;
Item 200 lb of Iron at 12s the C – £1 4s;
2,500 lb of welshe Iron at 12s the C – £15;
Item 67 peeces of Coulered Kerse at 32s by the peece
   £107 4s;
Item one Tabell borde & one presse £1 13s 4d;
Item one Iron beame & Skayles 16s;
Item one fflaunders beame and Skayles 6s 8d;
Item 3 C 3 quarters of wights £1 6s 8d;
Item halfe A hundred of Almens £1;

Item 5 C and halfe of Tynne at 48s the C – £13 4s;
Item 3 C of Rise £3;
Item one slyde 1s;
Sum £294 15s.

In the Stabell
Firstly one Racke and maunger 2s;
Item one Saddell & bridell 10s;
Item A brounge Ceve and 2 Trendels [?] 6s 8d;
Item 2 olde hodgsheades & 8 halfe barrells 12s 6d;
Item 3 bearers and one stoole 3s 4d;
Item 3 bordes and certain olde Tymber 4s;
Item 3 doosen of woode £1;
Item olde Haye 13s 4d;
Item 2 wenskouts 6s;
Item one olde Saddell 2s;
Sum £3 19s 10d.

In the Courte
Firstly one musterd mille one ledden stille and one Stoninge
   Trowe 10s;
Item one benche in the entery and one picke 3s 4d;
Sum 13s 4d.

In the Seller
Firstly 3 doosen of hard wood £1 10s;
Item 4 bearers 3s;
[m. 8] Item 2 littell Coastes 2 standerdes & 2 powdringe
   Tubbes 5s 8d;
Item one hodgshead for salte with one Tree and 5 Brewinge
   vessells 8s;
Item olde stufe aboute the house £1;
Sum £3 6s 8d.

In the Chest over the Kitchinge
Firstly one dameske Table Cloth & one doosen of naptkins £2
   15s;
Item one diaper Tabell Cloth with one doosen and halfe of
   Naptkins £2 3s;

Item one fine murles bord Clothe with one doosen and halfe of [blank] of the same £2;

Item 3 ffyne Normundy Canvas bord Clothes at 12s 6d a peece £1 16s;

Item 4 Table Clothes at 6s 8d A peece £1 6s 8d;

Item 3 other Table Clothes 10s;

Item one doosen and halfe of playne naptkins 9s;

Item one doosen and halfe of naptkins 10s;

Item one doosen of naptkins 5s;

Item one doosen of naptkins 6s;

Item one doosen of fyne naptkins 10s;

Item 10 naptkins 3s 4d;

Item halfe a doosen of napkins 3s;

Item 3 Tabell Towells £1 4s;

Item 2 diaper Towells £1;

Item 5 washinge Towels £1 4s;

Item 6 washinge Clothes £1;

Item 7 Small Tabell Clothes 17s 6d;

Sum £18 2s 6d.

In the Chamber over the pastery

Firstly 10 payre of Shits at 8s the payre £4;

Item 22 payre of Course Shites at 8s the payre £7 6s 8d;

Item 16 longe Tabell Clothes £3;

Item 10 short Table Clothe 15s;

Item 10 payre of Course pillities £1 2s 6d;

Item 6 hand Towells of dowlis 3s;

Item 6 Course hand Towells of Canvas 2s;

Item 6 shorte Couborde Clothes 9s;

Item 2 doosen and halfe of St malvis £1 5s;

Item one doosen and halfe of naptkins 4s 6d;

Item one doosen of dowles naptkins 6s;

Item one doosen of frenged naptkins 4s;

[m. 9] Item one doosen of olde naptkins 3s 4d;

Sum £19 1s.

In the parler Chamber

Firstly 6 payre of Shits £4;

Item one shite & halfe of Callacow 8s;

Item one payre of Hulland shites £1 6s 8d;

Item one payre of fyne shites 18s;

Item one halfe shite 10s;

Item one bearinge shite 6s 8d;

Item one Coubord Cloth 8s;

Item one shilfe Clothes with their frenge £1 6s 8d;

Item 3 wraught Towells £1 4s;

Item 6 payre of fyne pillities £3;

Item 3 payre and one pillitie 9s;

Item 9 shertes £1 16s;

Item 10 bandes with 6 hand Kerchers £2;

Sum £17 13s.

In the Countinge House

Item one litell Tabell & seate one nest of boxes 4 shelves one standage and one payre of gold wights 3s 4d;

Sum 3s 4d.

[m. 10] A note of the wight of the plate

Firstly 3 Tankerds doubell gilted weighin 63 and halfe;

Item 3 boules doubell gilte weighinge 53 ounces;

Item 3 littell boules doubell gilte weighinge 19 ounces & halfe;

Item 2 boules gilted weighing 34 ounces;

Item one salte gilte weighing 18 ounces;

Item 2 littell salts gilted weighinge 11 ounces & halfe;

Item one littell Ale cupe gilted weighinge 11 ounces & 3 quarter;

Item one Ale Cupe 11 ouncs;

The Sum is 211 ounces and one quarter at 6s the ounce amounteth unto the some of £63 7s 6d.

Item 3 Goblets parcell gilte weighinge 51 ounces;

Item 3 goblets parcell gilte weighinge 40 ounces & one quarter;

Item 2 Tankerds parcell gilte weighinge 33 ounces;

Item one salte parcell gilte weighinge 10 ounces;

Item 2 doosen and halfe of Spoones parcell gilte weighing 43 ounces;

The Sume is 175 ounces and one quarter which at 5*s* the ounce amounteth unto £43 16*s* 3*d*.

[m. 11] Item 3 littell white boules weighinge 22 ounces;

Item one white salte weighinge 14 ounces;

The Sum is 36 ounces at 4*s* 4*d* the ounce amounteth unto £7 16*s*.

Item 2 stones Cupes Covered & gilted £4 10*s*;

Item 1 stone Cupe with A white Cover and foote £1 13*s* 4*d*;

Item 4 stone Cups with plene white Covers £1 12*s*;

Sum [£1,303 – crossed through].

Item in money £1,303.

A Note of the leases

Firstly one lease of the Tenemente in Chidley called Cowtrige £30;

Item one lease of A wishe mede in the parishe of Broade Cliste for 99 yeres yf three lives so longe shall live valued £95;

Item one lease of one garden and stabell in the parishe of St Mary Stepes in reversion of one John Foye £7.

Item in god debts by specialtye £753 2*s* 1*d*.

Other debts by specialty

Item Anthony Clathworthy £8;

Item of John Fysher of Alfinton £36;

Item due by John Gratlinge £5;

Sum [blank].

[m. 12] Debts upon the bookes which are good debts £155 2*d*;

Other debts due upon bookes which are not good

William Mathew of Cliste £3 9*s*;

Item John Axe of Atrey £2 6*s* 8*d*;

Item Humfry Alsope £16 5*s*.

In the parlor

Firstly one Table borde one fforme 2 Joyne stooles and on side Table borde 20*s*;

Item one standinge presse 22*s*;

Item the seelinge 13*s*;

Item one Cheare and one foote stoole 2*s*;

Item 3 shilves in the Buttery 6*d*;

Item one Carpett for the Tabell borde & 4 Cuishings 5*s*;

Item one Iron barr for the Chimney 1*s* 8*d*;

Sum £3 4*s* 6*d*.

In the Chamber over the parler

Firstly one bed steed one bed performed & one Trouckell bed £4;

Item 8 payre of shites 4 Table Clothes 2 doosen of naptkins 6 hande Towells & 2 payre of pillities £2 6*s* 8*d*;

Item one Cheste 2 Cheares one stoole and towe shilfes 3*s* 4*d*;

Item one payre of doggs & one Toster 12*d*;

[m. 13] Item 2 payre of blankets one littell Coverlett one olde Gowne and one payre of Breeches £2;

Item one paire of Courtins with rodds 1*s*;

Sum £8 12*s*.

In the Chamber over the buttery

Firstly on duste bed one fflocke bed 2 Coverlets one bed steede and one Trouckell bed 20*s*;

Item one shelfe one Couste and one Hamper 1*s* 4*d*;

Sum £1 1*s* 4*d*.

In the Halle

Firstly 3 fflitches of Baken & one breste of Byeffe 30*s*;

Item one borde one fforme and 2 Cheares 6*s* 8*d*;

Item one Amerye with 2 Couberds 3*s* 4*d*;

Item one doosen of platters and poddingers one doosen of Sawsers and plates 6 porige dishes 2 Saltes one Tynninge Cupe one Tynninge boule & 3 Candlesticks 18*s*;

Item 3 brasinge Crockes 2 Iron Crockes 26*s* 8*d*;

Item one greate pan 3 littell Cawdrens & 2 skillets 20*s*;

Item 2 Goose pans 1 ffrienge pane one fleshe hooke one
 baster 2 broches & on ladell 5*s*;

Item one payre of Andirons one payre of doggs one fire pan
 one payre of Tongs one barr of the Chimney and 2 pott
 hookes 10*s*;

Sum £5 19*s* 8*d*.

In the Chamber over the Entry
Firstly one ffeather bed performed with one Trouckellbed &
 one fflocke bed £2;

Item 52 fflyses of old woolle £3;

Sum £5.

In the kitchinge
Item 1 ffurnis 30*s*;

Item one wringe for Cheeses 2*s* 6*d*;

Sum 32*s* 6*d*.

In the Chamber over the Entery
Firstly Shefe of Arrowes on bill & one sworde 6*s* 8*d*;

[*m. 14*] Item one douste bed with blankets & one Coverlett 10*s*;

Item 12 Cheeses and one Racke 5*s*;

Item 2 boushells of malte 6*s* 8*d*;

Sum £1 8*s* 4*d*.

In the milke house
Firstly 8 milke panes of brasse 25*s* 4*d*;

Item 4 gallons of Butter 10*s*;

Sum 35*s* 4*d*.

In the [blank]
Item 8 Coustes 6*s* 8*d*;

Item 7 bagges one sacke & one wimshite 10*s*;

Item 3 Serges 2*s*;

Item 4 leatheren bottells 20*d*;

Sum £1 4*d*.

In the barne
Firstly 6 bushelles of Wheate 2 bushells of Rye 2 bushelles of

beanes and wotes £2;

Item Rude in the barne 20*d*;

Item 2 barnegeseves [?] & 2 winnen seves 1*s*;

Sum 42*s* 8*d*.

Item one heape of dunge 20*s*;

Item one payre of Harrowes 3 payre of Crookes 2 while
 borowes 2 payre of dunge potts & one payre of Crookes 13*s*
 4*d*;

Sum 33*s* 4*d*.

Item 9 piggs 40*s*;

Item 3 stone Trowes 2*s*;

Item 3 peekes 2 dunge Evells one shovell one hooke 2 paren
 hatchets one hande hatchett with one Iron barre 2 mattocks
 & one pickise 6*s* 8*d*;

Item 2 Saddells with gisses and Ropes 10*s*;

Item a hodgshead and pipes & other Treinge vessells £2;

Item woode and other things 20*s*;

Item for ffacgott woode and harde woode £5;

Item 7 keye & 2 yerlings £18;

Item 42 sheepe £10;

Item 10 lambes 20*s*;

Item 2 horsses £5;

Item the Corne in grounde £10;

Item the puntry 6*s* 8*d*;

Item 4 butts of bees 4*s*.

[*m. 15*] The Inventory of the bargayne wherin Michaell
 Wynter late dwelled
Firstly the seelinge of the parler with a bed steede & one
 Table borde with A pourtall and one Couborde £5;

Item one bare of the Chimney 1*s* 8*d*;

Item one Tabell borde in the Halle 10*s*;

Item 2 hodgsheades one well buckett with a trous other olde
 Timber 6*s* 8*d*;

Sum [blank].

Sum total [blank].